Praise for netguide™

"Thanks to Wolff and friends, the cyberswamp may just have become a little less murky."—*Entertainment Weekly*

"*Net Guide* is the computer world's online *TV Guide*."—*Good Morning America*

"*Net Guide* will keep you from wandering around aimlessly on the Internet, and is full of good ideas for where to pull over."—*Forbes FYI*

"*Net Guide* is the liveliest, most readable online guide yet."—*USA Today*

"What you need to connect."—*Worth Magazine*

"*Net Guide* is the *TV Guide* to Cyberspace!"—Louis Rossetto, publisher/editor, *Wired*

"One of the more complete, well-organized guides to online topics. From photography to the Church of Elvis, you'll find it here."—*PC Magazine*

"The best attempt yet at categorizing and organizing all the great stuff you can find out there. It's the book people keep stealing off my desk."—Joshua Quittner, *New York Newsday*

"It's changed my online life. Get this book!"—Mike Madson, "Computer Bits," Business Radio Network

"My favorite for finding the cool stuff."—*The Louisville Courier-Journal*

"*Net Guide* focuses on the most important aspect of online information—its content. You name it, it's there—from erotica to religion to politics."—Lawrence J. Magid, *San Jose Mercury News*

"Not only did all the existing Net books ignore Cyberspace's entertaining aspects, but they were process-oriented, not content-oriented. Why hadn't someone made a *TV Guide* for the Net? Wolff recognized an opportunity for a new book, and his group wrote *Net Guide*."—Mark Frauenfelder, *Wired*

"Couch potatoes have *TV Guide*. Now Net surfers have *Net Guide*."—*Orange County Register*

"*Net Guide* is one of the best efforts to provide a hot-spot guide to going online."—*Knoxville News-Sentinel*

"An excellent guide for Internet adventurers. *Net Guide* is well-written and no subject remains undiscovered. *Net Guide* is indispensable for targeted explorations into Cyberspace."—*Het Parool*, the Netherlands

"Assolutamente indispensabile!"—*L'Espresso*, Italy

Voyage Into Cyberspace Aboard the Online Service That Has It All...

You've read the book. Now keep up-to-date online.

Every month hundreds of new games come online. How can you possibly keep up? It's easy. The Net Games online directory is updated round the clock. Call YPN for the latest offerings on the Net.

YPN is a service for data.comm.phobes

To watch your favorite show on TV you don't have to know about circuits and tubes. To have fun in Cyberspace you shouldn't have to know about "transmission-control protocols." YPN support makes it simple to navigate the Net— you'll get real help from real people.

Busy? No carrier? Host unavailable?

If you've been out in Cyberspace, you know the frustration of not connecting. YPN can handle the traffic! Call now for your local access number and make an easy connection.

Join us!

The Net is a new medium and a new world. Be a part of it. As a member of YPN you'll get 15 hours of time FREE, plus one of the lowest subscription costs anywhere in Cyberspace!

**Call 1-800-NET-1133 for Local Access Numbers!
15 Hours Free Online Time!
Call Today!**

✓ **Unique Forums**

✓ **Interactive Magazines**

✓ **Special Directories**
  • **Net Guide**
  • **Net Games**
  • **Net Chat**
  • **Net Money**
  • **Net Tech**
  • **Travel**
  • **Business**
  • **Shareware**
  • **Kids**

✓ **BBS Reviews**

✓ **Net News**
  • **Usenet Digest**
  • **Talk of the Net**

✓ **Easy Navigation Tools**

✓ **Usenet FAQ Archive**

✓ **Chat**

✓ **Games**

✓ **News**

✓ **Shopping**

Net Books!

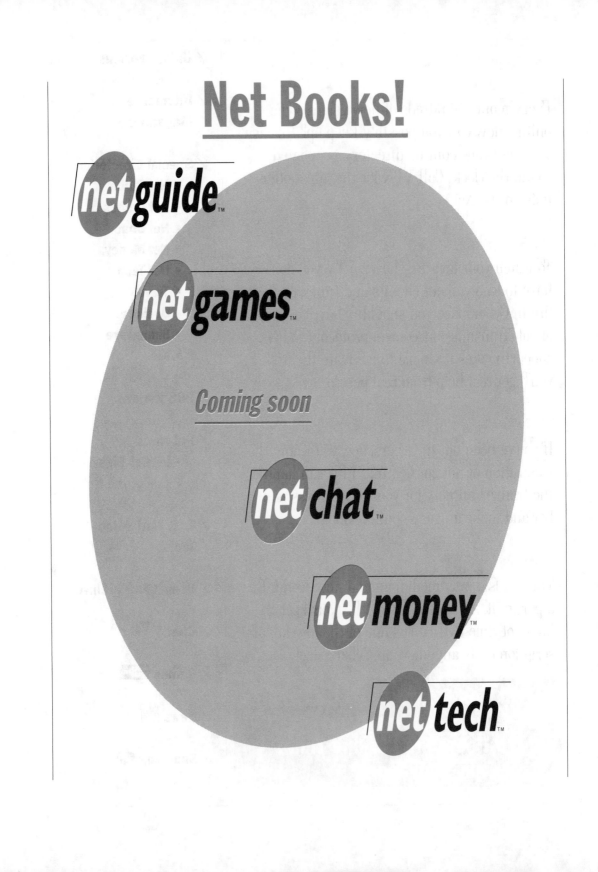

net games ™

Your Guide to the Games People Play on the Electronic Highway

---

A Michael Wolff Book

Kelly Maloni, Derek Baker,

and Nathaniel Wice

For free updates call 1-800-NET-1133

RANDOM HOUSE
ELECTRONIC PUBLISHING

MICHAEL
WOLFF
& COMPANY, INC.
DIGITAL
PUBLISHING

New York

The Net Books series is a co-publishing venture of Michael Wolff & Company, Inc., 1633 Broadway, 27th Floor, New York, NY 10019, and Random House Electronic Publishing, a division of Random House, Inc., 201 East 50th Street, New York, NY 10022.

Net Games™ has been wholly created and produced by Michael Wolff & Company, Inc. Net Games is a trademark of Michael Wolff & Company, Inc. All design and production has been done by means of desktop-publishing technology. The text is set in the typefaces Garamond, customized Futura, Zapf Dingbats, Franklin Gothic, and Pike.

Published simultaneously in the U.S. by Random House, NY, and Michael Wolff & Company, Inc., and in Canada by Random House of Canada, Ltd.

0 9 8 7 6 5 4 3 2

ISBN 0-679-75592-6

All of the photographs and illustrations in this book have been obtained from online sources, and have been included to demonstrate the variety of work that is available on the Net. The caption with each photograph or illustration identifies its online source.

The book jacket has been designed by Peter Rutten. Copyright © 1994 by Michael Wolff & Company, Inc.

The author and publisher have used their best efforts in preparing this book. However, the author and publisher make no warranties of any kind, express or implied, with regard to the documentation contained in this book, and specifically disclaim, without limitation, any implied warranties of merchantability and fitness for a particular purpose with respect to listings in the book, or the techniques described in the book. In no event shall the author or publisher be responsible or liable for any loss of profit or any other commercial damages, including but not limited to special, incidental, consequential, or any other damages in connection with or arising out of furnishing, performance, or use of this book.

Trademarks

A number of entered words in which we have reason to believe trademark, service mark, or other proprietary rights may exist have been designated as such by use of initial capitalization. However, no attempt has been made to designate as trademarks or service marks all personal-computer words or terms in which proprietary rights might exist. The inclusion, exclusion, or definition of a word or term is not intended to affect, or to express any judgment on, the validity or legal status of any proprietary right which may be claimed in that word or term.

Manufactured in the United States of America

New York   Toronto   London   Sydney   Auckland

A Michael Wolff Book

Michael Wolff
President and Editor in Chief

Peter Rutten
Creative Director

Kelly Maloni
Managing Editor

Senior Editors: Derek Baker, Nathaniel Wice

Assistant Editor: Maria Sturani

Research: David Heller, Robert Kenney, Kendra Wilhelm

Technical Editor: David Wood

Contributing Writers: Eric Berlin, Brad Friedman, Chris Weller

Production Editor: Jeff Hearn

Copy Editor: Matt Weingarden

Children's Editor: Elizabeth Wolff (age 10)

Special thanks:
Random House Electronic Publishing—Kenzi Sugihara, Tracy Smith, Steve
Guty, Dennis Eulau, Mark Dazzo, Alison Biggert, Jean Davis Taft, Holly
Pemberton, and Niki DiSilvestro

Alison Anthoine at Kay Collyer & Boose

Peter Ginsberg at Curtis Brown Ltd.

Stan Norton

Chip Bayers

And, of course, Aggy Aed

Grateful "waves" and "hugs" to the following Netters:

"Dante Adel," Peter Alexander, "Amradron," Amy Arnold, Shannon Ayers, Jonathan Baron (Blue Baron), Richard Bartle, Rick Beardsley, Marcia Bednarcyk, Gregory Blake, Janet Brodhead, Elizabeth Brown, Will Christie, Tyra Clymer, Steve Cohen, Gary "Moggy" Cooper, Laura Craighead, Frank Crowell, "del," John Dreher, Jerome Dubois, Anna Eklund (Vitastjern), Scott A. Ettin, Amy Fehringer (Tinkerbell), James Frazier (FlashForce), Joel Furr, Scott Geertgens, Chuck Gendrich, "Geo," R. M. Green, Jason Guy, Remmelt de Haan (Zarniwoop), Barbara A. Hare (RDI Kairee), Melanie Diamond Harper, Neil Harris, the Rev. William G. Hartwell, "Hazed," Douglas Hendrickson, Col. Richard Hymer, Kenneth Jackson, Tamela Johnson, Andrew Kantor, Liz "Green Eyes" Keough, James Kiley, Greg Kolanek (Pazu), Kirby Krueger (Aspen), Julia Ann Krute, "Kyrell," Lydia Leong (Amberyl), Yifun Liang (CheeseCoke), Greg Lindahl, "Lord Hakim," Bill Mackiewicz, Edward Malinowski (Alucard), "Matsi," Edmond L. Meinfelder, Patrick Moss (Granola), William Moxley, "Nightshift," Niilo Nuevo (Anipa), Janet O'Bryan (Mariana), "OGF Devron," "OGF Diamond," Thomas Ohrbom, Bruce W. Onder, Marisa Ong, Christopher Page (Fire), Scott Panzer, Jim Pascua, Jonathan Perret, Ken Pertcheck, "Pinkfish," Lisa Powell, Antonio Prats, Andrea Reed (OGF Coord), George Reese, Eric Romanik, "Rusty," "Rusty Chicken Meat," Kathy Sanguinetti, Amanda Schack (Iago), Michael Schoenbach, "Silkcut," Larry Singh, "Sketch the Cow," Jennifer Smith (Moira), "Sojan," Christina Sterman-Hack (Lady Squirrel), Frank Stolze (Phylax), Greg Swan, "Sweetea," Ashley Taft, "Talyessin," Thomas E. Terrill, J. T. Traub (Moonchild), "Trent the Uncatchable," Carol Wallace, Kim Weisman, Lisa Wetenkamp, "White Wolff," Jay Wilbur, Regis Wilson, Paul Wouters, Victor Zaveduk, and Z100 (for the rock).

The editors of *Net Games* can be reached at Michael Wolff & Company, Inc., 1633 Broadway, 27th Floor, New York, NY 10019, or by voice call at 212-841-1572, fax at 212-841-1539, or email at editors@ypn.com.

Contents

Frequently Asked Questions

1

Part 1. Shoot-'em-Up

Part 2. Role-playing & Adventure

Contents

Part 3. Strategy & Classics

Part 4. Puzzles, Trivia & Word Games

Part 5. Personal Computer & Video Games

Part 6. Sex, Hubs, MUDs & More

Appendices

FAQs

"Frequently Asked Questions" about the Net and Net Games

1. How are games you play on the Net different from ordinary video games?

The first computer games—stuff like *tic-tac-toe*, *chess*, and *Space Invaders*—were great because you didn't need a human opponent around to enjoy a good game. Games on the Net take the next level—you don't need a human opponent around because there are 20 million potential candidates out there in the elastic space created by the connections between computers and their users known as the Net.

2. Who's playing these online games?

Who isn't? The players include *Dungeons & Dragons* role-players who explore adventure, fantasy, and sci-fi universes; armchair strategists—from war generals to football quarterbacks—who plan, ally, trade, defend, attack, and put a premium on realistic details; chess (or *backgammon*, *Go*, *bridge*, *checkers*, *poker*, you name it) novices and masters getting their anytime, anyplace fix of human competition; puzzle lovers, you daily crossword-doing, *Jeopardy*-watching, *Rubik's Cube*-solving people out there; *Mortal Kombat* killers and other hand-eye shoot-first, check-the-score later types; and the gregarious gamers for whom it's not whether you win or lose but how good the company is.

3. If I get into this, what's it gonna cost me? Will I go bankrupt?

You might hear horror stories about GEnie users addicted to *Air Warrior* blowing $1,000 a month in WWII dogfights, but the truth is that most online games can be enjoyed as part of the monthly basic rate of a commercial service or a local BBS, or, even more cheaply, on the mostly unmetered Internet. And—just in case—this book marks games that involve extra costs with a $ symbol.

4. Before you go any further, what's "the Net," anyway?

The Net is the electronic medium spawned by the millions of computers linked (that is, networked) together throughout the world. Known as Cyberspace, the Information Highway, or the Infobahn, the Net encompasses the Internet, a global, noncommercial system with as many as 30 million computers communicating through it; the commercial online services like CompuServe, America Online, and GEnie; the thousands of local and regional bulletin-board services (BBSs); the networks of discussion groups, like FidoNet, that are carried over BBSs; and the discussion groups known as Usenet that traverse the Internet.

More and more, the Internet unites all these diverse locations that make up the Net.

5. Where are these games played on the Net?

Games can be played on a local network (your AppleTalk at the office, for instance); through a modem call to a friend's computer (just you, your telephone company, and your friend are involved); via a BBS that carries the game you want to play, and often maintains a high-scores bulletin where your scores are listed; on a commercial service, where you can hook up with someone in what's called a modem lobby and start playing any game you and your opponent share, or you can join a game on message boards and in the gaming forums; and on the Internet, using tools like email, telnet, and the World Wide Web (which we'll explain later).

6. I'm game. What do I need to get started?

Computer hardware and software, online access (or not—it's not a sine qua non), and a few tricks to find your way around.

7. Can you explain just exactly what hardware and software I'll need?

You'll need a personal computer (any flavor). If you've bought one fairly recently, it's likely that it came with everything you need. But let's assume you have only a PC. In that case you'll also need to get a modem, which will allow your computer to communicate over the phone.

So-called 14.4 modems, which transfer data at speeds up to 14,400 bits per second (bps), have become the latest standard. You should be able to get one for as little as $150. (Within a year, however, 14,400 bps will feel like a crawl next to faster speeds of 28,800 bps and higher.) Joysticks, soundcards, color monitors, and lots of RAM obviously add to the fun, but they're optional.

Next, you need a communications program to control the modem. This software will probably come free with your modem, your PC, or—if you're going to sign up somewhere—your online service. Otherwise, you can buy it off the shelf for under $25.

You may also need a copy of the game you want to play, or a graphical frontend or interface to access a game on another computer. This FAQ will tell you about easy, and cheap, ways to get a lot of great games. And sometimes you'll need so-called client software to make Internet games more fun (explained on page 17). Finally, you'll want a telephone line (or two if you plan on tying up the line a couple of hours per night).

Of course, if your office or school is hooked directly into the Internet or into a LAN (Local Area Network), you don't need the telephone line, the modem, or the software.

8. I'm ready. What kind of access should I get? A commercial service?

No, not necessarily. You have a number of options, varying in price, flexibility, speed, and bandwidth (the amount of data that can travel through a network):

Email Gateway

This is the most basic access you can get. It lets you receive messages from anywhere on the Net and allows you to send messages anywhere. Email gateways are

---

ONLINE SERVICES

America Online
- 1-800-827-3338 (voice)
- Monthly fee: $9.95, first month free
- Free monthly hours: 5
- Hourly fees: $3.50
- Email: joinaol@aol.com

CompuServe
- 1-800-848-8199 (voice)
- Monthly fees: $8.95, first month free (standard); $2.50 (alternative)
- Free monthly hours: unlimited basic (standard); none (alternative)
- Hourly fees: $6.- (standard) or $6.30 (alternative) for 300 bps; $8.- (standard) or $12.80 (alternative) for 1200/2400 bps; and $16.- (standard) or $22.80 (alternative) for 9600 bps
- Email: 70006.101@ compuserve.com

Delphi
- 1-800-695-4002 (voice)
- Monthly fees: $10,- (10/4 plan); $20,- (20/20 plan)
- Free monthly hours: 4 (10/4 plan); 20 (20/20 plan)
- Hourly fees: $4 (10/4 plan); $1.80 (20/20 plan)
- Setup: $19.- (20/20 plan)
- Email: info@delphi.com

GEnie
- 1-800-638-9636 (voice)
- Monthly fee: $8.95
- Free monthly hours: 4
- Hourly fees: $3.- (off-prime) or $12.50 (prime time) for 2400 bps; $9.- (off-prime) or $18.50 (prime time) for 9600 bps
- Email: feedback@genie.geis.com

→

often available via work, school, or any of the other services listed here.

BBSs

BBSs range from mom-and-pop hobbyist computer bulletin boards (often run from a basement) to large professional services. What the small ones lack in size they often make up for in cost and uniqueness, and many users prefer these scenic roads over the Info Highway. The large ones can be as rich and diverse as the commercial services.

BBSs are easy to get started with, and if you find one with Internet access or an email gateway, you get the best of local color and global reach. Games are really big on most BBSs—so big that this book contains lots of games created only for the BBS world. And remember: For every game listed in this book, there are dozens if not *hundreds* of variants playing on BBSs across Cyberspace.

You'll find BBSs for your area code in the back of this book. Other places to find local BBSs are the Usenet discussion groups alt.bbs.lists and comp.bbs.misc, the BBS forums of the commercial services, and regional and national BBS lists kept in the file libraries of many BBSs.

Once you've found a local BBS, contact the sysop to inquire about the game you want. BBS games are known as "door" games, a kind of customizable shareware unique to the BBS world. Even if the game of your choice is not on their board yet, many sysops are glad to add a door game that a paying customer has requested.

Many, if not most, local BBSs now offer Internet email, as well as message "conferences" or "echoes," file libraries, and some quirky database, program, or directory unique to their little corner of Cyberspace.

The ImagiNation Network
- 1-800-695-4002 (voice)
- Monthly fee: $9.95
- Free monthly hours: 5
- Hourly fee: $3.50
- Software: $5.95

MPGNet
- 1-800-GET-GAME (voice)
- Monthly fee: none (5 free hours at sign up)
- Hourly fee: $4 using local access numbers; $2 using direct-dial nodes (in N.Y. area) or telnetting from the Internet
- Email: info@mpgn.com

Prodigy
- 1-800-PRODIGY
- Monthly fees: $14.95 (Plan 1), $29.95 (Plan 2)
- Free monthly hours: unlimited in core services; 2 hours in plus services, which consist of the bulletin boards, EAASY Sabre, Dow Jones Co. News, and stock quotes (Plan 1); 25 hours on a specific service of choice—e.g., bulletin boards (Plan 2)
- Hourly fees: $3.60 for plus services (Plan 1), $1.80 (Plan 2)
- Email: prodigy@prodigy.com

USA Today Information Center
- 1-800-826-9688 (voice)
- Monthly fees: $14.95
- Hourly fees: $14.95 for Basic or $17.90 for Entertainment Center (day time); $2.95 for Entertainment Center (evening)
- Free hours: unlimited in Basic, 5 hours/month in Entertainment Center (evening)

Commercial Services

They're the priciest but also the easiest. The big ones are America Online, CompuServe, and Prodigy. Also popular are GEnie and Delphi.

Commercial services are big cyber-villages. The large ones have more "residents" (members) than most U.S. cities. They generally require their own special software, which you can buy at any local computer store or by calling the numbers listed in this book. (Hint: Look for the frequent starter-kit giveaways.)

Some of the most elaborate games are found on the commercial services. On the other hand, it can be hard to get from the commercial world out into the larger world of games in Cyberspace.

All the commercial services, however, provide an electronic-mailbox (email) address, with which you can communicate with people elsewhere in Cyberspace—important for playing certain Internet games.

On the commercial services, you'll also find areas for discussion, libraries for downloading files, and software-company representatives to answer questions.

Internet Providers

There is a growing number of full-service Internet providers (which means they offer email, IRC, FTP, Telnet, Gopher, WWW, and Usenet access), including Your Personal Network (YPN), run by the editors of this book. In practical terms, the Internet allows you to download a war-strategy game from a computer in Japan; enter a multiplayer fantasy world on a computer in Lawrence, Kansas; and play *VGA Planets* with someone next door or 12 time zones away.

A dial-up SLIP (serial line Internet protocol) account is positively the most fun you can have through a modem. It is a special service offered by some Internet providers that gets you significantly faster access and the ability to use point-and-click programs for Windows, Macintosh, and other platforms.

Direct Network Connection

Look, Ma Bell: no phone lines! The direct network connection is the fast track of college students, computer scientists, and a growing number of employees of high-tech businesses. It puts the user right on the Net, bypassing the phone connections, and has the advantage of tremendous speed and large amounts of bandwidth.

Make a connection without an online account

You don't necessarily need an online account, although your gaming life will be a lot less versatile without one. You can make connections using so-called Null Modem Connection (hook your computer directly to another computer with a serial cable); Modem-to-Modem (connect your computer to someone else's over the phone; and Local Area Network (play over the local area network in your school or office).

9. Great, I've got an account. What do I have to know about navigating the Net?

Basically, just a few tricks on how to get around. They're easy and they're all means by which numerous fantastic games are played. They are:

Email

You can talk to anyone on a commercial service, Internet site, or BBS with Internet access (and to people connected with email gateways, SLIP, and direct network connections).

Email addresses have a universal syntax called an Internet address. An Internet address is broken down into four parts: the user's name (e.g., Kelly), the @ symbol, the computer and/or company name, and what kind of Internet address it is: *net* for network, *com* for a commercial enterprise—as with Your Personal Network (ypn.com) and America Online (aol.com)—*edu* for educational institutions, *gov* for government sites, *mil* for military facilities, and *org* for nonprofit and other private organizations. The dictatorial cybermaven who drove this book to completion and herself and the staff to an early grave would therefore be kelly@ypn.com.

But she doesn't answer her mail.

I'm on a commercial service. How do I send Internet email?
Each of the major commercial services offers Internet email, with slight variations in form.

From CompuServe
Enter the CompuServe mail area by choosing the **go** command from the menu and typing **mail** (if you don't have CompuServe's Information Manager software, type **go mail**). If you want to send a message to someone on another comercial service, your email will be routed through the Internet, so you must address it with the prefix **internet:**. Mail to John Doe at America Online, for instance, would be addressed **internet:jdoe@aol.com**; to John Doe at YPN, it would be addressed **internet:jdoe@ypn. com**.

To CompuServe
Use the addressee's CompuServe I.D. number. If John Doe's I.D. is 12345,678, you'll address mail to **12345.678@ compuserve.com**. Make sure you replace the comma in the CompuServe I.D. with a period.

From America Online
Use AOL's Internet mail gateway (*keyword*: **internet**). Then address and send mail as you normally would on any other Internet site, using the **jdoe@ service.com** address style.

To America Online
Just address email to **jdoe@ aol.com**.

→

Telnet

When you telnet, you're logging in to another computer or network somewhere else on the Internet. You then have access to the programs running on the remote computer. If the site is running a library catalog, you can search the catalog. If it's running a BBS, you can chat with others logged in. And, to get to the point, if it's running a game, you can play the game. Most MUDs (multi user dimensions—later on them) and Internet servers, like the Internet Go Server, involve telnetting. In fact, just about any time you're playing a live multiplayer game on the Internet, you'll be telnetting to the game.

FTP

FTP (file transfer protocol) is a program that allows you to copy a file from another Internet-connected computer to your own. Hundreds of computers on the Internet allow "anonymous FTP": In other words, you don't need a password to access them. The range of material available is extraordinary—from books to free software to pictures to thousands of games!

Gopher

A gopher is a program that turns Internet addresses into menu options. Gophers can perform many Internet functions, including telnetting and downloading files. Gopher addresses throughout this book are useful for finding collections of information and collections of telnet links to game sites.

Gophers also come in handy for circumventing restrictions on MUD access from some large sites like schools—it's harder to trace a gopher path (the steps the gopher takes to reach the MUD). Gopher menus, however, are likely to be swallowed up by the very latest in Net navigation pleasure: the World Wide Web, a.k.a. WWW or the Web.

From GEnie
Use the keyword: **mail** and address email to **jdoe@service. com@inet#**. GEnie's use of two @ symbols is an exception to Internet addressing convention.

To GEnie
Address email to **jdoe@genie. geis.com.**

From Delphi
Use the command **go mail**, then, at the prompt, type **mail** again. Address mail to **internet"jdoe@ service.com"** (make sure to include the quotation marks).

To Delphi
Address email to **jdoe@delphi. com.**

From Prodigy
To send email from Prodigy, first download Prodigy's Mail Manager by using the command **jump: mail manager**. Address mail to **jdoe@service.com**. Mail Manager is currently available for DOS and Windows only, with a Mac version due soon.

To Prodigy
Address email using the addressee's user I.D. For John Doe (user I.D.: ABCD12A), for example, you would address it **abcd12a@prodigy.com.**

Frequently Asked Questions

Chat

Live chat registers an instant return—it's happening in real time. Every online service offers live chat areas, where you type to other people and they type to you. The Internet version is called IRC, which stands for Internet relay chat. Game-specific IRC "channels" and live "conferences" on the commercial services may serve as discussion forums, as opponent pickup (or pick-a-fight) joints, or as the actual "game server"—the place where you play the game. Many live chats are regularly scheduled; others never stop. MUDs and many multi-action games thrive on real-time chat within the game itself.

The Web

The World Wide Web is a hot new hypertext-based information structure on the Internet. Many believe the Web may become the standard navigational tool on the Net. The Web is like a house where every room has doors to every other room—or, more accurately, like the interconnections in the human brain. Highlighted words in a document link to other documents that reside on the same machine or on a computer anywhere in the world. You only have to click on the word—the Web does the rest.

You jump from the Netrek Home Page in Arizona to the Lagg U. Netrek team in Seattle with a click, over to a beginner's graphical walk-through of the opening play, and back to a loving history of the game's two-decade development. All the while you've FTPed, telnetted, and gophered with nary a thought to case-sensitive Unix commands or addresses.

Your dial-up Internet provider undoubtedly offers programs to access the Web. Lynx and WWW are pretty much the standard offerings. Usually you choose them by typing **lynx** and **www** and then **<return>**. What you'll get is a "page" with some of the text high-

1. Log in to your Internet site and locate the telnet program. Since telnet is a widely used feature, you will most likely find it in the main menu of your Internet access provider. On Delphi, for example, telnet is available in the main Internet menu. Just type **telnet**.

2. Once you've started the program, you should see a telnet prompt (for instance, **telnet>** or **telnet:**). Type **open <telnet address>**, replacing the bracketed text with the address of the machine you want to reach. (Note: Some systems do not require you to type **open**. Also, don't type the brackets.) Let's say you want to go to the Internet Go Server. The Internet Go Server is at the address hellspark.wharton.upenn.edu 6969, so after the telnet prompt you would type **open hellspark. wharton.upenn.edu 6969**. Many telnet addresses for games include a port number with the telnet address (e.g., **6969**); type a space to separate the port number from the address. (Port numbers are placed after the uninterrupted string. It's the only time when an Internet address contains a space.)

3. The telnet program will connect you to the remote computer—in our example, the Internet Go Server. Once you're connected, you'll see a prompt. Type the remote computer's log-in information as listed in the Net Games entry. The prompt may

→

lighted. These are the links. Choose a link, hit the return key, and you're off.

If you know exactly where you want to go and don't want to meander through the information, you can type a Web page's address, known as a URL (uniform resource locator), many of which you'll find in this book.

With the emergence of new and sophisticated so-called Web browsers (with a graphical point-and-click interface) like Mosaic and Cello, the Web is starting to look the way it was envisioned—pictures, colored icons, and appetizing text layouts. Unless you have a direct connection to the Internet, you'll need a SLIP for these browsers. But if you can't get direct access or a SLIP, do not despair: Dial-up versions of these browsers are expected soon.

be as simple as **login** followed by another prompt for a **password**, or it may ask for information like a character's name, a gender, or the type of creature you'd like to play. If no log-in is needed, the Net Games entry will not list one. Oh, and you may be asked about the type of terminal you're using. If you're unsure, vt-100 is a safe bet.

4. You're logged in. Now just follow the instructions on the screen, which will differ with every telnet site.

Discussion groups

The most widely read bulletin boards are a group of some 10,000-plus "newsgroups" on the Internet, collectively known as Usenet. Hundreds of these are related to computer games. Usenet newsgroups travel the Internet, collecting thousands of messages a day from whoever wants to "post" to them. More than anything, the newsgroups are the collective, if sometimes Babel-like, voice of the Net—everything is discussed here. And we mean everything.

Reading Usenet newsgroups is easy—all you need is an Internet, BBS, or commercial-service site that offers them. And most do.

The messages in a newsgroup, called "posts," are listed and numbered chronologically—in other words, in the order in which they were posted. You can scan a list of messages before deciding to read a particular message.

If someone posts a message that prompts responses, the original and all follow-up messages are called a "thread." The subject line of subsequent posts in the thread refers to the subject of the original. For example, if you were to post a message with the subject **Need help with Doom** in alt.games.doom, all responses would have the subject line **RE: Need help with Doom**. In practice, however, topics in a thread tend to wander off in many directions.

To read the newsgroups you use a program called a "reader," a standard offering on most online services. There are several types of readers—some let you follow message threads, others organize messages chronologically. You can also use a reader to customize the newsgroup menu to include only the newsgroups you're interested in.

Mailing lists are like newsgroups, only they're distributed over the Internet email system. The fact that messages show up in your mailbox tends to make the discussion group more intimate, as does the proactive act of subscribing. Mailing list are often more focused, and they're less vulnerable to irreverent contributors.

To subscribe to a mailing list, send an email to the mailing list's subscription address. Often you will need to include very specific information, which you will find in this book. To unsubscribe, send another message to that same address.

Local BBSs often carry what are known as "echoes" or "conferences," which are part of messaging networks among BBSs. You'll find several of these networks mentioned throughout the book: FidoNet, RelayNet, SimNet, WWIVnet. There are hundreds of BBS networks in Cyberspace, new ones are added daily, and no BBS carries them all—usually they don't even carry all the conferences on a single network.

Check with local BBSs in your area code to see whether they have the network you want. If they do, but they don't carry the conference you're looking for, ask for it. Most sysops will gladly add a conference for a paying customer.

Finally, every online service, including the commercial Goliaths, has its own bulletin boards, a.k.a. forums, categories, and topics. The boards are the primary area of discussion on the service, and games provoke some of the most passionate discourse.

HOW TO DOWNLOAD

How do I download from a commercial service?
The download command on each of the commercial services may differ slightly depending on the type of computer you use, but in most instances file downloads work as follows:

On **America Online**, once you locate the file you want, select the file name so that it's highlighted. Then select one of two buttons: **download now**, or **download later**. If you choose **download later**, the file will be added to a list of files, all of which you can download when you're done with your America Online session.

On **CompuServe**, if you're browsing a library list (using CompuServe's Information Manager), you can highlight a file you want and select the **retrieve** button to download it immediately. If you want to download it later, select the box next to the file name, then select **yes** when you leave the forum and a window will appear that says **download marked files?** (If you don't have Information Manager, type **down** and [return] at the prompt following the file description.)

On **Delphi**, after you read a file description in the file or "database" area, there are four commands available—**next**, **down**, **xm**, and **list**. Type **down** and [return] to download the file.

On **GEnie**, after you've chosen a file to download, select **download a file** from the RoundTable library menu. When
→

10. What does all this have to do with playing a game?

Well, the tools discussed above are the means by which many games are played. Here's how it works:

Connect-and-Play Games

Backgammon pickup games 24 hours a day, 7 days a week, 365 days a year on the Internet Backgammon Server; Jedi knight training on the *Star Wars MUSH*; and the *Who-Am-I* version of *Twenty Questions* in America Online's Game Parlor. What these games have in common is that they run on a remote computer that you connect to, whether it's a commercial service, an Internet host, or a stand-alone BBS. To play *Who Am I?*, for instance, simply connect to America Online and type a keyword to get to the Games Parlor. You're there. You're live. And you'd better be ready to play.

On the Internet, many of the connect-and-play games are so-called MUDs (multi-user dimensions, often text-based fantasy role-playing games). But the Net also contains a wide variety of other connect-and-play games. The *backgammon, chess, scrabble*, and *Go* servers, for instance, are formidable gaming institutions on the Net. All these games are accessed by telnetting to them.

Many Internet games allow you to use another client program instead of telnet. You may, for instance, want to get a client to better manage text flow or expedite frequent moves for Internet games (see the sidebar on page 17 for more details).

On the commercial services and BBSs some games come with fancy graphical "frontends" that you run on your computer. These frontends are usually available for downloading from the same menu or forum on the

you see the prompt **enter the download request**: type the file name and **[return]**. At the next prompt, which asks you to confirm your download, type **d** and **[return]** to download the file. At the next prompt, you'll be asked to choose a download "protocol"; your best choice, if available with your communications software, is Z-modem (number 4), so type **4** and **[return]**.

How do I download from the Internet?

Using FTP (file transfer protocol). Internet FTP sites open to the public (known as anonymous FTP sites) appear throughout this book, offering tens of thousands of games and game-related hints, instructions, and patches.

To FTP:

1. Log in to your Internet site. Then start the FTP program at that site—in most cases, by typing **ftp** or by choosing it from an Internet menu.

2. When you see the FTP prompt, type **open <ftp.address>** to connect to the other computer. The Monster Macintosh Gaming Archive, for example, is at the address mac.archive. umich.edu, so you would type **open mac.archive.umich.edu**. (By the way, sometimes you'll be asked for just the FTP site name, which means you wouldn't type **open**.)

3. Most FTP sites offer "anonymous login," which means you

→

service as the game itself.

Frontend programs replace typed commands and word descriptions with colorful pictures and point-and-click options. You can *see* your opponent's pieces, characters, spaceships, or, in the case of GEnie's *CyberStrike*—a multiplayer, futuristic pod combat game—the giant robotic machines that roam the terrain. Night after night, players (sometimes up to 100) log in to GEnie, launch their *CyberStrike* frontend, find their buddies, split into teams, and blast away at enemies.

Play-by-Email Games (PBeM)

Just about every "turn-based" game in this book, even the fancy strategy games with elaborate graphics, has an email variant. And, about every game you can play by postal mail—*chess, Diplomacy, rotisserie baseball,* you name it—you can also play by email.

What is often an impossible offline task—getting seven players together for a classic game of *Diplomacy*—is nothing special on the Net. PBeM requires so little effort that players are often involved in multiple *Diplomacy* games simultaneously. The popular fantasy-adventure game *Monster Island* has hundreds of players using their corporate email accounts to send in fart orders (yup, you heard right). If you joined an *E-wrestling Federation* on the Net and sent in your moves, you'd very likely get back reports of matches that make WWF commentary sound like Wimbledon. And yes, of course, there are chess opponents from every time zone, skill level, and age group.

These cyber equivalents of classic postal play-by-mail make finding adversaries easier and submitting moves faster. But the games don't have to be fast. You can play twice a day or once a week. Just set the schedule with the other players. When the game involves more than two players, there's usually a computer or human game master, who processes moves, enforces deadlines, and reports game progress.

won't need a personal account and password to access the files. When you connect to an anonymous FTP machine, you will be asked for your name with the prompt **name:**. Type **anonymous** after the prompt. Next you'll be asked for your password with the prompt **password:**. Type your email address.

4. Once you're logged in to an FTP site, you can change directories by typing **cd <directory name>**. For example, the Monster Macintosh Gaming Archive at **mac.archive.umich.edu** is in **mac/game**. After login, type **cd mac/game** to change to the directory. (To move back up through the directory path you came down, you type **cdup** or **chdirup**). You must move up one directory at a time.

5. To transfer files from the FTP site to your "home" or "files" directory at your Internet site, use the **get** command. For example, in the Monster Macintosh Gaming Archive, you can download a computer version of *Risk*. Retrieve it by typing **get risk** and **[return]**. The distinction between the upper- and lowercase in directory and file names is important. Type a lowercase letter when you should have typed uppercase and you'll leave empty-handed.

All you need is an email address—sometimes not even that if the game is being played on a message board or through a file library. Play-by-email games are the most leisurely of games on the Net, but often the most intense; it's not unusual to find "the next move" taking over your idle thoughts.

Network and Modem-to-Modem Games

This is the domain of arcade-style graphics and action, with flight-sim treasures like *Air Warrior* and the infuriating marble puzzles of *Oxyd* drawing players into head-to-head competition. Four-person *Spectre* death matches that make office networks sag under the high performance pressure; *Bolo* tank battles joined by Internet users from every corner of Cyberspace; head-to-head *Doom* destruction planned and played over CompuServe's network or via direct phone connections.

The only requirements are that the game you want to play has modem-to-modem capabilities (hundreds do), that each player has a copy of the game on his or her machine, and that the machines are connected to each other one way or another.

The game may be one that was downloaded from a shareware archive on the Net or one purchased at the local software store. It doesn't matter.

There are many ways to connect two or more computers—whether they're in the same building or on different continents—and play network and modem-to-modem games.

Two computers that are in each other's vicinity can be hooked up with a cable (called a null-modem setup) to play a game; in offices and schools, people play network games on PCs that are linked with a local area network; connecting to a fellow player's computer with a modem over the regular phone lines is popular among Net users in the same area code; commercial-

The live-chat service on the Internet is called Internet relay chat, or IRC. The chat is real-time, which means that if you type something, the people you're chatting with—in Sweden, Switzerland, or the Sudan—see your words appear immediately on their screens. People from around the world gather in "channels" that are usually focused on a specific theme or subject. When a channel is "hot," there may be as many as 50 chatters. Sometimes, though, it's just you and a friendly stranger. If you would like to join the gaming channel **#bolo**, for instance, do the following:

1. If your Internet site offers IRC (sometimes such a site is called an IRC client), follow the site's access instructions. This may be as simple as typing **irc** at the main-menu prompt.

2. Once you're there, you can go to a particular channel. For example, to go to the channel **#bolo** all you have to do is type **/channel #bolo** and **<return>**. (Whatever you type on IRC appears on the other users' screens as dialogue, so if you don't want to converse but want to give an IRC command, you have to first type a backslash.)

3. If you want to see a list of available channels, with the number of people participating, and a short description of what the channels are about, type **/list** and press **<return>**.

→

service members hook up their computers using the service's network; and more and more often Netters with Internet access establish a link between their PCs via the Internet, using special IHHD (Internet head-to-head daemon) software.

See the Modem-to-Modem page (page 216) for information about the gaming lobbies on CompuServe and GEnie, where people hook up using the service's network, as well as for information on where to get instructions for IHHD.

Offline CD, Cartridge, and Computer Games

You know all those magazines and books that purport to tell you the "secret" to winning at *Mortal Kombat*, *NBA Jam*, or *Sim City 2000*? Well, the real secret is that they crib their best tips from the Net, where amateur game mavens and professional designers share their insights in a spirit of free exchange. The reviews never stop, the Easter eggs are always revealed, and advice is easily found.

Even when you can't play a particular game online, that doesn't mean you won't find discussion, support, patch files, upgrades, and scenarios galore for the hottest, latest, and most explosive versions of these offline games. Much of the light and noise surrounds the best-selling commercial games, but there are also tons of shareware gems like *VGA Planets* and *Maelstrom* for personal computers. Haggard players of arcade and home game system hits fill up bulletin boards, newsgroups, and file archives with tips on how to win everything from *Sonic 3* to *Civilization*.

Some of these games—and soon even the video-game cartridges—include network or modem features to breathe human competition into the entertainment.

4. If you would like to create your own channel, follow the same steps you would to join an existing channel, but substitute the new channel name you want. If there isn't already a channel named **#hotgames** on IRC, for example, you would type **/channel #hotgames** to create it.

5. To quit IRC, type **/quit** and **<return>**.

On **CompuServe**, chat takes place in the CB Simulator, which you can reach by using the **go** command from the menu and typing **cb** (or, if you don't have CompuServe's Information Manager software, type **go cb**). You can choose one of 36 channels to join. To join a channel, type **/cha <channel number>** and **<return>**.

AOL's chat area is The People Connection, which can be reached by using the keyword **chat**. The first screen you'll see is called The Lobby Window. The left side of the window contains four icons: People, Rooms, Center Stage, and PC Studio. "People" provides information about the people in whatever room you enter. "Rooms" gives a list of the rooms where conversation is currently taking place. "Center Stage" takes you to an online "auditorium," where AOL presents online guests and games. "PC Studio" offers a schedule of Center Stage activities and an overall guide to the conversation and topics in each of the rooms.

→

11. I'm the kind of person who likes to read the instructions first.

Games on the Net, like most other games, come with instructions. You just have to know where to look for them. Often, on the commercial services, instructions are available from the game's opening menu. If they're not, look in the file library of that service's main gaming forum or post a message on the gaming bulletin boards asking for help.

If we found instructions for a game in a not-so-obvious place, we've provided the address after the word "info." We've also listed the in-game commands for many games. Of course, simply typing **help** in games on the Internet, and sometimes on the commercial services, usually brings you more than enough information to get started. Still wary? Don't be. One of the best aspects of gaming on the Net is the other players: They'll help.

12. All these games sound pretty straight-forward, but what the hell are MUDs, MOOs, MUSHes, and MUCKs?

> **GEnie**'s chat area is ChatLines. You can reach it by typing the keyword **chat**. ChatLines is part of the LiveWire area and is divided into channels that you enter by typing **/cha <channel number>** and **<return>**. Information on all the channels is available in Channel 1, the Welcome Lounge.
>
> **Delphi**'s Chat area is centered in the Main Conference Area (type **go gr** conference). Its subject areas are called groups. To see a list of available groups when you enter the area, type **who** after the conference prompt. When you've selected a group you want to join, type **join <group name>** or **join <group number>** to enter the group. You can create your own conference group by typing **join** followed by a name that isn't currently on the menu.
>
> **Prodigy**'s chat area is available to Windows and Mac users. **Jump: chat**.

Named for multi-user dungeon, but more accurately called a multi-user dimension, the text world of a MUD can just as easily be gaslight San Francisco, a space station orbiting Earth, or, yes, a medieval kingdom. Sometimes there's an actual holy grail to find; other times MUD life is more like an extemporaneous soap opera, an elaborate costume party, or a heavy-duty session of role-playing group therapy.

MUD citizens like to create their worlds just as much they enjoy playing in them. Overlapping MUD variants include the building, role-playing, and socializing MOO, MUSH, MUSE, and MUCK; or the adventure-combat LPMUD, DikuMUD, and AberMUD (see the glossary for what these acronyms mean).

There are more than 500 MUDs in Cyberspace. Some of them draw hundreds of players a night; others attract small, intimate groups of regulars. Most are public, with newbies constantly filling the closets, churches, and town halls—the places where new players are usually welcomed. Others stay semiprivate—known only through word of mouth.

The only gossip more common than news about a new MUD is news about a lost MUD. The MUD world is constantly changing. Players who've been around a long time in cyber terms—a year or two in RL time—nostalgically look back at the "good old days" when *Space Madness*, *Islandia*, and many other now-deceased MUDs were at their peak.

Today's MUDs are tomorrow's Islandia. Why do MUDs go down? Usually because a university administrator closes the MUD after the game has turned the institution's mainframe into a smoking piece of scrap metal. But quite often it's the players who bring doom to their own world in an all-too-familiar outburst of political infighting. For up-to-the-minute MUD announcements, monitor the rec.games.mud* newsgroups.

13. But how do I play a MUD?

Let's take a walk through a generic MUD. Enter the MUD's address, press the return key, and—if the MUD is up—the opening screen will appear. Since on a MUD you're never who you are in real life, the next thing to do is get a character. In many cases, you just type **connect <a character's name of your choice> <a password of your choice>**, but in others you have to choose a race, like elf or orc, and a gender (try the one you've had less experience with).

Sometimes you first have to register your character by email while exploring the MUD as a guest in the interim. The commands for getting the essential information (what you absolutely must know to play) are almost always listed on the opening screen. Also, a

---

MUD COMMANDS

- **emote <action>** *or* **pose <action>** *or* **<action>** Allows you to describe what your character is doing (varies with server).

- **help** Often gives a directory of help information. You would then type **help <a choice from the directory>** to get topical help.

- **home** Returns the character to his or her home location.

- **look** *or* **l** Displays the description of an area.

- **look <object>** *or* **l <object>** *or* **read <object>** Displays the description of an object or character.

- **news** *or* **faq** *or* **info** Often supplements the help command with more site information (varies with server).

- **page <player>=message** *or* **tell <player>=message** Sends a message that only the specified character can hear (varies with server).

- **quit** *or* **QUIT** *or* **@quit** Disconnects you from the game (varies with server).

- **say <message>** *or* **"<message>** Sends a message to everyone in the local area (e.g., the room) you're in (varies with server).

- **whisper <player>=<message>** Sends a message that only the specified local character can hear

- **who** *or* **WHO** *or* **@who** Displays a list of all the players currently connected to the MUD (varies with server).

newbie or public channel on a MUD is often a great source of information and an easy way to meet people.

When you enter a MUD, a description of your surroundings—often a poetic one—will immediately scroll onto your screen. It will sing of the land you have set foot on, tell you of mysterious objects in the area, show you exits for leaving, and announce the other characters going about their business in the same area as you are. Or are they? Don't be surprised if you're eaten alive by a monster or beheaded by a fellow player. Such is MUD life—and death.

If you're still in one piece, let's wander around a bit. There are many ways to move in a MUD (from riding a flying carpet to attaching yourself to another player to teleporting), but the most common—and simplest—way is by typing the name of an exit or by typing a direction: **n** (north), **s** (south), **e** (east), **w** (west), **ne** (northeast), **se** (southeast), **nw** (northwest), **sw** (southwest), **u** (up), **d** (down).

As you travel a MUD, you may find objects along your way. You can trade or sell them, give them to someone else, wear them or wield them in battle, discard them, or—if they appear to be alive—lock them up or kill them, whatever you fancy. There are many action commands—including some for text sex—and it is recommended that you use the help facility on your particular MUD to learn about them.

On some MUDs, you'll start out with a small inventory of items you can add to or discard from as you go along. On combat MUDs, you will also need need to monitor your experience and skill levels.

The amount of power you have to change the MUD—i.e., build in it—depends on the server (MOOs and MUSHes offer the most freedom to build) and the administrator. Building commands are usually preceded by an @ to remind you that when you're building, you're changing the world.

MUD CLIENTS

What do clients do?

Auto-login: automatically logs you into your favorite MUD (login and password).

Gag: suppresses selective text. As with highlighting, you can choose to suppress a certain player's "voice" or certain expressions.

Highlighting: applies emphasis to certain text. You could, for instance, select certain players to have what they say highlighted so that you do not lose track of their "voices" in the flood of chatter around you. Or you could highlight text triggered by certain expressions.

Line Wrap: provides a feature that prevents the messy breaks in words common to telnet sessions.

Logging: records your MUD session to a file.

Macro: attributes certain phrases or commands to a key stroke to save typing or stores mini-programs you can run on the MUD.

Multiple logins: provides multiple, simultaneous connections to different MUDs.

Trigger: generates an action when another action occurs on the MUD (e.g., waving when a player enters the room)

→

14. Where are all those free games I've heard about?

Which client should you get?

Some longtime favorites:

- **MUDCaller** A DOS client
- **MUDDweller** A Macintosh client
- **Mudling** A Macintosh client
- **TinyTalk** A Unix client for TinyMUDs
- **TinyFugue** A Unix client (a.k.a. tf) for TinyMUDs
- **Tintin++** A Unix client for DikuMUDs

Oh, boy. Every corner of Cyberspace—on the local BBS, on the commercial services, on the Internet archives—is overflowing with oceans of freeware (public domain) and shareware (pay if you like it) games. The major commercial services—except, currently, Prodigy—have thousands of files in large download areas, often in both a games area and a computer or software area. Many of these files are free games. Even better, there are often playable demos of many hot new games (e.g., *Doom*) before they appear in software stores.

The largest archives are usually on the Internet (but check out the Atari RoundTables on GEnie for an example of how formidable the commercial services can be) and are accessed by FTP. You'll also find downloadable files on BBSs.

15. Uh, a small detail before I take off: How do I find opponents?

You won't be able to escape from them. Log into the Internet Chess Server, and within minutes you'll be paged by someone looking to have you checkmated in 13 minutes. Connect to a MUD and there will be half a dozen people or more in the connect room alone—never mind in the pubs, caves, space ships, and private rooms throughout it. Or, when you're ready to play a game of *Bolo*, telnet to the Bolo Tracker, which lists everyone on the Internet who's playing *Bolo*, and where. (Other games have this service as well.)

Players also hang out in game-related IRC channels, waiting for friends—and foes—to connect so they can set up a game. Usenet newsgroups as well as the message boards on the commercial services are filled with "players wanted" posts.

Or someone else will find you an opponent! Read the rec.games.chess newsgroup, for example, and see the chess email pairing system in action.

When you browse the CompuServe or GEnie play-by-mail discussion topics, you'll find—amid the heated playing, chatting, strategizing, and flaming—places to join games or learn about them.

And there's more. Web pages now carry lists of players who play the site's games.

Lists with players names and gaming interests circulate on newsgroups and mailing lists (see the Modem-to-Modem page for the addresses of two such lists). And on CompuServe and Delphi, the gaming and modem-to-modem forums are designed to bring players together. You simply can't miss them.

DECOMPRESSION UTILITIES				
Downloadable games may have been compressed. These are the utilities to decompress them, listed by suffix and platform.				
	DOS	**Mac**	**Amiga**	**Atari**
.ARC	arc	arcmac	pkax	arc
.arj	unarj	unarjmac	unarj	unarj
.cpt		Compact Pro		
.gz	gzip	Macgzip	gzip	gzip
.lha			lz	
.lzh	lha	MacLHA	lz	lha
.sea		*Self-Extracting Archive* (no utility needed)		
.sit		Stuffit Expander	unsit	
.Z	comp	Macgzip		
.ZIP	pkunzip	unzip	pkazip	unzip
.zoo	zoo	macbooz	zoo	zoo

16. Sometimes I just like to watch or compare notes.

Many games have an option that lets you ask the players if you can be a spectator. On others, like the Internet game servers, all you have to do is type **observe <players' name>** to watch a game in progress. In multiplayer games like the MUDs, the games in AOL's Game Parlor, or the IRC games, you can "lurk" without being chased away.

If you want gaming advice and instruction, turn to the players or to the hundreds of message boards, mailing lists, newsgroups, IRC channels, and chat rooms throughout Cyberspace that cover gaming subjects. They are so active that "sites" are becoming more and more specialized—for example, not only is there a newsgroup for *Doom* players, alt.games.doom, but there's also one for new *Doom* players, alt.games.doom.newplayers.

A ton of mailing lists and message boards are set up just for talking about games—rules, challenges, strategies, character stories, fantasy-world news, and much, much more. For some, the free secrets, cheats, and advice are more exciting and urgent than the free games. Just about every game is subjected to relentless probing by Netters, who freely share adventure walk-throughs, fighting-game moves, and secret codes. Want free bonds in *SimCity 2000*, blow-by-blow instructions for *Sonic 3*, Jeffrey's elbow throw in *Virtua Fighter*? These secrets fill game bulletin boards and discussion groups all over the Net.

Finally, the Web is an incredible resource for reading about, discussing, and downloading games. Whenever a game listed in this book is noted as having a

"Web home page," you can bet that it's your best online resource for the game. Wait until you see the information on the Bolo home page, including pictures of many of the more active Bolo players on the Net.

17. Got everything. Know everything. But how do I use this book?

If you know the specific game you want to play, discuss, or analyze, turn to the index, where every entry, subject, and game genre in the book is listed alphabetically. If you're not sure, or you want to experiment, you can browse and check out sites as you go along.

The book is divided into six parts:

• Shoot-'em-up

• Role-playing & Adventures

• Strategy

• Puzzle, Trivia & Word Games

• Personal Computer & Video Games

• Sex, Hubs, MUDs & More

Each part is broken down by subject: Modern Flight Sims, Historical Flight Sims, Combat Flight Sims, Noncombat Flights Sims, etc. In most instances, we've gone a step further. The Horror subject, for instance, has subheaders for Vampire and Werewolf games.

All entries in *Net Games* have a site name, a site description, an address, and, where applicable, cost information, related addresses, requirements, commands, and stats.

The first element in all entries is the name of the site, which appears in boldface. If the entry is a mailing

---

BOOK TERMINOLOGY

Terms that identify specific site information in a *Net Games* entry:

• **Archives:** the address of an archive of a mailing list or newsgroup.

• **FAQ:** the address where the FAQ can be found.

• **Interface:** the address where a frontend for the game can be found.

• **Info:** the address where instructions for the game or more information about the site can be found.

• **Support:** the email address of someone willing to answer questions about the game.

• **Register:** the registration address if a game requires you to register by email.

Additional information about the game is usually broken up into three parts:

• Under **Requirements** you'll find listed anything special you need to play, such as a certain type of monitor.

• Below **Commands** are a few commands unique to the game, and some for getting gaming instructions.

• The **Stats** provide a quick overview of the game in terms of difficulty, number of players, the style of competition, the interface, and the platform.

• **Difficulty:** Games are rated "simple," "average," or "com-

→

list, "(ml)" immediately follows; if a journal, "(j)"; if a newsgroup, "(ng)"; if a BBS echo, "(echo)"; and if a BBS, "(bbs)." Then the description of the site follows. A $ indicates that there are additional costs involved when you're playing a game on this site.

After the description, complete address information is provided. The first part of an address consists of a check mark, the name of the network, and an arrow. The arrow means "go to…" followed by all the steps you have to take, such as typing a command, starting a program, searching for a file, subscribing to a mailing list, or typing a Web site's URL. (Additional check marks indicate the other networks through which the site is accessible; triple dots indicate another address on the same network; and more arrows mean more steps.)

An address is context-sensitive—it follows the logic of the particular network. So, if the entry describes a Web site, the address following the arrow would be a URL that you would type on the command line of your Web browser. If it is a mailing list, the address would be an email address followed by instructions on the exact form of the email message. An FTP, telnet, or gopher address consists of the site's name, followed by a log-in sequence and a directory path or menu path when necessary (see the sidebars on pages 8–15).

In a commercial-service address, the arrow is followed by the service's transfer word (e.g., keyword, go word, or jump word), which will take you to the site. More arrows lead you along a path to the specific area on the site.

IRC addresses indicate what you must type to get to the channel you want once you've connected to the IRC program.

The name of a newsgroup entry or BBS echo is also its address, so there is no address information other than the network for these types of sites.

The notation for BBS addresses differs slightly from that for the other sites. The address for a BBS is its modem number (or numbers) followed by, where applica-

plex" based on such aspects as technical set-up, rules, keyboard commands, and the ease of winning. Of course, it all depends on how experienced a player you are.

- The **number of players** is indicated as "1" for single-player games; "1+" for games that can be played solo or against other players (live or in a game-by-game high-score competition); and ranges such as "4–7"—the minimum and maximum number of players—for multiplayer games.

- The style of **competition** is characterized "live" for real-time play; "personal best" when you're competing against yourself; "turn-based" when this is a play-by-mail game or any other game in which moves are contemplated for minutes, hours, days, or weeks before being submitted or played online; and "high score" for games that you play solo but that let you compete with others through a standardized scoring system or challenge ladder.

- Finally there's info on the game's **interface**, and the required **platform**.

ble, a log-in sequence. BBS games are listed in *Net Games* with the notice "check local bulletin board systems for this or similar games." In many instances, we've gone ahead and followed that phrase with the phone number of a BBS that carries the game, but there may be a bulletin board in your own area code that carries the game as well.

At other times—for a game like *chess*, for instance—one example would misrepresent the many, many variations of the game available. (There are hundreds of BBS *chess* programs.) In such a case the book suggests you "check a local bulletin board system for a variation of this game."

One more thing: addresses in Cyberspace are often long and they aren't always in plain English. Internet addresses in particular consist of one uninterrupted string of characters, hyphens, and underline marks. (The occasional port number in an Internet telnet address is not part of the uninterrupted string.) If an Internet address breaks to the next line in a *Net Games* entry, *there will be no hyphen to indicate the break* (to avoid confusion with hyphens that *are* part of the address). The absence of a hyphen *does not mean that the address consists of two words*—just type the address as one uninterrupted string.

18. All right, I'm ready. Last question: How do I keep from making a fool of myself?

You won't. Games need players—allies, opponents, role-players, good guys, bad guys. Join a game and your mere presence will be welcomed. You'll feel like you've just made a hundred new friends. They'll wave you in, chat you up, take you on a tour, make a pass at you—and then shoot you down, literally. Have a blast!

19. Oh, yes—what if I want more than games?

Try *Net Guide*! You should find it in your bookstore right beside *Net Games*.

Part 1

Shoot-'em-Up

Arcadelike action

Get some Apogee stock. These people put demos on the Net of some really fun stuff,

get you hooked, and then they go for the throat: Prices range from $29.95 to $59.95. In the lead role: Commander Keen, who fights aliens, saves the Milky Way, and rescues the baby-sitters. If this involves too little ballistics for you, start shooting at people from a cyberpod in **CyberStrike**, or a tank in *Spectre*. If you'd rather have the enemy bite a fruit tart than a bullet, play **Food Fight**. But do get that stock!

On the Net

Across the board

comp.sys.ibm.pc.games.action (ng) Discuss MS-DOS action and arcade games, classified as such by their fast-paced emphasis on hand-eye reflexes. Until recently, MS-DOS games and games for the arcade and home game machines didn't have a lot in common, but hits on disk like *Mortal Kombat* have changed all that; the discussion now includes these games as well as the games from Apogee, id, and other action-game designers. ✓**USENET**

Apogee

Blake Stone: Aliens of Gold You're British agent Blake Stone, and your job is to take down the insane Dr. Goldstern, who has plans for the destruction of

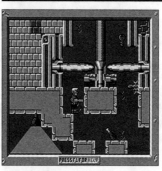

Screenshot from Duke Nukem—*from Apogee Software.*

mankind. A sci-fi setting for shoot-'em-up arcade-style adventures. ✓**COMPUSERVE**→*go* ibmnew→Libraries→*Search by file name:* BLAKE.ZIP ✓**GENIE**→*keyword* scorpia→Gamers Libraries→Set Library Category→ MS-DOS Games & Programs→*Download a file:* 7348 ✓**INTERNET**→ *ftp* wuarchive.wustl.edu→anonymous→<your email address>→/systems/ibmpc/msdos-games/Apogee→1bs20.zip

Stats
- Competition: personal best
- Number of players: 1
- Interface: graphical
- Platform: DOS

Commander Keen—Aliens Ate My Babysitter Demo. Keen must travel to the planet Fribbulus Xax and battle to save all the babysitters. ✓**AMERICA ONLINE**→*keyword* pcgames→Software Library→*Search by file name:* K6DEMO.ZIP ✓**COMPUSERVE**→*go* zenith→Libraries→*Search by file name:* KEEN6.ZIP ✓**GENIE**→*keyword* scorpia→Gamers Libraries→Set Software Library→MS-DOS Games & Programs→*Download a file:* 4705

Stats
- Difficulty: average
- Competition: personal best
- Number of players: 1
- Interface: graphical
- Platform: DOS
Requirements: *EGA or VGA graphics*

Commander Keen FAQ Not the best FAQ we've seen—more outline-bones than cheat-meat—but how else would you know to look for a surprise in Keen 4 by going to the Pyramid of the Crescent Moon and standing on one of the crescent moons? ✓**INTERNET**→ *ftp* ftp.uwp.edu→/pub/msdos/games/romulus/hints→keenfaq.zip

Commander Keen—Invasions of the Vorticons A huge shareware hit with 3D animation that's spawned several follow-up adventures. Eight-year-old Billy Blaze, aka Commander Keen, explores Mars in search of the secret city, while the alien Vorticons plan to conquer Earth. ✓**AMERICA ONLINE**→*keyword* pcgames→Software Library→*Search by file name:* 1KEENV3.ZIP ✓**COMPUSERVE**→*go* ibmnew→Libraries→*Search by file name:* A1KEEN.ZIP ✓**GENIE**→*keyword* scorpia→Gamers Libraries→Set Software Library→MS-DOS Games & Programs→*Download a file:* 3574 ✓**INTERNET**→*ftp* wuarchive.wustl.edu→anonymous→<your email address>→/systems/ibmpc/msdos-games/Apogee→1keen.zip

Stats
- Difficulty: average
- Competition: personal best
- Number of players: 1
- Interface: graphical
- Platform: DOS

Requirements: *EGA graphics or better; 640K*

Commander Keen—Goodbye Galaxy Once again Commander Keen finds himself on an alien planet—this time to rescue the keepers of the Oracle. The future of the Milky Way is at risk. ✓**COMPUSERVE**→*go* pbsarcade→Libraries→*Download a file:* GDBYE1. ZIP *and* GDBYE2.ZIP ✓**GENIE**→ *keyword* scorpia→Gamers Libraries →Set Software Library→MS-DOS Games & Programs→*Download a file:* 4095 ✓**INTERNET**→*ftp* wuarchive. wustl.edu→anonymous→<*your email address*>→/systems/ibmpc/msdos-games/Apogee→4keen.zip

Stats
- Difficulty: average
- Competition: personal best
- Number of players: 1
- Interface: graphical
- Platform: DOS

Crystal Caves Treasure hunter Mylo Steamwitz explores a star system for valuable crystals, but the planets are filled with dangerous monters and traps. Lots of action, adventure, and puzzles. ✓**AMERICA ONLINE**→*keyword* pcgames→ Software Library→*Search by file name:* #1crystl.zip ✓**COMPUSERVE**→*go* zenith→Libraries→*Search by file name:* CRYSTL.ZIP ✓**GENIE**→*keyword* scorpia→Gamers Libraries→Set Library Category→MS-DOS Games & Programs→*Download a file:* 3952 ✓**INTERNET**→*ftp* wuarchive. wustl.edu→anonymous→<*your email address*>→/systems/ibmpc/msdos-games/Apogee→1crystl.zip

Stats
- Difficulty: average
- Competition: personal best
- Number of players: 1
- Interface: graphical
- Platform: DOS

Requirements: *EGA or VGA graphics*

Duke Nukem You're Duke

> **"Keen must travel to the planet Fribbulus Xax and battle to save all the babysitters."**

Nukem, you're working for the CIA as a specialist (à la Rambo), and you have to stop Dr. Proton, a madman out to destroy Earth. Try to reach his hideout underneath the city. ✓**AMERICA ONLINE**→*keyword* pcgames→Software Library→*Search by file name:* #1DUKE.ZIP ✓**COMPUSERVE**→*go* ibmnew→Libraries→*Search by file name:* DUKE.ZIP ✓**GENIE**→*keyword* scorpia→Gamers Libraries→Set Software Library→MS-DOS Games & Programs→*Download a file:* 3568 ✓**INTERNET**→*ftp* wuarchive.wustl. edu→anonymous→<*your email address*>→/systems/ibmpc/msdosgames/Apogee→1duke.zip

Stats
- Difficulty: average
- Competition: personal best
- Number of players: 1
- Interface: graphical
- Platform: DOS

Requirements: *EGA or VGA graphics*

Duke Nukem II As Duke Nukem is being interviewed about his book, *Why I'm So Great,* he's abducted by aliens and must escape. ✓**AMERICA ONLINE**→*keyword* pcgames→Software Library→*Download a file:* #4DUKE.ZIP ✓**COMPUSERVE**→*go* ibmnew→Libraries→*Search by file name:* 4DUKE.ZIP ✓**GENIE**→*keyword* scorpia→Gamers Libraries→Set Library Category→MS-DOS Games & Programs→*Download a file:* 6916

Stats
- Difficulty: average

- Competition: personal best
- Number of players: 1
- Interface: graphical
- Platform: DOS

Requirements: *EGA or VGA graphics*

Keen Dreams Children are being held hostage by hostile vegetables. Commader Keen must enter the dream world of Tuberia to save them. ✓**AMERICA ONLINE**→*keyword* pcgames→Software Library→*Search by file name:* KEENDM01.ZIP ✓**COMPUSERVE**→*go* pbsarcade→Libraries→*Search by file name:* KEENDM.ZIP ✓**GENIE**→*keyword* scorpia→Gamers Libraries→Set Software Library→MS-DOS Games & Programs→*Download a file:* 5460 ✓**INTERNET**→*ftp* wuarchive. wustl.edu→anonymous→<*your email address*>→/systems/ibmpc/msdos-games/Misc→keendm01.zip

Stats
- Difficulty: average
- Competition: personal best
- Number of players: 1
- Interface: graphical
- Platform: DOS

Requirements: *EGA or VGA graphics; 640k+*

Major Stryker WWIII is history—it's the alien invaders that are now the big worry. Pilot a space ship into shoot-'em-up space action as you, Major Harrison Stryker, try to free the cryogenic hostages and destroy the alien headquarters on the planet of Kreton. ✓**AMERICA ONLINE**→*keyword* pcgames→Software Library→*Search by file name:* #1MAJR14.ZIP ✓**COMPUSERVE**→*go* fifthg→Libraries →*Search by file name:* #1MAJR.ZIP ✓**GENIE**→*keyword* scorpia→Gamers Libraries→ Set Library Category→MS-DOS Games & Programs→*Download a file:* 5755 ✓**INTERNET**→*ftp* wuarchive.wustl.edu→anonymous→<*your email address*>→/systems/ibmpc/msdos-games/

Apogee→1majr14.zip

Stats
- Difficulty: average
- Competition: personal best
- Number of players: 1
- Interface: graphical
- Platform: DOS

Requirements: *EGA or VGA graphics*

Wolfenstein-3D/Spear of Destiny FAQ

Wolfenstein-3D/Spear of Destiny FAQ The first monster action-adventure shareware games from id, the makers of *Doom*, explained. Internet discussion takes place on the comp.sys.ibm.pc.games.action newsgroup. Updates are frequent, so expect to find a higher version number replacing the 2_13 in the filename. ✓**INTERNET**→*ftp* ftp.uwp.edu→anonymous→<your email address>→/pub/msdos/games/id/home-brew/wolf3d→w3d-213.faq.Z

CyberStrike

Beginner's Tactical Guide Alternately titled "*CyberStrike* Survival: A Guide for New Players, Training and Beginner Cities." Compiled by other players, this concise rundown of strategic considerations covers everything from the obvious (take the high ground) to expert-level advice on topics such as advanced firefights, uses of launchpads, and heady power management. ✓**GENIE**→*keyword* mpgrt→Multiplayer Games Software Library→CyberStrike→*Download a file:* 3106

CyberStrike From your seat in a CyberPod, you're out to take control of as many cities as you can. Team up with other players—you'll need them when you're under attack. With a cockpit view from your chickenlike pod, scurry along the bleak, topologically varied 3D landscape collecting power-up modules, erecting energy towers, and dogfighting with ene-

CyberStrike *screenshot—downloaded from GEnie's Press RoundTable.*

my teams for territorial control. "Guppies" fly over head dropping new modules (no, you can't kill them), thunderstorms come in, day turns into night, and the fog rolls out.

Live (and die)

If the cockpit controls seem a bit daunting at first, just ignore them. Live (and die) a little. Go pick a few fights—you can pop right back into the same game almost instantly—before you even think about a strategy. Soon enough you can start cultivating your kill ratio and work your way up the informal ranks of the *CyberStrike* campaigns organized on GEnie. Up to 16 players can join in one game, the play is smooth even with a 2400-baud connection, and there's almost always a game to join after 6 p.m. EST, when GEnie's rates are lower.

Full stereo

The game takes full stereo advantage of your soundcard if you have one. The program is a free download, but it's no good until you join up with other *CyberStrike* players through a *CyberStrike* server (currently available only on GEnie, though it will probably be available on other services shortly). Instructions are available on the

same menu from which you download the game.

Newbie advice

Everything from newbie advice to advanced strategy is discussed in the *CyberStrike* area (category 15) of the MultiPlayer Games RoundTable. Informal tournaments and campaigns are also organized here. The RoundTable is an option off the *CyberStrike* menu, as are the CyberStrike Software Libraries, where players and the game designer Simutronics upload numerous help files. ✓**GENIE**→*keyword* cyberstrike

Stats
- Difficulty: average
- Competition: live
- Number of players: 2–16
- Interface: graphical
- Platform: DOS

Tank games

A-Maze-ing In this multiplayer game for the Mac on GEnie you're a tank in an underground maze with a lot of other tanks shooting at you. Download the graphic front-end software, then log back on to GEnie using the "dumb terminal" of the game or your own terminal software program. To play for scores and till death, select "Enter *A-Maze-ing*." For a more

> "Scurry along the topologically varied 3D landscape collecting power-up modules, erecting energy towers, and dogfighting enemies."

friendly area, where people are willing to help you learn the game, choose "Go to *A-Maze-ing* Training Area." Either way, you'll be in a maze with other tanks, picking up boxes of goodies, blowing each other up, and exploring the levels of the maze. (In the Training Area, you don't earn or lose points for kills, hence the more tolerant ambience.) The game was popular a few years back, but interest waned. It's experiencing a mild revival, and players now try to get together every night around 10 p.m. EST for some maze shoot-'em-up. ✓**GENIE**→*keyword* a-maze-ing *Interface:* ✓**GENIE**→*keyword* a-maze-ing→Download Software→Download a File→210 <or> 211

Stats

• Difficulty: average
• Competition: live
• Number of players: 2+
• Interface: graphical
• Platform: Macintosh

Combat Tanks v1.0 An animated, action battle game for Windows. Play either head-to-head or against the computer. The armies consist of soldiers, small tanks, bombers, and choppers. The terrain is configurable, and includes water, mud, and movable walls. ✓**COMPUSERVE**→*go* gamers→Libraries→*Search by file name:* TANK.ZIP

Stats

• Difficulty: average
• Competition: personal best *or* live
• Number of players: 1–2
• Interface: graphical
• Platform: Windows

Requirements: *Windows-compatible soundcard; joystick*

rec.games.xtank * (ng) *XTank,* a tank game for Xwindows, has two official newsgroups—rec. games.xtank.play and rec.games. xtank.programmer—but activity in both is minimal. Most of the

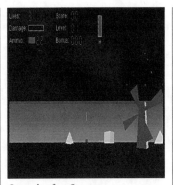

Screenshot from Spectre.

discussion in both groups revolves around compiling, installation, and where-do-I-find-the-code questions. ✓**USENET**

Spectre Challenge Ladder

The commercial 3D tank battle *Spectre* is one of those games that you use to show off your computer. Even the original version (superseded by *Spectre Supreme, Spectre VR,* and a CD version of the latter) has smooth, excellent graphics and, more important, ferocious game play. Play it by yourself or over your local network. Although not shareware, the game has a large Net following on CompuServe, where *Spectre* players use their store-bought game to compete with each other in the Modem Lobby—and to climb the challenge ladder posted regularly on the Message Board. The instructions for playing *Spectre* via CompuServe are in the Library. ✓**COMPUSERVE** ...→*go* mtmforum→ Libraries→Action Games ...→*go* mtmforum→Messages→Tank Sims & Games

Tank v2.4 An arcade game with 3D graphics, sound effects, and 15 missions. In addition to tanks, the game includes choppers, lasers, missiles, napalm, and flamethrowers. ✓**COMPUSERVE**→*go* gamers→Libraries→*Search by file name:*

TANK.ZIP

Stats

• Difficulty: average
• Competition: personal best *or* live
• Number of players: 1–4
• Interface: graphical
• Platform: DOS

Requirements: *286; EGA or VGA; MS mouse; 101 keyboard*

Xpilot

alt.games.xpilot (ml/ng) The art of flying, the art of killing, the art of finding more players to kill. Messages posted to the mailing list (below) are also gatewayed to here. (Xwindows or Unix only, thank you very much). The FAQ is focused on setting the game up and comes complete with an extensive troubleshooting section in case you can't get off the ground. Also included is information on how to create your own playable maps. ✓**USENET** ✓**INTERNET**→*email* xpilot-request@cs.uit.no ✐ *Write a request Archives:* ✓**INTERNET**→*ftp* ftp.cs.odu.edu→anonymous→<your email address>→/pub/news/alt. games.xpilot

Xpilot So there you are, just sort of flying around, enjoying the view, when all of a sudden some

> "Get hit points by throwing food at other players. You can purchase objects for your protection (like a raincoat or a table to hide under)."

bastards start firing at you! Good thing you've got your smart missiles and your heat seekers and your mines. Outmaneuver your opponents and blow 'em apart in this fast-paced multiplayer game. The FTP site carries the game code. ✓ **INTERNET**→*ftp* ftp.cs.uit.no→ anonymous→<your email address> →/pub/games/xpilot→xpilot-3.2.2.tar.gz

Stats
• Difficulty: average
• Competition: live
• Number of players: 2+
• Interface: graphical
• Platforms: UNIX, X Windows

XPilot Home Page Contains the whole shooting match, no pun intended: The FAQ is here, access to the Meta Server is available (not to mention several backup servers), information on the game's inventors, and access to sites that will let you play *XPilot* with sound effects! ✓ **INTERNET**→ *www* http://www.cs.uit.no/XPilot

---

XPilot Maps New maps lend variety to the game; and there are dozens to download from this site, incuding maps with names like "babe.map" and "Big_Bang.map" which sound like they add more than just variety. ✓ **INTERNET**→*ftp* xpilot.sdsu.edu→anonymous→<your email address>→/pub/xpilot-maps

---

XPilot Meta Server So you've got the game; now you need the players. *XPilot* is not on a single Cyberspace location, but the Meta Server helps to keep the *XPilot* universe a little organized. Telnetting here will get you a list of *XPilot* servers running on the Internet and the status of games in progress there. ✓ **INTERNET**→*telnet* xpilot.cs. uit.no 4400

Commands
• To get the email address of the registered *XPilot* servers, type: list

• To focus your queries on a specific server, type: server <server's telnet address>
• To query about a specific server (players, scores, etc.), type: status <server's telnet address>

Other action

Deluxe Chase ANSI arcade game similar to the old arcade game *Berserk*. Use all your wits— not to mention your laser—to escape from a maze with robots thirsty for your blood! ✓ CHECK LOCAL BULLETIN BOARD SYSTEMS FOR THIS OR SIMILAR GAMES ☎→*dial* 502-375-4657

Stats
• Difficulty: simple
• Competition: high scoring
• Number of players: 1+
• Interface: ANSI
• Platforms: all

Food Fight Silly fun. Get hit points by throwing food at other players. You can purchase objects for your protection (like a raincoat or a table to hide under). ✓ CHECK LOCAL BULLETIN BOARD SYSTEMS FOR THIS OR SIMILAR GAMES ☎→*dial* 408-229-0706

Stats
• Difficulty: simple
• Competition: live
• Number of players: 3+
• Interface: ANSI
• Platforms: all

Lemmings FAQ Game goal: to save as many lemmings from suicide as you can. There's a serious guide to this silly action game, with elaborate technical details to bring the game to its knees. Internet discussion takes place on the comp.sys.ibm.pc.games.action and the comp.sys.ibm.pc.games.misc newsgroups. ✓ **INTERNET**→*ftp* ftp. uwp.edu→anonymous→<your email address>→/pub/msdos/games/ romulus/hints→ lemfaq.zip

BattleTech & mecha

FASA's *BattleTech* games have inspired not only Net discussion—see rec.games.mecha

—but also intense online simulations of the *BattleTech* universe (where giant mech robots, the ultimate weapons of the 31st century, are more valuable than life). On the Internet, *BattleTech* MUSEs come and go (new ones begin at different points on the *Btech* time line), but they consistently draw more than 100 players an evening. **Btech 3056** has been around for a while, but if the battle's been won and the game has closed by the time you're ready to play, check the newsgroup for word of others.

A Mechwarrior—downloaded from GEnie's Scorpia RoundTable.

- Competition: turn-based
- Number of players: 2–5
- Interface: graphical
- Platform: DOS

Requirements: *Must download a frontend; color EGA/VGA terminal*

On the Net

Mech battles

Battle Grid After the world is nearly destroyed in an all-out nuclear world war, it is determined by law that the battlefield for future conflict resolution is an arena of huge machines ("mechs") that battle it out for world supremacy. You are a mech pilot with the responsibility of supplying and arming the finest mech possible. Players make their moves once a day and then wait till midnight, when the turns are processed. ✓CHECK LOCAL BULLETIN BOARDS FOR THIS OR SIMILAR GAMES ☎→*dial* 904-241-6301

Stats
- Difficulty: complex

Btech 3056 As the ComStar in the year 3056 gears up for its next battle with the Clans, it's a time of transition and intrigue in the *BattleTech* universe. Gigantic 10-meter robots, called the BattleMechs, duel for supremacy; mech warriors who pilot the BattleMechs are the heroes of this age. *Btech 3056* is huge, crowded, and complicated, but if you're a *BattleTech* junkie with a penchant for combat, it's a lot of fun. There's a sophisticated combat system that can support fights among dozens of robots at the same time (not that there won't be some lag) allowing players to battle opponents in simulations, skirmishes, and full-blown invasions. Your ability to kill and kill quickly is more important than your talent for role-playing. Come here to chat about *BattleTech*, kibitz with members of

your faction, and fight.

Join a faction

Your first goal on the MUSE will be to join one of the factions, which are always eager to recruit anyone who knows one end of a laser from another. Enter the hotel lobby, and read all the newbie topics you can. You'll be lost otherwise. Look at the Faction Leader Info to find out which leaders are connected. Then try to buy a ticket to visit the faction of your choice from Raglin's Robo-Vendor (not always easy, but you're in a room with other newbies, so talk it through). When you've bought your ticket, hop on the elevator and go talk to your preferred faction about recruiting possibilities. Don't worry. If they don't want you, the ticket's round-trip. Newbies have the run of the hotel—so do explore! Players are allowed to program on *Btech 3056* and it's recommended you learn how to—you'll go farther. Make sure you know something about *BattleTech* before you try this MUSE. ✓**INTERNET**→*telnet* mccool.cbi.msstate.edu 3056→create <your character> <password>

Stats
- Difficulty: complex
- Competition: live
- Number of players: 1+
- Interface: ASCII
- Server: MUSE
- Platforms: all

Commands
- To get instructions, type: newbie news
- To use the newbie channel for help, type: new <your message>
- To get a list of channels for the online communication system,

type: +channel
- To speak on a channel, type: +com <channel name> = <your message>
- To move an object or yourself to another area, type: @teleport <object or yourself> <area or room>
- To search for a player, type: @whereis <player>

Mech Warriors Played out on a 100x100 matrix, *Mech Warriors* offers 10,000 sectors you can explore in search of the computer controlled "drones" who must be destroyed and then salvaged for spare parts to increase your own power. There are 1,000 different "ports" throughout the universe where players can buy and sell their salvaged metals. Team play can be useful for spying and sharing information, but real player enemies can be much more destructive than the "drones," so be careful about whom you count on as a friend. ✓CHECK LOCAL BULLETIN BOARDS FOR THIS OR SIMILAR GAMES ☎→*dial* 919-489 9446

Stats
- Difficulty: complex
- Competition: live
- Number of players: 2+
- Interface: ANSI
- Platforms: all

MultiPlayer BattleTech Enter the world of the Inner Sphere around the year 3026, generate a character, and start your training as a mech warrior at the military academy. After graduating from the academy, you'll be transferred to a House military unit. You may go on missions for the House, operate as a mercenary, or fight on Solaris VII in the Inner Sphere equivalent of bullfight spectacles. Meanwhile, you can chat live with other players, engage in combat with other mech warriors, board trams to move across planets, or

travel between planets.

What it takes

You gotta have what it takes to be a mech warrior, and in GEnie's case, you gotta have an IBM-PC. If you do, download the program and data files (BTECH.EXE and MECHDATA.EXE, respectively) from an option on the opening menu. Besides reading the extensive game description (also available from the opening menu), newcomers would do well to visit the the Multiplayer Games RoundTable and root through the Multiplayer Games Software Library for beginners' advice. They should also check out the two bulletin boards (MP Battletech Solaris Warriors and MultiPlayer BattleTech) and attend the weekly live conference. ✓GENIE→*keyword* btech

Stats
- Difficulty: complex
- Competition: live
- Number of players: 2+
- Interface: graphical
- Platform: DOS

Requirements: *EGA or VGA graphics*

RL simulations

BattleTech VR (ml) Battle other mech warriors in *real life*. The list will give you the details. ✓INTERNET→*email* hen8@uchicago.midway.edu *Write a request*

Support material

The BattleTech Archive GIFs, shareware games for several computer platforms, alternate rules of play, documentation for the *Btech* MUSEs, and player aides—all related to FASA's *BattleTech* game—are archived here. ✓INTERNET→*ftp* soda.berkeley.edu→anonymous →<your email address>→/pub/ btech

---

BattleTech Files & Discussion

Stats for mechs and vehicles, tactical handbooks, images, fiction, maps, and a few programs, including an actual mech game (MECH11.ZIP). Not a lot of discussion on the message boards. ✓**COMPUSERVE**→*go* rpgames→ Libraries *or* Messages→SF/Near Future→*Search by keyword:* battletech

---

io.games.fasa.battletech A low-volume newsgroup with a representative from FASA as the moderator. More product information than discussion, but discussion is encouraged. ☎→*dial* 512-448-8950→<your login>→ <your password>→<choose a newsreader like "tin">→io.games. fasa.battletech ✓**INTERNET**→*telnet* io.com→<your login>→<your password>→<type a newsreader like "tin">→io.games.fasa.battletech

---

net.mekton.mecha.book A huge collection of mecha designs created by dozens of Net authors. The designs may be used in the *Mekton Mecha* combat/roleplaying game. ✓**INTERNET** …→*ftp* wais.com →anonymous→<your email address>→/pub/games/cyberpunk/ mekton …→*ftp* ftp.ccs. neu.edu→ anonymous→<your email address> →/pub/people/ratinox/mekton …→*ftp* ftp.netcom.com→ anonymous→<your email address>→ /pub/sandman/mekton

---

rec.games.mecha (ng) If killer robots are your passion, especially the ones in FASA's *BattleTech*, here's the place to discuss the books, cartoons, and games. From PC *BattleTech* to the MUSEs on the Internet, strategy and rule discussions are ongoing. Game updates are monitored closely, including site changes for the MUSEs. Role-playing in the form of mech challenges is also quite common. ✓**USENET**

Bolo

This tank battle game is dominated by college students

with handles like Flash Force, Wolverine, and Amoeba, who have direct (often Ethernet) Internet access—anything less via the Internet is just too slow for this lightning-paced game. Organized competitions between university *Bolo* teams take place every semester. Scandals over which teams cheated (hacked the game) are ongoing. But *Bolo* players are not just students. On **#bolo** and **rec.games.bolo**, you'll find *Bolo* fanatics from all walks of life, including office workers who avidly play the game over AppleTalk. *Bolo* is available as shareware and can be downloaded—as can the huge collections of *Bolo* maps and several map-making editors—from the **Bolo Archives** or from the **Bolo Libraries** on AOL, and CompuServe.

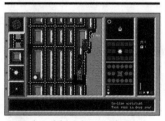
Screenshot of the Bolo map of Manhattan—from saloon.intercon.com.

On the Net

Bolo You, your allies, and your enemies are tanks. The little green men in the game, well, they just work for you—constructing bridges, walls, and buildings to help protect your bases. Survival, per se, isn't so important since you and the men have unlimited lives, but lose all your bases or find yourself unable to get to a base to refuel and it's all over. Tank battles—some can last for hours—only "end" or, more likely, wind down when you or your opponents can no longer access the all-important refueling bases. What's more, you need bases to get ammunition. (You need ammunition to fight.)

Swaps

There are swamps and water to cross and rubble and craters to move through. Fortunately, there are also bridges and roads to help your tank movement, as well as forests to hide in.

But beware! Your enemies will lay mines or hide in the forest to mount an ambush (advice: Yell to your allies for help), and you won't be able to see what they're planning—only their allies will. Double agents and traders will wreak all sorts of intrigue in the midst of the raging war. Perhaps most important, you'll need to capture some of the powerful pillboxes which are programmed to shoot and fight far better than you could ever do. (Hint: Run over a pillbox to make it yours—just disabling it isn't enough.)

It takes practice and often an allied strategy, but patience and co-operation pay off. A captured pillbox is a loyal pillbox, and loyal pillboxes are great for protecting your bases.

A Mac and a network

To play, you need a Macintosh, system 6.0 or higher (color monitor preferred), a network (a local or remote Appletalk connection will do, but to join Internet competitions you'll need a Mac-TCP connection), and the same version of *Bolo* as your opponents. The game comes with a map of Everard Island, but you can also use one of the several map-making editors to create new, challenging terrain. Or try someone else's map. The game begins with your tank in shallow water on a boat just off the coast of an island. Make your way to land... ✓**INTERNET** ...→*ftp* fpm.uchicago.edu→anonymous→ <your email address>→ Bolo992 package.sit.hqx ...→*ftp* aurora. alaska.edu→anonymous→<your email address>→/mac/games/ shareware/bolo→bolo-0-992-2-cpt.hqx ✓**AMERICA ONLINE**→*keyword* mgm→Software Libraries→ *Search by keyword:* bolo v.0.99.2 ✓**COMPUSERVE**→*go* mac fun→Libraries→*Search by file name:* BOLO.CPT

Stats
- Difficulty: average
- Competition: live
- Number of players: 1–16
- Interface: graphical
- Platform: Macintosh

Commands
- Read the documentation that comes with the game, including the Bolo.FAQ and the MacBolo

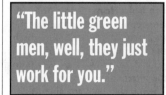
"The little green men, well, they just work for you."

Bolo Shoot-'em-Up

Instructions
- To move forward, press: q
- To stop, press: a
- To turn left, press in the number pad: /
- To turn right, press in the number pad: *
- To fire the tanks, press in the number pad: 0

Archives

Bolo Archives Carries the current *Bolo* program, which includes creator Stuart Cheshire's instructions on how to play, his FAQ, and a statement about plans for *Bolo*'s future. There are huge map collections, which differ by archive, including maps based on Atlantis, Florida, Harvard Yard, and Manhattan. Map editors for generating your own maps are also available. *Bolo* can be played with different versions of Brains (programs to help you control your tank or, if no other players are available, to serve as the enemy), several of which are included here. Strategy guides (see Puppy Love's Tactics & Strategy Guide), *Bolo* utilities, and other additions or enhancements to the game also end up in here. ✓**INTERNET** ...→*ftp* saloon.intercon.com→anonymous →<your email address>→/pub/ mac/bolo ...→*ftp* aurora.alaska. edu→anonymous →/mac/games/ shareware/bolo ...→*ftp* mac. archive.umich.edu→anonymous→ <your email address>→/mac/ game/war/bolo ...→*ftp* sumex-aim.stanford.edu→anonymous→ <your email address>→/info-mac/ game/bolo

The Bolo Home Page An excellent resource for discovering the *Bolo* scene. There are links to both the International and the European Bolo Trackers as well as to the international player registries. These include a searchable Multi-media Player Registry, with player images and hobbies, *Bolo* preferences, and email addresses; the Chicago Player Registry, with *Bolo* nicknames and email addresses; the European Player Registry, with names and email addresses of European *Bolo* players; and the Australian Player Registry with lots of information on Australian players. The *Bolo* Home Page also carries the indexes of Bolo FTP sites on the Internet; information on the Central Bolo League, including statistics and schedules, and news about the IRC channel and newsgroup. ✓**INTERNET**→*www* http:// compstat.wharton.upenn.edu:8001 /~frazier/Bolo/BoloHome.html

Bolo Libraries Includes *Bolo* maps, map editors, Brains, and the game itself. ✓**AMERICA ONLINE**→ *keyword* mgm→Software Libraries→ *Search by keyword:* bolo ✓**COM-PUSERVE**→*go* macfun→Libraries→ *Search by keyword:* bolo

The Official Bolo Archive Includes the latest version of *Bolo*, the FAQ for rec.games.bolo, a collection of maps, Mosaic with the *Bolo* Home Page in the hot list, IRC clients, Maven, Bolo Tracker, and Bolo Finder. ✓**INTERNET**→*ftp* fpm.uchicago.edu→anonymous→ <your email address>

Contacts

Stuart Cheshire Creator of *Bolo*. A virtual god to *Bolo* players. How does Cheshire rate himself in the *Bolo* players' multimedia registry? "...Honorary *Bolo* God (I'm not very good, but I do have the source code)." ✓**INTERNET**→*email* cheshire@cs.stanford.edu ✍ *Email with general correspondence*

Discussion

 # bolo Talk *Bolo*! Chat with others about strategy, find opponents, and track other games in progress. ✓**INTERNET** ...→*irc* /channel #bolo ...→*irc* /channel #bolo2

Bolo Discussion on AOL Discussion for people just discovering *Bolo* and for those already addicted. This group is far friendlier to newbies than the cutthroat rec.games.bolo newsgroup. ✓**AMERICA ONLINE**→*keyword* mgm→Message Boards→Let's Discuss–Mac Games→Strategy & Tactics→Bolo

Brain Programmers (ml) Discuss the programming of Brains (codes to control your tanks). Brains may be used to play a form of solitaire *Bolo* in which they're your enemies. ✓**INTERNET**→*email* listserv@ncrpda.curtin.edu.au ✍ *Type in message body:* subscribe brain <your full name>

rec.games.bolo (ng) Discuss *Bolo*, post and download *Bolo* maps and strategy guides, find tournament schedules, and look for opponents. The Top 40 List of *Bolo* maps is posted here monthly. A *Bolo* FAQ (covering computing requirements, Internet resources, strategy, and rules) is posted twice a month and archived. And if unwanted guests have intruded on your Internet *Bolo* game or lag time has slowed down a game, this is the place to gripe. While the newsgroup alt.netgames.bolo still exists at some sites, rec.games.bolo has almost completely superseded it. ✓**USENET** *FAQ:* ✓**INTERNET** ...→*ftp* cybercow.rh.uchicago.edu →anonymous→<your email address>→/pub/BoloFAQ ...→*ftp* fpm.uchicago.edu→anonymous→ <your email address>

Hints

Puppy Love's Unofficial Bolo Tactics and Strategy Guide A

guide packed with hints to improve your *Bolo* game. Features explanations ranging from "taking out a pillbox" to setting up a defense. ✓**INTERNET**→*ftp* fpm.uchicago.edu→anonymous→<your email address>→Tactics-&-Stretegy-Guide.txt

Utilities

Bolo Finder or Black Lightning's Fast Tracker Utilities for telnetting to the BoloTracker. ✓**INTERNET**→*ftp* mac.archive.umich.edu→anonymous→<your email address>→/mac/game/war/bolo/tracker

BoloTrackers Track *Bolo* games in progress on the Internet. Follow who's playing, where they're playing, the number of players, the name of the map they're using, and the number of neutral pills and neutral bases. (*Bolo* comes with a built-in option to update the BoloTracker about the status of your game, allowing the Internet community to follow the game.) Looking to join in? This is the place to find a raging battle. ✓**INTERNET** ...→*telnet* gwis.circ.gwu.edu 1234 ...→*telnet* ray.abo.fi 50000

Other info

The Chicago Player Registry A registry of *Bolo* players that includes both Internet and AppleTalk players. To register yourself, email your name, handle, and email address. The registry is updated weekly at the FTP and WWW sites. ✓**INTERNET** ...→*email* aaron_bratcher@fpm.uchicago.edu ✍ *Email with registration information* ...→*ftp* fpm.uchicago.edu→ anonymous→<your email address> ...→*www* http://ticker.wharton.upenn.edu:8001/Bolo/BoloHom.html

---

CYBERNOTES

Top Ten Mistakes by Average Players

1. Spiking with one pillbox, often unprotected
2. Sending the builder out to fix a pillbox without heed or protection
3. Building lots of walls to take a neutral pillbox
4. Ignoring bases and only trying to take pills
5. Attacking an enemy pillbox with two or fewer walls and no support, while the enemy is right next to it
6. Getting spiked while on a base, missing the builder, and then shooting the pillbox about 12 times and having it kill you; don't shoot it at all, just back off and take your time
7. Ignoring defense in a pill war
8. Not checking for mines before building
9. Attacking a pill and being forced to turn and run from fire
10. Being afraid to pick up a dead friendly pill

—**Puppy Love's Unofficial Bolo Tactics and Strategy Guide**

Doom

Doom is quite simply the hottest action game around for the personal computer. How to

explain the game's epidemic spread? It's not the story line—the classic spurious sci-fi setup for a blasting spree (you're a space marine, stuck on a Martian moon, battling to reclaim a military base overrun with alien baddies). So here's what's great: episodes like "Knee Deep in the Dead" that make *Mortal Kombat* look like Fischer Price; texture-mapped, animated, morphed, open-architecture graphics so real you can almost taste virtual reality; and most of all, a multi-user death match that gives new meaning to the term "friendly fire." And when accounting for *Doom*'s dominating popularity among shoot-'em people, don't forget the free Net distribution of the fully functioning first level, a marketing plan not so different from giving away trial-size samples of crack.

On the Net

Across the board

Doom on AOL Mucho megabytes of add-ons and cheats. The local discussions supplement AOL's access to the busier Usenet newsgroups by providing a patient community for answering the in-

Screenshot from Doom—*from America Online's PC Graphics Forum.*

evitable questions about modem-configuration problems. ✓**AMERICA ONLINE** …→*keyword* pcgames→ Message Boards→Other Games→ Doom: General Folder (for messages) …→*keyword* pcgames→Software Library→*Search by keyword:* doom (for files)

Doom on CompuServe CompuServe is riding *Doom* hard, setting up tourneys, assigning staff sysops, and keeping the downloads as current and complete as possible. Even better, the Modem-to-Modem Lobby (see separate entry) is a good place to find a *Doom* partner if you're in a palindromic *Doom* mood. You'll have to log off and connect directly, though, since the game-playing facility supports only 2400 baud, which really isn't good enough for *Doom*. The Gamers' Forum also supports active *Doom* discussions and files. ✓**COMPUSERVE** …→*go* mtmforum →Libraries *or* Messages→Action/ Arcade Games (for Modem Games Forum) …→*go* mtmlobby

(for the Modem-to-Modem lobby) …→*go* gamers→Libraries *or* Messages→Action Games (for the Gamers' Forum)

Doom on GEnie *Doom* discussion happens across several categories on the Games Bulletin Board. Launches are conducted in the "Category 3: Other Games in Scorpia's Games Roundtable." Games are organized in Topic 26, "DOOM Modem Tournament/ Network Stuff"; topic 40, "-= DOOM 3D =- Editor Use/Making Levels," is for talking about making new *Doom* map designs; topic 41, "DOOM 1.2: Our modems are DOOMED?" is the best place to puzzle out modem-configuration problems; topic 42 is filled with posts on "*Doom* Wish List for New Features"; more general discussion fills topic 46, "DOOM 3D—successor to Wolfenstein (id)." There is also a Doom Files library packed with patches, maps, FAQs, images, cheats, walk-throughs, audio files, and the program itself—files 7374 and 7375. ✓GENIE ...→*keyword* scorpia →Games Bulletin Board→ set 3 (for messages) ...→*keyword* scorpia→ Gamers Libraries→Set Library Category→DOOM FILES (for files)

Doom talk

alt.games.doom (ng) Daily posts number in the hundreds. And why shouldn't they? There are war stories and high scores to boast about, battles to coordinate, add-ons to discuss, and future versions about which to speculate. ✓USENET

Doom Stalkers (echo) Meet other players of *Doom*, and trade secrets and strategies. ✓ICENET

Players

alt.games.doom.newplayers (ng) Created to siphon some of the newbie noise away from the alt.games.doom newsgroup. The perfect place to pose that question you know you'd be able to answer if you bothered to read the FAQ. ✓USENET

#doom Cruise the channel to pick up IHHD game players. ✓IN-TERNET→*irc* /channel #doom

Doom Modem Contact List Should you be in short supply of *Doom* company, here's a directory of anonymous *Doom* modem players from practically every state and a few nasty long-distance possibilities from as far away as Australia and Hong Kong. ✓INTERNET→ *email* 73743.431@compuserve.com ✍ Type in *subject line:* DMCL-Add me *Type in message body:* <your state and country> <your area code and exchange> <your handle or first name> <your city> <death-match, cooperative, or either>

✓COMPUSERVE→*go* mtmgames→Libraries→Action/Arcade Games ✓INTERNET→*ftp* wuarchive.wustl. edu→anonymous→<your email address>→/pub/MSDOS-UPLOADS/ gmes/doomstuff→modplay.txt

Programs & files

alt.binaries.doom (ng) One of the brilliant touches in *Doom* is the open architecture for plugging in new features. Mini-programs that augment *Doom*—such as the popular multiplayer death hockey—are posted here all the time. Also check out the FTP sites for archives of *Doom* add-ons. ✓USE-NET

Doom The current version at press time is shareware, v1.2, which is the first to include support for modem play and the much vaunted Nightmare mode. The basic package is approximately 2 megabytes. The shareware version of *Doom* needs about 5 megs of hard-drive space. (To get the program, pick a site, any site.) The mail-order version needs about 12 megabytes of hard-drive space. *Doom* will make you hug yourself for having a soundcard. The game maker says it is working on a version for the Atari Jaguar. ✓INTERNET ...→*ftp* infant2.sphs. indiana.edu→anonymous→<your email address>→/pub/doom ...→ *ftp* ftp.uml.edu→anonymous→ <your email address>→/msdos/ Games/ID ...→*ftp* wuarchive. wustl. edu→anonymous→<your email address>→/pub/MSDOS_ UPLOADS/games/doom ...→*ftp* ftp.funet.fi→anonymous→<your email address>→/pub/msdos/ games/id

Stats
- Difficulty: complex
- Competition: live
- Number of players: 1–4
- Interface: graphical

- Platform: DOS
Requirements: *386sx or better; MS-DOS version 3.3 or higher; VGA graphics; 4MB of RAM*

Doom Archives You're not done downloading when you get the basic game (see Getting the Program). You need *Doom* add ons to cheat, edit maps, play with the sounds, and introduce entirely new features like Pong modules. Many add ons will work only on the registered version. ✓INTERNET ...→*ftp* infant2.sphs.indiana.edu→ anonymous→<your email address> →/pub/doom ...→*ftp* ftp.orst.edu→ anonymous→<your email address> →/pub/gaming/doom ...→*ftp* ftp.uwp.edu→anonymous→<your email address>→/pub/msdos/ games/id/home-brew/doom ...→*ftp* wuarchive.wustl.edu→ anonymous→<your email address> →/pub/MSDOS_UPLOADS/games /doomstuff

"Official Doom FAQ" Covers just about everything to do with the game and points to the rest. ✓INTERNET ...→*email* ap641@cleve land.freenet.edu→anonymous→ <your email address> ✍ *Type in subject line:* DOOM FAQ Request ...→*ftp* ftp.uwp.edu→anonymous→ <your email address>→/pub/ms-dos/games/id/home-brew/doom ...→*ftp* ocf.unt.edu→anonymous→ <your email address>→/pub/ doom/text ...→*ftp* wuarchive. wustl.edu→anonymous→<your email address>→/pub/msdos_ uploads/games/doomstuff

Support

Software Creations BBS (bbs) Official BBS of id Software. Home to the FAQ, shareware game program, and many other downloadable, *Doom*-related megabytes. ☎→*dial* 508-368-7036/508-368-4137/508-365-2359

Fighting games

Without virtual-reality goggles, CD-ROM, or even a plastic
gun, the Capcom arcade game *Street Fighter* single-handedly revitalized the Nintendo-eclipsed coin-op business in the early '90s, sucking more quarters than anything since the day that *Pacman* ate the brains of an entire generation. Its success spawned a whole genre of head-to-head fighting games replete with sequels, home cartridges, and product spin-offs for the exaggerated, stereotyped fighting characters. On the Net, clone after clone emerged—see *Kung Fu Louie, Stick Fighter 2, Sangho Fighter,* and *The Executioners*—and countless volumes of fighting moves were published. Check out the **Street Fighter 2 Guides**. And, for every *SF2* character analysis or move diagram, there was one for *Mortal Kombat 2*—the now-aging favorite, whose gore made headlines and embarrassed video-game manufacturers into establishing a rating system.

Street Fighter II's *Cammy—down-loaded from ftp.krl.caltech.edu.*

try rumors, speculation on new release dates, game-related fiction, and the ongoing *MK2* vs. *SF2* war, virtually anything goes here (video-game-related or not). See also *MK* discussions on rec.games.video.arcade, alt.sega.genesis, and rec.games.video.nintendo. ✓**USENET**

Mortal Kombat Guides Looking for help with *Mortal Kombat I* and *II*? Available files include the *Mortal Kombat* FAQs (mk.mov and mk1faq.txt), a single-page *MK2* list of moves (mk2_1pg.txt), the *MK2* FAQ (mk2.faq.v16—but check to see if the FAQ has been updated to a later version), a guide to beating *Mortal Kombat II* (mk2guide.txt), and information on the death punch (mkpunch. txt). ✓**INTERNET**→*ftp* ftp.netcom. com→anonymous→<your email address>→/pub/vidgames/faqs

Mortal Kombat Tips & Discussions (echo) Find out how to make the moves in *Mortal Kombat.* ✓**ICENET**

On the Net

Mortal Kombat

alt.games.mk (ng) Amid indus-

Mortal Kombat II (echo) Get the cheats for *Mortal Kombat II.* ✓**WWIVNET**

Street Fighter II

alt.games.sf2 (ng) From cheats to announcements, this newsgroup is always buzzing with the latest word about *SF2*. The *Street Figher 2* FAQ is standard fare for a hit video game, with rundowns of deviations from the arcade originals in the home game and computer versions (e.g., Nintendo censors changed blood to the color gray), special character moves, and pointers to other *SF2* caches including pictures. See also rec. games.video.arcade, alt.sega.genesis, and rec.games.video.nintendo for more *SF* discussion. ✓**USENET** *FAQ:* ✓**INTERNET** ...→*ftp* ftp. netcom.com→anonymous→<your email address>→/pub/vidgames/ faqs→sf2.faqs ...→*email* mlm@ mrcnext.cso.uiuc. edu ✍ *Write a request for a copy*

Street Fighter II Archive Home to a huge collection of *Street Fighter II* files. Subdirectories include cheats, character strategies, pictures, technical details on various versions, and even fiction based on the World Warriors. Read stories about the Balrog, pick up a beginner's guide or list of moves, download sound files (Sagat's Tiger Uppercut, for example) and, of course, the FAQs! There are lots of *Mortal Kombat II* files to be found as well. ✓**INTERNET** →*ftp* ftp.krl.caltech.edu→anonymous→<your email address>→ /pub/sf2

Street Fighter 2 Guides An archive of several FAQs, including the newsgroup's FAQ (sf2.faq) covering how Sagat got his scar, how he does the Tiger knee, and other *SF2* details. The alternative four-and-a-half-part FAQ (sf2faq. pt0, sf2faq.pt1, sf2faq.pt2, sf2faq. pt3, sf2faq.pt4) includes character info, trivia and tactics, home and arcade info, and FTP and Net hints. The *Super Street Fighter 2* FAQ (ssf2.txt) diagrams the moves and analyzes the fighting styles of the characters new to the "Super" edition of *Street Fighter 2*; as does its counterpart the *Super Street Fighter 2 Turbo* FAQ (ssf2tfaq. txt). There are also guides to Ken's character (sf2.ken) and a move list (sf2.moves). ✓**INTERNET**→*ftp* ftp.net-com.com→anonymous→<your email address>→/pub/vidgames/ faqs

Street Fighter II Tips & Discussion (echo) Many tips on great moves in *Street Fighter II*. ✓**ICENET**

Windows Games WAVs The definitive place to go for *Street Fighter II* sounds. ✓**AMERICA ONLINE**→*keyword* video games→Windows Games WAVs

Other fighting games

Art of Fighting 2 Carries the "Art of Fighting 2 Dictionary" (aof2dict.txt), the "Art of Fighting 2 Move List" (aof2move.txt), a short list of moves (aof2quik.txt), the *Art of Fighting* FAQ, and a scan of the *Art of Fighting 2* CD. ✓**INTERNET**→*ftp* ftp.netcom.com→ anonymous→<your email address> →/pub/vidgames/faqs

The Fighter's History Lists of moves for all the characters in *The Fighter's History* (fighthst.txt) and *The Fighter's History Dynamite* (fighthst.dyn). ✓**INTERNET**→*ftp* ftp.netcom.com→anonymous→ <your email address>→/pub/ vidgames/faqs

Fighting Warriors A clone of

Street Fighter II. ✓**INTERNET**→*ftp* wuarchive.wustl.edu→/systems/ amiga/aminet/game/shoot→Fighting Warriors.lzh

Stats
- Competition: personal best
- Number of players: 1
- Interface: graphical
- Platform: Amiga

Requirements: *244k+*

Martial Champion A short list of moves. ✓**INTERNET**→*ftp* ftp.net-com.com→anonymous→<your email address>→/pub/vidgames/ faqs→martlchp.txt

Virtua Fighters Scans of the *Virtua Fighters* CDs (vfcd*), a FAQ (vf-25.txt), a quick FAQ (vf-qk25.txt), and a list of moves (vf-pg25.txt) ✓**INTERNET**→*ftp* ftp. netcom.com→anonymous→<your email address>→/pub/vidgames/ faqs

Pong Kombat

Pong Kombat A combination of *Pong* and *Mortal Kombat*. ✓**AMERICA ONLINE**→*keyword* pcgames→ Software Library→*Search by file name:* PONGKOMB.ZIP

Stats
- Competition: live *or* personal best
- Number of players: 1 *or* 2
- Interface: graphical
- Platform: DOS

Pong Kombat An official file (pongkmbt.faq) and unofficial file (pongkmbt.txt) containing the FAQ for the *Pong Kombat* game. For discussion of the game, check out alt.games.mk. ✓**INTERNET**→*ftp* ftp.netcom.com→anonymous→ <your email address>→/pub/ vidgames/faqs

Shareware

The Executioners Two-level demo of a *Street Fighter*–like game.

✓**COMPUSERVE**→*go* ibmnew→Li-braries→General Fun & Games→ execut.zip

Stats
- Competition: personal best
- Number of players: 1
- Interface: graphical
- Platform: DOS

Kung Fu Louie A karate action game. ✓**INTERNET**→*ftp* wuarchive. wustl.edu→anonymous→<your email address>→/systems/ibmpc/ msdos-games/Misc→kflouie1.zip

Stats
- Competition: personal best
- Number of players: 1
- Interface: graphical
- Platform: DOS

Requirements: *EGA graphics or better*

Sangho Fighter A *Street Fighter II* clone. ✓**INTERNET**→*ftp* wuarchive. wustl.edu→anonymous→<your email address>→/systems/ibmpc/ msdos-games/Misc→ sanfight.zip

Stats
- Competition: personal best
- Number of players: 1
- Interface: graphical
- Platform: DOS

Requirements: *VGA graphics or better*

Stick Fighter 2 A martial-arts game with the traditional punches and blockings and the less traditional blade kicks and fireballs. ✓**AMERICA ONLINE**→*keyword* pc games→Software Library→*Search by file name:* SFII.ZIP ✓**INTERNET**→*ftp* wuarchive.wustl.edu→ anonymous→<your email address> →/systems/ibmpc/msdos-games/ Misc→sf2.zip

Stats
- Competition: personal best
- Number of players: 1
- Interface: graphical
- Platform: DOS

Requirements: *EGA graphics or better*

Flight simulators

A WWI battle in the sky over France. A perfect landing at Kennedy International Airport.

A mission in galaxies well beyond our present reach, if not imagination. Those who thrill to piloting in simulated flight scenarios, who seek the "ultimate flight scenario" and the most skilled opponents, need to be online. America Online's **Flight Sim Resource Center** is a hotbed of pilots looking for head-to-head duels. The Internet's **Flight Simulation Monster Archives** are unsurpassed in materials—scenarios, scenery, and utilities—to enhance the experience. Flying alone at home on your PC? You don't know what you're missing.

On the Net

Across the board

AIR_ACES (echo) Covers modem-to-modem flight simulation games. ✓**FIDONET**

comp.sys.ibm.pc.games.flightsim (ng) This unmoderated group is for the discussion of air and space flight-simulation games, including *X-Wing, Aces Over Europe, Air Warrior, Falcon 3.0*, and the venerable *Microsoft Flight Simulator*. ✓**USENET**

flight_sim A collection of flight-sim newsgroup postings. ✓**INTERNET**→*wais* flight_sim.src

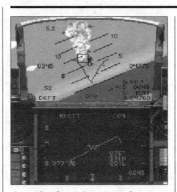

Screenshot from Falcon 3.0—*from CompuServe.*

Flight-Sim (ml) Seasoned *Microsoft Flight Simulator* pilots discuss their travels, hardware and software issues, and product rumors. ✓**INTERNET**→*email* flight-sim-request@grove.iup.edu ✍ *Write a request Archives:* ✓**INTERNET**→*ftp* ftp.iup.edu→anonymous→<your email address>→flight-sim.archive

FLIGHTSIM (echo) For sim pilots to talk about their recent flights in the virtual blue yonder. ✓**RACENET**

FLIGHTSIM (echo) Talk to others who fly the virtual sky. ✓**INTELEC**

Flight Sim Resource Center On the message board in the flight-sim topic, you can talk specs, hardware, and the pros and cons of different sim programs, like *Fleet Defender, TFX: Tactical Fighter*, and *Falcon 3.0*. Once you've flown, take your bragging to the Brag Board area, where you can recount your jet-jockey exploits, and find others in your area code for some head-to-head butt-kicking. There's even a folder just for *Falcon 3.0* opponents.

After-flight chatter
To join a club of fellow pilots, where you'll receive a rank, missions to fly, and rights to engage in after-flight chatter, check the message board's Organizations folder. Among the library choices filled with flight-sim goodies: Add-Ons with pilot files for *X-Wing* and custom aircraft for *Secret Weapons of the Luftwaffe; Flight Simulator 4.0* aircraft and scenery; and Utilities & Miscellaneous with programs that add capabilities to your sim, such as Falconer to boost your *Falcon 3.0* management of squads and pilots, and the X-Wing Pilot Revive Utility, which allows you to defeat the Grim Reaper and still keep your points and rank. ✓**AMERICA ONLINE**→*keyword* pc games→Flight Sim Resource Center

Flight Simulation Forum If you can't get an answer to your flight-sim question here, an answer doesn't exist. Whether you're discussing historical simulations, à la *Air Warrior*, modern sims, such as *Falcon* and *Fleet Defender*, or even space-combat sims, like *X-Wing*, you'll find a wealth of knowledgeable, no-nonsense pilots to help you out. Players who want to boast about missions they've flown may be disappointed, however. There's more detailed tech talk than swagger on the message boards. In the libraries, you can download scenery of Milwaukee airports—Mitchell, Kenosha, and Delavan—for *Flight Simulator 4.0* and *5.0*. Or download the replay of an F4U-1 Corsair packing 20mm cannons against some top

WWII Japanese pilots for *Aces Over the Pacific*; GIFs of aircraft; mission replays; utilities to camouflage your Falcon F-16 for jungle flight; and tons of bug fixes, patches, and editors to get you up in the air. ✓**COMPUSERVE**→*go* fsforum

Flight Simulation Monster Archives Archived discussions and tips related to *Flight Assignment ATP*, *Falcon*, *Flight Simulator v4.0* and *v5.0*, and various simulations. Also includes scenery, sound files, patches, images, and codes. ✓**INTERNET** ...→*ftp* ftp.iup.edu→anonymous→<your email address>→/flight-sim.dir ...→*ftp* cactus.org→anonymous→<your email address>→/pub

Flight Simulators Have an opinion on *F-14 Fleet Defender* versus *Hornet*? Think you can handle a little *Falcon* head-to-head? Overstressing the aircraft in *Flight Simulator 5.0*? Check the *Flight Simulators* topic for discussions like these—serious or silly, every post is full of flyboy braggadocio. Because modem-to-modem charges can get expensive long distance, flight sim clubs that rely on offline flying have grown in popularity on Prodigy.

Real-world hot spot

Most club commanding officers define missions—usually some real-world hot spot—for the squadron commanders, or SCOs, to pass on to the pilots, who fly the mission offline, then debrief their SCO online, who report back to the CO, who keeps tabs on individual pilots and awards rank promotions accordingly (got it?). Also popular are *X-Wing* and *Wing Commander* clubs for Jedi Knight wannabes. The largest and most venerable of these clubs is the American Military Forces,

known as the AMF, although you'll find other clubs starting up almost daily, and lasting about that long as well. ✓**PRODIGY**→*jump* games bb→Choose a Topic→Flight Simulators *or* Flight Sim Clubs

Flight Simulators Serious discussion by actual pilots and knowledgeable pilot wannabes about the major Flight Simulators and their uses for training. The emphasis is on realism and how the sim relates to true-life situations. *Air Transport Pilot*, *Flight Simulator 4.0* and *5.0*, and *Falcon 3.0* seem most popular with this crowd. Software Library holds modeled aircraft, scenarios, and utilities such as the *ATP* Flight-Planner (ATPutil3.zip) for "extremely detailed flight/frequency/radial/fuel stats." For more game-oriented discussions and files organized by software publishers, see also GEnie's "Games RoundTable." ✓**GENIE** ...→*keyword* aviation→Aviation Bulletin Board→set 18 (for messages) ...→*keyword* aviation→Aviation Software Library→*Search by search string:* sim (for files)

Flight Simulator Topics (echo) Devoted to flight simulations. ✓**WWIVNET**

FS (echo) In the Flight Simulators conference, discuss all facets of combat and non-combat flight simulations. ✓**FIDONET**

H2H_ACS (echo) The Head-to-Head Air Combat Simulations Echo is a forum where air-combat players discuss tactics, air-combat maneuvering, and upcoming tournaments. Requests for assistance and flight tales are the norm. ✓**FIDONET**

PC Pilots (echo) Meet hardcore sim pilots on the PC trail. ✓**ICENET**

rec.aviation.simulators (ng) Devoted to discussion about air and spacecraft simulators, especially PC and workstation sims. There are nine other rec.aviation* newsgroups but sim talk happens here. ✓**USENET** *FAQ:* ✓**INTERNET**→*ftp*

ACRONYMS YOU'LL ENCOUNTER	
Acronym	**Game title**
AOE	Aces Over Europe
AOTP	Aces of (Aces Over) the Pacific
ATP	Air Transport Pilot
AW	Air Warrior
BH or BH1942	BattleHawks 1942
BOB	Battle of Britain
F15SEIII	F-15 Strike Eagle III
F3	Falcon 3.0
FD, F14FD	F-14 Fleet Defender
FS, FS4, FS5	Flight Simulator, 4.0 or 5.0
FSTK	Flight Sim Toolkit
PAW	1942: Pacific Air War
RB	Red Baron
SWOTL	Secret Weapons of the Luftwaffe
TF	Tie Fighter
WC	Wing Commander
XW	X-Wing

rtfm.mit.edu→anonymous→<your email address>→/pub/usenet-by-group/news.answers/aviation→flight-simulators

SimNet A growing BBS network dedicated to flight-sim discussions, especially military sims. The list of SimNet conferences includes the 510th Tactical Fighter Wing (for simmers in California area code 510), Spectrum HoloByte Sims, Domark Sims, MicroProse Sims, World War II Sims, and Thrust-Master Support. See the "BBS Bar" for a partial list of BBSs that belong to SimNet. ✓CHECK LOCAL BULLETIN BOARD SYSTEMS

Pilot talk

Computer Programs for Aviators Real-world, pilot-to-pilot discussions of flight sims, especially *Flight Simulator 4.0* and *5.0* and *MiG-29*. Frequently, sim talk evolves into discussions about air-foil-plotting software, map software, and other non-sim software. For more flight-sim chat on Delphi, see also the GameSIG, the Modem-to-Modem Gaming area, and the various "games" topics in the Computing Groups sigs. ✓DELPHI→*go* gro avi→Forum→clear*→set comp

Software companies

LucasArts Sims For discussions of LucasArts sims, especially *Secret Weapons of the Luftwaffe* and *X-Wing*. In the Software Library, you'll find pilot files and missions for *X-Wing*, SWOTL scenarios, and utilities to "resurrect" pilots. ✓**GENIE** ...→*keyword* scorpia→Gamers Libraries→Set Software Library→LucasArts (for files) ...→*keyword* scorpia→Games Bulletin Board→set 27 (for messages)

MicroProse Simulators Along with MicroProse game discussions on the Bulletin Board, discuss *F-15 Strike Eagle III, F-14 Fleet Defender, 1942: Pacific Air War*, and other sims. Software Library has archives of conference discussions, updates, patches, demos, and more. ✓**GENIE** ...→*keyword* scorpia →Gamers Libraries→Set Software Library→Microprose (for files) ...→*keyword* scorpia→Games Bulletin Board→set 12 (for messages)

Utilities

Aviation Log Book As an ace pilot, you'll need to keep track of your flights. This spreadsheet program is laid out like a standard logbook and includes such entries as date, time, origin and destination, description, type of flight (day, night, etc.), and more. A logbook program has a big advantage over a standard book: It does all the math for you. ✓**AMERICA ONLINE**→*keyword* pc software→File Search→*Search by keyword:* LOGBOOK.XLS **Requirements:** *Windows 3.1; Excel 4.0 or higher*

AvPlan Flight Planner v3.0 Sim pilots who want to make their virtual flights look more realistic can download this program to plan flights, routes, way points, and winds. Includes a database of information on airport facilities and a feature that allows you to print your plans. ✓**GENIE**→*keyword* aviation→Aviation Software Libraries→*Download a file:* AVPLAN.ZIP

Mach Numbers Nineteenth-century Austrian physicist Ernst Mach had no idea flight-sim pilots would someday be throwing his name around. One "mach" is the speed of sound. Tricky thing is, the speed of sound varies with the altitude. To translate your in-flight mach number to miles per hour,

knots per hour, and vice versa, download this helpful GIF file. ✓**COMPUSERVE**→*go* fsforum→*Search by file name:* MACH.GIF

XtraSlow You never thought your revved-up 486 PC would put you at a disadvantage, did you? Well, many 486s let you fly a little too fast for your own good in a computer flight sim. This utility allows you to slow down. ✓**COMPUSERVE**→*go* fsforum→Libraries→*Search by file name:* XTRASL.ZIP

SimNet BBSs

Afterburner BBS
817-292-4193
Beta
805-528-6829
Check Six
714-362-8299
The Contrails
817-355-9242
Cyber Space BBS
503-654-4645
The Fast Tracks
408-739-5781
The Fox Den
203-223-5217
Fox One BBS
918-251-3160
Gamma On-line
804-565-3503
Modem CONNECTion
404-952-8981
NM Railroad Conn.
505-865-8412
Powerline BBS
912-249-9585
Reverse Polarity
203-620-0001
Silver Software
505-268-8502
The Spacedock
203-666-4999
32 Bit Bus BBS
215-949-2701
The Trade Center
415-340-0197

Historical flight sims

No historical air-combat sim has as big a presence in Cyberspace as *Air Warrior*. A sub-

culture of ace bravado has grown up around *AW*, especially on GEnie, where you'd swear you were listening to Army Air Corps radio transmissions of 1942 coming through your modem as Air Warriors fly in the Pacific and European theaters of WWII, and *Red Baron* pilots on the ImagiNation Network take to the sky when Wilson was president and Sopwith Camels were the planes of choice. There's some sort of irony, perhaps, in the use of the Net by thousands of virtual pilots to fly, discuss, and upgrade sims of combat planes and jets that half a century ago made the world safe for democracy but never saw a silicon chip.

On the Net

Air Warrior

Air Warrior *Air Warrior* is the current king of remote multiplayer shoot-'em-ups, but it's not the program—it's the people. The screen layout is run-of-the-mill flight sim; the maps are your basic air carrier, distant mountain, and lone runway; the interface couldn't nauseate a hung-over freshman, but then you notice the text chatter coming over the radio. Those other planes on your radar— friend and foe—are real people.

Air combat—from CompuServe's Flight Sim Forum.

Ah, the thrill of downing an opponent with feelings—a chat system in which you can also shoot at people! The GEnie skies fill every day at six p.m. EST when the non-prime rates go into effect, with as many as 20 planes and three teams battling in one "conference room."

Heroic bombing runs

Stick with a friendly squadron and pick off stragglers, or set out on your own heroic bombing runs as the teams skirmish over territorial control. Send messages to single players, teams, or just the whole darn game—but don't take your hands off the yoke for too long! There's almost a decade's worth of files in the Air Warrior Software Library, with instructions; patches for the Mac, IBM PC, and Amiga front-ends; player-created maps; images; utilities; and loads of mission films.

AW Training course

Just as F-14 Navy pilots don't want to mess around with one-prop dweebs, the *Air Warrior* players would prefer you know your stuff before you take to the air. That's why many flyboy-wannabes take GEnie's 7-week, 21-hour AW Training Academy course. There

you learn about *Air Warrior* aircraft, air-combat maneuvering, gunnery, communications, radar, bombers, capturing airfields, aircraft carriers, and ground vehicles.

Maneuver tips

Interested in sharing maneuver tips or recounting missions won and lost? Check out the Multiplayer Games Bulletin Board (an option on the *Air Warrior* menu) for active *Air Warrior* discussions. When you've been around for a while and, perhaps, have signed on with a specific flight squadron, you'll have access to its private message areas and libraries. Cost conscious *Air Warrior* addicts should know that Internet play tends to be much cheaper, if harder to set up, then GEnie action.

✓**GENIE**→*keyword* air

Stats
- Difficulty: complex
- Competition: live
- Number of players: 1–50+
- Interface: graphical
- Platforms: all

Air Warrior Archives Fly into

> **"As a dweeb, expect to get your butt kicked. But Cooper shares some of the tips that he says have saved his 'Virtual Crotch™'"**

this archive for *Air Warrior* scenarios, patches, images, FAQs, information on IHHD, and utilities. ✓**INTERNET** ...→*ftp* rex.pfc.mit.edu→ anonymous→<your email address> →/pub/genie/airwar ...→*ftp* cactus.org→anonymous→<your email address>→/pub/genie/airwar

Air Warrior Challenge Ladder Rules A great pilot, huh? How are you with 1940s-era sky iron? Prove your stuff against other CompuServe Air Warriors. These rules give instructions for joining the SVGA Air Warrior Challenge Ladder. Competition takes place either in the Modem-to-Modem Lobby at 2400 bps, or by skipping CompuServe and making a direct phone call at, one would hope, higher speeds than 2400 bps. ✓**COMPUSERVE**→*go* mtmforum→Libraries→*Search by file name:* AW-CIS.RUL

Air Warrior FAQ Gary Cooper's entertaining FAQ focuses mainly on GEnie *Air Warrior* play, but that's not all. Written with "dweebs" (newbies) in mind, it offers some cold, hard facts about the *Air Warrior* world, which basically all boil down to this: As a dweeb, expect to get your butt kicked. But Cooper shares some of the tips that he says have saved his "Virtual Crotch™" many a time. ✓**INTERNET** ...→*ftp* rex.pfc.mit.edu→ anonymous→<your email address> →/pub/genie/airwar→ FAQ-rev2 ...→*ftp* ftp.center.osaka-u.ac.jp→ anonymous→<your email address> →/news.answers/games→ AirWarrior-faq.gz ...→*ftp* cactus.org→ anonymous→<your email address> →/pub/genie/airwar→ FAQ-rev2

666th-etal (ml) GEnie flight masters and those flying solo on their home PCs swap tails and tips about surviving the Net's most popular flight simulation. ✓**INTER-**

NET→*email* listserv@cactus.org ✍ *Type in message body:* subscribe 666th-etal <your full name> *Archives:* ✓**INTERNET**→*ftp* cactus.org→anonymous→<your email address>→/pub/genie/airwar/666th-etal

Air Warrior Review The Electronic Gamer's review of SVGA *Air Warrior* by Kesmai, examining only the stand-alone (not network or modem-to-modem) aspects. ✓**COMPUSERVE**→*go* fsforum→Libraries→*Search by file name:* AIRWAR.REV

Trevor Myler's Air Warrior Help File Good file for beginners, includes pros and cons of each aircraft choice, tactics advice, and handy radio and keyboard tips for online play against a real-live opponent. ✓**COMPUSERVE**→*go* mtmforum→Libraries→*Search by file name:* AW-HLP.ZIP

On the Internet

Big Hank's Guide to Air Warrior Through the Internet: Practical Instructions for Total Dweebs If you're interested in playing *Air Warrior* on the Internet, you'll need to use the IHHD (see page 216 for more info). Get a copy of Big Hank's Guide for step-by-step instructions on how to play. ✓**INTERNET** ...→*ftp* rex.pfc.mit.edu→anonymous→<your email address>→/pub/genie/airwar→Internet_H2H ...→*email* liangh@eniac.seas.upenn.edu ✍ *Request a copy*

Internet SVGA Air Warrior Ladder The boys that subscribe

to the *666th-etal* mailing list meet for head-to-head competition on the Internet using the IHHD. Challenges and outcomes are logged through this scoring ladder and posted to the *666th-etal* list. Pilots may challenge those holding positions up to two rungs higher on the ladder, and the winner assumes (or maintains) the higher position.

Europe and The Pacific

Most people duel three or four times a month; if you're challenged you are required to fight within two weeks of the challenge. The theater alternates monthly between Europe and the Pacific theaters and the planes flown must be historically accurate. About 25 people compete regularly. To join the ladder, send your name, nom de guerre, email address, time zone, and maximum baud rate. Once you've proved you can fly on the Internet, you'll be added to the bottom of the ladder. There are very specific rules for flying in ladder competitions—get a copy of the instructions. If you're having difficulties with the IHHD software and you've read all the documentation, Will Christie, who runs this ladder, may be able to answer a few questions. ✓**INTERNET** →*email* chrstie@cc.UManitoba.CA ✍ *Write a request* *Info:* ✓**INTERNET** →*ftp* cactus.org→anonymous→ <your email address>→/pub/ genie/airwar→InternetLadderRules

Red Baron

Red Baron The online, multiplayer, real-time version of Dynamix/Sierra Online's popular WWI sim gives you three levels of difficulty: Novice, Normal, and Expert. At Novice level, the planes are easiest to fly, and it takes a lot of bullets to shoot you out of the air. The more difficult levels have smaller target areas, and allow you to sustain less damage. Be careful: You may black out at high altitudes. Also at the more difficult levels, under Options, you can choose from five German planes or nine American planes, set the weather, time of day, and starting positions. Check the Sierraland. doc files in the INN directory on your hard drive for complete instructions. ✓**THE IMAGINATION NETWORK**→*select* Sierraland

Stats
- Difficulty: average
- Competition: live
- Number of players: 1+
- Interface: graphical
- Platform: DOS

Commands
- To fire the machine gun, use either: spacebar, left mouse button, or joystick button 1
- To unjam the machine gun, press: U
- For flight control help, press: Alt-H
- To challenge others: Select play-

ers' name tags in the Waiting Room, then select Invite.
Requirements: *2400-bps modem or faster*

1942: Pacific air war

1942: Pacific Air War When you're not fighting Japanese pilots—or American pilots, if you're flying for the Japanese—come here to talk about the single- and campaign-mode sorties you've flown, the naval battles you're planning, and the missions you're building for the Microprose game *1942: Pacific Air War*. ✓**AMERICA ONLINE**→*keyword* industry connection→Games→Microprose→Let's Discuss→1942 - Pacific Air War

Forums

Historic Air Combat Discussion and files about *Air Warrior*, as well as *Pacific Air War*, *Aces Over the Pacific*, *Aces Over Europe*, and other sims depicting the golden (and bloody) years of air combat. ✓**COMPUSERVE** ...→*go* fsforum→Libraries *or* Messages→Historic Air Combat ...→*go* mtmforum→Libraries *or* Messages→Historic Air Combat

Game developers

LucasArts Historical Flight Sims Discuss, with other pilots and company reps, the LucasArts line of historic flight sims: *Battle-Hawks 1942*, *Battle of Britain*, and *Secret Weapons of the Luftwaffe*. ✓**AMERICA ONLINE**→*keyword* industry connection→Games→LucasArts Games→Let's Discuss→BH1942/BOB/SWOTL

Sierra/Dynamix Historical Sims *Red Baron*, *Aces Over the Pacific*, and *Aces Over Europe* flyers will want to check out the Bulletin Board for technical support, as

well as pilot chatter. From the Software Library, you can download additional planes for *AOTP* —the file name is 1946II.zip— patches, *Red Baron* films, and utilities. ✓**GENIE** ...→*keyword* scorpia →Gamers Libraries→Set Software Library→Sierra Online (for files) ...→*keyword* scorpia→Games Bulletin Board→set 22 (for messages)

Hellcats

Hellcats Over the Pacific Tips-FAQ includes FAQs, hints, easy "cheat" methods, and suggestions of things to try. If you don't want to know all the game's secrets, don't read this—if you do, it's all here. ✓**INTERNET** ...→*ftp* chemo taxis.biology.utah.edu→anonymous →<your email address>→/Hell cats_Feats→hellcats-faq.txt ...→ *www* http://chemotaxis.biology. utah.edu/hellcats/index.html

Shareware

Sopwith1 Fly the Sopwith Camel. ✓**GENIE**→*keyword* aviation→ Aviation Software Libraries→ *Download a file:* sopwith1.com

Modern air combat

"We both realized that it is now do or die! I have never seen such flying by anyone

ever! We matched each other's turn to perfection! It was definitely 'The Dance of Death!' Eventually I had the angle and kept shooting snapshots until Mongoose was spiraling down in flames!" The best modern air-combat flight simulators—Spectrum HoloByte's *Falcon, MiG-29*, and *Hornet*—may be available only in stores, but while you won't find the programs themselves on the Net, you'll find just about everything else: discussion, lobbies to meet potential opponents, support from Spectrum HoloByte, etc. See the **Falcon 3** mailing list for nonstop hints and *Falcon 3* Utilities sites for add-ons galore. To fuel competition, CompuServe players have created challenge ladders for *Hornet, MiG-29*, and *Falcon* pilots. Start climbing.

On the Net

Battlefield series

The Electronic Battlefield Series FAQ + The FAQ is a must-have reference guide to both Net and commercial products for *Falcon 3.0*. It also extensively covers Falcon flying techniques, program features, and product support in-

Operation Fighting Tiger—*from CompuServe's Flight Sim Forum*

formation. Both the WWW and FTP site also carry the separate "Falcon 3.0 Modem Bible" with step-by-step instructions for head-to-head play of *Falcon, MiG-29*, and *F/A-18 Hornet*. If you're looking for the IHHD dialer software needed for head-to-head Internet flying, that's carried at the FTP site, but for visuals, check out the web site with a graphical browser. ✓**INTERNET** ...→*www* http://www. hh.sbay.org/~krismon/public.html ...→*ftp* hh.sbay.org→anonymous→ <your email address>→/user/kris mon

Falcon

Falcon 3 (ml) *Falcon 3.0* pilots share mission, strategy, and dogfighting tips. ✓**INTERNET**→*email* majordomo@onion.rain.com *Type in message body:* subscribe falcon 3 *Archives:* ✓**INTERNET** ...→*ftp* neon.rain.com→anonymous→<your email address>→/pub/falcon3 /maillist ...→*wais* falcon3.src

Falcon 3 Utilities If you're a *Falcon 3* pilot, you'll want to stop by these Archives. Goodies include the *Falcon 3* FAQ (dated but a good source of info), scenery files, utilities (for editing pilot stats, assisting with mission planning, etc.), the Usenet Guide to *Falcon*

3.0, and *Falcon 3.0* instructions. ✓**INTERNET** ...→*ftp* onion.rain.com→ anonymous→<your email address> →/pub/falcon3 ...→*ftp* ftp.infor matik.uni-rostock.de→anonymous→ <your email address>→/pub/ms dos/falcon3

Falcon 3.0 and Modem Lobby Help Download this file for detailed, step-by-step instructions for hooking up your *Falcon 3.0* to the Modem-to-Modem Lobby, where you can compete against other *Falcon* pilots in real time. ✓**COMPUSERVE**→*go* mtmforum→ *Search by file name:* F3.MTM

Falcon 3.0 Challenge Ladder Rules If you enjoy knocking guys out of the air, you'll want to join the CompuServe Falcon Challenge Ladder and compete for top rankings. The rules explain how the ladder works and whom you need to write to get on it. Actual flying takes place in the Modem-to-Modem Lobby on CompuServe. Ladder leaders recommend, but don't require, that players have the "Operation Fighting Tiger" scenario disks in addition to *Falcon 3.0*. ✓**COMPUSERVE**→*go* mtmforum→Libraries→*Search by file name:* FAL CON.RUL

Falcon 3.0 Competition Ladder If you subscribe to the credo that "real men fly jets," you can back that up by competing head-to-head and posting your results on the message boards, showing the AOL world just how real a man (in a virtual world) you are. ✓**AMERICA ONLINE**→*keyword* flight→ Message Board→List Categories→ Organizations→Falcon3 AOL Competition Ladder

#falcon3.0 Chat about *Falcon 3.0* with other pilots. ✓ **INTERNET**→ *irc* /channel #falcon3.0

Falconer 3.1 A popular utility for *Falcon 3.0* that allows you to resurrect dead pilots, put together flawless squadrons, issue supplies and medals to your squad members, and import pilot faces from PCX files. ✓ **COMPUSERVE**→*go* fsforum→Libraries→*Search by file name:* FALCNR.ZIP ✓ **AMERICA ONLINE**→ *keyword* pc software→File Search→ *Search by file name:* FALCNR.ZIP

F/A-18

F/A-18 FAQ First question: "How do I avoid missles?" This FAQ jumps into the tactical issues of flying *F/A-18*. Starting with defensive and offensive strategies, covering mission hints and scenery reviews, and ending with some troubleshooting advice, it answers the questions and offers several sim stories along the way. ✓ **INTERNET** ...→*ftp* chemotaxis.biology. utah.edu→ftp→<anonymous><your email address>→/Hellcats_Feats →fa18-faq.txt ...→*www* http:// chemotaxis.biology.utah.edu/ hornet/index.html

Hornet

Hornet Challenge Ladder Rules If you can land your F/A-18 on a popsicle stick, you're ready to show your stuff. Download these rules for instructions on competing head-to-head in the Modem-to-Modem Lobby. ✓ **COMPUSERVE**→*go* mtmforum→Libraries→ *Search by file name:* HORNET.RUL

MiG-29

MiG-29 Challenge Ladder Rules So, Comrade, you've got

36,600 lbs. of deadly thrust blowing out of twin Isotov RD-33 engines—but so does the other guy. See who should win accolades from the Central Committee and a virtual pic in Pravda when you compete against other MiG aces on the Challenge Ladder. Download this file for complete details. Competitive fly time takes place in the Modem-to-Modem Lobby. ✓ **COMPUSERVE**→*go* mtmforum→Libraries→*Search by file name:* MIG29.RUL

Companies & support

Modern Air Combat The nitty-gritty of the sims—from *Falcon 3.0* to *F-14 Fleet Defender*—gets discussed on the Flight Sim Forum's Message board. For utilities and flight films, check out the Forum's Library. Need more utilities? Visit CompuServe's Modem-to-Modem Forum Library. Modem-to-Modem Message board discussion related to flight sims centers around the challenge ladders—this is a competitive place! ✓ **COMPUSERVE** ...→*go* fsforum→Libraries *or* Messages→Modern Air Combat ...→*go* mtmforum→Libraries *or* Messages→Modern Air Combat

Spectrum HoloByte BBS (bbs) If you can't figure out how to get *MiG-29* to work with *Falcon 3.0*, go directly to the source: Spec-

trum HoloByte's BBS has technical support, recent news of the Electronic Battlefield series, and official updates, patches, and third-party utilities, including "coolie hat utilities" for Thrust-Master Flight Control Systems, allowing you to switch cockpit views more easily and efficiently. ☎→*dial* 510-522-8909

Spectrum HoloByte Simulators Discuss Spectrum HoloByte's Electronic Battlefield Series, including *Falcon 3.0*, *MiG-29*, and Hornet. File library has upgrades and patches from Spectrum HoloByte to update your programs to the latest version, as well as shareware contributions from other sim jockeys. ✓ **GENIE** ...→*keyword* scorpia→Games Bulletin Board→set 18 (for messages) ...→ *keyword* scorpia→Gamers Libraries →Set Software Library→Spectrum HoloByte (for files)

Shareware

Corncob 3D v3.42 Fight for your life in the cockpit of a Corsair. Awarded *Shareware Magazine*'s Editor's Choice in 1993. ✓ **COMPUSERVE**→*go* fsforum→Libraries→*Search by file name:* CC3D34.ZIP
Stats
• Number of players: 1
• Interface: graphical
• Platform: DOS
Requirements: *286 or better; VGA or SVGA*

Strike Jets v.2.05 A tactics simulation "board game" of modern air combat. Lead several aircraft at once into combat. ✓ **COMPUSERVE**→ *go* fsforum→Libraries→*Search by file name:* STRIKE.SIT
Stats
• Number of players: 1
• Interface: graphical
• Platform: Macintosh

> "You've got 36,600 lbs. of deadly thrust blowing out of twin Isotov RD-33 engines—but so does the other guy."

Non-combat air sims

There's a whole class of flight sims in which you don't shoot anyone down—you don't

have time. In Microsoft's **Flight Simulator**, for example, you have your hands full flying and landing a wide-body jet. Realism is the hallmark for these sims, taking them to a level beyond conventional gaming. As the pilot, you're managing drag, lift, latitude, longitude, weather, air traffic, and much more. And there are tons of add-ons, increasing the reality factor even more. You can visit CompuServe's Scenery Design library in the **Flight Simulation Forum** and download digital views of places like Kenosha, Wisconsin, and Tokyo, Japan, enabling you to attempt airport landings all around the world. In addition, these simulators often allow you to add on and fly "modeled aircraft," programs that mimic the handling of everything from a Piper Cub to an Airbus jet.

Screenshot of MS Flight Simulator 5.0 *—from GEnie's Aviation Forum.*

Grand Canyon, travel past hot-air balloons or air-traffic-control towers, or land at San Francisco International Airport, to name but a fraction of the scenes. ✓**INTERNET** …→*ftp* ftp.uml.edu→anonymous→ <your email address>→/msdos/ Games/FltSim/Scenery …→*ftp* wuarchive.wustl.edu→anonymous→ <your email address>→/systems/ ibmpc/msdos-games/FltSim/ Scenery …→*ftp* ftp.ulowell.edu→ anonymous→<your email address> →/msdos/games/FltSim/Scenery …→*ftp* acorn.grove.iup.edu→ anonymous→<your email address> →/flight-sim.scenery

Mallard Software Those Mallard folks down in Flower Mound, Texas, have carved a niche for themselves creating scenery and utilities for Microsoft's *Flight Simulator 4.0* and *5.0*. In these message boards and libraries, discuss and download update patches to Real Weather Pilot and other popular *FS* add-ons. Of interest is the file FS4FS5.txt, which gives instructions for installing Mallard-created *FS 4.0* scenery in *FS 5.0*.

✓**COMPUSERVE**→*go* gambpub→Libraries *or* Messages

Microsoft Flight Sim 4.0 Files Download aircraft and scenery for use with Microsoft *Flight Simulator 4.0*. You'll find scenery for airports and flight patterns from Liverpool, England, to Yakima, Washington, and a wide assortment of aircraft to fly between them. Among the more original: an Icarus motorized hang glider, the Spruce Goose, and for the holiday-inclined, Santa's Sleigh. The sleigh software's author suggests you use a tower view for takeoff and a full view of your craft in flight, for the complete effect. ✓**AMERICA ONLINE**→*keyword* flight→ MSFS 4.0

Scenery Design Just what makes good scenery? Sim artists discuss commercial, shareware, and their own flight scenery for *Flight Simulator 4.0* and *5.0*. The Library holds scenery for both. A few of the more interesting choices are Shanghai; Queensland, Australia; and Austria. ✓**COMPUSERVE**→*go* fsforum→Libraries *or* Messages→Scenery Design

On the Net

Microsoft flight sim

Flight Simulator Scenery Archives *Flight Simulator* pilots should check out these archives full of scenery files. Grab files that let you fly over Hong Kong or the

> "Grab files that let you fly over the Grand Canyon, travel past hot-air balloons, or land at San Francisco airport."

Upgrade Patch for FS5.0 To update your Microsoft *Flight Simulator 5.0* to *5.0a* status, download this file and follow the README.txt file instructions. ✓**GENIE**→*keyword* microsoft→Download Flight Simulator 5.0a Update

Air Traffic Controller

Air Traffic Controller You are an FAA traffic controller. Planes come into your sector to land at one of your two airports, or they take off from your airports to fly to another sector. Some planes may just be passing through your airspace, and you have to get them from entry point to exit point. You'll have to keep track of each plane's altitude and position. Your goal is to gain points by getting planes to their destination with a minimum of fuel use. Any plane leaving your airspace with less than 150 units of fuel will cost you points. If you've got a plane with low fuel on your hands, redirect it toward one of your airports—marked by % and # on your 12x12· grid—and give it the "arrival" command. If the players in adjoining sectors are humans (instead of programs), you'll want to notify them of planes arriving in their sector. (You get extra points for notification.) And you lose points for crashing into another plane...just like in real life. ✓**COMPUSERVE**→*go* atcontrol

Stats
- Difficulty: average
- Competition: live
- Number of players: 1+
- Interface: ASCII
- Platforms: all

Commands
- To see which other sectors are controlled by real people, use the command: P
- To move a plane up or down a level of altitude, use the commands: U *or* D

> ## "You lose points for crashing into another plane...just like in real life."

- To direct a plane to the left or right, use the commands: L *or* R
- To notify an adjoining sector of a plane's arrival, use the command: N
- To clear planes for takeoff or arrival, use the commands: T *or* A

Air Traffic Control Simulation

Try your hand at getting planes in the air and to the ground safely. The uploader says, "If you can consistently beat the game at level 20, you should consider applying for a job with the FAA." ✓**GENIE**→*keyword* aviation→Aviation Software Libraries→*Download a file:* ATC.ARC ✓**COMPUSERVE**→*go* fsforum→Libraries→*Search by file name:* ATC.ZIP

Stats
- Difficulty: complex
- Competition: personal best
- Number of players: 1
- Interface: graphical
- Platform: DOS

Air Transport Pilot

Air Transport Talk flight patterns, runways, and scenery with other *Air Transport* pilots and *Flight Simulator 4.0* and *5.0* sim jockeys. The Library has scenery and aircraft files for non-combat sims, especially *FS 4.0*. ✓**COMPUSERVE**→*go* fsforum→Libraries *or* Messages→Air Transport

Air Transport Pilot Help Help file for subLogic's Flight Assignment: *Air Transport Pilot*. ✓**COMPUSERVE**→*go* gamapub→Libraries→*Search by file name:* ATPHLP.ZIP

ATPUTIL If you're not taking advantage of *Air Transport Pilot's* editing capability, you're not fully using *ATP*. It is considered "the ultimate" editing tool for *ATP*. Included are a career-assignment editor, a career-result editor, a logbook editor, a flight planner with route and fuel calculations, a node and route editor, a scenery editor, and several patches. ✓**COMPUSERVE** →*go* fsforum→Libraries→*Search by file name:* ATPUTI.ZIP

Scenedit for ATP To make your own *Air Transport Pilot* airport scenery, you'll want to use Scenedit. For use with ATPUTIL, for which a tutorial is also included in this download. ✓**COMPUSERVE**→*go* fsforum→Libraries→*Search by file name:* SCENED.ZIP

CYBERNOTES

"Does anyone know why dynamic scenery is only available at Miegs Field?"

"Shouldn't be if you have more DY1 files in your directory...

"Sometimes the system locks onto Miegs and will not release it. If you select 1, J and disable the option saying 'auto load dynamic scenery,' then go into your dynamic scenery library (4, D) and select the area you want, this should break the stranglehold."

—From the **Scenery Design Message board**, **CompuServe Flight Sim Forum**

Netrek

Netrek is almost as old as the original *Star Trek* TV series

and undoubtedly the most popular multiplayer shoot-'em-up on the Internet, with more elaborate playing and programming subcultures than any other game on the Net.

Players can log in over the phone, but all across the world eight-person teams of Netrekkies crowd into underused campus and corporate computer labs to get at the high-powered workstations and network connections that give them an edge in battle. Placed in a world of ships and planets and the "final frontier," tournament-level game play (90 minutes) resembles a Cyberspace version of rugby with dogfights. Teamwork is key, as squadrons fight in formation for control of the galaxy.

Netrek has been through many evolutionary steps. Born in 1972 as *Empire* on a Plato terminal system at the University of Illinois, it was imitated on an IBM mainframe as *Conquest* in the early '80s. These adaptations and others that followed are still in use, including *Netrek*'s immediate predecessor, *Xtrek*. And

U.S.S. Starship Enterprise—downloaded from lajkonik.cyf-kr.edu.pl.

even now *Netrek* is giving way to a flashier, more intricate real-time *Star Trek* combat game called *Paradise*.

On the Net

Find a game

Netrek Metaserver You have the software; now log into this server to find a live game. The server tells you who's playing and where. ✓INTERNET→*telnet* metaserver.ecst. csuchico.edu.

rec.games.netrek (ng) *Netrek*'s rabid following is evidenced in the daily activity on this newsgroup, the locus of the international *Netrek* community. Newbies pick up connection and strategy tips that are usually buried in the middle of *Netrek* manuals, and old-timers organize and report the results of major battles they're involved in. The FAQ functions as the *Netrek* manual, but it also points to a host of oth-

er useful strategy and tip files that will prevent you from ever actually playing the game if you try to read them all. ✓USENET *FAQ:* ✓INTERNET ...→*ftp* soda. berkeley. edu→anonymous→<your email address>→/pub/netrek→netrekFAQ ...→*www* http://www.cis.ohio-state.edu/hypertext/faq/usenet/ games/netrek/top.html.

Archives & info

"FTP List" FAQ The guide to all other *Netrek* FAQs. Everything's here, from basic tips to instructions for starting your own *Netrek* server. ✓INTERNET ...→*ftp* soda. berkeley.edu→anonymous→<your email address>→/pub/netrek→ netrekFTP ...→*ftp* rtfm.mit.edu→ anonymous→<your email address> →/pub/usenet/rec.games.netrek→ netrekFTP

Netrek Archives Most files are accessible and browsable via the *Netrek* Web Site. The Carnegie Mellon site has *Netrek* documentation galore: detailed advice for beginners, high-level strategic analysis for the experienced. The site archives old *XTrek* files, as well as standard compendiums of rec. games.netrek wisdom. Must-see files include the newbie's guide, Grey Elf's Guide to Planet Taking, and Ship Facts, for the bottom line on torp and plasma velocities. ✓**INTERNET** ...→*ftp* gs69.sp.cs.cmu.edu→anonymous→ <your email address> ...→*ftp* soda.berkeley.edu→anonymous→ <your email address>→/pub/ netrek *Info:* ✓**INTERNET**→*www* http://obsidian.math.arizona. edu:8080/ftp.html

Netrek Home Pages If you've got a good enough network connection to play *Netrek*, you've got access to the World Wide Web. Maybe this is why the Web is blanketed with *Netrek* coverage. ✓**INTERNET** ...→*www* http://obsidi an.math.arizona. edu:8080/netrek. html ...→*www* http://www.cs. cmu.edu:8001/afs/cs/user/jch/ netrek/README.html ...→*www* http://www.cis.ufl.edu:80/~thoth/ paradise/

Clients

Netrek Client List *Netrek* is a client/server game.The server acts as the host for players who are running client programs. The server coordinates commands from all the players and reports the game situation. There are plenty of *Netrek* servers on the Internet, but you need a client program for your machine (most are X-Windows based, but there are a number of implementations) and a direct connection to the Internet (i.e., you have to have your own IP address), through a dial-up SLIP or PPP account or through a direct network connection. (See the Net Games FAQ and glossary (page 251) for an explanation of these terms.) There is a WWW page listing clients as well as an accurate and up-to-date list of pro-

grams available from *Netrek* FTP sites. ✓**INTERNET** ...→*ftp* gs69.sp. cs.cmu.edu→anonymous→<your email address>→ftp-list.Z ...→*www* http://obsidian.math.arizona.edu:8 080/client.html

INL

Intercollegiate Netrek League
The Intercollegiate Netrek League (INL) organizes team battles with players from all over the world. Elaborate cultures have grown up around the older teams. One championship L.A. team calls itself Will Riot for Food; the best Seattle team calls itself Lagg U, a play on their once slower network connection. Team captains decide on new drafts. Applications are posted on rec.games.netrek or sometimes emailed directly to a team captain. Get acquainted with the INL by rifling through their files at the FTP site. Documents include current rosters and schedules. ✓**INTERNET**→*ftp* soda.berkeley.edu→

anonymous→<your email address>→/pub/netrek/INL

Newbies

Beginners Must-read file for *Netrek* beginners. Anticipates and answers newbie questions. ✓**INTERNET** *ftp* →anonymous→<your email address>→ beginners.Z

The History of Netrek Legendary *Netrek* Ace Andy McFadden (aka Shadow Spawn) has drafted an authoritative history of *Netrek* that is fascinating reading for players and students of computer-game history. Posted regularly to rec.games.netrek. ✓**INTERNET**→*www* http://obsidian.math. arizona.edu:8080/History.html

Tour of Netrek Take the *Netrek* tour, a walk-through of the Metaserver, with explanations on choosing your "persona" and ship, joining a league, etc. ✓**INTERNET**→*www* http://obsidian.math. arizona.edu:8080/nttour.html

---

NETREK VOCABULARY

DI	Destruction Inflicted. The index for *Netrek*'s scoring and ranking system.
T-mode	Tournament Mode. A "t" signifies that there are enough teams with enough players (the specific number depends on the server you are using) to play a tournament.
ogging	Kamikazi (suicide attack)
genocide	Occurs when a race loses its last planet
pregnant	Carrying armies (said of a ship)
<blank> scum	Name for someone who uses <blank> tactic more than you
XTrek	Precursor to *Netrek*
Paradise	*Netrek: The Next Generation*. New ships, new rules, new game.
Netrek For Morons mode (-M)	Newbie help, available on some servers
borg	Robot players, disallowed on standard servers
server god	The person who maintains and often customizes a *Netrek* server.

Space combat

"Cover me, Red Leader, I'm going in..." You are Luke Skywalker fighting the Evil Empire,

piloting an X-Wing fighter, a celestial Top Gun ace. Take your X-Wing on a fly-by of the authoritative **Internet Guide to X-Wing Strategy**, buckle yourself into the **TIE Fighter Demo**, and relive the pre-*Pong* days of computer game history with **SpaceWar**.

X-Wing *fighter—downloaded from wpi.wpi.edu.*

On the Net

Across the Board

Space Combat If you've shot down too many Confeds in *Privateer* and want to get back on the side of good, ask here how to convert it and where to find the pirates. (Tip: It takes about five badguy kills for every Confed you've downed.) Also, ask your *Wing Commander* and *X-Wing* questions here, or join a squadron of Rebel pilots. The file library has mostly *X-Wing* files—films, pilots, missions—but also *Privateer* maps and a few shareware space-sim programs to try out. ✓**COMPUSERVE** →*go* fsforum→Libraries *or* Messages→Space Combat

Companies

LucasArts Space Flight Sims Regardless of which side of the Force you're on—Empire or Rebellion—you'll find like-minded sim jockeys here with whom you can hash out strategies, trade files, and create missions. ✓**AMERICA ONLINE**→*keyword* industry connection→Games→LucasArts Games→ Let's Discuss

Origin Space sims The *Wing Commander* universe is thoroughly thrashed out on the Bulletin Board in a number of discussion topics, whether you're viewing that universe from the perspective of a Wing Commander or from its seamy underside as exhibited in *Privateer*. The Software Library has archives of *Privateer* spoiler messages, help files for *Wing Commander*, and the WCVIEW2.zip file, an easy-to-use *Wing Commander* ship editor. ✓**GENIE** ...→*keyword* scorpia→Gamers Libraries →Set Software Library→ Origin Systems (for files) ...→*keyword* scorpia→Games Bulletin Board→set 16 (for messages)

TIE Fighter

TIE Fighter Demo Demo and information about the PC action flying game *TIE Fighter*, in which the sympathies lie with the Empire (you remember, Darth Vader's former gang). ✓**INTERNET**→*ftp* wpi. wpi.com→anonymous→<your email address>→/starwars/TIE_Fighter

Wing Commander

K'tihrak mang: Wing Commander (echo) For *Wing Commander* pilots. ✓**ICENET**

> **"Throw a bajillion TIE fighters at your squad and see what they're really made of."**

X-Wing

Internet Guide to X-Wing Strategy Comprehensive manual for the first flight simulator to unseat Microsoft's dominance of this game category. Updates were frequent, so expect to find a higher version number replacing the ten in the filename. Internet discussion takes place on the comp.sys. ibm.pc.games.action and comp. sys.ibm.pc.games.flight-sim newsgroups. ✓**INTERNET**→*ftp* wpi.wpi. edu→anonymous→<your email address>→/starwars/X-Wing→ X-WingGuide 10.Z

X-Wing Archive A one-stop center for *X-Wing* missions, patches, programs, hints and downright cheats. Includes guides to the maze (Maze-Guide.Z), difficult

> "Ever feel like you're alone, with the entire Evil Empire on your back and no one to cheer for your side? Then join a Rebel Squadron. Squadron leaders create missions for you to fly, and you report back to them when you've brought the Empire down another notch."

missions (X-WingGuide10. Z), and combat strategy (X-Wing-Combat10.Z). ✓**INTERNET**→*ftp* wpi.wpi.edu→anonymous→ <your email address>→/starwars/X-Wing

X-Wing Mission Builder Create missions for *X-Wing* pilots with this shareware utility. Throw a bajillion TIE fighters at your squad and see what they're really made of. Also supports *B-Wing*. ✓**AMERICA ONLINE**→*keyword* pc software→File Search→*Search by file name:* XMB.ZIP ✓**COMPUSERVE** →*go* fsforum→Libraries→*Search by file name:* XMB.ZIP ✓**INTERNET**→*ftp* wpi.wpi.edu→anonymous→<your email address>→/starwars/X-Wing→ xmb20.zip

X-Wing Ship Editor Freeware utility that allows you to modify ship attributes, including its rapid-fire weapons, Instalok target-acquisition system, and the feature that lets you print ship's data functions. Also supports *B-Wing*. ✓**COMPUSERVE**→*go* fsforum→Libraries→*Search by file name:* XWS-ED.ZIP ✓**INTERNET**→*ftp* wpi.wpi.edu→anonymous→<your email address>→/starwars/X-Wing→ xwse4a.zip

X-Wing Silly Tour Admiral Ackbar is selling his Rebel Ships to the Empire, he's got heavy gambling debts, and he's generally become a lout. Your job: Escort him to his next gambling match, destroy other Rebel Ships, thereby cutting down on fleet overhead, and perform a number of other, cynical missions—there are 12 in all—for a satirical view of *X-Wing*. The mission authors recommend you back up the missions in your TOD 1 directory before installing this program, as it will overwrite them. ✓**AMERICA ONLINE**→*keyword* pc software→File Search→*Search by file name:* STOUR.ZIP

X-Wing Squadrons Ever feel like you're alone, with the entire Evil Empire on your back and no one to cheer for your side? Then join a Rebel Squadron. Squadron leaders create missions for you to fly, and you report back to them when you've brought the Empire down another notch. ✓**AMERICA ONLINE**→*keyword* flight→Message Board→List Categories→Organizations→Rebel Squadrons

Other

Spacewar Shareware to run an early version of *SpaceWar* for the PC. ✓**COMPUSERVE**→*go* fsforum→Libraries→*Search by file name:* SPACEW.ZIP

Stats
- Difficulty: average
- Competition: personal best
- Interface: graphical
- Platform: DOS

VGA Planets

Galactic empires clash over planet mining and celestial

colonization in this 11-player strategy game that is played through email. The game boasts thousands of dedicated players across the Net with a fanatical following in the BBS community, where it took root and where its popularity is perhaps rivaled only by that of *TradeWars 2002*. Much of the thrill comes from the elaborate sci-fi battle confrontations displayed in full color and the ease of automated move-making and report-processing. Players either (a) send their move by email to a game master host, who computes clashes and then returns result reports, or (b) upload their turn report to a BBS and then download the most current result report, which they then feed into their local program to size up the situation and prepare orders for the next turn. (Missed deadlines are simply computed as continuations of the previous orders; e.g. ships maintain their speeds and headings.) Games typically last for more than 50 turns, with move deadlines of one to three days, which adds up to several months or

Screenshot from VGA Planets—*CompuServe's Play-by-Mail Forum.*

even a year of absorbed, offline strategizing for a single game. Elaborate strategy guides, such as the Hints File, have been prepared by experienced masters and there is lively newsgroup coverage in **alt.games.vga-planets**.

On the Net

Planet play

VGA Planets There are plenty of *VGA-P* players to get a game going on America Online, CompuServe, and GEnie, but serious players will eventually want to venture out through email and other forms of Internet access to explore the wider, more competitive action on the Internet. Meanwhile, you can download copies of the frontend, pick up utilities, and find opponents on these three.
✓ **AMERICA ONLINE** ...→*keyword*

gaming→PBM & Strategy Messaging→VGA Planets Messaging (discussion and play) ...→*keyword* pcgames→Software Libraries→ *Search by keyword:* planet (for files)
✓ **COMPUSERVE**→*go* pbmgames→Libraries *or* Messages→Other/ PBM/PBEM→*Search by keyword:* planets (for messages, play, and files) ✓ **GENIE** →*keyword* scorpia→ Games Bulletin Board→set 19→Topic list→PBM VGA Planets: Players Wanted (for discussion and play) ...→*keyword* scorpia→Games Bulletin Board→set 9→Topic list→VGA Planets* (for messages) ...→*keyword* scorpia→Gamers Libraries→ Set Category→ALL Libraries→ *Search by keyword:* vga planets (for files)

VGA Planets A popular multiplayer galactic BBS war game and one of the first that is played offline with full VGA graphics. Take your time working out a strategy and make moves without the constraint of BBS time limits. Then upload your "packet of moves" to the BBS. At night, the turns are processed and the results are available for download the next day.
✓ CHECK LOCAL BULLETIN-BOARD SYSTEMS FOR THIS OR SIMILAR GAMES ☎ →*dial* 703-709-6691/817-539-4751/ 612-572-2587/505-334-6483
Stats
• Difficulty: complex
• Competition: turn-based
• Number of players: 2-11
• Interface: graphical
• Platform: DOS
Requirements: *Requires a frontend*

VGA Planets at the Gamer's Den There's always a new game of *VGA Planets* about to begin, or you can choose to set up a private, customized game with some friends. Pick your racial preferences, turn frequency, and game type and start sending in your turns. You'll be updated with emailed turn results. Game turns can be processed as often as you like—from once a week to every day. *Info:* ✓**INTERNET**→*email* vgap @den.com ✍ *Type in subject line:* readme

Stats
- Difficulty: complex
- Competition: turn-based
- Number of players: 2–11
- Interface: graphical
- Platform: DOS

Requirements: *Requires a copy of the program*

Planet talk

alt.games.vga-planets (ng) Where new games are started and old strategies analyzed. Effectively functions as the Worldwide HQ for the *VGA Planets* community. To start a game, just answer (or post, once you've got some *VGA-P* experience, an announcement to the newsgroup with the subject "players wanted." The post should include information on the game version, whether it's shareware or registered, skill level, deadlines, and the method of assigning the galactic races. The FAQ explains the game, tells you where to find the latest shareware version, and answers such vital questions as "Why did the colonists I dropped on a planet vanish?" and "What's the deal with science ships?" *VGA-P* fans may also wish to check out the related but more general rec.games.pbm and comp.sys. ibm.pc.strategic newsgroups. Updated versions of the FAQ and Hints files are posted to the newsgroup on a monthly basis. ✓**USENET** *FAQ:* ✓**INTERNET** ...→ *email* vgap-bin-get@slammer. atl.ga.us ✍ *Type in message body:* get vga-faq ...→*ftp* risc11.cahs. colostate.edu→anonymous→<your email address>→/pub/planets/ vga-info→vga-faq

VGA Planets Players' Pub (echo) Sysops and players discuss *VGA Planets.* ✓**WWIVNET**

VGA Planets Players Pub (echo) For *Planets* players to come and be themselves. ✓**ICENET**

Program

Tim Wisseman Creator of *VGA Planets.* You may register your version with him (currently at no cost) or let him know about any bugs. He runs a BBS called Tim's Continuum with local conferences covering tech support and general discussion about the game. There is also a file library with everything you need for *VGA Planets* and more. Looking for a BBS near you that runs *VGA Planets* games? Wissman's board carries a listing (BBS1994.ZIP) of all registered BBSs. ☎*dial* 209-877-4921 ✓**INTERNET**→*email* cocomax@gorn. echo.com ✍ *Email with general correspondence*

VGA Planets Archive Besides the FAQ and the Hints file in the /vga-info subdirectory, the site also carries the unregistered version of *VGA Planets 3.0*, the host program, and a slew of *VGA Planets* utilities. ✓**INTERNET**→*ftp* risc11.cahs. colostate.edu→anonymous→<your email address>→/pub/planets

Support

National VGA Planets Help/ Support (echo) Everything you ever wanted to know about *VGA Planets.* ✓**WWIVNET**

VGA Planets—HINTS *VGA Planets* guru Gary Grothman maintains this extensive, seven-part strategic guide to playing the game. The guide gives general advice ("Don't piss off a cloaking race early in the game"; "Always

use large freighters—the little ones are just too small to do anything") and specific strategies for particular sides ("Fireclouds can't fight enemy ships, though they can take out an all beam craft"; "There is nothing scarier to a Borg than a fully loaded Biocide Carrier"). The file is posted twice a month to the alt.games.vga-planets newsgroup. ✓**INTERNET** ...→*ftp* risc11.cahs. colostate.edu→anonymous→<your email address>→/pub/planets/ vga-info→vga-strat ...→*email* vgap-bin-get@slammer.atl.ga.us ✍ *Type in message body:* get vga-strategy

> *"VGA Planets guru Gary Grothman maintains this extensive strategic guide to playing the game. The guide gives general advice ('Don't piss off a cloaking race early in the game'; 'Always use large freighters—the little ones are just too small to do any-thing') and specifc strategies for particular sides."*

Part 2

Role-playing & Adventure

Fantasy role-playing

Ever wonder about those '80s stories of college students dying in real-life *D&D* quests

through city sewer systems? One section of the **rec. games.frp** FAQ deconstructs vilification of the gaming world by right-wing religious types. If battling televangelists is not your thing, check out the 21st-century fascists in the **Cyberpunk 2020 Archive**, the super-bad guys in the **DC Comics Role Playing Game**, or the literary combat of the medieval MUSH **Tela Magica**.

Wielding the sword—downloaded from wuarchive.wustl.edu.

On the Net

Across the board

Delphi GameSIG Role-playing gamers will find free-form role-playing in the conference rooms. Go to the conference room, choose a nickname for your "character," and just start typing. Players tell stories, order virtual drinks, and cavort in real-time conversation. To play a specific, such as *AD&D*, go to the Forum and look for a game announcement in the Role-Playing Games topic. Then contact the game master for information on creating a character. Turns are posted back and forth and eventually compiled and put in the GameSIG Database. The Forum also carries the Computer RPG's topic for discussion and a general-chatter topic, where RPG discussions are often found. The GameSIG Database (Delphi's name for a library) includes pro-

grams to help you create characters for role-playing games or, if you're a game-master, to keep track of combat or monsters.
✓ **DELPHI**→*go* ent game

GEnie TSR RoundTable TSR Inc. moderates this RoundTable, which features both message-based and conference-based (real-time) games, as well as news, a mail-order hobby shop, product information, announcements of coming attractions, and free-form gaming in the Red Dragon Inn. Check out the TSR Online Bulletin Board for discussions on playing or serving as DM for any TSR role-playing game: *Dungeons and Dragons, Advanced Dungeons and Dragons, Marvel Superheroes, Buck Rogers,*

and others.

The Bulletin Board offers dungeon-master training at the Dungeon Masters Academy, where you'll learn the tricks of the trade to make your campaign more exciting.

Monsters & spells

The AD&D Game Support Center offers game supplements like the Complete Book of Races and Drow R Us. Look here for new character classes, monsters, and spells. This is also the campaign-setting headquarters for all TSR campaign worlds for *AD&D,* with new locations, spells, and rules for every campaign setting that allow you to expand your campaign. Questions about campaign themes, mood, and geography are skillfully answered.

Universe design

All the *AD&D* game settings are represented here: Forgotten Realms, Ravenloft, Dark Sun. There's also a Universe Construction Club, where DMs trade their campaign settings and talk about the finer points of designing a campaign universe. And if you want to add some real-world history to *AD&D*, there's historical information on the age of Charlemagne, the Roman Empire, the Celts, and the Vikings.

Look in the software libraries for computer aids, downloadable graphics of player characters, and compiled message and conference game logs. Want to go to a gaming convention? Look up the information on GenCon, the world's largest role-playing convention, and register on the Conline if you like.

Special events

While you're here, check the Special Events listing for guest speakers in the conference rooms. If you have the itch to play, go to the Real-Time Game Information and Sign Up, where you can choose your game by the genre, game setting, and method—conference chat or play-by-message. Or, if you can't wait to play, go to the Red Dragon Inn and play sans the rules—just be a character as you type. ✓ **GENIE**→*keyword* tsr

Illuminati Online Offers local newsgroups for role-playing discussions. There are about a dozen newsgroups for Steve Jackson Game's GURPS (io.games.sjg. gurps*) as well as discussions about *Toon*, FASA's *BattleTech*, *Wizards of the Coast* games, and others. Discussions are enhanced by the presence of game designers

from Steve Jackson Games and other role-playing-game publishers. ☎ →*dial* 512-448-8950→ <your login>→<your password>→ <choose a newsreader like "tin"> ✓ **INTERNET**→*telnet* io.com→<your login>→<your password>→tin <choose a newsreader like "tin"> *Info:* ✓ **INTERNET**→*www* http://io. com/root.html

---

rec.games.frp.advocacy (ng) Not sure which game to buy? Ever thought about changing game systems? Or are you just so happy with the game that you want to tell the world? This is the place for the great debates: *Hero* or *Gurps*? *Ars-Magica* or *D&D*? *Cyberpunk 2020* or *Shadowrun*? Gaming systems and materials are compared and rated in this forum for the highly opinionated. You'll learn the pros and cons of just about any gaming system out there. Just be careful—it's a free-for-all in here! Take your Vorpal Blade (or your Ingram, Elder Sign, or battle armor…). ✓ **USENET**

---

rec.games.frp.announce (ng) For announcements of new games, Net-books, FTP sites, gaming conventions, live-action games, and other role-playing news. Discussions of specific role-playing games should be directed to their appropriate newsgroups, not this one. The rec.games.frp.* FAQ, which is posted here and to other frp newsgroups, is a ten-part wonder covering the gamut of role-playing.

Part 1 explains the structure of the frp newsgroups and gives posting guidelines. Parts 2 and 2a answer frequently asked questions about role-playing games, explain such terms as "munchkinism" and "Monty Haul," and provide some background on important role-playing-game figures, such as Gary Gygax and Steve Jackson.

Stackpole's Defense

Part 2b is also called "Stackpole's Defense of Gaming" and addresses parental concerns about role-playing games and pointedly answers charges against gaming put forth by various religious organizations. It also dispels a few "urban legends" about gaming. Part 3 lists FTP archive sites containing role-playing-game-related materials. Parts 4, 5, and 5a list mailing lists and digests on the Net. Part 6 is a directory of non-Internet BBSs of interest to role-playing gamers, and part 7 describes the various Net-books out there and tells you whom to contact to get updates

> "Gaming systems and materials are compared and rated in this forum for the highly opinionated. You'll learn the pros and cons of just about any gaming system out there. Just be careful— it's a free-for-all in here! Take your Vorpal Blade (or your Ingram, Elder Sign, or battle armor…)."

for the FAQ. Probably the best place to start when looking for game-related information on the Net. ✓**USENET**

rec.games.frp.misc (ng) The catch-all discussion group for role-playing games without their own newsgroup. Talk about *Runequest, Call of Cthulhu, Star Trek, Toon,* and *Macho Women With Guns* here. Discuss rules, evaluate supplemental material (published by either the gaming company or the Net), and swap story ideas. If you're not sure which newsgroup to post to about a role-playing game, start here. ✓**USENET**

REECFRP (echo) Discuss all types of role-playing games, including board, war, sci-fi, fantasy games, and more. ✓**FIDONET**

ROLEPLAY (echo) Create a character and join in the adventure. ✓**ILINK**

Role-Playing Game Discussion Forum (echo) Forum for discussing all kinds of RPGs. ✓**WWIVNET**

ROLE PLAYING GAMES (echo) Compare role-playing-game systems. ✓**RELAYNET**

Role Playing Games Forum Members of this forum like to conduct play-by-message and play-by-conference campaigns—from medieval fantasy to cyberpunk systems. Games are announced in the Playing/Recruitment section of the messages and then played in the section dedicated to the genre, such as Fantasy, Horror/Occult, or Heroes. Each game's messages have a header abbreviating the title of the campaign, and you can browse through them and follow the game.

Man on Pegasus—downloaded from lajkonik.cyf-kr.edu.pl.

Lively chat
Games are also held in the two conference rooms dedicated to the forum—players meet at a preset time and play using real-time chat. Logs of these adventures, and the completed message-based games, are then put in the gaming library according to genre, where they are preserved for members to download. You'll also find lively chat about the games in the Gamemastering and Crossroads messaging sessions.

Look in the various libraries to find artwork and game statistics for player characters, submissions guidelines from role-playing-game publishers, discussion archives, and programs for your home computer to help you create characters or track combat information. The *Crossroads Gazette,* an electronic gaming magazine written by and for forum members, is chock-full of reviews, regular gaming columns, and news from game publishers. And like the forum, the newsletter caters to all kinds of role-playing games. ✓**COMPUSERVE** →*go* rpgames

Role-Playing Gaming Forum Information about live (i.e., chat room) and message-based RPG games on AOL. Check the Game

Schedules for when and where games are played (listed by game system, by day for live games, and by board for message-based games). The General Information message board contains posts from game-seekers. You'll find descriptions of ongoing games in the Live Game Descriptions and the Message-Based Game Descriptions. For a general overview of live games, select the Live Games folder, which contains How to Play Live Games, the Live Game Schedule, a Live Games Updates message board, and links to the six chat rooms where live games take place. Choose the Message-Based Games folder for message-board role-play talk.

Druidic priestesses
The RPG Forum General Library carries equipment and spell lists, *Robotech* damage-information tables, *Star Wars* control power lists, and more. For more character-specific files, including weapons, character sheets, and other files for games from *AD&D* to *BattleTech* to *Kult* and *WarHammer,* select the Character Information Library. You'll also find PC-only, Macintosh-only, and Apple II–only files in their own libraries on the Gaming Libraries window. And for fantasy fans, GIF after GIF of druidic priestesses, muscled berserkers, raven ladies, dragon battles, and evil mages is in the D&D Graphics library. ✓**AMERICA ONLINE**→*keyword* rpg

RPG Discussion (echo) Discuss any and all. ✓**ICENET**

RPG Forum (echo) Discuss the pros and cons of role-playing games. ✓**WWIVNET**

RPG_PLAY (echo) Talk to others about role-playing on the Net. ✓**INTELEC**

The RPG Thang (echo) Anything-goes role-playing discussions. ✓**WWIVNET**

Archives

Fantasy Art Archives Fantasy art serves as an inspiration to players and game masters alike. Here you'll find art from the various *Dungeons and Dragons* books and Tolkien calendars, as well as paintings by Boris Vajello and other fantasy artists. ✓**INTERNET** ...→ *ftp* ftp.sunet.se→anonymous→<your email address>→/pub/pictures/fantasy ...→ *ftp* lajkonik.cyf-kr.edu.pl→anonymous→<your email address>→/agh/reserve/gifs/fantasy

---

Monster RPG Archives Material for several role-playing-game systems, including character sheets, game-master-assistant programs, home-brewed rules, archived threads from usenet newsgroups, and original fiction. ✓**INTERNET** ...→*ftp* ftp.cs.pdx.edu→anonymous→<your email address>→/pub/frp ...→*ftp* ftp.funet.fi→anonymous→<your email address>→/pub/doc/games/roleplay ...→*ftp* ftp.umd.umich.edu→anonymous→<your email address>→/pub/frp ...→*ftp* ftp.mpgn.com→anonymous→<your email address>→/Gaming/Fantasy ...→*ftp* ftp.csua.berkeley.edu→anonymous→<your email address>→/pub

---

rec.games.frp.archives (ng) The frp discussion lists generate volumes of information. Digests of interesting threads, Net-books, stories, and even binaries of useful programs for role-playing games are posted here. ✓**USENET**

Wizards of the Coast Archive FTP sites for *Wizards of the Coast* role-playing materials. The first site includes *GURPS* material and translation rules allowing you to move player characters from *Runequest* and *Chaosium* games to *GURPS* fantasy and horror games. If you're an aspiring game designer or illustrator, look here for author and artist submission guidelines. The second site stores archives of dozens of mailing lists related to *WotC* games. ✓**INTERNET** ...→*ftp* altair.acs.uci.edu→anonymous→<your email address>→/pub/wizards ...→*ftp* ftp.wizards.com→anonymous→<your email address>→/pub/wizards

Ars Magica

Tela Magica Based on the *Ars Magica* role-playing-game system (the MUSH is fully supported by *Wizards of the Coast*). The setting is France around A.D. 1200, a time of legends and folklore, magic, and battles in the name of God. Every player is entitled to one magus or faerie companion character, one companion character, and an unlimited number of grogs. To create a character, you must go through a five-room character-concept-building process. Enter through the OOC lounge.

Character creation

Character creation is complicated—you really must be familiar with *Ars Magica*. Role-playing is taken very seriously here, and all plots and building must be in keeping with the theme and the historical period. Most role-playing happens in Paris, especially in the magi covenants, where politics and personal relationships fuel the role-playing on Tela. Players (unfortunately relatively few) develop the tinyplots, and approved story lines affect "history" in the MUSH. One of the elements of RPGs is combat, and *Ars Magica* has an elaborate combat system. If *Ars Magica* is your game, if you enjoy debating rules, and if you don't mind investing a lot of time learning how to play, this is the place to be. ✓**INTERNET**→*telnet* tela.wizards.com 6250→connect guest guest

Stats
- Difficulty: complex
- Competition: live
- Number of players: 1+
- Interface: ASCII
- Server: MUSH
- Platforms: all

> "Nowadays, chummer, if you ain't got the intel you're street pizza. Plug in here to get the latest on role-playing games of the ugly future, especially *Shadowrun*, *Cyberpunk 2020*, and *GURPS Cyberpunk*. These Netboys are talking game mechanics, and plotlines, and they're serving up their home-brew rules for hungry GMs."

Commands
- To get information, type: news *or* news intro
- To get a list of wizards, type: news wizards
- To get a list of story guides, type: +who/sg

Computer RPGs

comp.sys.ibm.pc.games.rpg (ng) Discussion of role-playing games that evolved from two intertwined strands—the board game *Dungeons & Dragons* and the text-based computer game *Adventure*. Popular examples include: *Dark Sun*, *Shattered Lands*; *Lands of Lore*; and *Ultima VII* Part 2. See also comp.sys.ibm.pc.games.adventure—it's often more lively. ✓**USENET**

Cyberpunk

rec.games.frp.cyber (ng) Nowadays, chummer, if you ain't got the intel you're street pizza. Plug in here to get the latest on role-playing games of the ugly future, especially *Shadowrun*, *Cyberpunk 2020*, and *GURPS Cyberpunk*. These Netboys are talking game mechanics, and plotlines, and they're serving up their homebrew rules for hungry GMs. So if you need the factfax, like quick, this is the place. ✓**USENET**

Cerebus Shadowrun Archive Cerebus is the official data haven for *Shadowrun* players. You'll find the errata for the *Shadowrun* rules published by FASA, Net-books, other home-brewed rules for *Shadowrun*, character sheets, computer programs to aid the GM, and tons of other material for Shadowrunners and GMs. This FTP site was formerly known as "teetot." ✓**INTERNET** ...→*ftp* cerebus.acusd.edu→anonymous→<your email address>→/pub/Role-Play

The Terminator—downloaded from lajkonik.cyf-kr.edu.pl.

ing/Shadowrun ...→*gopher* cerebus.acusd.edu→Role-Playing→Shadowrun

Cyberpunk 2020 Archive This is *Cyberpunk*'s data haven. You'll find character sheets, weapons tables, optional rules, computer programs to help you create characters, a dictionary of *Cyberpunk* slang, and much more. ✓**INTERNET**→*ftp* wais.com→anonymous→<your email address>→/pub/games/cyberpunk

Jayhawk Stories The Jayhawk story is a collection of postings about a real *Shadowrun* campaign with a "hero" whose name was Jayhawk Davies. ✓**INTERNET** ...→*ftp* ftp.cs.pdx.edu→anonymous→<your email address>→/pub/frp/stories/jayhawk ...→*ftp* ftp.white.toronto.edu→anonymous→<your email address>→/pub/frp/shadowrun/jayhawk

Neo-Anarchists' Guide to Everything Else This *Shadowrun* Net-book attempt to cover everything that was not dealt with in the *Neo-Anarchist's Guide to Real Life*, published by FASA. There are six volumes. Volume one includes a description of Los Angeles, Las Vegas, the Neo-Anarchist's Online Grimoire, rules for

dead zones (areas where technology doesn't work), and many other articles and reviews. ✓**INTERNET** ...→*ftp* cerebus.acusd.edu→anonymous→<your email address>→/pub/Role-Playing/Shadowrun/NAGEE ...→*gopher* cerebus.acusd.edu→Role-Playing→Shadowrun→NAGEE

NERPS Mailing List (ml) NERPS is short for Net Enhancements to Role Playing Shadowrun. Experienced game masters—some of whom have connections to the original author of *Shadowrun* (the Dark Lord on High, Tom Dowd)—collaborate in developing new rules anthologies (Net-books) for the *Shadowrun* system. *Shadowlore* was the first completed project of this group. You can subscribe and lurk, but if you want to post you must obtain an author i.d. (instructions are in the FAQ, which is sent when you subscribe). ✓**INTERNET**→*email* listserv@hearn.bitnet ✍ *Type in message body:* subscribe nerps <your full name> *Archives:* ✓**INTERNET** ...→*email* listserv@hearn.bitnet ✍ *Type in message body:* index nerps ...→*ftp* hearn.nic.surfnet.nl→anonymous→<your email address>→/archive

RTal List Covers R. Taslorian Games products, including *Cyberpunk 2020* and *Mekton*. Discussion encompasses rules, upcoming products, Net-books in the works, and campaign development. ✓**INTERNET**→*email* archive-server@runic.via.mind.org ✍ *Type in message body:* join rtal *Archives:* ✓**INTERNET**→*email* archive-server@runic.via.mind.org ✍ *Type in message body:* archive rtal

Shadowlore *Shadowlore* is the first publication of the NERPS mailing list. It covers new races, such as halflings and minotaurs, totems for shamans, spells, and rules for bioware and magic. This very well-done Net-book was written as a supplement to the *Shadowrun* rules. No game master should be without it. ✓**INTERNET** ...→*ftp* cerebus.acusd.edu→anonymous→<your email address>→ /pub/Role-Playing/Shadowrun/ NERPS ...→*gopher* cerebus.acusd. edu→Role-Playing→Shadowrun→ NERPS

ShadowMUSH Based on *Shadowrun* Second Edition rules, this MUSH will let you play your favorite *Shadowrun* character in a multiplayer, real-time setting. The centerpiece of this MUSH is the Net of the Shadowrun world, where players with decker characters can glom intel from the datahavens and sell it to whoever has the cred. Very role-playing-intensive—don't leave the OOC lounge unless you're IC. ✓**INTERNET**→*telnet* yacht.slip.andrew.cmu.edu 4201→ connect guest guest *Register:* ✓**INTERNET**→*email* srun-reg@yacht.slip. andrew.cmu.edu ✍ *Write a request:* <your character's name and a brief concept>

Stats
- Difficulty: average
- Competition: live
- Number of players: 1+
- Interface: ASCII
- Server: MUSH
- Platforms: all

ShadowRun Discussion List (ml) Full of sammys, riggers, cowboys and wu-jen, this is not the kind of place you wanna stroll into with a 'tude. But if you need tips or campaign ideas, or you wonder what a full-auto Ingram is going to do to your cyberarm, this is the place. You'll also find real-life experts on encryption, weapons, and Internet issues. ✓**INTERNET**→*email* listserv@hearn. bitnet ✍ *Type in message body:* subscribe shadowrn <your full name> *Ar-*

chives: ✓**INTERNET** ...→*email* list serv@hearn.bitnet ✍ *Type in message body:* index shadowrn ...→*ftp* hearn.nic.surfnet.nl→anonymous→ <your email address>→/archive

Shadowrun WWW Pages *Shadowrun* Web pages are linked as FTP and gopher sites, archives of the listserv lists, and other *Shadowrun* resources (e.g., a *Shadowrun* time line). A great place for one-stop shopping for *Shadowrun* inspiration. ✓**INTERNET** ...→*www* http://www.oat.ts.astro.it/marcucci/sr2/index.html ...→*www* http:// yoyo.cc.monash.edu.au/~wigs/ shadowrun.html ...→*www* http:// www.cs.odu.edu/~mark/shadow. html

ShadowTalk Mailing List (ml) Can't get a team of runners going at home? Check here for *Shadowrun* role-playing. List members develop characters and play the game via email. Posts follow a very specific format, taken from FASA's *Shadowrun* game books. List members pretend to be on a secret BBS in Seattle—that's where they're reading these posts. Each post mentions who is not supposed to see the message—anyone else is assumed not to have seen the message (even if they have) and cannot act on it. The upshot of this is that you get to see the entire story, including plots against your character. The FAQ (which arrives as soon as you subscribe to the list) will let you know how to post. Also, be sure to sign up for the Plot-D mailing list. ✓**INTERNET**→*email* listserv@ hearn.bitnet ✍ *Type in message body:* subscribe shadowtk <your full name> *Archives:* ✓**INTERNET** ...→*email* listserv@hearn.bitnet ✍ *Type in message body:* index shadowtk ...→*ftp* hearn.nic.surfnet.nl→ anonymous→<your email address> →/archive

Stats
- Difficulty: average
- Competition: turn-based
- Number of players: 2+
- Interface: ASCII
- Platforms: all

(ShadowTalk) Plot Development Mailing List (ml) An out-of-character environment to develop story plots for the Shadowtalk Mailing List (which is strictly in character!) ✓**INTERNET**→*email* list serv@hearn.bitnet ✍ *Type in message body:* subscribe plot-d <your full name>

Free-form

alt.pub.dragons-inn (ng) Welcome to the Dragon's Inn! Pull up a chair while someone pours you an ale. Now sit and listen to the other patrons. Outlandish, isn't it? Seems everyone here has survived incredible journeys fraught with peril. And it's true. Everyone here is a hero. The Dragon's Inn newsgroup thrives on bravery and story-telling ability. Each author/ player controls one character in a story that is collectively written via email by several adventurers. Finished sections are posted to the newsgroup.

Generica

All stories transpire in the city of Generica, where anything can happen. In addition to storytelling, there's ongoing free-form role-playing in the Dragon's Inn (or as "free-form" as message-based role-playing can get). Participants post their character's actions and dialogue to the newsgroup and respond without the limits of a specific plot.

Here's how to get in on the action yourself. First, get hold of the FAQ and read a few stories on alt.pub.dragons-inn. There are other files available at the FAQ site that describe *Generica* and its inhabitants. Once you have a feel for the setting, write up a character description for your adventurer—an elf, a wizard, a troll, or whatever you want. When a new thread (story) is announced, contact the instigator of the thread and ask to join in. Later, you can return to the Inn and brag yourself. ✓**USENET** *FAQ:* ✓**INTERNET**→*ftp* rtfm.mit.edu→ anonymous→<your email address> →/pub/usenet-by-hierarchy/ alt/pub/dragons-inn *Info:* ✓**INTER-NET**→*www* http://wwwcip.infor matik.uni-erlangen.de/user/ fkschmid/dragon.html

Stats
- Difficulty: simple
- Competition: n/a
- Number of players: 2+
- Interface: ASCII
- Platforms: all

The Arena A spin-off of the Free-Form Gaming Forum, but *The Arena* has rules and a game master. First, create a character from the character-classes folder (your character must have the same screen name as you sign on with). Then, pick a hand-to-hand weapon and a missile within your class limitations. Send your character-class and weapon choices to OGF Devron via AOL email. OGF Devron will figure out your hit points, your spell points and your rank points and post all this information in the Character Information folder.

New characters are posted on Saturdays and you may begin competing the following Sunday. Refereed matches take place Wednesday through Sunday, 8–11 p.m., EST. "Entry fees" are charged at the beginning of a match (10 gold pieces for common matches, 100 gold pieces for tournaments). Characters can borrow the money from *The Arena*, but that money is deducted from

any winnings until the balance is paid. Read the rules before you enter a match; otherwise you won't know whether to "Attack," "Spell-<spell name>," "Advance," "Retreat," "Pass," or "Use-<item>." ✓**AMERICA ONLINE**→*keyword* ffgf→ The Arena

Stats
- Difficulty: simple
- Competition: live
- Number of players: 2+
- Interface: ASCII
- Platforms: all

Commands
- To get instructions, choose Rules for the Arena
- To get support, leave a message on the Arena Messaging board
- To roll dice, type the command: //roll-sides<# of sides>.0-dice<# of dice>.0 —or— //roll-dice<# of dice>.0-sides<# of sides>.0

Dragon Rampant Inn Harold of the Blue Shield leaps onto the table and makes an announcement: *"The Dragon Rampant Inn is now open and drinks are on me!" The Dragon Rampant Inn* on Delphi is the place to go for free-form role-playing in a medieval fantasy setting. Just make up a character and jump into the fray, where everyone acts out their characters in real-time chat. The Inn's hours are posted in the GameSIG banner. ✓**DELPHI**→*go* ent gamesig→conference

Stats
- Difficulty: simple
- Competition: live
- Number of players: 2+
- Interface: ASCII
- Platforms: all

Duel of Swords The FFGF's basic combat game, played in the People Connection room and via email. The whereabouts of the rules are not always clear, but the FFGF's message boards are usually a good bet. Using ten basic maneuvers—Thrust, High Cut, Slash, Low Cut, Disengage, Lateral Parry, Sidestep, Circular Parry, Duck, and Stop Hit—opponents score a hit (1 point), a miss (0 points), or an advantage (½ point). No maneuver other than Disengage may be played twice consecutively. Because the Free-Form Gaming Forum characters take the screen names of AOL members, nobody is allowed to die. Good duelists rise in rank from Commoner to Overlord. Once a month an Overlord Challenge takes place in the Dreamweaver's Lair. ✓**AMERICA ONLINE**→*keyword* pc→RDI Duel of Swords *Info:* ✓**AMERICA ONLINE**→*keyword* ffgf→ Dreamweaver's Lair

Stats
- Difficulty: average
- Competition: live
- Number of players: 2+
- Interface: ASCII
- Platforms: all

Commands
- To get instructions, go to the Red Dragon Innsights message board

---

Fable's Guide to Free-Form Gaming

Fable, a self-proclaimed master of free-form role-playing, gives his seven cardinal rules for enjoying *Red Dragon Inn*'s character role-playing. He admits, however, to having violated, at one time or another, rules 2 through 7. A good guide for beginners, though short on how-to information. ✓**AMERICA ONLINE**→*keyword* ffgf→More→Free-Form Gaming Forum Library→Fable's Guide to Free-Form

---

Free-Form Gaming Forum

A game that's all about role-playing a character to the hilt. There are no rules, other than AOL's Terms of Service and some simple conventions. All conversation takes place "in character," no one's allowed to question another's creativity, the

DragonLance—*downloaded from lajkonik.cyf-kr.edu.pl.*

---

general layout of the place is whatever the collective consciousness suggests it is, and there are no winners and losers.

The center of the FFGF is the *Red Dragon Inn*, a quirky place that can accommodate up to 23 people. (You get there with the keyword "PC.") In the evenings, there's a bartender on duty, known as an RDI; at other times, it's self-serve.

Half-baked characters

Players show up, with well-formed or half-baked characters in mind, and interact. Lately there's been a plague of vampires, but you're just as likely to see werewolves (Garous), Cheysulies, rangers, jesters, cowboys, mysterious ladies whose beauty is exceeded only by their cunning, warriors, and sci-fi "spacers." It's much like improvisational acting.

Players type their characters' actions within double colons (e.g., "::nods in direction of Jester, and smiles to herself::"), and spoken words as normal chat-room conversation. Some players like to flirt (several weddings have taken place), joke, or speak mysteriously. Others show up with characters they've developed in a game or from fantasy fiction; for quite a number of them, this is their first

experience with role-playing games.

Duel of Fists

Two rooms have been set up for battles—Duel of Swords and Duel of Fists. People will often go off to "the Lake" or "the Road" (meaning they create a private chat room) to live out their fantasies—whether social, amorous, or combative—without being interrupted by other patrons in, for example, the *Red Dragon Inn*. Characters and story lines are further developed in collaborative writing efforts in the FFGF message boards. Incidentally, the FFGF may hold the distinction of having the highest ratio of female characters to male creatures of any online role-playing game around. Wait, wait: We said female *characters*—not players. ✓**AMERICA ONLINE**→*keyword* ffgf

Stats
- Difficulty: simple
- Competition: live
- Number of players: 2+
- Interface: ASCII
- Platforms: all

Commands
- To get support, leave a message on the Red Dragon Innsights board
- To indicate action of your character, describe action within double colons. E.g., ::walks in and sidles up to the bar::
- To roll dice, type the command: //roll-sides<# of sides>.0-dice<# of dice>.0 —or— //roll-dice<# of dice>.0-sides<# of sides>.0

The New Dimension

Create a character and start a life in the New Dimension, an ongoing story where adventure and intrigue rule the day. Play the game via the forum's message boards. ☎→*dial* 216-368-3888→A visitor→Explore the system→go dimension ✓**INTER-**

NET→*telnet* freenet-in-a.cwru.edu→ A visitor→Explore the system→go dimension

The Pendragon Inn (echo) A free-form story line RPG. ✓**WWIV-NET**

The Red Dragon Inn (echo) Play the WWIVnet's version of free-form RPG. ✓**WWIVNET**

Vostag's Tavern (echo) Create a character and come on in for a drink. ✓**ICENET**

Game masters

GMAST-L (ml) Are you a game master? This list is for you. GMs from all role-playing games talk about rules, creating a campaign, dealing with "munchkin" players, and the best music to play during a game. List volume is heavy, and the discussion is lively and helpful. Have a question or a problem? Members of this list can help. ✓**INTERNET**→*email* listserv@ utcvm.bitnet ✍ *Type in message body:* subscribe gmast-l <your full name>

Heroes

Champ-L Want to find out how far a six-inch character will fly when hit by a superstrong villain? Find the answers to all your questions about the rules of *HERO*, and *Champions* in particular, plus ideas for campaigns, villains, and player characters. ✓**INTERNET**→ *email* champ-request@omg.org ✍ *Type in message body:* subscribe champ-l <your email address>

Comics-L (ml) Bone up on your superhero classics and spice up your *Champions* or *GURPS Supers* campaigns. ✓**INTERNET**→*email* listserv@unlvm.bitnet ✍ *Type in message body:* subscribe comics-l <your full name>

> "Harold of the Blue Shield leaps onto the table and makes an announcement: 'The Dragon Rampant Inn is now open and drinks are on me!'"

DC Comics Role Playing Game (echo) Be a superhero or a supervillain in this RPG based on DC Comics. ✓**ICENET**

HERO System Archive The "official" Internet archive for the *HERO* games system. You'll find sample characters, *Fantasy HERO* spells, character sheets, computer aids for creating players, and more. Contains subdirectories for *Ninja HERO*, *Space HERO*, *Fantasy HERO*, and *Champions*. ✓**INTERNET**→*ftp* ftp.cs.pdx.edu→anonymous→<your email address>→ /pub/frp/hero

io.games.sjg.gurps * The source! Steve Jackson Games has its own BBS with several local newsgroups related to *GURPS*. Designers, developers, and Steve Jackson himself are here to answer your *GURPS* questions and to ask you for suggestions and feedback on *GURPS* rules revisions, sourcebooks, and other products. You have to be a member of the Illuminati Online. ✓**INTERNET**→*telnet* io.com→<your login>→<your password>→<select a newsgroup reader like "tin">→ io.games.sjg.gurps

Superguy (ml) The most outlandish superhero stories ever, of-fering a mixture of comic relief and solid adventure ideas for some superhero games. ✓**INTERNET**→ *email* listserv@ucf lvm.cc.ucf.edu ✍ *Type in message body:* subscribe superguy <your full name>

ImagECastle

ImagECastle Less a game than an evolving stage play wherein each character authors and enacts his or her own part. The world is quite small, consisting of areas in and around the Castle D'Image. Most of the castle denizens are "ordinary" citizens—courtiers, swordsmen, rogues, courtesans, and gypsies. The focus of the MUD is more on social interaction and intrigue than on combat and exploration. Activity tends to center in the Salon and the Foyer, where gossip is exchanged, romances born, tempers ignited, and villainous plots revealed. Roleplaying is considered quite good here and the chat channels are always buzzing. ✓**INTERNET**→*telnet* fo gey.stanford.edu 4201→connect guest guest

Stats
- Difficulty: average
- Competition: live
- Number of players: 1+
- Interface: ASCII
- Server: MUSH
- Platforms: all

Commands
- To get information, type: news *or* help topics

Marketplace

rec.games.frp.marketplace (ng) Looking to hock your old *Champions* rule books because you just bought the new edition? Want to find mint-condition first printings of the *Dungeons and Dragon* rules? And what about that obscure game you saw in the back of a store years ago? Come to the role-playing market, where items are traded, bought, and sold. Put "For Sale" or "Wanted: X" in the subject line. ✓**USENET**

Mythus

Mythus-L (ml) The role-playing game *Mythus* is set in Ærth, a place not unlike our own antiquity. Vikings, Ægyptians, and Celts undertake dangerous journeys in this game, and list members discuss campaign settings, adventure ideas, and the rules (lots and lots of rule discussion). ✓**INTERNET**→ *email* listserv@brownvm.brown. edu ✍ *Type in message body:* subscribe mythus-l <your full name> *Archives:* ✓**INTERNET**→ *email* listserv@brownvm.brown. edu ✍ *Type in message body:* index mythus-l

News & reviews

Electronomicon AOL's online gaming newsletter, concentrating on RPGs, with interviews, reviews, and articles (e.g., "Genericsville: Urban Setting in RPGs"). ✓**AMERICA ONLINE**→ *keyword* ogf→ Electronomicon Library

Organizations

Fellowship of Online Gamers The AOL chapter of the Role-Playing Game Association Network. For members of the RPGA only (for applications, see the Fellowship's main window). FOG members can participate in various RPGA Network events, FOG activities, and contests. They can also use the FOG's message board, library, and conference room. ✓**AMERICA ONLINE**→ *keyword* fog

Talislanta

Talislanta-L (ml) Discussion of the *Talislanta* fantasy role-playing

> ## "A million million invaders, and a million million attempts to crush them."

game, a game without the usual cast of fantasy characters. Rules and design discussions are quite common on this list and members spend a lot of time discussing what they want to see improved. But there are still no elves allowed. ✓**INTERNET**→ *email* listserv@wiz ards.com ✍ *Type in message body:* subscribe talislanta-l <your full name> *Archives:* ✓**INTERNET**→ *ftp* ftp.wizards.com→anonymous→ <your email address>→/pub/wiz ards/archive/talislanta-l

Torg

alt.games.torg (ng) There has been a terrible side effect to a human resistance group's attempt to thwart alien invaders—the Earth has been duplicated a trillion times. A million million Earths. A million million invaders. And a million million attempts to crush them. Should one Earth fail, then maybe another can succeed. If all Earths succumb, all will be lost.

Torg is not a computer-based game, it's a face-to-face role-playing game, and the Net brings *Torg* players together to reconcile events in the millions of realities called the Infiniverse. The *Torg* gaming groups are related to one another in a unique way—each one of them exists on an Earth duplicate, and the events on one Earth can greatly influence the course history takes on another Earth.

The newsgroup has a lot of "here's what's happening in my universe" type of posts, along with discussions of new gadgets, rules,

characters, etc. It's a great place to get ideas for adventures, or to get an answer on your in-game questions. An informative FAQ is posted here every couple of weeks— find out just what a Black Marble Wombat is! ✓**USENET**

Masterbook (ml) For the discussion of all West End Games MasterBook-based role-playing games, including *Torg*, *Shatterzone*, *BloodShadows*, and the *World of Indiana Jones.* ✓**INTERNET**→ *email* masterbook-request@ speed.intecom.com ✍ *Type in subject line:* subscribe

TORG (echo) Discuss the RPG *Torg.* Includes hints. ✓**WWIVNET**

Torg Archive Nothing new here for quite a while, but the site carries archives of the former *Torg* mailing list, spreadsheet programs for managing the game, a guide to the Infiniverse, variant rules, *Torg* magic information, and more. ✓**INTERNET**→ *ftp* morticia.cnns.unt. edu→anonymous→<your email address>→/pub/lists/torg

Torg on GEnie A smattering of *Torg* guides and product information is available in the library, including an introduction to the game (WHATTORG.TXT). West End Games, creator of *Torg*, has its own discussion category on GEnie, where a hefty amount of *Torg* conversation takes place. ✓**GENIE** …→*keyword* scorpia→ Gamers Libraries→Set Library Category→ Role-Playing Games Archives→ *Search by keyword:* torg (for files) …→*keyword* scorpia→Games Bulletin Board→set 17 (for messages)

Torg Spells Spells, spells, and more spells. ✓**INTERNET**→ *ftp* ftp.ias tate.edu→anonymous→<your email address>→/pub/frp/incoming/ Archives/Othersys→ torg_spl.tar.Z

Dungeons & Dragons

There are so many *D&D* riches on the Net that new players must wonder how role-

playing games ever existed before the advent of the modem. America Online's **Neverwinter Nights** is one of the most elaborate online multiplayer *AD&D* games going, but even if you play offline, there's heavy-duty discussion of TSR products in **rec.games.frp.adnd** and GEnie's **TSR Bulletin Board** (see the Fantasy Role-Playing pages). You'll also want to check out downloadable game utilities on **alt.games.frp.dnd-util**, which in effect turn your PC into the world's most expensive 20-sided die.

Battle of the Dragonriders—downloaded from lajkonik.cyf-kr.edu.pl.

---

modules, and FAQs about fantasy role-playing. ✓**INTERNET**→*www* http://www.acm.uiuc.edu/adnd/

ADND-L (ml) Hail, weary traveler! Come back from the caves with nary a piece of electrum for your trouble? Perhaps you need a few hints. Try the ADND-L, where veteran adventurers and dungeon masters talk rules, new monsters, spells, tricks, and role-playing experiences. TSR publications are also frequently reviewed. You'll get more than one answer to any question posted here, and perhaps you'll find players for a play-by-email game. The listserv archive for this list includes not only past discussion but also several Netbooks with new spells, monsters, and skills. Just what you need before you descend into the depths again. ✓**INTERNET**→*email* listserv@pucc.princeton.edu ✉ *Type in message body:* subscribe adnd-l <your full name> *Archives:* ✓**INTERNET** →*email* listserv@pucc.princeton.edu ✉ *Type in message body:* index adnd-l

On the Net

Across the board

AD&D (echo) For playing and discussing *Advanced Dungeons and Dragons.* ✓**FIDONET**

AD&D_CHAT (echo) Discuss *AD&D*, including spells, artifacts, monsters, gaming strategies, and experiences. Tips and hints are also available. ✓**FIDONET**

AD&D Web Pages A one-stop shop for *AD&D* players who are new to the Net. This Web site offers descriptions of many of the Net resources available to *AD&D* players as well as links to several FTP sites where you'll find Net books, character sheets, adventure

Dungeon and Dragon Debate (echo) Are you pure evil, or just misunderstood? Share your whines and hisses here. ✓**WWIVNET**

International Dungeons and Dragons Echo (echo) Discuss all aspects of *D&D*. ✓**WWIVNET**

Realms of Fantasy (echo) A national *AD&D* discussion conference. ✓**WWIVNET**

rec.games.frp.adnd (ng) Discussion of *Dungeons and Dragons*, from basic boxed-set rules to second-edition *Advanced Dungeons and Dragons* and its supplements—from the World of Greyhawk to Dark Sun. You'll find rules talk, stories, home-brewed rules, reviews of new TSR products, and rumors a plenty. The largest *Dungeons and Dragons* discussion anywhere. ✓**USENET**

Dark Sun

Dark Sun Mailing List (ml) DM's of Dark Sun campaigns discuss rules, geography, and survival. Dark Sun is a departure from traditional *AD&D* campaigns, with unusual races, classes, and monsters, and a much tougher desert world. Members post stories, adventure scenarios, and home-brewed rules. TSR supplements for Dark Sun, novels, and adventure modules are always food for discussion. ✓**INTERNET**→*email* listserv@leicester.ac.uk ✉ *Type in message body:* subscribe dark-sun <your full name>

Forgotten Realms

Forgotten Realms Mailing

List (ml) Lost in the Forgotten Realms? This list will help you find your way around TSR's enormous campaign setting for *Advanced Dungeons and Dragons*. The Forgotten Realms campaign setting covers all the classic fantasy role-playing themes and adventures from previous *AD&D* material, including dark elves, undead armies, and woodland elves. Dungeon Masters flesh out parts of the map not detailed by campaign supplements, post their own rules, create adventure scenarios, and write stories set in the Forgotten Realms. You'll also find reviews of Forgotten Realms novels, and fascinating adventure modules and realms for your players to explore. ✓**INTERNET**→*email* majordomo@ossi.com ✍ *Type in message body:* subscribe realms <your email address> *Archives:* ✓**INTERNET**→*email* majordomo@ossi.com ✍ *Type in message body:* index realms

Forgotten Realms Unlimited Adventures Artwork, monsters, patches, and other binaries that allow you to create an adventure game. Forgotten Realms is a game-authoring/playing program that allows you to design your own computer games based on the AD&D Forgotten Realms setting. The result will resemble the Gold boxed commercial *AD&D* games available in stores. Look in the /Misc directory for the Mac or DOS version of Unlimited Adventures game. Look in the /Modules directory for adventures written by other gamers. And once you have designed your own, you can upload it into the /Uploads directory. ✓**INTERNET**→*ftp* ccosun.caltech.edu→anonymous→<your email address>→/pub/UA

Neverwinter Nights *D&D* diehards look no further. Sometimes attracting more than 100 players an evening, *AD&D* on America Online is a multi-player role-playing adventure that uses SSI's Gold Box series. The large world consists of 28 regions, each a 16x16 grid with woods, dungeons, cities, and hills. Explore, join guilds, fight monsters and other players (yes, it's allowed here and very popular), and participate in the weekly quests and events organized by the game masters—usually held in the Great Hall Tavern. The Neverwinters Nights Forum features real-time chat in Lord Nashers lounge (where you can always find someone to help you or to roll dice with), message boards for discussing Neverwinter events, a library full of *D&D* images, program documentation, an events board (where you can find out when newbie tours of Never-

winter are being given and the next quests are being held). To purchase the required $14.95 kit, go to the Download and Ordering Center. ✓**AMERICA ONLINE**→*keyword* ad&d

Stats
- Difficulty: complex
- Competition: live
- Number of players: 1–200
- Interface: graphical
- Platforms: DOS, Windows

Commands
- To view a list of people in the same quadrant as you are, press: F2
- To view a list of everyone in the game, press: Shift-F2
- To push the chat screen back up to the top, press: F3

Ravenloft

Ravenloft (echo) Discuss the *Dungeons & Dragons* RPG *Ravenloft.* ✓**ICENET**

RuneQuest

RuneQuest Archives Archived discussions, character sheets, game master's aid programs, articles on *RuneQuest* from the newsgroups, *RuneQuest* fonts, and a compiled Net-book on the cults of Glorantha. ✓**INTERNET**→*ftp* ftp. csua.berkeley.edu→anonymous→<your email address>→/pub/runequest

RuneQuest Daily Digest (ml) The *RuneQuest* "in-crowd" discuss the world of Glorantha, *RuneQuest* rules, and upcoming products. New explorers are welcome. ✓**INTERNET**→*email* runequest-request@glorantha.holland.sun.com ✍ *Type in message body:* subscribe <your full name> <your email address> *Archives:* ✓**INTERNET**→*ftp* ftp.csua.berkeley.edu→anonymous→<your email address>→/pub/runequest/archives/digests

> "Hail, weary traveler! Come back from the caves with nary a piece of electrum for your trouble? Perhaps you need a few hints. Try the ADND-L, where veteran adventurers and dungeon masters talk rules, new monsters, spells, tricks, and role-playing experiences."

Spell books +

The Almost Complete List of AD&D Wizard Spells A listing of all the spells from all currently published *AD&D* 2nd edition handbooks, campaign supplements, and adventure modules published by TSR. Note: This is a list and not a reprinting of all spell descriptions and information. ✓ **INTERNET**→*ftp* ftp.cs.pdx.edu→ anonymous→<your email address> →/pub/frp/net-books→tacloaws. zip

Alpha's Book of Spells A spell book written and published on the Net by Alpha the Mage, a prolific spell researcher and the inventor of spells such as "Alpha's Sheet Lightning" and "Alpha's Starlight Citadel." The book is a collection of 61 spells of first to sixth level, published for *AD&D* 2nd Edition Rules. ✓ **INTERNET**→*ftp* ftp.iastate. edu→anonymous→<your email address>→/pub/frp→ Alpha_Spells.Z

The Great Net Spell Book More than 400 new spells and cantrips are described in this, the largest Net-book for *AD&D*. Includes such curiosities as "Sillvatar's Dragon Claw," "Valcon's Spectral Army," and "Ding Shu's Marvelous Chopsticks." Wizards all over the Internet contributed the best spells from their tomes to bring you this excellent collection of magic. ✓ **INTERNET** ...→*ftp* ftp.iastate.edu→anonymous→<your email address>→/pub/frp→Net. Spell. Book.tar.Z ...→*ftp* ftp.cs.pdx. edu→anonymous→<your email address>→/pub/frp/net-books/ magespells

Net Monster Manual Dungeon Masters! Do your players' eyes glaze over when you trot out yet another manticore, lich, or green dragon? Do they routinely cast a

Mage duels with demon—downloaded from wuarchive.wustl.edu.

spell or produce the magic item to kill the monsters you're sending their way? You need the *Net Monster Manual*, a book of all-new monsters packed with variations of werebeasts, dragons, and undead! Give your players the willies with something they've never seen before. Contributed by Dungeon-Masters from all over the Net, these are guaranteed to keep them on their toes. ✓ **INTERNET**→*ftp* ftp.iastate.edu→anonymous→<your email address>→/pub/frp→Net_ Monster_Manual.Z

Net Monstrous Compendium A collection of new monsters for *AD&D* from various Net gamers. Includes 14 new subspecies of dragons and a few other nasty surprises for the dungeon adventurer. Written specifically for *AD&D* 2nd edition rules. ✓ **INTERNET**→*ftp* ftp.iastate.edu→anonymous→<your email address>→/pub/frp→Net_ Monstrous_Compendium.tar.Z

Net Munchkin Handbook Role-playing humor comparing the different styles of role players.

They save the punch line for "munchkins"—those annoying people who always have to win. ✓ **INTERNET**→*ftp* ftp.cs.pdx.edu→ anonymous→<your email address> →/pub/frp/net-books/misc_ books→munchkin.handbook.Z

Net Plots Book Creative energy running a little low? Need an idea—any idea—for a fantasy role-playing adventure? Go to the *Net Plots Book* for help. It has hundreds of plot ideas taken from mythology, literature, and movies to inspire desperate game masters. An excellent compilation to keep the campaign interesting. ✓ **INTERNET** ...→*ftp* ftp.cs.cdx.edu→anonymous→<your email address>→ /pub/ frp/net-books/misc_books→ net.plots.1.Z ...→*ftp* ftp.funet.fi→ anonymous→<your email address> →/pub/doc/games/roleplay/texts →net.plot.books.ascii.Z

Net Trap Book A collection of dungeon traps for any fantasy role-playing game. Sinister traps so evil we're not even going to mention them by name. Guaranteed mortality! Only for the heartless game master! ✓ **INTERNET**→*ftp* ftp.cs.pdx.edu→anonymous→<your email address>→/pub/frp/net-books/misc_books→net.traps.book.Z

Net Weapons Book A compilation of ancient, medieval, and imaginary weapons described in *AD&D* terms. Adds an exotic flavor to any gladiator match. ✓ **INTERNET** ...→*ftp* ftp.cs.pdx.edu→anonymous→<your email address>→/pub/frp/net-books/misc_books→net.weapons.Z ...→*ftp* ftp.funet.fi→anonymous→<your email address>→/pub/doc/games/roleplay/texts/net.books→weapons book.tar

Pilpin's Book of Evil Spells The evil arch-mage Pilpin the Black has published his book of evil spells on the Net. Thanks to him, do-gooders have to contend with spells like "Pilpin's Acidball," "Pilpin's Soul Exchange," and "Noska Trade's Selective Death Spell." A nasty collection of spells of first to ninth level. Somewhere far below the material plane, Pilpin is looking up and laughing. ✓ **INTERNET**→*ftp* ftp.iastate.edu→anonymous→<your email address>→/pub/frp→Pilpin_Spells.Z

Poison Digest Compilation of poisons, both real (e.g., arsenic) and imaginary (e.g., dog demon poison). Damage is described in terms of *AD&D* rules, but this guide is also useful for assassins and other evil characters in fantasy games. ✓ **INTERNET**→*ftp* ftp.cs.pdx.edu→anonymous→<your email address>→/pub/frp/net-books/misc_books→Poison.Digest.Z

Thom's Monster Manual A compilation of *AD&D* monsters with a mixture of extra-deadly dragons, tougher undead, six-foot bunnies, and a monster known only as "Another Mid-Level Creature." The undead will please the sadistic Dungeon Master; the bunnies are for the softies. ✓ **INTERNET**→*ftp* ftp.funet.fi→anonymous→<your email address>→/pub/doc/games/roleplay/texts→Thom_Monster_Manual.txt

Spin-offs

Fiery Dragon Inn (echo) Join this interactive RPG of the *AD&D* variety. ✓ **ICENET**

Swords & Sorcery Although open to discussions about all fantasy role-playing games (see the "From the Sages" board), the forum has its own ongoing campaign set in the world of Marjhann, based on the rules of *AD&D*, 2nd edition. After you've posted a move on the message board, the Dungeon Master will respond within a week. There has been, at times, a waiting list to get a character. See the "Request a Character" topic for information. ☎→*dial* 216-368-3888→A visitor→Explore the system→go swords ✓ **INTERNET**→*telnet* freenet-in-a.cwru.edu→A visitor→Explore the system→go swords

Stats
- Difficulty: average
- Competition: turn-based (play-by-message boards)
- Number of players: 2+
- Interface: ASCII
- Platforms: all

Wizardry 6 FAQ Covers the classic *D&D*-style graphic adventure game. Also look for a guide to *Wizardry 7*, which should surface soon. Discussion takes place on comp.sys.ibm. pc.games.rpg. *FAQ:* ✓ **INTERNET**→*ftp* ftp.uwp.edu→anonymous→<your email address>→/pub/msdos/games/romulus/hints→wizardry6.Z

Utilities

alt.games.frp.dnd-util (ng) Tips on where to find and how to program utilities to make the world of *Dungeons and Dragons* a smoother place. ✓ **USENET**

CYBERNOTES

Ding Shu's Marvelous Chopsticks

"This spell brings into existence a pair of huge chopsticks, 30 feet long, which attacks all creatures as if they were AC 10 (modified by dexterity). These giant chopsticks attack with the caster's THAC0. Victims weighing more than 5 tons are immobilized by the chopsticks, while those of lesser weight will be picked up, and may be deposited, within the same round, at any point in the spell's range. Those who successfully roll to bend bars manage to free themselves, but they may suffer falling damage as a result. Most probably, the caster will choose to deposit the victims into a gargantuan mouth which appears above his head. This mouth can hold 2 size L, 4 size M, or 8 size S creatures at one time."

—from **Net Spell Book**

Gemstone III

GEnie's text-based online fantasy game is for the most

intrepid of explorers. Kalthea, the world in which the game takes place, is everchanging, thanks to the GameMasters, who are continually modifying her to surprise players.

Players start off by choosing one of eight classes and races, and then mold their character by allocating Skill Points (there are 28 skills from which to choose, from Lock Picking to Body Training). Skills are quite expensive if they are abnormal for your character (say, if you wanted your fighter to cast spells), but there are plenty of things your character can do that others can't. You'll need to start "earning" experience points quickly to pay for the skills you want.

Get killed

Once you've got your character established, it's off to the main town of Kelfour's Landing. You can stick around town and build up experience or go off into the large Kalthean world and get killed. We recommend you do the former. There are plenty of people to talk to, including GameMasters, who sometimes drop in to see how you're doing. Otherwise, typing "advice" will steer you in the right direction, as opposed to "help," which will tell you how to steer in the first place. If you truly need personal assistance and the GameMasters haven't noticed, "assist" will get their attention. Of course, you might read the online instructions that are available via *Gemstone*'s main menu before you enter the game.

You can have only one character

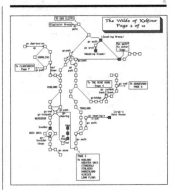

Map for Gemstone III—*from GEnie's* Gemstone III *Software Libraries.*

at a time, so treat him or her with great care. However, if you just want to get your feet wet, you can also "QuickGen" a character, which lets you skip all the niceties, and get right to the game. Once you have a better understanding of how things work, you can retire that character and go back and create yourself a keeper.

A familiar

People take their characters very seriously; after all, the evolution of a character is the whole idea of the game. Oh, there are the usual ways to grow—killing monsters, finding magic treasure, and the like (you may even find a familiar, a pet who'll stay by your side)—but don't overlook your social skills. Characters have actually married other characters in on-line ceremonies, but more important, if you get yourself into a jam, who else is going to help you but your fellow players?

As the game is text-based, movement is simply a matter of typing "east" or "west" or whatever. The standard commands are all

here—"get," "open," "close," 'look," "inventory," etc. A graphical interface for DOS machines is available from the *Gemstone* Download Library, and while this gives you some nice reference points, it's by no means required to play the game. The library also includes maps of the *Gemstone* world uploaded by players—make sure you get a map that's up to date, or the strange world you're a stranger in will be even stranger than you thought.

GameMasters' mischief

Unlike other FRP worlds, which have a single main quest and a bunch of subquests, *Gemstone* is a free-form world. This does not mean that there's nothing to do. The GameMasters are constantly making mischief, and if you pass a door where once there was none, you can bet you're about to get into an adventure.

Another of the GameMasters' tricks comes up once a year in the form of the *Gemstone* Tournament. Gems are hidden in the online world, and if you find one, you will actually receive that gem in the mail. Mind you, we're not talking emeralds here, but it's still a nice twist to actually receive the treasure you're alter ego has discovered. ✓**GENIE**→*keyword* gemstone *Interface:* ✓**GENIE**→*keyword* gemstone→GemStone Software Libraries→Set Software Library→IBM Graphics Front End

Stats
- Difficulty: average
- Competition: live
- Number of players: 1+
- Interface: ASCII, graphical
- Platforms: all

Commands
- To get hints on what to do next, type: advice *or* help
- To send out a call to all GameMasters for help, type: assist

Horror

We've all heard of an American werewolf in London, but vampires in Manchester (**City of Darkness**), a haunted Albuquerque, New Mexico (**The Masquerade**), and a supernatural, David Lynch–like New Hope, Maine (**AmarynthMUSH**)? Time to enter the hexed worlds of game manufacturer **White Wolf**'s RPGs.

On the Net

Chaosium

alt.horror.cthulhu (ng) An excellent source of supplementary information for those who play Chaosium's *Call of Cthulhu* role-playing game, or other horror games. Discussion centers on literary works of H. P. Lovecraft, August Dereleth, and Robert Bloch, but may also include gaming discussions and dark, Cthonian humor. ✓**USENET**

Chaosium Archives This archive covers the major games put out by Chaosium, especially *Call of Cthulhu*. You'll find rules additions, background information, and even GIFs of Lovecraft's grave. You'll also find material for Chaosium's fantasy games, Pendragon and Elric, and a complete Chaosium catalog. ✓**INTERNET**→*ftp* ftp.csua.berkeley.edu→anonymous →<your email address>→/pub/chaosium

Chaosium Digest (ml) What's the best way to skin a Yoggoth? How does one employ the elder sign? The answers are here in the

Vampire carries victim—lajkonik.cyf-kr.edu.pl.

Chaosium Digest, including articles and discussion of all of Chaosium's games, especially *Call of Cthulhu*. Discussions center on rules interpretations, inspirational reading, and upcoming Chaosium products. ✓**INTERNET**→*email* appel@erzo.berkeley.edu ✍ *Write a request Archives:* ✓**INTERNET**→*ftp* ftp.csua.berkeley.edu→anonymous →<your email address>→/pub/chaosium/archives/ascii

Necronomicon FAQ For players and game masters of Chaosium's *Call of Cthulhu* game and fans of H. P. Lovecraft. This FAQ covers *The Necronomicon*, a legendary book of magic that is the basis for Lovecraft's Cthulhu mythos. Addressing speculation that the book never existed, the FAQ covers the four commercially available books called *The Necronomicon* and provides a bibliography for those interested in reading more about Cthulhu, Babylonian mythology, and Mesopotamian magic. ✓**INTERNET**→ *ftp* ftp.csua.berkeley.edu→anonymous→<your email address> →/pub/chaosium/cthulhu/books→necronomicon-FAQ.Z

Mage: The Ascension

The Awakening One of the MUDs that were created specifically for role-playing the White Wolf games. On this one you can play the game *Mage: The Ascension*. In conflict are the four Mage sects (Traditions, Technocracy, Marauders, and Nephandi) who seek to impose their evil vision on Earth's reality. Each Mage yearns for the ultimate prize: ascension. The MUSH is set in the industrial city of Fort Duquesne and is still being developed. ✓**INTERNET**→*telnet* cestus.gb.nrao.edu 9999→connect guest guest *Register:* ✓**INTERNET**→*email* awakebgs@sadira. gb.nrao.edu ✍ *Type in subject line:* Awakening: <your character's name> *Type in message body:* <your character's name> <your password> <a character description>

Stats
- Difficulty: complex
- Competition: live
- Number of players: 1+
- Interface: ASCII
- Server: MUSH
- Platforms: all

Mage-L (ml) A discussion list for the *Mage: The Ascension* role-playing game. Discussion ranges from the intricate rules of the magic system of Mage to magic systems of the real world. You'll also find game ideas, stories about characters, and discussion of White Wolf supplements to Mage. Very heavy volume on this list, largely due to the rules discussions. ✓**INTERNET**→ *email* listserv@wizards.com ✍ *Type in message body:* subscribe mage-l <your full name> *Archives:* ✓**INTERNET** ...→*ftp* illuminati.io.com→

anonymous→<your email address> →/pub/usr/ebartley/Storyteller/ Archive/Mage …→*ftp* ftp.wizards. com→anonymous→<your email address>→/pub/wizards/archive/ mage-l

Vampires

alt.vampyres (ng) A newsgroup for those who believe in vampires, or believe they are vampires. Discussion ranges from Anne Rice's novels to vampire films to the metaphoric interpretations of vampire lore. Great for learning about vampires and invaluable to the horror role-player. ✓**USENET**

AmarynthMUSH Set in a small Maine college town called New Hope with a "David Lynch kinda feel." This is one of the many VampMUSHs based on the White Wolf vampire role-playing games. At first glance, New Hope seems like your average, quirky little college town. Wandering around the town, you won't find any obvious evidence of vampires. Perhaps just a candleabra or a gargoyle here and there, or a Gothic style bedroom to make things a little eerie. But they're here!

And you're here to role-play adventures and stories based on the White Wolf world. Getting a character on *Amarynth* is a detailed process—the MUSH administration wants interesting and unique characters. Type "news registration" for an explanation. Then, when your ready, contact a staff member about getting involved in a story (tinyplot). ✓**IN-TERNET**→*telnet* pharos.acusd.edu 9999→ connect Tourist Tourist *Info:* ✓**INTERNET**→*gopher* pharos.acusd. edu 70
Stats
- Difficulty: average
- Competition: live
- Number of players: 1+

- Interface: ASCII
- Server: MUSH
- Platforms: all
Commands
- To get informaiton, type: news
- To get a list of staff members online, type: +staff

Camarilla-L (ml) The *Camarilla* is a live-action role-playing group and fan club for *Vampire: The Masquerade*. Their mailing list, Camarilla-l, is for the discussion of *V:TM*. You'll find discussions on the various vampire clans, rules modifications, story ideas, and news about upcoming LARP games. ✓**INTERNET**→*email* listserv@ wizards.com ✍ *Type in message body:* subscribe camarilla-l <your full name> *Archives:* ✓**INTERNET**→

> "In this polarized gothic punk world, a vampire may have taken the identity of a regular in one of the town's obscure bars, it may hide behind the face— often corrupt—of a politician, or the bloodsucking creature may pose as an only marginally less harmful gang member."

ftp ftp.wizards.com→anonymous→ <your email address>→/pub/wiz ards/archive/camarilla-l

City of Darkness If you are intrigued by misery and despair, check out this MUSH's interpretation of present-day Manchester, England. You are warned at the beginning of the game that the MUSH deals with adult themes and that your character may die. *City of Darkness* is based on the vampire role-playing games, and the vampires indeed rule Manchester, but garou, mages, and the incredibly powerful "creatures of the outside" also roam this world and battle one another.

They're in disguise though and use all their powers to keep their existence secret. The administrators are insistent that if your character is a mortal you must role-play as though you're not aware of the existence of such monsters. Sharing information OOC or using that information IC is frowned upon as it destroys the intrigue of the game. An elaborate gaming system based on the White Wolf system is used to mediate combat, blood-bond relationships, and power struggles. The Main Room of the Cuckoo's Nest is a popular hangout. ✓**INTERNET**→*telnet* melan dra.cs.man.ac.uk 2000→connect guest guest
Stats
- Difficulty: average
- Competition: live
- Number of players: 1+
- Interface: ASCII
- Server: MUSH
- Platforms: all
Commands
- To get instructions, type: news newbie
- To get help, type +staff
- To get help from other players, type: +ooc
- To get a description of character concepts, type: +concept

The Masquerade Set in the city of Albuquerque, N.M. in the near future, and based on White Wolf's storytelling RPG *Vampire: the Masquerade, Masq* is in its second incarnation. Hugely popular the first time around, it has recently reopened with the promise of more supernatural characters (the lack of which was a big complaint). Most players hang out in bars and clubs about the city, often as their RL selves—it's an extremely social place.

Masq implements almost the entire range of White Wolf's game system, and character creation can be quite time-consuming (don't get bogged down by it unless you're really into creating the ultimate killing machine). Role-playing was not a strong point in the first implementation, but if you're a *Masquerade* fan and you want to play with others who've also memorized game author Mark Rein-Hagen's rules, this may be the place for you. If you haven't played the tabletop version of the game, you should definitely read the rules for combat in the MasqTech Nexus. And, warn the MUSH admins, "remember, there are no such things as monsters…" ✓**INTERNET**→ *telnet* phobos.unm.edu 4444 →connect guest guest

Stats
- Difficulty: average
- Competition: live
- Number of players: 1+
- Interface: ASCII
- Server: MUSH
- Platforms: all

Commands
- To get information, type: +MasqTech *or* help
- To get a list of staff members willing to help newbies, type: +staff
- To get a list of wizards, type: +wizards
- To call a judge to solve a dispute, type: +judge

Vamps—downloaded from America Online's PC Graphics Forum.

"The DAMNED" Based on White Wolf's *Vampire: The Masquerade,* "*The DAMNED*" is set in a very dark and grim Pittsburgh with a supernatural presence. In real life, most mortals don't believe in vampires, and on this MUSH, they don't talk about them. Players are very serious about their role-playing and it would be completely out of character for everyone to believe that vampires roam the city.

That's not to say that vampires and ghouls (often IC spouses or lovers, who share blood with vamps but don't go all the way) aren't there. If your character is looking for vampires, you'll find them—but you're also likely to die shortly afterward. In this polarized gothic punk world, a vampire may have taken the identity of a regular in one of the town's obscure bars, it may hide behind the face—often corrupt—of a politician, or the bloodsucking creature may pose as an only marginally less harmful gang member.

Tiny-Sex

And what's to do in this dark Pittsburgh? Visit people's apartments for conversation or Tiny-Sex. Hang out in the the Corrosion, a converted warehouse-turned-club with industrial music all day and night, where you can even request a favorite Metallica song, order a drink, and sit with friends at a private table. Or visit the Scream, a bar run by the gang the Fallen.

On the other side of town, check out Elizabeth's—a jazz club for the more artsy types. Then, of course, there are concert halls, churches, or the nude show at Spanky'z.

Dead means DEAD

The abandoned warehouses and dark alleys are dangerous. Beware! Dead on this MUSH means DEAD, and you'll lose a character you may have spent a long time developing. Therefore, the admins demand that a player be first asked OOC if his character can be killed. For general OOC chat or to find the ghosts of those killed, go to the Spam and Grill. From there, go to "The Damned" Night School, a free coding room, or the TP Room, where you can learn how to take part in a TinyPlot.

To learn how to build in the MUSH world, take the building tutorial (news buildtut) and create your own apartment in the process. You arrive in downtown Pittsburgh at the intersection of Grant and Liberty where the Amtrak station is located… ✓**INTERNET**→ *telnet* janus.library.cmu.edu 6250→connect guest guest

Stats
- Difficulty: average
- Competition: live
- Number of players: 1+
- Interface: ASCII
- Server: MUSH
- Platforms: all

Commands
- To get information, type: news *or* help
- For a list of staff members on call, type: +staff
- To go in character to where you

last left off, type: +ic
- To go out of character and to the OOC Spam and Grill, type: +ooc
- To speak to just the people at your local table, type: tt <message>
- To sit down at a table, type: sit at #<table number>
- To leave a table, type: stand

Vampire-L (ml) For detailed discussion of *Vampire: The Masquerade*. Topics center on rules interpretations, real-life belief in vampires, religions, game ideas, and anything that might add life to your vampire game. ✓**INTERNET**→ *email* listserv@wizards.com ✍ *Type in message body:* subscribe vampire-l <your full name> *Archives:* ✓**INTERNET**→*ftp* illuminati.io.com→ anonymous→<your email address> →/pub/usr/ebartley/Storyteller/Archive/Vampire

---

Vampire/White Wolf Discussion (echo) Join in the discussion about White Wolf's Vampire games. ✓**ICENET**

Werewolves

GarouMUSH Set in the 1990s in and around the fictional city of St. Claire, Washington, *GarouMUSH* focuses on the conflicts and culture of the *Garou*—the werewolves from White Wolf's *Werewolf: The Apocalypse* game. The *Garou*, who are fighting a losing battle to save the earth, have come to St. Claire to protect an abandoned Caern, holy land that has been found on the wooded areas to the east of the city.

Vicious serial killers, vampires, a chemical company, and conflicts among the *Garou*'s tribes threaten the *Garou*'s very existence. *GarouMUSH* probably offers the best and most intensive role-playing on the Net. Players take only

occasional OOC breathers, usually in the OOC Lounge.

Feature stories

Besides the free-form role-playing common to most MUSHes, *Garou* has instituted Feature Stories: players whose stories are approved by the wizards are given the power to communicate more easily with other players in their stories. Story lines can affect the entire MUD or a small group of players.

If you don't want to role-play—if you're just looking for a place to kick back, chat about the RPG, and do things OOC—*Garou* isn't for you. It's also not a good place for beginning players. To play, you must send a developed character concept (personality, background, and motivations) to the administration, who admit to being picky. They might reject someone whose grammar, spelling, or punctuation is subpar. You can also expect feedback and recommendations regarding your character from them.

Background reading

Newbies should spend some time in the OOC Lounge, which is full of background reading material. Expect to encounter difficulties in the forest. It's extremely hard and frustrating to navigate through—you may want to page a veteran player to help you. It's also dangerous, of course! Strong language, sexual situations, and graphic violence are everyday occurrences. ✓**INTERNET**→*telnet* party. apple.com 7000→connect guest guest *Info:* ✓**INTERNET** …→*email* garou-reg @cygnus.com ✍ *Request a copy of the Newbie Guide* …→*www* http://nyx10.cs.du.edu:8001/~ whartwel/garou.html *Register:* ✓**INTERNET**→*email* garou-reg@ cygnus.com ✍ *Email a character concept*

Stats
- Difficulty: complex
- Competition: live
- Number of players: 1+
- Interface: ASCII
- Server: MUSH
- Platforms: all

Commands
- To get general background information, type: news
- To get a list of wizards online, type: +wizard
- To go to the OOC room where people will generally be helpful, type: +ooc

GarouMUSH Player List (ml) Discuss the MUSH, voice concerns, and suggest improvements. MUSH news is also posted to this list. ✓**INTERNET**→*email* garou-request@cygnus.com ✐ *Write a request*

Werewolf: The Apocalypse (echo) Talk to people involved in White Wolf's popular RPG. ✓**ICENET**

Werewolf: The Apocolypse (echo) Where werewolves like to gather outside the RPG to discuss history, lore, game rules, and more. ✓**WWIVNET**

Werewolf-L (ml) *Garou* lope this way to talk about the Werewolf role-playing game from White Wolf games. Learn more about the werewolf's place in nature. Find out the secrets behind the disappearance of the Roanoke colony. Lots of talk about rules, scenario ideas, and real-life werewolf mythology. ✓**INTERNET**→*email* listserv@wizards.com ✐ *Type in message body:* subscribe werewolf-l <your full name> *Archives:* ✓**INTERNET** ...→*ftp* illuminati.io.com→anonymous→<your email address>→/pub/usr/ebartley/Storyteller/Archive/Werewolf ...→*ftp* ftp.wizards.com→anonymous→<your

Werewolf attack—from CompuServe's Quick Pictures Forum.

email address>→/pub/wizards/archive/werewolf-l

White Wolf

A World of Darkness (echo) A conference for vampire RPG discussion. ✓**WWIVNET**

alt.games.white-wolf (ng) Vampires, werewolves, and occultists are rarely found in the same place, at least peacefully so. But they have established this newsgroup as the hallowed ground for discussing White Wolf's storyteller role-playing games. Inspirational material, game ideas, and rules are the main course (no matter what your natural appetite may call for). ✓**USENET**

Discussion of White Wolf Games (echo) Communicate with other White Wolf enthusiasts about the games—learn rules, tips, and clues. ✓**WWIVNET**

White Wolf Archive This is the "official" archive site for White Wolf gamers. What dusty tomes will you find on the shelves? The digests of the White Wolf games mailing lists, humorous stories, and parodies of the World of Darkness, alternate rules that allow you to incorporate Clive Bark-

er's Hellraisers into your game, and databases to aid the storyteller in running the game. ✓**INTERNET**→*ftp* illuminati.io.com→anonymous→<your email address>→/pub/usr/ebartley/Storyteller

Worlds of Darkness FAQ This large FAQ covers the various storyteller games from White Wolf, including rules, errata, and reviews of storyteller supplements. The initial explanations of the games are excellent, but at some point the FAQ gets too cryptic for the beginner. ✓**INTERNET** ...→*ftp* illuminati.io.com →anonymous→<your email address>→/pub/usr/ebartley/Storyteller/General ...→*ftp* cerebus.acusd.edu→anonymous →<your email address>→/pub/Role-Playing/Horror ...→*gopher* cerebus.acusd.edu→/pub/Role-Playing→Horror→World of Darkness

Inspiration

Horror Mailing List (ml) Are your players hohum when Nyarlothep knocks? Does the strange, pale man with no reflection in the mirror fail to wake them? Perhaps you need to put the scare back in your horror role-playing. This mailing list covers the horror genre extensively—from Shelley to Barker, Stoker to King, Nosferatu to Croenenberg. Discuss books, film, and television, and get scared! ✓**INTERNET**→*email* listserv@pacevm.bitnet ✐ *Type in message body:* subscribe horror <your full name>

Horror RPG (echo) Discuss Horror RPGs. ✓**WWIVNET**

Horror RPGs (echo) Whether a kult, a vampire, or a werewolf, you'll find someone to talk to here. ✓**ICENET**

Magic: the Gathering

It's a card game with pictures, but it ain't Old Maid. Your goal in MtG (that's *Magic:*

the Gathering for those of you not already obsessed) is to summon the most powerful creatures you can to attack and finish off your opponent. A magic duel from start to finish, the game actually begins before you sit down and start drawing the cards. First you have to collect the cards that make up your deck—with the result that the Internet has turned into a marketplace for *MtG* players looking to buy, sell, trade, and auction cards in a never-ending quest to make their Wizard the most powerful guy on the block. Check out the Web, especially **Whicken's Page**, for the details, the variations, and the explanations.

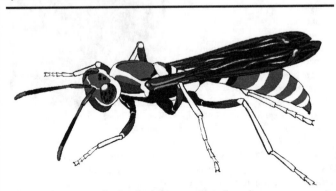

Close-up of an MtG *card—downloaded from anubis.ac.hmc.edu.*

On the Net

Bret Larwick's Page The real gem here is the card database—a list of cards linked to descriptions of their power and relationships to other cards. The site is also developing a telnet link to the Magic Merchant, a server dedicated to trading, purchasing, and selling Magic cards. Other options include the FAQs, links to the FTP site and newsgroup, and product information about Deckmaster card games. ✓**INTERNET**→*www* http://www.public.iastate.edu/~blarwick/games/magic.html

GG-Auction-L (ml) For players looking to find a steal. ✓**INTERNET**→*email* listserv@wizards.com ✍ *Type in message body:* subscribe gg-auction-l <your full name>

GG-L (ml) General rules discussions and lots bantering about the game. ✓**INTERNET**→*email* listserv@wizards.com ✍ *Type in message body:* subscribe gg-l <your full name> *Archives:* ✓**INTERNET** …→*ftp* marvin.macc.wisc.edu→anonymous→<your email address>→/deckmaster/archive.for.gg-l …→*ftp* ftp.wizards.com→anonymous→<your email address>→/pub/wizards/archive/gg-l

GG-Trading-L (ml) For players looking to find a deal. ✓**INTER-NET**→*email* listserv@wizards.com ✍ *Type in message body:* subscribe gg-trading-l <your email address>

Home Page for Deckmaster Offers links to the Magic: the Gathering FAQ, the Arabian Nights FAQ, the Deckmaster FTP archive, Duelist's Convocation Tournament Rules, and other Magic Web sites. Novices should

check out the Revised Edition Rules for both an overview and detailed information about the game. ✓**INTERNET**→*www* http://marvin.macc.wisc.edu/deckmaster/wotc.html

io.games.wotc (ng) News and discussion about game plans by Wizards of the Coast. Low volume. ☎→*dial* 512-448-8950 →<your login>→<your password> →<choose a newsreader like "tin">→io. games.wotc ✓**INTERNET**→ *telnet* io.com→<your login>→<your password>→<type a newsreader like "tin">→io.games.wotc

io.games.wotc.magic News and discussion about the game *Magic: the Gathering*. Low volume. ☎→*dial* 512-448-8950→<your login>→<your password>→<choose a newsreader like "tin">→io.games. wotc.magic ✓**INTERNET**→*telnet* io.com→<your login>→<your password>→<type a newsreader like "tin">→io.games.wotc.magic

Magic: the Gathering Archive Besides an FAQ about the game, this is the place to go for an

> **"Marketplace central. Trade your Ancestral Recall for someone's Mahamoti Djinn. Sell your Urza's Avenger and your Jandor's Saddlebags. Seek out a Demonic Attorney or a Veteran Bodyguard. Or, if you have no idea what any of this means, just ask questions about the game."**

overview of several of the hard-to-find cards, some strategy hints, an electronic catalog from Wizards of the Coast (the Magic-makers), and a ton of other stuff. ✓**INTERNET**→*ftp* marvin.macc.wisc.edu→anonymous →<your email address>→/deck master

---

Magic: the Gathering on GEnie In the Other Games message category, *MtG* is a steady topic of discussion. Look for subjects like *Magic: The Gathering* Trades and Magic: The OnLine League. Files are rather sparse, but you'll find the usual FAQs and lists as well as some card utilities. ✓**GENIE** …→*keyword* scorpia→Gamers Libraries→Set Category→All Libraries→*Search by keyword:* gathering (for files) …→*keyword* scorpia →Games Bulletin Board→set 3 (for messages)

MtG Files & Discussion The library carries digests of the GG-L mailing list, the FAQs, lots of card lists, rule booklets, pricing guides, and more. Discussion is predominantly trading talk. ✓**COMPUSERVE** →*go* rpgames→Libraries *or* Messages→Board/Card RPGs→*Search by keyword:* gathering *or* magic

---

rec.games.deckmaster (ng) Marketplace central. Trade your Ancestral Recall for someone's Mahamoti Djinn. Sell your Urza's Avenger and your Jandor's Saddlebags. Seek out a Demonic Attorney or a Veteran Bodyguard. Or, if you have no idea what any of this means, just ask questions about the game. ✓**USENET**

Thoth's Page Somewhat smaller than other Magic Web sites, but contains official tournament rules, and something people on the Usenet group are always clamoring for: a complete list of Magic cards, along with their rarity levels. FAQs and product information are also available. ✓**INTERNET**→ *www* http://www.cis.ufl.edu/ ~thoth/magic/

Whicken's Page An extensive collection of material related to *Magic: the Gathering* and its variations, including rules variations (check out the *Solitaire* version), pricing lists, strategy and deck-building hints, alternate card sets, and links to other Magic Web pages and FTP sites. If you're new to the game, the overview and glossary are excellent introductions. If it's not here, it's probably not on the Net. ✓**INTERNET**→*www* http://www.parasoft.com/whicken /magic/magic.html

---

Middle Earth

J.R.R. Tolkien's world come to life from a *Lord of the Rings* RPG to discussions devoted

to the Elvish Old English of **Tolkien Language** and the original texts in **rec.arts. books.tolkien**. Mythologized by the Net, Tolkien himself regularly appears as a kind of provincial deity reigning over his corner of Cyberspace.

On the Net

Adventure

Genesis LPMud You enter *Genesis* as a ghost looking for a body. Numbered bodies of different races and genders lie before you. Look at them. Compare their statistics. Pick one. The beginning of your adventure on this MUD depends on the race you chose. Elves, for instance, begin in the land of Greenoaks while dwarves begin in what looks like Tolkien's Middle Earth.

Each continent in the medieval world of *Genesis* can be visited by land or water routes. Boats can transport you to many of the major cities. In each of them, you will find several quests ranging from small (kill something, find an artifact) to average (such as "touristing," in which you need to find a specific place) to elaborate (tasks that require several players to cooperate).

Guild

The world you enter will be relatively silent. You are not immediately thrust into a chat line. In fact, you must first join a guild before you may talk to anyone not in the same room as your character.

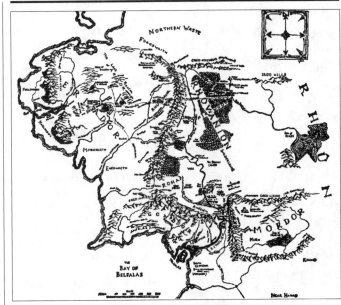

Middle Earth—downloaded from wuarchive.wustl.edu.

Each character may join up to three types of guilds, with only the race guild being predetermined. The other two are occupational and laymen guilds.

Unlike other MUDs, *Genesis* requires your character to first introduce himself to other players before you can see their names (you don't automatically know people's names in RL, do you?). For newbies it is often difficult to get someone to answer a question—you have to gain for your experience here. *Genesis* lays claim to being the first LPMUD. ✓**INTERNET**→*telnet* 129.16.226.142 3011→ guest→[return]

Stats
- Difficulty: average
- Competition: live
- Number of players: 2+
- Interface: ASCII
- Server: LPMud
- Platforms: all

Commands
- To get a description of the MUD, type at the login: gameinfo
- To introduce yourself to another player, type: introduce myself
- To introduce a friend to another player, type: introduce <friend's name>

Role-playing

Elendor "You have entered the lands of J.R.R. Tolkien's imagination." Once you've "locked" your character so that no one else can control it, specified your gender, and given your email address, you are transported to the "Hall of Races," where you may choose to be a hobbit, elf, dwarf, or another creature from the world of Tolkien. Use of names from the book is prohibited—or everyone would login as Gandalf.

Based in the third age, shortly after the events in *The Hobbit*, the MUSH is less about reenacting the books and more about exploring "what would happen if..." questions. By necessity, an alternate timeline has evolved, but great pains have been taken to stay true to the themes and "rules" of the books (Sauron is still the bad guy).

To cater to new players who are learning about the MU*s, the MUSH offers coding classes, role-playing classes, and friendly support. Besides role-playing, there is also a combat system featuring timed healing and stats. Dead really doesn't mean dead here. Just keep playing. The MUSH is large and detailed and a fun place for Tolkien fans. ✓ **INTERNET**→*telnet* ghost.cse.nau.edu 1892→connect nomad nomad

Stats
- Difficulty: average
- Competition: live
- Number of players: 1+
- Interface: ASCII
- Server: MUSH
- Platforms: all

Commands
- To get a list of wizards and royals, type: +admins
- To get a list of people in charge of your immediate area, type: +rulers
- To get information on commands type: +help
- To get a list of unique commands, type: +commands
- To whisper to someone with the random chance of being overheard by someone nearby, type: +whisper=<message>
- To chat out of character in the OOC Room, type: +ooc
- To return in character to the room you were last in , type: +ic

---

Lord of the Rings RPG—Evil

Chat (echo) Let the darker half out as you chat with others in this RPG ✓**ICENET**

Lord of the Rings RPG—Good Chat (echo) As the light of goodness comes your way, join in this RPG. ✓**ICENET**

MUME IV *Multi-Users in Middle Earth*, or MUME, simulates Tolkien's world of Middle Earth. Sauron's a mobile. The orcs and trolls support each other, and the "whities"—elves, dwarves, humans, and hobbits—are forced to defend their town from daily orc attacks, commonly referred to as "orc and whitie wars."

Role-playing is encouraged, but this is primarily an adventure and combat MUD. You need to acquire a set amount of travel points (leave the town and explore other areas) and experience points (kill mobiles or players) to advance, and that's exactly what most players are intensely focused on.

There are more than 25 levels in the game. Advice: If you're new to the MUD, don't play an orc. Most orcs are experienced players, and since orcs and trolls are on a different chat channel from the other players, you'll be cut off from communication with other newbies. ✓**INTERNET**→*telnet* 128.178.77.5 4242→ <your character's name>→<y *or* n>→<your password>→<your password>→<f *or* m>→<your race>→<your class>→ <your alignment>

Stats
- Difficulty: complex
- Competition: live
- Number of players: 1+
- Interface: ASCII
- Server: Diku
- Platforms: all

Commands
- To get information, type: help
- To send a public query, type: narrate <your question>

- To get a list of gods online, type: who ainur
- To get a list of the points required for each level, type: level

Inspiration

rec.arts.books.tolkien (ng) Freudian analysis of the hobbit? Female orcs? Music of Middle Earth? The discussion never stops here—elves, orcs, wizards, and Tolkien himself. ✓**USENET** *FAQ:* ✓**INTERNET**→*ftp* rtfm.mit.edu→ anonymous→<your email address> →/pub/usenet-by-hierarchy/rec/ arts/books/tolkien

Tolkien Language (ml) From Old English to Elvish vocabulary, discuss the use of language in Tolkien's works. ✓**INTERNET**→*email* tolklang-request@lfcs.ed.ac.uk ✍ *Write a request*

Tolkien Mailing List (ml) For an in-depth discussion of the writings of J.R.R. Tolkien, including *The Hobbit*, the *Lord of the Rings* trilogy, and *The Silmarillion*. Analyze the setting, history, characters, and language of Middle Earth. Tolkien experts can supply you with fascinating and detailed information that will bring a fantasy game set in Middle Earth to life. ✓**INTERNET**→*email* listserv@jhuvm.bitnet ✍ *Type in message body:* subscribe tolkien <your full name>

Tolkien Web Page This WWW page links numerous Net resources relevant to J.R.R. Tolkien, including mailing lists discussing his literature, the mythology he developed, and the languages he invented. A great resource for anyone playing the Middle Earth role-playing system or incorporating Middle Earth into a fantasy role-playing game. ✓**INTERNET**→*www* http://herald.usask.ca/~friesend/ tolkien/rootpage.html

Pern

For fans of Ann McCaffrey's *Dragonriders of Pern* novels, the Net is filled with role-playing possibilities. There are MUSHes and MOOs exclusively devoted to things Pernese as well as a newsgroup, **alt.fan.pern**, which obsesses on the interpretations and other issues that arise in these virtual environments. On the MUDs, players join one of three social structures—Weyrs, Crafts, or Holds—through which they meet people and gain more responsibilities. The mammoth *PernMUSH* is by far the most active and long-standing of the sites; the other sites all have their own unique communities based on local Pern interpretations. Of course, many players have characters on multiple sites. Immerse yourself in Pern without the intrusion of spacemen and elves. Meanwhile, clear skies!

On the Net

MUSHes

PernMUSH One of the oldest and biggest MUSHes on the Net, *PernMUSH* consistently draws more than 100 players an evening, some of whom never go to bed. *PernMUSH*, or *Northern Conti-*

Dragon overhead—downloaded from wuarchive.wustl.edu.

nent, as it is also known, covers the Northern Continent of Pern in a time period well after the era described in the books. Pernese society is menaced every 250 years by deadly Threads that fall from a neighboring planet. Role play becomes feverish when the Threads begin to fall. Other common RP events include "mating flights" of the dragons and "hatchings," which are often staged for the enjoyment of the MUSH members. Yet *PernMUSH* is probably more about socializing than role-playing. It is also newbie-friendly—there's a large staff to help players with problems. On your first trip to *PernMUSH*, you'll enter the Birthplace where you can read about *PernMUSH* and meet other unborns. Then get out and spend some time in the public areas—commands like '+where' and '+who' will help you find other players. Finally, join a Craft, Hold, or Weyr, but spend some time on the MUSH before you commit yourself to a new way of life. ✓INTERNET→*telnet* cesium.clock.org 4201→create <your character's name> <your password> *Info:*

✓**INTERNET** ...→*email* shill@emc next.tamu.edu ✍ *Request a copy of the guide* ...→*ftp* caisr2.caisr.cwru. edu→anonymous→<your email address>→/pub/mush/pern→intro.kit *Register:* ✓**INTERNET**→*email* nc-wiz @cygnus.com ✍ *Email with character name if site doesn't allow you to create a character upon connection*

Stats
- Difficulty: average
- Competition: live
- Number of players: 1+
- Interface: ASCII
- Server: MUSH
- Platforms: all

Commands
- To get instructions, type: news misc *or* help
- To find online support staff, type: +swho
- To find online wizards, type: +wizards
- To locate other players on the MUSH, type: +where

Pern-RP (ml) Covers role-playing and other issues on *PernMUSH*. ✓**INTERNET**→*email* listserv@cornell. edu ✍ *Type in message body:* subscribe pern-rp <your full name>

DragonsDawn Set at the beginning of the Second Pass, approximately 250 years after the events in McCaffrey's novel *Dragons-Dawn*, this MUSH has an intimate player base and small world—you won't get lost here. Role-playing is encouraged, but no one is obsessing about it. ✓**INTERNET**→*telnet* cashew.enmu.edu 2222→connect guest guest

Stats
- Difficulty: average
- Competition: live
- Number of players: 1+
- Interface: ASCII
- Server: MUSH
- Platforms: all

Commands
- To get information, type: help *or*

news
- For more information, go to the Dragon Dawn Information Center

Shards A relatively small MUSH that covers the western portion of the Northern Continent and that's based on the Seventh Pass in Pernese history, a time following a plague in which much of society's populace has perished and its knowledge has been lost. There are dragons, fire lizards, hatchings, and the Dreaded Thread. Dragonriders practice for thread flaming, crafts are flourishing, and players hang out in the Great Hall at Tillek, the Pub, and the Living Caverns at High Reaches Weyr. As a newbie you are greeted by a Guide who will get you started. Role-playing is encouraged here, but you can be OOC as long as you don't bother the ICs. ✓**INTER-NET**→*telnet* vesta.unm.edu 7777→ connect guest guest *Register:* ✓**IN-TERNET**→*email* rerwey@acs.ucalgary.ca ✍ *Send request to register your character*

Stats
- Difficulty: average
- Competition: live
- Number of players: 1+
- Interface: ASCII
- Server: MUSH
- Platforms: all

Commands
- To get instructions, type: news *or* help
- To get help, type: ask <your question>

SouCon This is the Southern Continent of Pern, which is set in the same era as *PernMUSH* but is slightly younger and less populated. In fact, for most of its early history, *SouCon* served as both a MUSH in its own right and a refugee camp for *PernMUSH* players whenever their own game went down—which led to the Great

Flame War and to the full recognition of *SouCon* as a sovereign entity. This finally came to an end after a long, involved flame war on alt.fan.pern. The atmosphere on *SouCon* is laid-back although there's more emphasis on role-playing here than on you'll find on *PernMUSH*. The smaller player base, however, makes finding RP companions somewhat difficult. ✓**INTERNET**→*telnet* beechnut.enmu.edu 4201→connect guest guest *Support:* ✓**INTERNET**→*email* scwiz@cygnus.com ✍ *Write for help & support*

Stats
- Difficulty: average
- Competition: live
- Number of players: 1+
- Interface: ASCII
- Server: MUSH
- Platforms: all

Commands
- To get information, type: news *or* help
- To get a list of wizards, type: news wizards
- To get a list of wizards currently online, type: +wizards
- For more instructions, go to the Information Center

MOOs

Dragonsfire! For the purposes of this MOO, it is 500 years after *The White Dragon* and events in *All the Weyrs of Pern* never occured. Role-playing is intense here, but, as with *Harpers Tale*, its appeal is its intimacy. ✓**INTERNET**→*telnet* moo.eskimo.com 7777→connect guest

Stats
- Difficulty: average
- Competition: live
- Number of players: 1+
- Interface: ASCII
- Server: MOO
- Platforms: all

Commands
- To get general information, type:

help *or* news
- To get a list of staff members, type: help staff
- For background information, go to the DF Information Center

Harpers Tale Set in the Fort Weyr area, this MOO is based on events immediately preceding the Tenth Pass of the Red Star (not considering the events in *All the Weyrs of Pern*) and appeals to those looking for a more intimate setting. Join the "@party" chat channel to find out where your fellow players are hanging out—one of the taverns in Harper Hall or the Great Hall at Fort Hold are likely bets. The MOO is very proud of its player dragons—they're controlled by a second player, making the rider-dragon relationship unpredictable and more interesting. ✓**INTERNET**→*telnet* netman.widener.edu 8888→ connect guest guest

Stats
- Difficulty: average
- Competition: live
- Number of players: 1+
- Interface: ASCII
- Server: MOO
- Platforms: all

Commands
- To get a list of members willing to answer questions, type: who (look for the % sign next to the name)
- To get a "newspaper" log of the events on HT, type: news

Other

alt.fan.pern (ng) Discuss the fictional world of Pern. The MUSHes get a lot of attention, especially *PernMUSH*. The FAQ covers everything from Pernese time lines to dragon sex. ✓**USENET** *FAQ:* ✓**INTERNET**→*ftp* rtfm.mit.edu→anonymous→<your email address>→ /pub/usenet-by-group/alt.fan.pern

Shadow of Yserbius

Other areas of Sierra's ImagiNation may turn you into a cardshark or a trivia whiz,

but **Shadow of Yserbius** turns you into a hero. Create a character—choosing among four different races and six different classes. You can be an elfish wizard, for instance, or a human ranger. In fact, you have a whole Rogue's Gallery of characters at your disposal, but you can play only one character at a time. Next, you round out your character with the customary ability scores, acquire a helpful skill or two (depending on your class you could find yourself good at leadership, archery, or what have you), and learn a few magic spells. (Magic is by no means restricted to wizards.)

When your MedievaLand persona is more or less complete, it's off into the world of Yserbius. The main attraction of Yserbius is a multileveled volcano, which you can explore alone or with the assistance of other online adventurers. You can join a party by "walking" over to them and then clicking "view" followed by "party." If there's no one at the dungeon entrance ("de" in Yserbius lingo), you can always head to the tavern and try to scare up a party of up to three other adventurers. When you've joined a party, the party leader decides which path to take through the various dungeons inside the volcano. If you're the leader of the party (which you

Screenshot from Shadow of Yserbius— *from The ImagiNation Network.*

should try to avoid if you're a newbie) or if you're adventuring solo, movement is controlled with six directional keys accessed by clicking on the "Map" button. This also gives you an overhead map of where you are, where you've been, and what you're walking into.

Time elemental

The main goal of Yserbius as told to us by a Shadowrune, a 15-year-old who also happens to be a 294th-level Knight, is this: "This dude named Arnakkian Slowfoot tried to become immortal and control time by subjecting En-li-kil, the time elemental. En-li-kil didn't like that and he squashed the place, burying the castle under lava. The volcano is still active. Your goal is to beat Arnakkian, get the blue gem, then get all the other gems, which are red, green, and yellow. Gems make the rainbow bridge which uncovers En-li-kil's dimension. Then get the Golden Boat and the Moon Prism, and go after En-li-kil."

Got that? Well, don't worry if you don't. It's perfectly acceptable to have a grand old time in Yser-

bius without ever thinking about time elementals and Moon Prisms. There are several dungeons to explore from the first level of the volcano and they are all approximately the same level of difficulty, except for the Labryinth and the Hall of Doors—avoid those if you're a beginner.

Battling bad guys

Battling bad guys is a matter of clicking on the desired action icon, then on the bad guy. The sword icon will, with luck, wallop the enemy; the spellbook icon brings up your list of magic spells; and if that doesn't work, you can flee by clicking on the boot icon. (Only leaders of a party can flee; if you're a follower in a losing battle, you're stuck.)

Winning battles will earn you treasure and experience, both of which can be cashed in at Guild Hall, located on the same opening screen as the volcano and the tavern. The hall also includes a shop where you can buy armor, weapons, and magic items. Your inventory is limited to about a dozen items, so make sure you need everything you're carrying.

Observant explorers will start paying attention to the various hints and riddles that pop up in the dungeons. They lead to various subadventures, which in turn take you to En-li-kil. ✓ **THE IMAGI-NATION NETWORK**→*select* MedievaLand

Stats
* Difficulty: average
* Competition: live
* Number of players: 1+
* Interface: graphical
* Platform: DOS

Sci-fi

If extant Cyberspace isn't fantastic enough, enter the **OTHER_SUNS** role-playing subworld or plug into the mighty **Science Fiction Archive**, home to FAQs on just about every sci-fi show that was ever beamed.

The alien in Aliens—*downloaded from ftp.sunet.se.*

On the Net

Beyond the Stars A board that's dedicated to space gaming with separate areas for exploration (assume the role of a crew member aboard a starship) and for battle (learn starship combat tactics). Rules for both areas as well as descriptions of character classes and Starfleet hierarchy are available. There's a lot of background info, but often there aren't a lot of players. ☎→*dial* 216-368-3888→A visitor→Explore the system→go beyond ✓**INTERNET**→*telnet* freenet-in-a.cwru.edu→A visitor→Explore the system→go beyond

Stats
- Difficulty: average
- Competition: turn-based (play-by-message boards)
- Number of players: 2+
- Interface: ASCII
- Platforms: all

Federation II An easy game to get started in, but your character can soon be engaged in complex economic, social, and political intrigue. After you've bribed an official for your ship permit, buy a ship at the Jarrow Shipbuilders.

Since you've just hocked yourself into debt, you'll need to accept a few jobs. Ignore, for the moment, the job descriptions that keep flashing by—they're a little too demanding for a newbie. Instead, type "job" to accept a job carrying a load from Earth to somewhere else, then "load" to get the stuff in your cargo bay. Follow the simple map found at the end of the QuickStart Kit to get to Mars. After you've "unload"-ed your cargo (and gotten paid), head for Chez Diesel, the happeningest place in the solar system, for fun and chatter.

Social ladder

As you rise in rank, you'll become a Trader, buying your own cargo, and then a Merchant, with your own factories. Rise far enough on the social ladder, and you'll be allowed to create your own planets, which other players can visit and explore. Watch out! If she's playing that night, a character named Hazed may very likely "grope" you somewhere along the game. (Just sit back and enjoy it.) The game is full of sound and picture files for the optional front-end software that's available for IBM and the Amiga. The Multi-Player Games RoundTable has out-of-game chatter. ✓**GENIE**→*keyword* fed *Interface:* ✓**GENIE**→*keyword* fed→Federation II Software Library→Download a File→32 *or* 102

Stats
- Difficulty: average
- Competition: live
- Number of players: 1+
- Interface: ASCII, graphical
- Platforms: all

OTHER_SUNS (echo) For players interested in the *Other Suns* science fiction role-playing game. Topics include new races, backgrounds, and rule revisions. ✓**FIDONET**

VegaMUSE II It's been a hundred years since the fourth planet from the star Vega was colonized by explorers from Earth. That was in 1998 after an environmental disaster wiped out all life on Earth. Now, with three empires, a mystical sect, academies in each of the empires for training and studying science and math, and a combat system, Vega might be an interesting place to visit. Recently the leader of the first colonists was assassinated and a being has emerged that possesses superpowers. ✓**INTERNET**→*telnet* planck.sos.clarkson.edu 2095→connect guest guest

Stats
- Difficulty: average
- Competition: live
- Number of players: 1+
- Interface: ASCII
- Server: MUSE
- Platforms: all

Science Fiction Archive Was Deckard really a Replicant in *Blade Runner*? How do the aliens in the movie *Alien* reproduce? What is the *X-Files* TV show about? Movie and television FAQs answer these questions and offer ideas for developing replicant concepts in *Traveller*, alien characters in *Star Wars*, or UFOs in *Storyteller*. You'll also see lists of books, archives of SF mailing lists, and many other sources. ✓**INTERNET** ...→*ftp* elbereth.rutgers.edu→anonymous→<your email address>→/pub/sfl ...→*www* ftp://gandalf.rutgers.edu/pub/sfl/sf-resource.guide.html

Dune

Enter into the galaxywide
wars of Frank Herbert's sci-fi epic, either as reader of his novels in **alt.fan.dune** or as a role-playing participant in the *Dune* universe in the **DuneMUSH**. No word yet on whether Sting has dropped by.

Dune *Sandworm—downloaded from lajkonik.cyf-kr.edu.pl.*

On the Net

DuneMUSH

DuneMUSH Shuttles leave regularly from the Space Platform Lucidity to the worlds of Frank Herbert's *Dune*. In the year 10,201, before the events in *Dune Messiah*, several factions are engaged in a battle for control of the galaxy. They need new recruits, and you'll have to ally with one of them. Getting a character on *Dune-MUSH*, in fact, is dependent upon joining a faction.

Also be sure to check out the Newbie Assistance Room, where you can find newbie helpers hanging out. A helpful FAQ for the MUSH is stored there, and there is a panic button for the truly desperate.

Want to meet new friends in a relaxed atmosphere? Type @tel #6615 to teleport to the Hot Tub of Ill Repute. This is strictly an out-of-character area, but you can ask players about *Dune* (they will certainly tell you that their faction is the best) or just hang out and chat. ✓**INTERNET**→*telnet* mellers 1. psych.berkeley.edu 4201→connect guest guest *Info:* ✓**INTERNET** ...→*www* http://www.ksu.ksu.

edu/~kxb/dunemush.html ...→*ftp* mellers 1.psych.berkeley.edu→ anonymous→<your email address> →/pub/DuneMUSH *Support:* ✓**IN-TERNET**→*email* dunemush@mellers 1. psych.berkeley.edu ✍ *Email with problems and inquiries*

Stats
- Difficulty: average
- Competition: live
- Number of players: 1+
- Server: MUSH
- Platforms: all

Commands
- To get instructions, type: events
- To get to the newbie room, type: newbie
- To read signs, type: inspect <sign name>
- To get information on factions and faction leaders, type: events factions

Dune Mailing Lists (ml) Subscribe to one of four public lists for *DuneMUSH*. Publish your role-playing logs or read those of other players on the *Dune* Readers list. On the *Dune* Players list, *Dune* players chat out of character. *DuneMUSH* coders and builders brainstorm on their respective lists. If you subscribe to any of these four, you are automatically added to a fifth list carrying official *DuneMUSH* announcements. ✓**INTERNET** ...→ *email* listproc@ mellers 1.psych.berkeley.edu ✍ *Type in message body:* subscribe dune-

readers <your character's name> ...→*email* list proc@mellers 1.psych. berkeley.edu ✍ *Type in message body:* subscribe dune-players <your character's name> ...→*email* list-proc@mellers 1.psych.berkeley.edu ✍ *Type in message body:* subscribe dune-coders <your character's name> ...→*email* listproc@mel lers 1.psych.berkeley.edu ✍ *Type in message body:* subscribe dune-builders <your character's name>

Zensufi Information Service
This Web site is filled with background material, from the Zensufi doctrine to role-playing logs to a collection of prayers. Also provides links to other *Dune* Web sites and the *DuneMUSH* FTP archive. ✓**INTERNET**→*www* http://S128_190.MNSMC.EDU/Zensufi.html

Inspiration

alt.fan.dune (ng) Never stop talking *Dune*—the books, movie, images, and MUSH. ✓**USENET**

Dune Home Page Sounds and images from the movie, images of the book covers, an assortment of *Dune* documents, information about the *DuneMUSH*, and the *Dune* FAQ. ✓**INTERNET**→*www* http://www.princeton.edu/~cgil more/dune/dune.html

Video game

Dune 2 FAQ & Strategy Guide Tricks and tactics for conquering the *Dune* universe. expect to find a new version every other month or so. ✓**INTERNET** ...→*ftp* ftp.uwp.edu→anonymous→<your email address> ...→*www* http:// wcl-rs.bham.ac.uk/~djh/dune2/ dune faq 1.html *FAQ:* ✓**INTERNET** →*ftp* ftp.uwp.edu→anonymous→ <your email address>→/pub/ms-dos/games/romulus/hints→dune2_13.lzh

Star Trek

There are many role-playing worlds on the Net, based on works of drama, literature, and art, but none compare with the popularity of the *Trek* realms. America Online's **Ten Forward Lounge** puts the *Deep Space Nine* promenade to shame, and there are two separate versions of the **TrekMUSE**, one for fans of Picard and Data, another for the Kirk and Spock generation. Go boldly.

On the Net

Role-play

Final Frontiers Ferengi? Klingon? Q? Join a race from the *Star Trek: the Next Generation* universe, then an organization, and then work your way up the ranks (from Starfleet cadet to admiral). The MOO offers flight and combat simulation, an economy, role-playing, and active discussion groups on the nature of space travel. ✓INTERNET→*telnet* trekmoo. microserve.com 2499→connect guest *Support:* ✓INTERNET→*email* pmoss@gxeng.microserve.com ✍ *Write for help & support*

Stats
• Difficulty: average
• Competition: live
• Number of players: 2+
• Interface: ASCII
• Server: MOO

Commands
• To get more information, type: help trekmoo
• To get a list of online wizards, type: wiz

Locutus, formerly Picard—from GEnie's Science Fiction RoundTable.

Star Trek: The Role-Playing Game (echo) The BBS Network Icenet offers almost a dozen conferences devoted to their *Star Trek: Role-Playing Game,* including ones for the Klingons, the Borg, the Federation, the Ferengi, the Cardassians, the Romulans, subspace news, and free traders. While the conference *Star Trek: the Role-Playing Game* is used by all the Trekkie races, each of the conferences has become part of the role-play. ✓ICENET

STARGAME (ml) Admiral Kirk wants you! Join Starfleet and boldly go where no other email role-playing game has gone before. Players fulfill the role of Starfleet officers and conduct their actions by email to this list. Each story is moderated by a coordinator, who acts as gamemaster, and is set in any of the *Star Trek* time periods. Numerous postings every day by players and GMs make this a fast-paced game. The FAQ lists the various ships you can sign aboard, as well as important etiquette. So set a course for excitement at warp

nine. Engage! ✓INTERNET→*email* list serv@pccvm.bitnet ✍ *Type in message body:* subscribe stargame <your full name> *Archives:* ✓INTERNET→*email* listserv@pccvm.bitnet ✍ *Type in message body:* index star game *FAQ:* ✓INTERNET→*email* listserv@pccvm.bitnet ✍ *Type in message body:* get stargame faq

STARTREK (echo) A role-playing scenario for *Star Trek* enthusiasts. No general *Star Trek* discussions. ✓FIDONET

TNG TrekMUSE Make it so, number one. Travel to the universe of *Star Trek: The Next Generation,* join a race, and work your way up the ranks of the Romulan Empire, the Ferengi Alliance, Starfleet, or one of several other empires. The pride of *TrekMUSE* is its fully functional space system, including ships that are unique to each empire. Space combat takes place, but role-playing is the primary activity here. So if you think like a Vulcan or scheme like a Ferengi, this is the place to travel to. ✓INTERNET→*telnet* grimmy.cnidr.org 1701 *Info:* ✓INTERNET ...→*ftp* grim my.cnidr.org→anonymous→<your email address>→/trek/docs ...→ *www* http://grimmy.cnidr.org/ *Register:* ✓INTERNET→*email* register @grimmy.cnidr.org ✍ *Email request to register a character:* <your character's name>

Stats
• Difficulty: average
• Competition: live
• Number of players: 1+
• Interface: ASCII
• Server: MUSE
• Platforms: all

Commands
• To get information, type: help *or* news
• To register, type: +register <your character's name>=<your email address><your first name><your last name>

TOS TrekMuse A role-playing game based on the original *Star Trek* series. Choose to join one of the five empires—Federation, Klingon, Orion, Rihannsu, or Tholian. The internal struggles and relationships within the empires offer the most fertile grounds for role-playing on this MUSE. Although there are always lots of newbies, the "help" information is not nearly as helpful as many MUDs. Logon more than once to see the opening design ASCII change. Neat! ✓**INTERNET**→*telnet* ed-ce-034.stanford.edu 1701→guest

Stats
- Difficulty: average
- Competition: live
- Number of players: 1+
- Interface: ASCII
- Server: MUSE

Commands
- To get information, type: help or news

Free-form role-play

Ten Forward Lounge If you're thirsty for some Romulan blue ale—and gosh, who isn't?—some player will "serve" you a glass here. The *Ten Forward Lounge* is the haven for *Star Trek* live role-play and chat—you'll find this member-created room full of people every night. ✓**AMERICA ONLINE**→ *keyword* pc→Member Rooms→Ten Forward Lounge

Stats
- Difficulty: simple
- Competition: live
- Number of players: 2-23
- Interface: ASCII
- Platforms: all

Inspiration

rec.arts.startrek* (ng) Seeking source material or inspiration for your *Star Trek* RPG? Several active newsgroups are devoted to *Star Trek*: rec.arts.startrek.current (gos-

> ## "Are you thirsty for some Romulan blue ale—gosh, who isn't?"

sip and convention notices), rec.arts.startrek.info (official, not speculative, info about *Star Trek*), rec.arts.startrek.misc (general discussions), rec.arts. startrek.reviews (book and movie reviews), and rec.arts.startrek.tech (what's probable, what's not). The collection of FAQs that are posted periodically to this newsgroup cover everything—and we mean everything—you could possibly want to know about *Star Trek* and its spinoffs. ✓**USENET** *Archives:* ✓**INTERNET**→*ftp* rtfm.mit.edu→anonymous →<your email address>→/pub/ usenet-by-hierarchy/rec/arts/ startrek

thIngan Hol (ml) Learn and practice the Klingon language. ✓**INTERNET**→*email* thlingan-hol-request@village.boston.ma.us ✍ *Write a request*

Star Fleet battles

Star Fleet Battles Online Players of the board game *Star Fleet Battle* and its variations—*Federation*, *Empire*, and *Prime Directive* —hang out on the "Messaging" board to swap war stories, find other players for face-to-face games (offline), and talk about the latest game modules. They also ask questions of *Amarillo Design Bureau* and *Task Force Games*. In the "File Library," players can download ship stats and programs, such as a computerized "Damage Allocation Chart" for the PC or the Macintosh. (Look for library files beginning with the subject

"DAC.") ✓**AMERICA ONLINE**→*keyword* PBM→Star Fleet Battles Online

Starfleet Battles File library for *Star Fleet Battles*, maintained by *Star Fleet* developer Amarillo Design Bureau. Download the official prototype or play-test files of new ships, scenarios, and rules. The incredibly active discussion about *Star Fleet* games—board, play-by-mail, online, card, etc.—takes place in 39 topics of the Star Fleet Universe category of the Scorpia RoundTable. Players revel in the intricacies of the game—rules are analyzed and interpreted incessantly. Amarillo has an online rep to field questions. ✓**GENIE** ...→*keyword* sfb (for files) ...→*keyword* scorpia→Games Bulletin Board→set 10

Star Wars

Star Wars online, offline, and neither—it's all here. Online role-players will find they're

needed in the battle between the New Republic and the Empire on the **Star Wars MUSH**. Real-lifers can play by mail or meet offline to war in universum ad infinitum in the **STARWARS–RPG**. And currently neither off- or online are the two **Jedi MUDS** that have been chased out of Cyber-Paradise (political turmoil, word has it). Look on **rec. arts.sf.starwars** for notice of their return.

Yoda—downloaded from wpi.wpi.edu.

On the Net

Star Wars The Emperor and Darth Vader are dead, and the second Death Star has been destroyed. The universe is split between the New Republic (what was once the Rebel Alliance) and the Empire. Enter: you! You could be the one to tip the scales. This is a large MUSH and there is a lot to discover. You can log on only as a guest, but once you have read up on what is going on, you can set up a character right there by getting in touch with an admin on the registration channel. Access to the MUSH is restricted until you get a character and a faction. Head into Kosari, where you can mill about and meet people—and stop by the Lookout, the local bar in Kosari. For OOC chatting, hang out in the the Walkway (a small hop from where you entered.) ✓**INTERNET**→*telnet* techno.stanford. edu 4402→connect guest *Support:*

✓**INTERNET**→*email* sw-mail@came lot.acf-lab.alaska.edu ✍ *Write for help & support*

Stats
- Difficulty: complex
- Competition: live
- Number of players: 1+
- Interface: ASCII
- Server: MUSH
- Platforms: all

Commands
- For instructions, type: swinfo *or* news
- To find an online member of the staff, type: +onstaff
- To request a character on the registration channel, type: =reg <your request>
- To chat on the public channel, type: =public <your message>

STARWARS_RPG (echo) A play-by-echomail conference set up to play the *Star Wars RPG* by West End Games. ✓**FIDONET**

rec.arts.sf.starwars (ng) It's been…how many years?—and the discussion just doesn't stop. Lots of game talk—from *TIE Fighter* space sims to *Star Wars* RPGs (particularly people looking to start local groups) to the Star Wars level in *Doom*. ✓**USENET**

Star Wars Archive A repository of *Star Wars* images, magazine articles, scripts and original fiction, RPG logs, *X-Wing* and *TIE Fighter* material, and lists, lists, and more lists (bloopers, quotes, actors, comics, music, etc.). ✓**INTERNET** →*ftp* wpi.wpi.edu→anonymous →<your email address>→/starwars

Star Wars Home Page Everything is here—lists, images, news, sounds, collectibles info, etc. For the role-player, there are links to extensive RPG system reviews, equipment and skill charts, a guide to the Imperial Planet, character-attribute forms, and more. ✓**INTERNET**→*www* http://stwing. resnet.upenn.edu:8001/~jruspini/ starwars.html

Live-action role-playing

Live-action role-playing (LARP), interactive literature, and historical reenactments

are forms of gaming, sort of. A little like improv acting, in which "events" happen in outdoor fields, auditoriums, hotels, and other places where large groups of people can physically gather. On the Net, however, where they virtually gather, events are planned and discussed and gaming materials and story lines traded. While LARPers enact fantasy adventures or corporate power struggles on Wall Street, SCAers stage Renaissance fairs and historical reenactments—and both groups flood the Net with rules, ideas, images of members in costume, and schedules. See the **SCA Archive** on the Internet and the **History RoundTable** on GEnie for the largest collections of SCA information online.

An SCA reenactment—downloaded from ftp.luth.se.

On the Net

Across the board

History RoundTable The libraries are packed with information on the SCA, and several categories on the bulletin board are devoted exclusively to the SCA, its kingdoms, and its events. Historical reenacting is another category worth checking out, especially if the Civil War is your kind of era. √GENIE→*keyword* sca

IL-Info (ml) Discuss various LARP and interactive literature games. √INTERNET→*email* il-info-request@han.unisysgsg.com ✍ *Write a request*

LARP Archive Look here for game announcements, LARP FAQs, and information on local LARP groups. Small site at the present. √INTERNET→*ftp* cs.uwp.edu→anonymous→<your email address>→/pub/larp

Living History Forum Relive several historical eras. The forum supports historical re-creation from periods as different as Edwardian England and the American Civil War. The libraries are packed with handbooks, images, historical texts, time-period recipes, and Renaissance festival announcements. √COMPUSERVE→*go* living

rec.games.frp.live-action (ng) Whether you'd rather explore dungeons or ride the *Titanic* on its maiden voyage, role players with a penchant for improv acting will find ideas and the latest news on LARP events in this newsgroup. LARP veterans, game designers, and enthusiasts discuss the mechanics of game play and the finer points of writing and post announcements of upcoming games by area. They're extremely friendly to newcomers and those with no previous role-playing experience. The FAQ will let you in on the jargon and help you find a LARP group in your area. √USENET *FAQ:* √INTERNET→*ftp* rtfm.mit.edu→anonymous→<your email address>→/pub/usenet-by-hierarchy/rec/games/frp/live-action→Live_Role playing_FAQ

News

Electronic Adventurer (j) A bimonthly e-zine dedicated to live-action role-play. Covers event listings, game and event reviews, LARP community news, information about suppliers for costumes and other accessories, and an updated list of LARP events in the UK. √INTERNET→*email* jay@dsbc.icl.co.uk ✍ *Write a request Archives:* √INTERNET→*ftp* etext.archive.umich.edu→anonymous→<your email address>→/pub/Zines/E-adventurer

Organizations

Interactive Literature Foundation The ILF was founded to provide resources to LARP gamers, including a library of games. √INTERNET→*email* jim@visix.com ✍ *Email with general correspondence*

Society for Interactive Literature The Society for Interactive

Literature (SIL) is one of the largest LARP organizations in the United States. If you are interested in interactive literature and want to learn of upcoming SIL events, contact SIL at either of the following addresses. They might also be able to refer you to a smaller LARP group in your area. ✓**INTERNET** ...→*email* oneil@husc.harvard.edu ✍ *Email with general correspondence* ...→ *email* srb@helix.com ✍ *Email with general correspondence*

Society for Interactive Literature Announcement List (ml) Find out about the next SILI-CON, the Society for Interactive Literature's annual convention for weekend-long "I-L" games. Then register immediately—it's the key to getting the best character to play. ✓**INTERNET**→*email* tad@inter con.com ✍ *Write a request*

Regional

New England Roleplaying Organization Think you're as tough as your D&D character? Find out by playing with the New England Roleplaying Organization (NERO), a group dedicated to live fantasy role-playing. NERO has chapters throughout the East Coast and Midwest. Check out their WWW page, which has an introduction to NERO and schedule information for the New York City area. Then dust off your spellbook and get ready for action! ✓**INTERNET** ...→*www* http://web. mit.edu/afs/athena/user/e/n/ enolagay/www/nerony/n-home. html ...→*email* ravenhrst@ace.com ✍ *Email with general correspondence*

New England Roleplaying Organization (echo) A conference for New England role-playing enthusiasts. ✓**WWIVNET**

SCA

The Consultant's List An email address list of lords and ladies who volunteer to answer any questions about the SCA or its activities. ✓**INTERNET**→*ftp* bransle.ucs.mun. ca→anonymous→<your email address>→/pub/sca→ consultants

The Frostheim Archive While not an "official" archive of the SCA, this site carries medieval music and poetry, the Corpora, information on Drachenwald, heraldry, rules of combat, introductory information about the SCA, and images. ✓**INTERNET**→*ftp* ftp.luth. se→anonymous→<your email address>→/pub/misc/frostheim

Nimbus Archive Home to the rules and governing documents of the SCA. Carries decisions of the board of directors, a recent copy of the armorial, and letters of acceptance and return (personas officially registered with the SCA). This archive is not the place to start if you are new to the SCA. ✓**INTER-NET**→*ftp* nimbus.gp.cs.cmu.edu→ anonymous→<your email address>→/usr/kvs/pub

rec.org.sca (ng) Find out about SCA events, hear kingdom news from all over the world, and talk to others about fleshing out your persona. It's all here. The mailing list, called Rialto (in reference to the marketplace in Venice where people gathered to exchange news, gossip, and ideas), is available in a digest format. All submissions are cross-posted to the newsgroup, so no need to get both. The FAQ is geared toward the newcomer and contains information about the SCA, its jargon, and local groups. ✓**USENET** ✓**INTERNET**→*email* SCA-Request@mc.lcs.mit.edu ✍ *Write a request FAQ:* ✓**INTERNET**→*ftp* rtfm.mit.edu→anonymous→<your

email address>→/pub/usenet/ rec.org.sca

SCA Archive Gentles will find herein everything they need to know about the SCA. The site stores the FAQ, the consultants list (the names of SCA members who consult on specific topics), an intro to the SCA, the Rolls Ethereal (a directory of SCA members on the Net), the Corpora (or bylaws) of the SCA, notices about the annual Pennsic event, and archives for some of the SCA-related mailing lists. There are also references for those interested in period music and lyrics, and rules for submitting your own heraldry. ✓**IN-TERNET**→*ftp* bransle.ucs.mun.ca→ anonymous→<your email address>→/pub/sca

SCA-West (ml) Primarily for SCA members of the West Kingdom, which includes northern and central California, northern Nevada, Alaska, Australia, and Japan. ✓**INTERNET**→*email* sca-west-request @mrfrostie.ecst.csuchico.edu ✍ *Type in message body:* subscribe <your full name>

Siege List Need tips for storming that castle this weekend? Let the SCA experts in pregunpowder warfare help you lay plans. Perhaps you can get someone to lend you a ballista or a team of sappers... ✓**INTERNET**→*email* siege-request@bransle.ucs.mun.ca ✍ *Type in message body:* subscribe siege <your full name> *Archives:* ✓**INTER-NET**→*ftp* bransle.ucs.mun.ca→ anonymous→<your email address>→/pub/sca

St. Olaf Archive Well met! Info on archery and the SCA, including where to find a group near you. ✓**INTERNET**→*ftp* ftp.stolaf.edu→ anonymous→<your email address>→/pub/sca

Adventures

Joseph Campbell would have a field day interpreting the hero's journeys on that construct of consciousness we like to call the Net. Many games such as **Adventurer's Maze** and **Excalibur II** follow the medieval monster motifs of D&D, but other legends are also re-created, including a Taiwanese MUD called **Eastern Stories** and a futuristic industrial megalopolis in **Future Runner**.

On the Net

3 Kingdoms The town of Pinnacle in the center of *3K* (as the MUD is commonly called) connects three separate realms: Fantasy, Science Fiction, and Chaos. Fantasy features *Dungeons & Dragons*; in the Science Fiction realm you can travel by MegaTech train to parts of the United States or through outer space; and in Chaos you'll find anything but the ordinary. On a trip to the grocery store, you'll meet old commercial favorites like Toocan Sam, the Lucky Charm Rabbit, Mr. Clean, and Mr. Whipple.

Flirting and jesting

The Login Room, where you enter the game, is located in a huge white marble building in the center of Pinnacle. It's a popular hangout, with more flirting and jesting than hack-'n'-slash. While you're in the Login Room, it's a good idea to "read map" to get a feel for the general layout of the MUD. Pinnacle, however, is a

Adventurers—downloaded from lajkonik.cyf-kr.edu.pl.

small town, so you can just as well wander around and get acquainted. Newbies are quite welcome here—there is even a special newbie land at the south end of the city to build a character's experience. You'll move around in newbie land by passing through mirrors, with an Alice in Wonderland effect. While there, you can visit a farm or a Disney area where Bambi and Ariel can be found.

Romp a Smurf

When you have gained some experience, you can leave newbie land. But leave Pinnacle and the killing begins…. Go off and fight the feared Goblin King, try to kill the president of MegaTech, Inc., or romp on a few Smurfs! When an adventurer has passed the fifth level, he may choose to join a guild—clerics, witches, animals, necromancers, etc. Occasionally Pinnacle will be invaded with only minutes' notice, and everyone will have to come to defend their guild. Be prepared to die. Even high mortals are killed in invasions! Injured after combat? Seek a

cleric for free healing. Or buy a drink with healing power in the pub. In a real emergency, use the "shout" command. It can be heard across all three kingdoms. For quieter moments go to the museum, read or post poetry, or marry another MUDder in the chapel. ✓**INTERNET**→*telnet* marble.bu.edu 5000 →guest *Info:* ✓**INTERNET**→*ftp* marble.bu.edu→anonymous→<your email address>→/pub/lp/doc→ 3k.ps.gz

Stats
- Difficulty: average
- Competition: live
- Number of players: 1+
- Interface: ASCII
- Server: LPMUD
- Platforms: all

Commands
- To get a list of topics with background information, type help
- To get a map of *3 Kingdoms*, type in the Login Room: read map

Adventurer's Maze Standard role-playing, *D&D*-type fare where players establish a character (either human, elf, half-elf, dwarf, or gnome) and work their way up the maze to slay the feared dragon. While many adventure games allow you to explore forever, this BBS adventure limits the number of moves you are allowed per day, though not the time you can spend there. ✓CHECK LOCAL BULLETIN BOARD SYSTEMS FOR THIS OR SIMILAR GAMES ☎→*dial* 804-587-4289/ 804-587-4382

Stats
- Difficulty: complex
- Competition: high scoring
- Number of players: 1+
- Interface: ANSI
- Platforms: all

Alatia In the Common World, players must earn the keys to the lost worlds by solving key quests. Then, through sacred portals deep underground, they can move from the medieval/fantasy setting to the shadow world of vampires and ghosts, and the Stone Age world of dinosaurs. In the lost worlds there are quests and adventures as well. Complete them to earn the "big points" and climb the levels of *Alatia*. When you reach level 20, you may continue to play the game as a "high-level player" or move on to wizardom. As a newbie, you'll enter in the church in the town of Celest. Find your way to the adventurer's guild and start reading about the quests. When you need a break from your adventures, drop by the pub in town. ✓**INTERNET**→*telnet* aann.tyrell.net 3000→1→<your character's name> →<your password>→<your password>

Stats
• Difficulty: average
• Competition: live
• Number of players: 1+
• Interface: ASCII
• Server: LPMUD
• Platforms: all

Commands
• To get instructions on how to play, type: help

Ancient Anguish (AA) Navigating the wilderness of *Ancient Anguish* is dangerous. You may want to explore it with other players instead of going off on your own. In any case, first spend some time in town preparing your character. After choosing from five races—human, orc, elf, half-elf, or dwarf—you should try to acquire some essentials: a compass and a pocket map, for instance, will help you find your way around; a magic stone will help gauge the strength of monsters before you decide to attack; and, a weapon will help kill a monster.

Money

To get the money for these pur-

> "**BatMUD** is for hard-core MUDders, featuring hundreds of skills and spells! Player killing is common, and the only time a wizard would intervene, explains one player, is 'if there's a random mass murdering (i.e., summoning 30 random players into a room without exits and killing them all—for no reason).'"

chases, you'll either have to kill a weak monster and steal from the corpse or work as a delivery person in the village. Without money you'll never get anywhere on *AA*. Before joining a class or a guild, you should be aware of the nuances: all the guilds have class and race restrictions of some sort, and there are good guys and bad guys. For instance, the Knights of Drin is the "good" guild based on the Code of Chivalry, while the Chaos guild is for necromancers and other evil magic users. You may travel alone, but there's safety in numbers—the monsters on *AA* can be aggressive and clever, and enemy

players are often devious.

Promiscuous

AA is very social (and rather promiscuous). More than thirty players are often logged on at once. Every time you logon, you start out in the church, where many players just hang out waiting for friends. There are public boards where you can post and read on topics ranging from poetry to jokes to the laws of *AA* all over the MUD. More than likely someone will pass you a pink, cuddly elephant. When it's in your possession, you can do some rather sensitive things to other players. Examine the elephant to see your options! ✓**INTERNET**→*telnet* end2.bedrock.com 2222→guest

Stats
• Difficulty: average
• Competition: live
• Number of players: 1+
• Interface: ASCII
• Server: LPMUD
• Platforms: all

Commands
• To get instructions, type: help newbie *or* help newbie 2
• To get a map of Ancient Anguish, go to Hanza's map shop and type: read map
• To read the map's legend, type: read legend

BatMUD With dozens of races to choose from (each with different skills), a newbie on *BatMUD* can join right in—that's if they can get in. No registration is required, but the MUD is often full. Newbies should definitely read the extensive help information. There's a lot to learn. *BatMUD* is for hard-core MUDders, featuring hundreds of skills and spells! Player killing is common, and the only time a wizard would intervene, explains one player, is "if there's a random mass murdering (i.e., summoning 30 random players into a room without exits and killing them all—for no reason).''

Do what you want

If you're looking for a place where you can say and do what you want, *BatMUD* may be appealing. As a visitor, you'll begin at Church Hall. Go east into a room where a tour guide is waiting. Type "look at tour guide" for instructions on how to take a tour of *BatMUD*. You'll also want to get to Digga's newbie area (3 moves east of church, look for the sign), where you can get free newbie armour and a weapon. Once you've become part of the community, you can pick up mail at the post office (e, e, n, n, w from Church Hall) or join the ongoing discussions via the news system, which features over 30 topics. You can also read the rec.games. mud* newsgroups in the newsroom (e, e, n, n, e, s from Church Hall). People usually socialize and form groups in their castles—it's the Middle Ages, after all. With these groups or "parties," they fight the tougher monsters.

Wimpy monsters

If you're a solo adventurer, *Bat-MUD* is probably not your game. You'll need to form alliances, ask for help (you'll probably have to pay back the favor later), and pick your fights carefully. Check the sewers for wimpy monsters. If you're killed, ask a cleric to ressurrect you. One last tip: Newbies get hungry often. Learn where to get food (Ugly Joe's should be a last resort). ✓**INTERNET** ...→*telnet* bat. cs.hut.fi 23→2→[return] ...→*gopher* bat.cs.hut.fi→Enter BatMUD *Info:* ✓**INTERNET** ...→ *ftp* bat.cs.hut.fi ...→*www* http://bat.cs.hut.fi *Support:* ✓**INTERNET**→*email* batmud@ bat.cs.hut.fi ✍ *Email with questions or problems*

Stats
• Difficulty: complex

Pure evil—downloaded from lajkonik.cyf-kr.edu.pl.

• Competition: live
• Number of players: 1+
• Interface: ASCII
• Server: LPMUD
• Platforms: all

Commands
• To get information, type: help topics
• To get help, type: bat <your question>
• To see the size and number of locations in the city, type: map
• To get started reading the newsgroups in the newsroom, type: list
• To judge the strength of monster, type: consider
• To determine which channels you are listening to, type: channels

British Legends This multi-player text game is so popular that it supports live discussion groups two days a week in CompuServe's MPGAMES Forum, an active bulletin board, and a whole slew of library files (including lots of help for the newcomer). *British Legends* is a quest for immortality—or Wizdom—which you can achieve by collecting valuable items and dumping them, logically enough, in a swamp. This gains you points; get enough points (without ever dying!) and you become a Wizard (or a Witch), a character so powerful that you don't play the game

anymore, you help run it. But die and you'll be taught the humility of starting over.

Subquests

En route to Wizdom are many subquests—complete them for much needed experience. Players can either team up or stab each other in the back, but in either instance there's a lot of friendly chatter going on. The interface is much like any text-adventure game—n, s, e, and w is your basic steering wheel. Commands will fill you in on some of the more esoteric stuff you can do. Be sure to keep a map of things as you got— the game isn't going to do it for you. And be ready to dedicate some real time to this game, because while you can save your character's general progress, you cannot save your inventory. Quitting for the evening will leave you empty-handed the next day. ✓**COMPUSERVE**→*go* gam-153

Stats
• Difficulty: average
• Competition: live
• Number of players: 1+
• Interface: ASCII
• Platforms: all

Dragon's Gate When you enter *Dragon's Gate*, you'll create a character using the online Character Generator. You choose your race (from among 20), your god, your occupation, and several other aspects your character needs to start off with. New players generally accept the invitation to go to the Training Grounds, an interactive introduction to the game. Head north to reach the Training Square, where you can buy torches from the General Store, weapons from the Armory, and other items you'll want to take on your adventure. Heading north, out of the square, you'll hit a crossroads, with three different areas to explore in the game: a city slum to the east, a cemetery to the north, and a woodsy area to the west. Back south, toward the Training Square, and east are the Training Guilds, where you'll pass through the Arch to take you into the town of Spur, the center of the actual game.

Spur

Once you pass through the Arch, you can't go back. In Spur you'll find other players to talk to or battle with—but don't battle in the Town Square; it's off-limits for combat. To gain experience, head north for the Guild District, provided you've joined a guild, south for the Noble District, where the well-to-do live, east for the temples to hook up with like-minded religionists, or west for the Merchant District, where you can buy more stuff. There are other regions to explore—the Poor Quarter to the northwest, the civic Arena east of Town Square for show-off battle, and even sewers under the city, but word is they're not for the newbie.

Explanation

For a good, condensed explanation of the game and its commands, download the Quick_Start.file from the *Dragon's Gate* Archives on the game's main menu. Or, if you've got the time, the entire *Dragon's Gate* manual (revised) is available either as ManualRev.zip or ManualRev.arc. Also available are ASCII maps, back issues of the game's newsletter, the *DragonFire Chronicles*, and a number of other, more specific manuals for thieving, buying and selling, and "living and dying." From the game's main menu, you'll find a link to the Multi-Player Games Round-Table (MPGRT), with its own bulletin board topic for *Dragon's Gate* and a file library of more *Dragon's Gate* maps, guides, and

newsletter archives. ✓**GENIE→** *keyword* dgate

Stats
- Difficulty: average
- Competition: live
- Number of players: 1+
- Interface: ASCII, ANSI
- Platforms: all

DragonMUD If you're keeping track of MUD servers (a true MUDder does), then we probably don't have to tell you that *Dragon-MUD* is the only remaining site running the TinyMUD code. But, if code isn't your thing, suffice it to say that *Dragon* is probably the oldest MUD on the Net. Set in 18th-century London, *Dragon* has no elves, orcs, or vampires. Adventurers, however, don't despair! Stop by the Questors' Rest, where you can get word of dozens of individual quests. There are lots of places to explore. Go west from the hotel to the Ticket Booth, where you can buy passage to many sites in Engand, including Wales, the Moors, and Camelot. Many players come here just to hang out, and the Town Square and the White Hart Pub are the popular places for doing just that. ✓**INTERNET→** *telnet* satan.ucsd.edu 4201→ connect guest guest

Stats
- Difficulty: average
- Competition: live
- Number of players: 1+
- Interface: ASCII
- Server: TinyMUD
- Platforms: all

Commands
- To get information, type: help *or* new topics
- To be added to a mailing list that will notify you if Dragon moves, type: gripe put me <your email address>

Eastern Stories Fantasy and Chinese culture—there's a scholars guild—merge into a world where

players (mostly from Taiwan, where the MUD is based) gather to fight, pursue adventure, and chat. The good people of Noden —you and the other players— have discovered strange lands to the east, including lands of riches and a land of the undead. Monsters wander the night, so beware. The real danger on *Eastern Stories*, however, are the invasions from the Moorth Empire whenever the magical barrier between the Moorth Empire and Noden is weakened. In fact, your first stop on *Eastern Stories* is the Knight's Guild in Nodania, capital of Noden, where you'll be recruited to help fight the invaders. Many of the areas on *Eastern Stories* have English translations, but in some areas, such as Eastland, only Mandarin descriptions are available (you must type "chinese" during login if you have a terminal capable of Big 5 code and you'd like to see Chinese descriptions). Most players chat in English. The wine shop located north of the Cemetery Farwind is often touted as the place to have the most fun. Re-

> "If another player has done you wrong, you can bring him or her to trial, and all the other players will serve as jury— unless, of course, the king throws out your suit and throws you in jail."

member the time difference when you're looking for friends! ✓**INTER-NET**→*telnet* 140.113.23.32 8000 →guest

Stats
- Difficulty: average
- Competition: live
- Number of players: 1+
- Interface: ASCII, ANSI
- Server: LPMUD
- Platforms: all

Commands
- To get information about the MUD, type: help topics

Excalibur II A medieval multi-player game chock full of features for the knight who aspires to the throne. You'll manage your fief-dom in and about the town of Camelot, traverse mountains and deserts, search for potions, kill dragons, joust at the court, and—if need be—overthrow the king. If another player has done you wrong, you can bring him or her to trial, and all the other players will serve as jury—unless, of course, the king throws out your suit and throws you in jail. It's a good idea to make friends in this game. ✓CHECK LOCAL BULLETIN BOARD SYSTEMS FOR THIS OR SIMILAR GAMES ☎→*dial* 717-868-5435

Stats
- Difficulty: average
- Competition: turn-based
- Number of players: 2+
- Interface: ANSI
- Platforms: all

Future Runner The giant indus-trial complexes of the mid–21st century are continually trying to steal technology from each other, and when they want a job done they look to you, the *Future Run-ner*. *Future Runner* has over 100 variations built in, so that each time the game is won, the theme, objects, and clues are in different locations. ✓CHECK LOCAL BULLETIN BOARD SYSTEMS FOR THIS OR SIMILAR

> "The monsters are smart. They can comfort you when you cry (or laugh at you), they can answer basic ques-tions like how many points you have, and they engage in a slightly more sophis-ticated form of com-bat than on other adventure MUDs."

GAMES ☎→*dial* 810-231-1207/503-624-7904

Stats
- Difficulty: average
- Competition: turn-based
- Number of players: 2+
- Interface: ANSI
- Platforms: all

Genocide War is hell, and *Geno-cide* is in a state of constant war, not to mention that it is—quite fittingly—one of the most confus-ing MUDs we've encountered. Player killing is encouraged—in fact, you probably won't survive your first two minutes in the world. The enemies aren't mon-sters here—worse, they're human. (At times, given the number of ghosts floating about, it seems as if everyone's been killed.) We strong-ly recommend that you read the Newbie's Introduction to *Geno-cide* in the Genocide War Com-plex (south from where you enter)

and then just jump in. If combat is what you're looking for and you're not put off by crass lan-guage, violence, and a hefty amount of information to take in, *Genocide* offers some of the best player-killing entertainment around. ✓**INTERNET**→*telnet* pip.shsu.edu 2222→<your character's name>→<y *or* n>→<your pass-word>→<your password>

Stats
- Difficulty: complex
- Competition: live
- Number of players: 1+
- Interface: ASCII
- Server: LPMUD
- Platforms: all

Commands
- To get information, type: help topics
- To get a list of the local news-groups on genocide, type: news

---

Gold Hunt! A simple adventure game in which the goal is to find gold in a mine. Items you discover along the way may prove helpful, but beware potential disasters. ✓CHECK LOCAL BULLETIN BOARD SYSTEMS FOR THIS OR SIMILAR GAMES ☎→*dial* 508-765-9387

Stats
- Difficulty: simple
- Competition: high scoring
- Number of players: 1
- Interface: ASCII, ANSI
- Platforms: all

Holy Mission Far less serious than its name implies—tickle at-tacks, winking, and flirting are more common than Jihads. On the other hand, it's not all socializ-ing—to wiz you must complete a large number of quests and score one million points. The MUD is huge, and as on most LPs, you won't get very far if you don't join a guild. You'll have to begin with a weak guild, like the adventurer's, but you can switch later. Newbies should start by trying to kill the insects in Jake's garden (east of the start area) or the fairies in the mage's tower (ask other players for directions). The MUD is located in Austria, and the English descriptions are not very well written. ✓**INTERNET**→*telnet* 140.78.3.1 2001→guest→[return]→1

Stats
- Difficulty: average
- Competition: live
- Number of players: 1+
- Interface: ASCII
- Server: LPMUD
- Platforms: all

Commands
- To get information, type: help
- To see a list of actions you can perform remotely, type: rsoul
- To see where another player is from in real life, type: rwhere
- To get a list of quests, type: list all
- To get a list of quests with descriptions and hints, type: list long

IgorMUD A popular and typical LPMUD setting with a fair number of quests. Newbies should begin in the Newbie Area (north of the church) and read the bulletin board. The Guild and the Church are the places to socialize. Be sure to ask an experienced player to see the Dragon Jousting if you enjoy combat. ✓**INTERNET**→*telnet* ny.mtek. chalmers.se 1701→guest

Stats
- Difficulty: average
- Competition: live
- Number of players: 1+
- Interface: ASCII
- Server: LPMUD
- Platforms: all

Commands
- To get information, type: help

Island Adventure, monsters, quests—seems a bit standard at first glance. But the quests here are hard, very hard, and getting lost in the tricky mazes is fairly common. What's more, the monsters are

smart. They can comfort you when you cry (or laugh at you), they can answer basic questions like how many points you have, and they engage in a slightly more sophisticated form of combat than on other adventure MUDs. Instead of just typing "kill monster" and sitting back to wait for the result, you have to actually fight it by choosing moves. As a beginner, you'll start in the Island Beginner's Zone in an area quite similar to Oxford, England. What awaits you? The *Enterprise* and Deanna Troi, who will spout psychological clichés at you ("I sense great guilt. Shouldn't you be working?"). The Planet of the Lost Dogs—a play on *Peter Pan*. And, well, Canada. ✓**INTERNET**→*telnet* teaching4. physics.ox.ac.uk 2093→<your character's name>→ <y or n>→<m or f>→<your password>→<your password> *Support:* ✓**INTERNET**→*email* islandad.teaching@physics. oxford.ac.uk ✍ *Write for help & support*

Stats
- Difficulty: average
- Competition: live
- Number of players: 1+
- Interface: ASCII
- Server: OxMUD
- Platforms: all

Commands
- To get information, type: help
- To get a list of people you can page for help, type: whoswho
- To get hints about quests, go to the pit and type: quest

Island of Kesmai You know a game has a steep learning curve when there are five file libraries on the subject, in this case in CompuServe's MPGAMES Forum. First of all, make your life easier and download one of the front-end shareware programs. You'll also want to download maps of the various areas, so you know where you're going.

Fluid world

Once you get the hang of all this, you'll find Kesmai to be a remarkably fluid world—there's no main goal to achieve, just adventure after adventure. And when you're not on a particular quest, join others in a hunting party and go after some big-time game (and treasure). Get enough experience points and you can find your way out of Kesmai and into the other segments of the game, eventually leaving the basic game entirely for the more-challenging Advanced Game.

Kesmai is a multiplayer game in the truest sense: killing other players is forbidden, and stealing from them (even if you're a thief) is frowned upon. There are so many other ways to perish here, however, that you'll probably be thankful you have to leave fellow players alive—they can help you. ✓**COMPUSERVE**→go gam-26 ✓**GENIE**→*keyword* iok *Info:* ✓**COMPUSERVE**→go mpgames→Libraries→ KOMPAN.ZIP ✓**GENIE**→*keyword* mpgrt→Multiplayer Games Software Library→Island of Kesmai→ 3896

Stats
- Difficulty: complex
- Competition: live
- Number of players: 1+
- Interface: ASCII
- Platforms: all

Kingdom of Drakkar You begin life here as a simple merchant in the town of Nork. Will you become a fighter or a martial artist? Maybe you'd rather be a mentalist, or a healer, or a thief, or a barbarian. As a newcomer to Nork, go to the "Weapon Training Center" in the northwest corner of the Town Square and ask the trainer to instruct you in the art of fighting. As you explore the kingdom, you'll encounter monsters guarding treasure. You can also join other players on this or that quest. And then there are exotic cities and the Steel Flower Tavern, where you can sit and chat, share tales of your adventures, whisper to another visitor, and retire with someone to a private table for uninterrupted conversation. When you exit from the game, your character is stored—but the story continues despite your absence, so expect new developments when you return. ✓ **MPG-NET**→*go* drakkar

Stats
- Difficulty: average
- Competition: live
- Number of players: 1+
- Interface: graphical
- Platforms: all

Commands
- To talk to other players, type: <player letter *or* name>, <message>
- To ask the trainer for instruction, type: <trainer's name>, train me

---

Land of Devastation *LOD* is a very popular game in BBS wasteland that's exactly where you'll find yourself—roaming about, battling mutants and other players as you attempt to find the "puritron" that was stolen by bad guys after a devastating nuclear war. As you roam the apocalyptic landscape, you'll need to collect weapons and build up experience to save the world. The game offers an optional EGA terminal program, allowing for full-color maps, inventories, and a rich graphical environment. ✓ CHECK LOCAL BULLETIN BOARD SYSTEMS FOR THIS OR SIMILAR GAMES ☎ →*dial* 904-483-2498/ 913-422-7345 /602-544-4655

Stats
- Difficulty: complex
- Competition: live
- Number of players: 2+
- Interface: ASCII, ANSI, graphical
- Platforms: all

Legend of the Red Dragon An easy-to-learn medieval roleplaying game set in a small town where children are disappearing. Your task: to rise to level 12 and defeat the dragon. You'll fight monsters along the way and slaughter other players, but you may also enjoy a few steamy dalliances—if you're charming enough. Lots of surprises keep the game interesting. Can be played by oneself or, if the BBS has multiple lines, with other players. ✓ CHECK LOCAL BULLETIN BOARD SYSTEMS FOR THIS OR SIMILAR GAMES ☎ →*dial* 504-383-2864/503-838-6171

Stats
- Difficulty: average
- Competition: live *or* personal best
- Number of players: 1+
- Interface: ANSI
- Platforms: all

Lost Souls Have weapon, will kill. *Lost Souls* is not for the faint of heart. Combat may result in the—nonfatal—loss of limbs, but with a sucking chest wound that won't stop bleeding, your spirit will take a trip to the church (where it must pray to be resurrected), and if you lose your head, you're dead. You're likely to die a lot at the beginning, and there's a lot to learn: races, quests, guilds, and languages. At the center of this large world is the neutral city of Losthaven, where the races mix. But outside the city, each race controls a different area—hidden in these areas are the guilds that may offer advantages to the player. ✓ **INTERNET**→*telnet* ronin.bchs.uh.edu 3000→guest→guest *Info:* ✓ **INTERNET**→*email* msheahan@carroll1.cc.edu ✍ *Write a request to be added to a mailing list with updates on* Lost Souls

Stats
- Difficulty: complex
- Competition: live
- Number of players: 1+

- Interface: ASCII
- Server: LPMUD
- Platforms: all

Monkey Island 2 Walkthru Explicit, step-by-step instructions on completing the game. ✓ **AMERICA ONLINE**→*keyword* mgm→Software Libraries→*Search by file name:* How To\Monkey Island ✓ **GENIE**→*keyword* scorpia→Gamers Libraries→Set Library Category→LucasArts→*Download a file:* 4434 *and* 4435 *and* 4436

Monster Island You're a monster venturing forth on Monster Island (an area three times the size of Australia) and encountering treasure and hundreds of other monsters, played by other people. Monsters are coarse folk generally, and the game has a decidedly bent sense of humor. In fact, one of the more popular actions is the "NF" command: "Let loose a Nasty Fart." The ABM computers keep track of over 2,100 statistics for each monster. Turns are three times a month, and your reports are sent via U.S. mail, even though you can send in your "Turn Entry" online. You'll find helpful information in the AOL file library, but many players enjoy just learning the ropes as they go along. Each turn costs $4. ✓ **AMERICA ONLINE**→*keyword* pbm→Adventures By Mail $ ✓ **INTERNET**→ *email* bob@abm.com $ *Archives:* ✓ **AMERICA ONLINE**→*keyword* pbm→Adventures by Mail→ABM File Library

Stats
- Difficulty: average
- Competition: turn-based
- Number of players: 1+
- Interface: ASCII
- Platforms: all

Monster Island Mailing List (ml) The mailing list for monsters who're roaming *Monster Island*. ✓ **INTERNET**→*email* warden@triton.

unm.edu ✍ *Type in subject line:* subscribe Monster Island

MooseHead MUD *MooseHead Mud* is set in A.D. 400 to 900.
You may play a dwarf, elf, giant, human, or a dragon that wanders the land. Though everyone chooses to become either a cleric, thief, mage, or warrior, you may dabble or even double in the skills of other classes. If you choose to join a Clan, you may participate in killing other player. If you're not a Clan member, you will only be threatened by nonplayer characters. The world is broad and deep and continually growing. Take a trip through MUD school if your new to MUDding. ✓ **INTERNET**→ *telnet* eskinews.eskimo.com 4000→ <your character's name>→<y or n>→<your password>→<your password>→<your race>→<m or f>→ <your class>→<good, neutral, or evil>

Stats
- Difficulty: average
- Competition: live
- Number of players: 1+
- Interface: ASCII
- Server: DikuMUD
- Platforms: all

Commands
- To get information, type: help
- To get a list of wizards, type: wizlist

Mud II: The Quest for Immortality When you think about it, why quest for anything else? Earn enough experience in GEnie's MUD by solving various puzzles and staying alive, and with any luck you'll reach the status of Immortal Wiz. After that you can help run the game instead of playing it. Of course, in any Multi-User Dungeon, there are players looking to get their experience by defeating other players—you, for instance, so beware. ✓ **GENIE**→*keyword* mud

Stats
- Difficulty: average
- Competition: live
- Number of players: 1+
- Interface: ASCII
- Platforms: all

Nightmare Mighty giant? Nimble fairy? A hobbit, perhaps? Begin by choosing your genetic make-up. Choose carefully because you're stuck for life with the attributes of your character (intelligence, dexterity, strength, etc.), its preferences (e.g. well-lit castles or dark, enclosed areas). Over time you may enhance some skills, but you then will lose some as you age.

You must also pick a profession: cleric, fighter, kataan, mage, monk, or rogue (read the online descriptions of each). And, you may choose to join a guild that will offer you the rewards of association, though there are dangers as well. Known guilds are the witches, the philosophers, and the druids, but there are rumored to be secret ones, too.

Bankrolls

As a newbie, you should probably go northeast from the center of town until you get to NewbieLand, where you can practice your skills and build your bankrolls. You can stay there until you reach level six. (Keep your ears open for word of the underground world in Praxis and the dark caves west of town).

Nightmare is a magical world where players marry, make friends, join parties, elect leaders, perform spells, go on adventures, kill monsters, fight their enemies, and even fish! Throughout your life, a biography is maintained, tracking your birthday (in *Nightmare* time), your marriages, divorces, deaths, significant accomplishments, and other data. Take a trip on the flying ships and visit the islands! ✓ **INTERNET** ...→*telnet* nightmare.connected.

com 4000→<your character's name>→<y or n>→<your password>→<your password>→<male or female>→<your email address> ...→*www* http://abacus.bates.edu/~greese→Try Nightmare! *Info:* ✓ **INTERNET**→*ftp* nightmare.connected.com→anonymous→ <your email address>→/pub/mud/docs

Stats
- Difficulty: average
- Competition: live
- Number of players: 1+
- Interface: ASCII, ANSI
- Server: LPMUD
- Platforms: all

Commands
- To get instructions, type: faq *or* help
- To leave a question, go to the post office and type: mail advocate
- To leave a public message for advocates, go to the board monitored by advocates: east east east south down

Northern Crossroads A large map, a small player base, and plenty of objects for newbies to find. As soon as you enter, you'll be asked to choose a class, sex, and race. In a later stage you'll also join a guild. There are weekly scavenger hunts, and occasionally the MUD is invaded or a princess is kidnapped to keep life interesting. ✓ **INTERNET**→*telnet* ugsparc13.eecg.toronto.edu 9000→<your character's name>→<y or n>→ <your password>→<your password>

Stats
- Difficulty: average
- Competition: live
- Number of players: 1+
- Interface: ASCII
- Server: DikuMUD
- Platforms: all

Commands
- To get information, type: help *or* info

• To get a list of wizards, type: wizlist

Overdrive A lot of horsing around goes on here—snowball fights (even in the summer) are a favorite pastime. Not that MUD-ders here are softies. They are quite focused on their objectives: gaining experience points, trading them in for better stats, and solving quests. The combat system is fairly complex, and death can be quite descriptive. Corpses, for instance, rot differently depending upon how they died. You can compete as long as you'd like, but you may apply to become a wizard when you reach level 30 and you've completed all the quests.

Fair game

At level four you may join a class. Each class has its own strengths and powers, and class rivalry is intense. Player killing is allowed if you sign up for it, but then you're fair game as well—unless, of course, it's a party war. *OD* has party wars every couple of weeks where people can kill each other without worrying about death—the results of these wars aren't permanent. ✓**INTERNET**→*telnet* castor.acs.oakland.edu 5195→guest→ [return]→ <male, female, or neuter>

Stats
• Difficulty: average
• Competition: live
• Number of players: 1+
• Interface: ASCII
• Server: LPMUD
• Platforms: all
Commands
• To get info, type: help

Quest You don't play one character, you play 6-15 characters in this popular play-by-mail, one-turn-per-week fantasy game. You submit your turns via the "Turn Entry" form for *Quest* on AOL, and you receive your turn reports

Morgoth—downloaded from lajkonik. cyf-kr.edu.pl.

---

via U.S. mail.

In the world of Kharne, characters engage in intrigue, magic, or combat. For an additional fee you can have up to two more parties. Your turn reports will reveal towns to explore, wilderness, dungeons, and encounters with up to a thousand other players. Your six starting characters are drawn from four races (human, elf, dwarf, and half-blood) and four professions (priest, fighter, thief, and mage).

Talk to people or rob them

A typical turn entry would include instructions to buy items; investigate locations, people, or parties; talk to people or rob them; pray to the gods or one particular god; take weapons practice; accept an offer to go on a quest; and mess around with spells (up to 15 orders per turn).

It may take a few turns to become familiar with the turn entry abbreviations and codes, but once you do, you'll find that the game expands enough to satisfy your characters' wandering natures. Each turn costs $3. ✓**AMERICA ON-LINE**→*keyword* pbm→Adventures By Mail $ ✓**INTERNET**→*email* bob@ abm.com *Archives:* ✓**AMERICA ON-LINE**→*keyword* pbm→Adventures By Mail→ABM File Library

Stats
• Difficulty: average
• Competition: turn-based
• Number of players: 1+
• Interface: ASCII
• Platforms: all

Realms of the Dragon (RotD)
Based loosely on Robert Jordan's *Wheel of Time* series. If you've chosen a race other than Drow, you'll be dropped into the Red Dragon Tavern in the town of Liarth—its walls are lined with pictures of famous adventurers who've roamed these parts before you.

Drow, on the other hand, start in the Main Square of Sreen, the Underdark city, and life is not easy for them—two powerful monsters stand between them and the surface. Says ThrashBarg, the High Immortal, "Theme is *AD&D*, with rapiers and whatnot, but the immortals of the MUD don't mind getting a bit silly every now and then." Chat on the gossip channel or join a guild; there's one for every trade from occultists to ninjas. For information about the guilds, go to the Library and ask the autolibrarian. ✓**INTERNET**→*telnet* 141.215.69.7 3000→guest

Stats
• Difficulty: average
• Competition: live
• Number of players: 1+
• Interface: ASCII
• Server: LPMUD
• Platforms: all
Commands
• To get information, type: help newuser

Sol III *Sol III* actually consists of five different games, all taking place on the same planet at different times in history or the future. When you join a campaign, you choose in which year you'd like to play.

A.D. 1203 is a low-magic fantasy campaign set in the time of Robin Hood and King Arthur. A.D. 1893 takes place on the Barbary Coast in California and contains a mixture of the Old West, Chinese mysticism, and Victorian-era gaslight culture. A.D. 1988 is a modern setting with a cyberpunk twist and also has a touch of magic. A.D. 2023 combines elements from all the other campaigns and takes place in Houston in a post-holocaust world that's rebuilding, with magic and feudal warlord states. And A.D. 2603 provides high space fantasy with the entire universe against the human race.

Time travel

To spark things up even more, time travel occasionally takes place among these five campaigns. Once in the middle of an adventure, you can schedule a one-to-two-hour live game with the game master to further your adventure. Designed to be as appealing as possible to people new to play-by-mail games, without offending experienced gamers, the game uses no turn sheets and no turn formats—in fact, it's more interactive fiction than a PBeM game. There are no charts to refer to, and the rules are, by and large, immediately apparent to the players.

Think creatively

The game master handles all rules and all dice rolls, based on the first-person descriptions of your character's actions. Since you're not keeping track of hit points or character levels, your only responsibility is to think creatively for your character.

To start playing, choose a time frame and a character type. Your AOL screen name or your Internet address will be your character's name. In addition, AOL players can download start-up files from the file library, which give details on the different settings, character types, maps of Houston, and more. ✓**AMERICA ONLINE**→*keyword* sol iii $ *Support:* ✓**AMERICA ONLINE** →*email* soliiigm

Stats
- Difficulty: average
- Competition: turn-based (play-by-email)
- Number of players: 1+
- Interface: ASCII
- Platforms: all

Tron When the occasional evil forces attempt to overrun the town of Darkwind, you must prevent them from destroying it. Darkwind is for hard-core, player-killing gamers and is set in a medieval fantasy world. The theme is consistent, but war can break out on the map, whereas in most other MUDs battles take place in fixed locations. Says a Darkwind admin, "If you don't like accidentally appearing in loony-toon land, then suddenly finding yourself on the bridge of a starfighter, then this is the place for you." Yes, the MUD is based on the movie. ✓**INTERNET**→ *telnet* 141.241.84.65 4000→guest→ [return]

Stats
- Difficulty: complex
- Competition: live
- Number of players: 1+
- Interface: ASCII
- Server: LPMUD
- Platforms: all

Commands
- To get information, type: help newuser
- To display the proportion of the map you occupy (if you are on the game grid), type: plan
- To display the entire game grid, type: masterplan

Valhalla Once registered, join a guild (either one located in town, such as the fighter's guild or the priest's guild, or one that's hidden, such as the druids or bards) and strive to reach the status of noble (adventures for nobles are being developed). Nobles may petition for wizard status and, if approved, will then be allowed to build on the MUD. Your personal statistics determine your character strength. The equipment you have with you and your character's attributes determine how well you do in combat. Remember: Good guys don't always win. ✓**INTERNET**→ *telnet* midgard.valhalla.com 2444→guest →<choose one of the guest name's offered> *Register:* ✓**INTERNET**→ *email* register@midgard.valhalla. com ✍ *Email within the first 12 hours of playing time to validate character*

Stats
- Difficulty: complex
- Competition: live
- Number of players: 1+
- Interface: ASCII
- Server: LPMUD
- Platforms: all

MORE ADVENTURES

For even more adventures, telnet to these MUDs:

AbyssMUD
helpmac.its.mcw.edu 8888
AlexMUD
marcel.stacken.kth.se 4000
Death's Domain
wizard.ece.miami.edu 9000
Deeper Trouble
alk.iesd.auc.dk 4242
Hercules MUD
sunshine.eushc.org 3000
The Last Outpost
kimiyo.summer.hawaii.edu 4000
MEDIEVIA Cyberspace
medievia.netaxs.com 4000
OpalMUD
opal.cs.virginia.edu 4000
StRaNgEMuD
sprinkle.cray.com 7900
TubMUD
morgen.cs.tu-berlin.de 7680

AberMUDs

Solve puzzles. Kill monsters. Find treasures. Sound famil-

iar? An AberMUD is the quintessential adventure game in a fantasy/medieval setting. Abers are divided into "zones," with some, such as the Elven Forest and Camelot, standard to all, and others, such as the "Femmenazi" zone and Oz, found only on a few. In the zones, players complete quests (a requirement on most Abers), collect valuable objects, and kill mobiles for points. A player is "mortal" until she scores enough points and completes the required quests to become an apprentice wizard. She will become a wizard at the discretion of the immortals. Once a player's wizzed, she can "run" (play) on another Aber or stick around to socialize and build new zones. The MUD's chat system and its long list of "actions"—from massaging another player's shoulders to dancing—make playing on an Aber a very social experience. For wizzes, who enjoy access to more chat lines and greater mobility, the MUD often turns into a social club where friends who've together climbed the levels of the AberMUD hang out.

A map of Northern Lights—from ftp.luth.se.

On the Net

BadLandsII A very chatty and social AberMUD. Players are young and friendly. Help is given freely, and the word has it that wizzing is fairly easy. The MUD is still new, and its growth has been affected by restricted hours (after 5 p.m. on weekdays). Immortals are on quite often and interact regularly with the players. ✓**INTERNET**→*telnet* alpha.dsu.edu 6789→<your character's name>→<y or n>→<your password>→<your password>

Stats

• Difficulty: average
• Competition: live
• Number of players: 1+
• Interface: ASCII, ANSI
• Server: AberMUD
• Platforms: all

Commands

• To get information about how to play, type: help *or* info
• To get a list of top powers, type: powers
• To send a message to all wizards, type: wish <message>
• To talk on the gossip channel,

type: gossip <message>
• To automatically see the exits when you enter a room, type: autoexit

BladeRunner You begin as a peasant in the Grindstone, an old English pub. Your objective is to become an apprentice Wizard, but first you must acquire the status of Over Lord. To do so, you'll need to amass 250,000 points and solve seven quests. *BladeRunner* is a relatively small and new Aber, but players are friendly and helpful to newbies, and the atmosphere is anything but uptight. Immortals mix freely with mortals. Many of the traditional zones have been customized, and the unique zones include one modeled after the video game *Street Fighter* and another after the game *Doom*. ✓**INTERNET**→*telnet* rm205.lindgren.neshall.nwu.edu 5000→<your character's name>→ <y or n>→<your password>→<your password>

Stats

• Difficulty: average
• Competition: live
• Number of players: 1+
• Interface: ASCII, ANSI
• Server: AberMUD
• Platforms: all

Commands

• To get information about playing the game, type: help *or* info
• To send a message to all wizards, type: wish <message>
• To get a list of wizards, type: wizlist
• To chat on the gossip channel, type: gossip <message>
• To view the game map, type: info map

Budapest Formerly a by-invitation-only MUD, *Budapest* is one of the oldest Abers still around. In fact, it's so old that most of its player base has wizzed. It's not a particularly good place for newbies (the player base is small and there are usually few people available to help), but for those with some Aber experience it can be one of the most difficult. To wiz here requires the completion of 37 quests—and many of the zones are unique—and a total of 260,000 points! If you're looking for a challenge and you don't mind going it alone, take a run on *Budapest*. ✓**INTERNET**→*telnet* prometheus. bsd.uchicago.edu 6789→<your character's name>→<y or n>→<your password>→<your password>

Stats
- Difficulty: complex
- Competition: live
- Number of players: 1+
- Interface: ASCII, ANSI
- Server: AberMUD
- Platforms: all

Commands
- To get information about how to play, type: info *or* help
- To get a list of wizards, type: wizlist
- To send a message to all wizards, type: wish <message>
- To get information about quests, type: qinfo
- To get a list of quests that are available, type: qdone

Dirt A smaller MUD—located in Norway—that nobody seems to know about. Standard Aber quests. ✓**INTERNET**→ *telnet* alkymene.uio.no 6715→<your character's name>→<y or n>→<your password>→<your password>

Stats
- Difficulty: average
- Competition: live
- Number of players: 1+
- Interface: ASCII, ANSI
- Server: AberMUD
- Platforms: all

Commands
- To get information on how to play, type: help *or* info
- To get a list of wizards, type: wizlist

- To send a message to all wizards, type: wish <message>

DragonMUD The oldest Aber-MUD, *Dragon* is a great place for newbies who need a lot of hand holding to begin their Aber adventures. Until you figure out how to silence "Puff," the robot dragon, he'll keep shouting, complaining, and mocking players. Quieting Puff is not an official quest, but it may well be the first thing you want to do! ✓**INTERNET**→*telnet* fermina.informatik.rwth-aachen.de 6715→<your character's name>→<y or n>→<your password>→<your password>

Stats
- Difficulty: average
- Competition: live
- Number of players: 1+
- Interface: ASCII, ANSI
- Server: AberMUD
- Platforms: all

Commands
- To get information about how to play, type: help *or* info
- To send a message to all wizards, type: wish <message>
- To get a list of all wizards, type: wizlist

Eclipse A friendly, medium-size AberMUD. Most active during the day. ✓**INTERNET**→*telnet* mud.bsd. uchicago.edu 6715→<your character's name>→<y or n>→ <your password>→<your password>

Stats
- Difficulty: average
- Competition: live
- Number of players: 1+
- Interface: ASCII, ANSI
- Server: AberMUD
- Platforms: all

Commands
- To get information about how to play, type: info *or* help
- To get a list of top powers, type: policy powers
- To send a message to all wizards, type: wish <message>

Infinity MUD A midsized Aber-MUD with all the traditional quests as well as its own *Infinity* quest. Once you've wizzed (eight quests and 300,000 points), you can hang out in the Wiz Dungeon. ✓**INTERNET**→*telnet* sirius.nmt.edu 6715→<your character's name>→<y *or* n>→<your password>→<your password>

Stats
- Difficulty: average
- Competition: live
- Number of players: 1+
- Interface: ASCII, ANSI
- Server: AberMUD
- Platforms: all

Commands
- To get information about how to play, type: help *or* info
- To send a message to all wizards, type: wish <message>
- To get a list of all wizards, type: wizlist
- To talk on the chat channel, type: chat <message>
- To automatically see the exits when you enter a room, type: autoexit
- To follow another player, type: follow <player>
- To stop a player from following you, type: lose <player>
- To get a map of the game, type: info map

Kender's Kove *Kove* has a reputation in the Aber community for matchmaking, in that its male players seem to spend as much time seeking female companionship as they do the answers to quests. Rumor has it that if you're looking for a MUD-marriage proposal, you should play a female character on *Kove*! The MUD is also known for many of its unique quests and zones. Besides the standard Aber quests, you have to solve the secret of Pirate's Kove, drive a stake through the heart of the Vampire leader, find Pooh's honeypot and return it to him,

slay the magical unicorn, and steal the God's most prized possession. Visit the "Femmenazi" zone, featuring, among others, Joan of Arc, Tipper Gore, and Catwoman. You need to score 300,000 points and complete 15 quests to become a wizard here. ✓**INTERNET**→*telnet* harvey.esu.edu 6715→<your character's name>→<y *or* n>→<your password>→<your password>

Stats
- Difficulty: average
- Competition: live
- Number of players: 1+
- Interface: ASCII, ANSI
- Server: AberMUD
- Platforms: all

Commands
- To get information about how to play, type: info *or* help
- To get a list of game administrators, type: powers
- To send a message to all wizards, type: wish <message>

Kove MUD Development List (ml) Keep up with what's going on at *Kender's Kove*. ✓**INTERNET**→*email* majordomo@cohl.llnl.gov ✍ *Type in message body:* subscribe kovedev

Mustang MUD *Mustang* is a huge AberMUD without set quests. But there are still plenty of mobiles to kill and objects to find. Wizard status is reached as soon as you score 300,000 points. As far as AberMUDs go, *Mustang* is not very social, but new management promises to bring changes. Check out the Rose zone (also found on *Northern Lights*) while you're here. The zone is based on Umberto Eco's *The Name of the Rose*, and the objective is to find the lost book in the monastery. The zone is laid out according to the map of the monastery in the book. Among the many other zones on *Mustang* are Atlantis, Chryos, the Icecave, and Heaven. There is also

a pawn shop to swap your objects. ✓**INTERNET**→*telnet* mustang.us.dell.com 9173→<your character's name>→<your email address>

Stats
- Difficulty: average
- Competition: live
- Number of players: 1+
- Interface: ASCII, ANSI
- Server: AberMUD
- Platforms: all

Commands
- To get information about how to play, type: help *or* info
- To get a list of wizards, type: wizlist
- To send a message to all wizards, type: wish <message>

Northern Lights While consistently one of the most popular and stable AberMUDs on the Net, the flip side to *Northern Lights'* large player base is that there are more players taking the treasures and solving the quests that you need to advance. With a heavy emphasis on questing and puzzle solving (it's a hard "run"), *NL* is not known as the most social of AberMUDs. Rumor has it that if you're looking to wiz, it can be a very political place. For those looking for "a good run," *NL* is a tried-and-true favorite, with original zones and a well-thought-out world. Located in northern Sweden, it also may very well be the world's northernmost MUD. ✓**INTERNET**→*telnet* aber.ludd.luth.se 6715→<your character's name>→<y or n>→<your password>→<your password> *Info:* ✓**INTERNET** ...→*www* http://www.ludd.luth.se/mud/aber ...→*ftp* ftp.luth.se→anonymous→<your email address>→/pub/misc/aber *Support:* ✓**INTERNET**→*email* aber@ludd.luth.se *Email for help & support*

Stats
- Difficulty: complex
- Competition: live
- Number of players: 1+

- Interface: ASCII, ANSI
- Server: AberMUD
- Platforms: all

Commands

- To get information on how to play, type: help *or* info
- To send a message to all wizards, type: wish <question>
- To get a list of game administrators, type: info powers

PrairieMUD *PrairieMUD's* quests tend to be harder than the norm and players are required to complete 13 of them, but they're "compensated" by receiving wiz status at 200,000 points—a lower score than the average Aber requires. The MUD features over 50 zones, including the Galaxy Zone, based on Douglas Adams's *The Hitchhiker's Guide to the Galaxy*. A small group of steady players run on *PrairieMUD*, but many come just to socialize. The MUD has segmented off an area devoted entirely to kicking back and chatting—just go south when you login to the Last Chance Cafe. ✓**INTERNET**→*telnet* prairienet.org 6715→ <your character's name>→<y *or* n> →<your password>→<your password>

Stats

- Difficulty: average
- Competition: live
- Number of players: 1+
- Interface: ASCII, ANSI
- Server: AberMUD
- Platforms: all

Commands

- To get information about how to play, type: info *or* help
- To get a list of wizards, type: wizlist
- To send a message to all wizards, type: wish <message>

Rainbow Immortals are friendly and chatty on *Rainbow*, setting the tone for a laid back and very social Aber. New players are asked to run through a tutorial. If you're new to

> **"Dragon is a great place for newbies who need a lot of hand holding to begin their Aber adventures. Until you figure out how to shut "Puff", the robot dragon, up, he'll keep shouting, complaining, and mocking players."**

AberMUD's, you'll appreciate this entertaining overview. *Rainbow's* own Newbie Trainer, a robot that hollers instructions like an exercise coach, will guide you through it. Once you've exited the training program, you'll hop on a tour bus and begin your adventures. Check out the casino and, when you're ready, the challenging Cliff and Middle Earth zones. In the works are quests that require teamwork—quite a novel idea considering the solo adventure style of Abers. ✓**INTERNET**→*telnet* rm205. lindgren.res-hall.nwu.edu 6715→ <your character's name>→<y *or* n> →<your password>→<your password>

Stats

- Difficulty: average
- Competition: live
- Number of players: 1+
- Interface: ASCII, ANSI
- Server: AberMUD
- Platforms: all

Commands

- To get information about how to

play, type: help *or* info
- To get a list of wizards, type: wizlist
- To send a message to all wizards, type: wish <message>
- To chat on the gossip line, type: gossip <message>

SilverMUD Many of the players on *Silver* are in their mid-20s, slightly older than the average Aber player, and the MUD prides itself on being a mature place to play. Since there isn't a quest requirement and the world is relatively small, players can usually wiz here in a few weeks. It's also a small, friendly community and probably a good place to learn the ropes. ✓**INTERNET**→*telnet* dante.ex ide.com 6715→<your character's name>→<y *or* n>→<your password>→<your password>

Stats

- Difficulty: average
- Competition: live
- Number of players: 1+
- Interface: ASCII, ANSI
- Server: AberMUD
- Platforms: all

Commands

- To get information about how to play, type: help *or* info
- To get a list of wizards, type: wizlist
- To send a message to all wizards, type: wish <message>

Sleepless Nights A very different style of AberMUD. More for running than socializing, *Sleepless Nights* with its guilds and spells is touted as the next step in Abers. The MUD also includes *PK* tournaments set up as a separate game, *Highlander*. The winner of each tournament is awarded several thousand points on *Sleepless Nights*. The game is still in development, and activity is often low. ✓**INTERNET**→*telnet* cs3.brookes. ac.uk 6789→<your character's name>→<your character's gender>

→<your email address>→<your password>

Stats
- Difficulty: complex
- Competition: live
- Number of players: 1+
- Interface: ASCII, ANSI
- Server: AberMUD
- Platforms: all

Commands
- To get information about how to play, type: info *or* commands
- To get a list of wizards, type: wizlist
- To send a message to everyone on the MUD, type: shout <message>
- To get hints on playing here, type: info hint
- To get a map of the MUD, type: map
- To talk on the gossip channel, type: gossip <message>

Temple II Solve five quests and score 160,000 points to become a wizard. The land is tough and players are allowed to kill each other. ✓ **INTERNET**→*telnet* yoda.cis. temple.edu 6715→<your character's name>→<y *or* n>→<your password>→<your password>

Stats
- Difficulty: average
- Competition: live
- Number of players: 1+
- Interface: ASCII, ANSI
- Server: AberMUD
- Platforms: all

Commands
- To get information about how to play, type: help *or* info
- To send a message to all wizards, type: wish <message>
- To get a list of all wizards, type: wizlist

The Terradome If easy wizzing is your goal, *Terradome* is not the place to do it. To wiz, the MUD requires a score of 200,000 points and the completion of several quests—not in itself prohibitive—

but the wiz hierarchy can be quite political. Wizzes are not given as much power as they're given on other MUDs—sometimes to the detriment of newbies who can't find powerful enough wizzes to help them out. (Newbies should go north as soon as they enter *Terradome* to take the introductory course.) With a larger than average

GETTING AROUND ON AN ABERMUD

INFO

who .... lists the players on the Aber
wizlist .... lists players that have obtained wizard status
levels .... shows the number of points required for each level
quests .... shows either the quests you have to complete or those presently available on the MUD
info quests .... describes the quests
score .... shows the number of points you've acquired
inv .... shows the items in your possession

COMMUNICATE

" <message> .... sends your message to everyone in the same room
tell <player> <message> .. sends your message to a specific player anywhere on the MUD
shout <message> .... sends your message to everyone on the MUD
wish <message> .... sends your message to all the wizards on the MUD
actions .... lists all the actions available on the MUD

EXPLORING

look .... describes the room
examine <object> .... describes a specific object and often offers hints on how to use it
exits .... lists available exits
get <object> .... picks up object
give <player> <object> ..... gives an object to another player
drop <object> .... drops an object (usually into the pit)
lock <object> .... locks an object (you must have a key)
unlock <object> .... unlocks an object (you must have a key)
open <object> .... opens an object

COMBAT

kill <mobile *or* player> ..... enters into combat
wield <object> .... wields your weapon (if you don't "wield" a weapon, it is not effective)
wear <object> .... puts on armour (if you don't "wear" armour, it is not effective)
flee .... run from combat

OTHER

mudlist *or* info mudlist ..... prints a list of other AberMUDs and addresses.
color .... adds color to the text display

world, *Terradome* is home to some colorful places and several unique zones. Check out the Village Store, where you can barter found objects for items you need. If you're feeling brave, try the East Coast zone. The Island zone is in full working order here (unlike most other Abers). Higher-level players are allowed to kill—with the permission of the MUD Gods. ✓**INTERNET**→*telnet* cmssrv-gw.brookes. ac.uk 8888→<your character's name>→<y or n>→<your password>→<your password>

Stats
- Difficulty: average
- Competition: live
- Number of players: 1+
- Interface: ASCII, ANSI
- Server: AberMUD
- Platforms: all

Commands
- To get information about how to play, type: help *or* info
- To get a list of the administrators, type: toplist
- To send a message to all wizards, type: wish <message>
- To get a map of Terradome, type: info map
- To beep another player, type: beep <player>
- To follow another player, type: follow <player>
- To lose another player, type: lose <player>

Ulrick Player killing, usually banned on Abers, is allowed here. Unfortunately it's difficult to find other players. *Ulrick* has five quests and a low points requirement, but it's not unusual to have the whole MUD to yourself—lots of objects to find, but not a lot of talk. ✓**INTERNET**→*telnet* alkymene.uio.no 6715→<your character's name>→<y or n>→<your password>→<your password>

Stats
- Difficulty: average
- Competition: live

- Number of players: 1+
- Interface: ASCII, ANSI
- Server: AberMUD
- Platforms: all

Commands
- To get information about how to play, type: help *or* info
- To send a message to all wizards, type: wish <message>
- To get a list of all wizards, type: wizlist

Virtual Sun A very quiet AberMUD—better for "running" than socializing. To wiz, you need to score 250,000 points and complete ten quests, including a few unique ones. While there's a Beginner's Welcome Center, accessible from the login, newbies would probably do better to start on a MUD with more players (and more help). ✓**INTERNET**→*telnet* babar.ksl.umn.edu 6715→<your character's name>→<y or n>→<your password>→<your password> *Support:* ✓**INTERNET**→*email* mud@rainbow.mitre.org

Stats
- Difficulty: complex
- Competition: live
- Number of players: 1+
- Interface: ASCII, ANSI

> "The lemmings roaming this MUD are dangerous not just to themselves (e.g. possessing suicidal tendencies), but to players as well. Do them before they do you."

- Server: AberMUD
- Platforms: all

Commands
- To get information about how to play, type: help *or* info
- To send a message to all wizards, type: wish <message>
- To get a list of all wizards, type: wizlist
- To talk on the chat channels, type: chat <message>
- To follow another player, type: follow <player>
- To lose another player, type: lose <player>

WhirlWind The lemmings roaming this MUD are dangerous not just to themselves (e.g. possessing suicidal tendencies), but to players as well. Do them before they do you. *WhirlWind* also has a newbie zone, a rather difficult Fairy Book Land, a zone based on Sherwood Forest, and a namesake funnel quest with tons of mobiles and several deathtraps throughout the maze. ✓**INTERNET**→*telnet* bubba. ucc.okstate.edu 6715→<your character's name>→<y or n>→<your password>→<your password>

Stats
- Difficulty: average
- Competition: live
- Number of players: 1+
- Interface: ASCII, ANSI
- Server: AberMUD
- Platforms: all

Commands
- To get information about how to play, type: help *or* info
- To send a message to all wizards, type: wish <message>
- To get a list of administrators, type: powers
- To view a map of the game, type: info map
- To speak on the gossip channel, type: gossip <message>
- To automatically view exits as you an enter a room, type: auto-exit

Other worlds

The optimist says, "This is the best of all possible worlds";

the pessimist says, "You're right"; and the Net says, "How about a living Toon Town (**ToonMUSH II**) right out of *Roger Rabbit*, a virtual *Hitchhiker's Guide* (**ApexMUSH**), or the *Narnia* wardrobe of C. S. Lewis made into an interactive, open-ended adventure?"

On the Net

Bits of everything

ApexMUSH From virtual Paris to the *Starship Enterprise*, *ApexMUSH* has an eclectic mixture of themes. From the central hub you can choose among seven independent areas, including the Snow Crash area with its R-rated futuristic cyberpunk atmosphere based on the book by Neal Stephenson, and Periland, where you can walk through the insides of a dragon. (Warning: not for the squeamish!)

Or stroll through Paris, seek adventures in the Hidden Worlds area, take a trip back through time to Celtic Magic, or visit Starbase, which uses space themes from *Hitchhiker's Guide to the Galaxy*, *Star Trek*, and others. Be sure to check out the library in Islandville, which contains a map, an index of adventures, information on puzzles, themes, social areas, and directions on how to get everywhere. If you intend to keep coming back to *Apex*, make your way to one of the virtual hotels, where you can set up your own room. √**INTERNET**→*telnet* apex.ccs.yorku.ca 4201→connect guest guest

By the portal—downloaded from lajkonik.cyf-kr.edu.pl.

Stats
- Difficulty: average
- Competition: live
- Number of players: 1+
- Interface: ASCII
- Server: MUSH
- Platforms: all

Commands
- To learn how to play, type: mud lessons
- To get back to the hub from anywhere on the MUSH, type: hub

Metaverse Need to get away for the evening? Stop by the *Metaverse*. Visit an orbital space station, knock back some ale at Saucy Jack's Pub, or cheer on the Freegate University "Fightin' Freegate Flatworms." This is a pay-for-play MUD—you must belong to the Illuminati Online—and the different areas of the world are accessible through a portal in the giant pyramid known as Freegate. They include horror, science fiction, and adult areas.

Noteworthy is the Freegate business district, where real-world businesses can set up areas for players to visit and learn about their products and services. New players will find the *Metaverse* an extremely friendly place. √**INTERNET**→*telnet* metaverse.io.com 7777 →connect guest $ *Info:* √**INTERNET** ...→*www* http://io.com/root.html ...→*email* info@io.com ✉ *Email for automated info*

Stats
- Difficulty: average
- Competition: live
- Number of players: 1+
- Interface: ASCII
- Server: MOO
- Platforms: all

TinyCWRU Claims to be the second oldest MU* in the world. When you get there, follow the Newbie Trail for a general intro to MUSHing. Visit Simpsonland, explore intestines, or witness the beginning of time, to mention just a few of the possibilities. Creation has been given free reign here, so you just don't know what you'll find. Look in the Map Room near Nexus Nexus for some tips on interesting sites—or just wander around. Consider checking into the Grand Hotel, especially if you're planning to come back and would like your own room. The hotel has 555 rooms, 65 floors, a working virtual phone system, and its own indoor mall. Look in the fine-art shop at the mall; there are original works there you can view. If you get lost, which is pretty easy, you can always type "home" which will take you back to the steam tunnels. √**INTERNET**→*telnet* caisr2.caisr.cwru.edu 4201→connect guest guest

Stats
- Difficulty: average
- Competition: live
- Number of players: 1+
- Server: MUSH
- Platforms: all

Commands
- To get more information, go to Information Central
- To get help, type the emergency number: 100

Cartoons & Comics

ToonMUSH II This zany cartoon MUSH is a great place for exploring. Guests connect as the character Eddie Valliant from the movie *Who Framed Roger Rabbit?* First head for the Square (just type "Square"), which is a central gathering place and has a bulletin board with announcements of new areas and things to do.

From the Square just type "WALT" and you'll be at the entrance to the Magic Kingdom and Epcot Center. Most of your favorite features of the Magic Kingdom are here, including the Pirates of the Caribbean ride. Be sure to "look left" and "look right" as you float along to get compelling descriptions of scenes from the bayou.

You can also catch the Toon Trolley (you have to wait for it to come), which will transport you to the main areas of the MUSH, including Warner Studios, Disney's Main Gate, Miscellaneous Square, and Toon Purgatory. There are several places where you can claim a space of your own and do some building, but the Disneyland Hotel is a good place to start. The cartoon theme gives you the freedom to create just about anything. ✓**INTERNET**→*telnet* merlin.mit.edu 1941→connect guest guest

Stats
- Difficulty: average
- Competition: live
- Number of players: 1+
- Interface: ASCII
- Server: MUSH
- Platforms: all

Commands
- To move to the square in the center of town, type: town
- To move to the gates of Walt Disney World, type: WALT

Two Moons MUSH Based on the *Elfquest* comics created by Wendy and Richard Bini and the corresponding RPG, MUSH life centers around the conflicts between elves and humans and the disputes among different groups of elves on the World of Two Moons. You can choose to join a group of elves (or humans or trolls) while creating your character, but you need approval of the player in charge of that group before you become an "official" member—probably the process serves as an idiot filter. The elf settlements are a bit difficult to navigate through and the theme is a bit bizarre, but if you're an *Elfquest* fan, there's a lot of noncompetitive, quality role-playing here. ✓**INTERNET**→*telnet* lupine.org 4202→connect guest guest

Stats
- Difficulty: average
- Competition: live
- Number of players: 1+
- Interface: ASCII
- Server: MUSH
- Platforms: all

Commands
- To get information, type: news *or* help
- To get a list of online wizards, type: +wizards

Novel-based MUDs

Discworld *Discworld*—"the land of the midnight frog, the place to be if you're a frog in a person's clothing"—is the setting. Based on the *Discworld* series of books by Terry Pratchett, the MUD is as social and light-hearted as an LP gets, albeit with constant bar brawls and killing sprees. For the adventurous, there are close to 40 quests based on the Pratchett stories. Check out the infamous Mended Drum, a favorite hangout. ✓**INTERNET**→*telnet* mud.com-pulink.co.uk 4242→<your character's name>→<y or n>→<your password>→<your password>→<male *or* female>→[return]

Stats
- Difficulty: average
- Competition: live
- Number of players: 1+
- Interface: ASCII
- Server: LPMUD
- Platforms: all

Commands
- To get information on how to play, type: help
- To get a list of people who are devoted to helping players, type: finger liaison
- To get a list of administrators, type: finger admin
- To see a list of actions you can perform, type: l souls

DragonLance A fairly new MUSH based on the popular *DragonLance Chronicles* and the fantasy world of Krynn. The year is 353, shortly after the *DragonLance Chronicles* conclude. The War of the Lance is drawing to an end, and the people of Krynn are trying to rebuild their lives. The emphasis is on role-playing (you're encouraged to stay "in character"), and your statistics influence the results of simple conflicts. Statistics measure strength, ability, endurance, intelligence, and willpower. You can strengthen your statistics by spending points on them, some of which you receive at the beginning, the rest to be earned with good role-playing. ✓**INTERNET**→*telnet* yacht.slip.an drew.cmu.edu 6250→connect guest guest

Stats
- Difficulty: average
- Competition: live
- Number of players: 1+
- Interface: ASCII
- Server: MUSH

Commands
- To get information about the MUSH, type: news *or* help
- To nominate a character for good role-playing, type: +nom

<name of character you're nominating>

Elenium MUSH Enter a time of religious upheaval and political intrigue. This world is based on David Eddings's *Elenium* books and is dated about 100 years after the events in *The Sapphire Rose*. The Elene church is divided over doctrinal issues, the King of Elenia has killed himself, and the Zemochs (who lost their God in the war 100 years earlier) are in a state of confusion. You'll begin by choosing a nationality: Chyrellan, Zemoch, Styric, Arcium, or Elenian. Voilà! You've generated a character; now go save the church. "*Deus vult!*" ✓**INTERNET**→*telnet* clayton.ru.ac.za 4201→connect Guest Guest *Info:* ✓**INTERNET**→*ftp* mary.iia.org→anonymous→<your email address>→/pub/mush/elenium

Stats

- Difficulty: average
- Competition: live
- Number of players: 1+
- Interface: ASCII
- Server: MUSH
- Platforms: all

Commands

- To get information, type: news or events

NarniaMush *NarniaMUSH* is based on the classic children's series *The Chronicles of Narnia* by C. S. Lewis. As a new player, you begin in the Spare Room, just as the four children began their adventures in *The Lion, the Witch, and the Wardrobe*. From there you proceed into a world of fauns, beavers, warrior mice, and the Sons and Daughters of Adam and Eve. The MUSH is set in an era just after King Caspian X's voyage to the end of the world, as told in *The Dawn Treader*.

Careful reconstructions

Much of the land of Narnia, as well as the foreign lands of Calormene, Archenland, Ettinsmoor, and the Islands of the Great Eastern Sea, are careful reconstructions of the lands in the book. Players can choose to portray characters from the books or invent new characters. There is very little combat in the MUD, and the few sparrings that do occur take place in a narrative style to advance the ongoing story. Most of the game play is centered on role-play, socialization, exploration, and the creation of new parts of the world. A fairly new trend on the MUSH is to offer TinyQuests (standard adventures and puzzles) in addition to the improv role-playing already going on.

> "Shhhhhhh... Amid the smell of incense and the sound of gongs and chanting, you have come upon the glorious *Zen MOO*. Please be quiet, and enjoy your meditation.'"

Storybook world

The land of Narnia is tamer than most other MUDs, and although most of the players are college age and older, children should like this storybook world. Familiarity with the stories is suggested—check out the books in the Ketterlys' attic (the room in which you first appear) for summaries. Then take the Tour Wagon from the Lamppost or from the town of Beaversdam for a brief introduction. Be patient, you may have to wait for it. And do pay a visit to the MouseTrap Tavern—a regular gathering place. ✓**INTERNET**→*telnet* argo.unm.edu 6250→connect Guest Guest *Register:* ✓**INTERNET** ...→*email* peters@muff.cs.mcgill.ca ✍ *Email to register your character* ...→*email* VanceB@eworld.com ✍ *Email to register your character* *Support:* ✓**INTERNET**→*email* narnia-request@sadria.gb.nrao.edu

Stats

- Difficulty: average
- Competition: live
- Number of players: 1+
- Interface: ASCII
- Server: MUSH
- Platforms: all

Commands

- To get information, type: news
- To get a list of places to which you can travel, type: +travel
- To get hints about what to do, type: +hints

Zen MOO

Zen MOO Dedicated to the "weary Internet wanderer," says its owner. Occasional mutterings will be heard as well as the announcements of people coming and going on the MOO, but other than that, it's you, your Karma, and your screen. "Shhhhhhh... Amid the smell of incense and the sound of gongs and chanting, you have come upon the glorious *Zen MOO*. Please be quiet, and enjoy your meditation." Need we say more? Ahh, but there is more. It's not quite as it seems.... ✓**INTERNET**→*telnet* cheshire.oxy.edu 7777 →create <your meditation name>→<your meditation password>

Stats

- Difficulty: simple
- Competition: live
- Number of players: 1+
- Interface: ASCII
- Server: MOO
- Platforms: all

Roguelike games

The old beggar with the eye patch whispered to me of treasures buried deep in the

Internet—of adventures to be had and gold to be won. He told me there would be great dangers but great glory as well. I tossed him a piece of silver for his trouble and headed out to find these lost dungeons and make my fortune in the world. First I found the **Dungeons of Moria**. I was a half-elven wizard with dreams of killing the Balrog at the bottom of the pits. Then I discovered *Mazes of Menace* and **NetHack**. Then the *Pits of Angband* and the Caverns of **Larn**. Eventually I ended up in a sewer in Seattle.

On the Net

Angband

Angband Fans of J.R.R. Tolkien's works will certainly want to try this one. You are a lone adventurer—perhaps a hobbit, dwarf, or high elf—descending into the Pits of Angband to try to defeat the evil Morgoth. The game's monsters and magical artifacts have been taken directly from *The Lord of the Rings, The Hobbit,* and the *Silmarillion,* so having read the books is an advantage! The *Angband* quest will probably take you weeks, maybe even months, to finish, not to mention the number of times you have to start over again because you've perished. One word of advice: Be

The Balrog—downloaded from lajkonik. cyf-kr.edu.pl.

careful before putting on any strange rings. The game uses letters and keyboard symbols to represent the map of the dungeon, the player, and the various monsters and treasures. As with most roguelike games, the rules are based loosely on Dungeons and Dragons. ✓**INTERNET**→*ftp* ftp. cis.ksu.edu→anonymous→<your email address>→/pub/Games/ Angband ✓**AMERICA ONLINE**→*keyword* mgm→Software Libraries→ *Software search by file name:* Angband2.0.2.sea (for Macs) ...→*keyword* pgm→Software Libraries→*Search by file name:* ANGEXE14.EXE (for DOS)

Stats
- Difficulty: complex
- Competition: personal best
- Interface: ASCII
- Number of players: 1
- Platforms: DOS, Amiga, Atari, Macintosh, UNIX

The Angband Home Page Link into the *Angband* archives or read the game's official newsgroup. Bone up on your *Angband* knowhow by studying the several infor-

mation-packed lists available from this site: the Complete Artifacts List, a list of magic spells, a list of unique monsters and their abilities, a list of good items, etc. Don't forget to peek at the giant Angband Strategy Guide—it may be just what you need, especially if you're a newbie. ✓**INTERNET**→*www* http://www.cen.uiuc.edu/~tm826 4/angband.html

"Wizards and Warriors? Ha! In this game you can be an alien con artist or a sexy female wrestler. Wander through the tunnels beneath eight cities, starting with Seattle, and fight off mad scientists and crazed junkies as you look for the BOSS. Whack him and you win. Otherwise you're food for worms."

Roguelike Games **Role-playing & Adventure**

The Official Angband Archive
Look here for the latest versions of *Angband* for several platforms. And if the game has you stuck, look in directory /doc for tips, spoiler FAQs, and other clues to help you defeat the evil Morgoth. ✓**INTERNET** ...→*ftp* ftp.cis.ksu.edu→ anonymous→<your email address> →/pub/Games/Angband ...→*ftp* ftp.engg.ksu.edu→anonymous→ <your email address>→/pub/ Games/Angband ...→*gopher* gopher.engg.ksu.edu→ENGG FTP Archives→Angband ...→*email* mailserver@cis.ksu.edu ✍ *To get info about accessing files via email, type in message body:* help

---

rec.games.roguelike.angband (ng) Features the best discussion and latest information on *Angband*. Not sure whether you should keep the Black Dragon Scale Armor or throw it out and don the Blue Dragon Armor? Need to know how to kill a Druj? Perhaps if you buy an ale for a surly *Angband* veteran, you can pick up some tips for surviving the Pits of Angband. ✓**USENET** *FAQ:* ✓**INTERNET**→*ftp* ftp.cis.ksu.edu→ anonymous→<your email address> →/pub/Games/Angband/doc→A NGBAND.FAQ

BOSS

BOSS Like forget all the dungeon hype, chummer. The future is where it's at. Wizards and Warriors? Ha! In this game you can be an alien con artist or a sexy female wrestler. Wander through the tunnels beneath eight cities, starting with Seattle, and fight off mad scientists and crazed junkies as you look for the *BOSS*. Whack him and you win. Otherwise you're food for worms. Perhaps the most original of the roguelike games, this *Moria/Angband* offshoot has a new setting, no magic, and a sick

sense of humor to boot. Uses the standard ASCII map and wandering @ symbol to illustrate the game action. ✓**INTERNET**→*ftp* ftp. cis.ksu.edu→anonymous→<your email address>→/pub/Games/ Moria/boss ✓**AMERICA ONLINE**→ *keyword* mgm→Software Libraries→ *Search by file name:* MacBOSS.sea
Stats
• Difficulty: average
• Competition: personal best
• Number of players: 1
• Interface: ASCII
• Platforms: Macintosh ,VMS

Crossfire

Cardiff's Crossfire Pages You bring the web browser, Cardiff's Web Site will do the rest. Not only does this web site feature downloadable source code and links to all the Net Crossfire servers (for Internet multiplayer *Crossfire* games), it also has spoilers. Looking for a general guide to surviving? Map making? Spell casting? Prayer? There are guides for all these and more. Links to two other *Crossfire* web pages—with unique content—are available as well. ✓**INTERNET**→*www* http:// www.cm.cf.ac.uk/Crossfire/

Crossfire *Crossfire* is a multiplayer roguelike game (one of the few multiplayer games in the genre), with several hundred maps and a dizzying array of monsters—some are smart, others aggressive, and others trainable as pets! There is no specific theme, other than accruing power and money, but there are many quests that must be completed. While *Crossfire* offers a shared world—players run copies of the game on their computer and connect to servers via the Internet—if players are exploring different regions, they might not even know someone else is on unless they see that telltale icon approach their window. ✓**INTERNET** …→*ftp* ftp.world.net→anonymous→ <your email address>→/pub/ crossfire …→*ftp* yoyo.cc.monash. edu.au→anonymous→<your email address>→/pub/crossfire …→*ftp* ftp.ifi.uio.no→anonymous→<your email address>→/pub/crossfire

Stats
• Difficulty: complex
• Competition: live
• Number of players: 1+
• Interface: graphical
• Platforms: UNIX, X Windows
Requirements: *Requires an ANSI C compiler*

Hack

ChrHack *ChrHack* is a program for editing *NetHack's* ASCII symbols and replacing them with graphic representations of monsters and treasures. ✓**INTERNET**→*ftp* wuarchive.wustl.edu→anonymous→ <your email address>→/systems/ ibmpc/msdos-games/Utils→ chrhac23.zip DOS
Requirements: *386 or better*

Hack Lite If you can't "hack" it, try this: *NetHack* with training wheels. Definitely for beginners. ✓**INTERNET**→*ftp* wuarchive.wustl. edu→anonymous→<your email address>→/systems/amiga/aminet/ game/role→ HackLite2_1.lha

Stats
• Difficulty: simple
• Competition: personal best
• Number of players: 1
• Interface: ASCII
• Platform: Amiga

NetHack After years of study at the adventurer's guild, you're ready to do the impossible. Which is exactly what the adventurer's guild expects you to do as a "graduation exercise." Stand at the entrance to the Mazes of Menace. Once you enter there is no turning back until you retrieve the Amulet of Yen-

dor. According to legend, the Gods will grant immortality to whoever braves the mazes to retrieve it. Ignoring the shaking of your knees, you take that first step down the stairs, knowing you will find either death or glory below…. *NetHack* is a dungeon adventure game that uses letters and symbols to represent a map of the Mazes of Menace. Commands are entered using one- and two-stroke keyboard commands. In addition to the major platforms, *NetHack* has been ported to OS/2, NT, and VMS. Source code is also available. Called *NetHack* because it was written by several programmers in the Net community. ✓**INTERNET**→ *ftp* linc.cis.upenn.edu→anonymous →<your email address>→/pub/ NH3.1/binaries (for source code) ✓**AMERICA ONLINE**→*keyword* mgm→ Software Libraries→*Software search by file name:* NetHack v.3.1.3 (for Mac) …→*keyword* pgm→Software Libraries→*Search by file name:* NH313PC.ZIP (for DOS) ✓**COMPUSERVE**→*go* gamers→Libraries→ *Search by file name:* NH3132.ZIP or NH3133.ZIP (for DOS) ✓**GENIE**→ *keyword* scorpia→Gamers Libraries →Set Software Library→MS-DOS Games & Programs→*Download a file:* 2250 or 7748 (for DOS)

Stats
• Difficulty: complex
• Competition: personal best
• Number of players: 1
• Interface: ASCII
• Platforms: DOS, Amiga, Atari, Macintosh, OS/2, UNIX, X Windows ,VMS

The NetHack Archive Looking for dungeon descriptions? Perhaps tips for a beginner? Maybe a list of artifacts? Spoilers? Versions of the official guidebook? Source code? It's all here. ✓**INTERNET**→*ftp* ftp.krl. caltech.edu→anonymous→<your email address>→/pub/nethack

Hot Hints

• Brush up on your Tolkien.

• Check out an artifact (magic items with a unique name) in a Tolkien dictionary or in a spoiler FAQ before using it. Your found artifact might be cursed!

• Buy extra light and rations in town before starting.

PC Hack The predecessor to NetHack. ✓**COMPUSERVE**→*go* gamers→Libraries→*Search by file name:* HACK36.ZIP

Stats
• Difficulty: average
• Competition: personal best
• Number of players: 1
• Interface: ASCII
• Platform: DOS

rec.games.roguelike.nethack (ng) Lost in the Mazes of Menace? Follow a ball of string to this newsgroup, where NetHackers gather after a hard day in the dungeons. Someone will be able to help you, you can be sure. And when you finally reach the amulet, here is where to tell the world. Also look here for news regarding new versions and ports of *NetHack.* ✓**USENET**

Larn

Larn Your daughter is sick with a mysterious disease. Nothing seems to halt her deterioration. In your desperation you decide to gamble on a legend. There was once a mighty wizard called Polineaus, who made his home in the Caverns of Larn. Although the mage died many years ago, the caverns are rumored to contain many wondrous magical artifacts. Perhaps there you can find something to cure her—but you had better hurry. *Larn* is a roguelike game that imposes a time limit. You don't have forever to finish your quest. ✓INTERNET ...→*ftp* wu. archive.wustl.edu→anonymous→ <your email address>→/systems/ amiga/aminet/game/role→ larn.zoo (for Amiga) ...→*ftp* nic. funet.fi→anonymous→<your email address>→/pub/msdos/games/ adventure→larn123e.zoo (for DOS) ✓**AMERICA ONLINE**→*keyword* pgm→Software Libraries→*Search by file name:* larn123e.zip (for DOS) ✓**COMPUSERVE**→*go* gamers→ Libraries→*Search by file name:* LARN12.ARC (for DOS) ✓**GENIE**→*keyword* scorpia→Gamers Libraries→Set Software Library→MS-DOS Games & Programs→*Download a file:* LARN12A.ARC (for DOS)

Stats
- Difficulty: average
- Competition: personal best
- Number of players: 1
- Interface: ASCII
- Platforms: DOS, Amiga, Atari, UNIX

Moria

Jamoria *Jamoria* is a work-in-progress version of *Moria* that adds outdoor adventuring, multiple dungeons and towns, and the druid character class. ✓**INTERNET**→ *ftp* wuarchive.wustl.edu→anonymous→<your email address>→/systems/mac/info-mac/game→jamoria-10d.hqx (for Macs)

Stats
- Difficulty: average
- Competition: personal best
- Number of players: 1
- Interface: ASCII
- Platforms: Macintosh, UNIX

Moria Gather your gold, your mettle, and your sword. Then descend into the Dungeons of Moria, where you will find treasures

and monsters galore—and, if you have the right stuff, the Balrog as well. Veterans of early Dungeons and Dragons will feel at home in this "hack and slash" adventure game, which borrows its setting and theme equally from D&D and Tolkien. The quest? To face the Balrog and live to tell about it. Merely surviving a battle with him wins the game. But there are plenty of dangers to face and treasures to accumulate in order to do that. *Moria* uses keyboard symbols and letters to map out the dungeon and tell you what monster is killing you and what treasures you have found. A highly popular and very addictive adventure game. *Moria* is available for most platforms. ✓**INTERNET**→*ftp* ftp.cis.ksu.edu→ anonymous→<your email address> →/pub/Games/Moria ✓**COMPUSERVE**→*go* gamers→Libraries→ *Search by file name:* MORIA.SIT <or> MOR54C.ZIP (for Mac and DOS, respectively) ✓**GENIE**→*keyword* scorpia→Gamers Libraries→ Set Software Libarary→All Libraries →*Download a file:* 4120 or 4121 ✓**AMERICA ONLINE**→*keyword* pgm→ Software Libraries→*Search by file name:* moria5.zip (for DOS)

Stats
- Difficulty: complex
- Competition: offline
- Number of players: 1
- Interface: ASCII
- Platforms: DOS, Amiga, Atari,

> **"A dizzying array of monsters—some are smart, others aggressive, and others trainable as pets!"**

Macintosh, UNIX

The Official Moria FTP Site The Dungeons of Moria descend deep into this archive. Delving here will turn up treasures for the explorer, including the latest *Moria* game for your platform, survival guides, source codes for programmers, and spoiler FAQs for cheaters. Also look for "unofficial" variations of *Moria* like *Jamoria*. ✓**INTERNET** ...→*ftp* ftp.cis.ksu.edu→ anonymous→<your email address> →/pub/Games/Moria ...→*email* mailserver@cis.ksu.edu ✍ *To get info about accessing files via email, type in message body:* help ...→*gopher* gopher.engg.ksu.edu→ENGG FTP Archive→Moria ...→ *www* file://ftp.engg.ksu.edu/pub/Games /Moria/

rec.games.roguelike.moria (ng) Not many have faced the Balrog and survived, but those who have, and those who hope to, congregate here. Share tricks, tips, and stories of your adventures in *Moria*. (Note: Although *Angband* was originally discussed here, all *Angband* discussion and questions should be directed to rec.games. roguelike.angband.) ✓**USENET** *FAQ:* ✓**INTERNET**→*ftp* ftp.cis.kis.edu→ anonymous→<your email address> →/pub/Games/ Moria/doc

Omega

alt.games.omega (ng) From where to look for the Star Gem to how to compensate for the program's bugs (this is shareware, after all!), the newsgroup offers low volume coverage of the game *Omega*. If your news reader does not carry it, try rec.games.rogue like.misc for discussion. ✓**USENET**

Omega *Omega* is in a class by itself. The game offers richer, more detailed descriptions than the other roguelike games, several developed villages outside the main city, multiple dungeons (each with a unique monster lurking at the very bottom), and an oracle to send you on various quests. But perhaps the best feature of this game is the chance to play as yourself! Choosing this feature at the start of the game will lead you through a series of questions that convert your real-life traits into game characteristics. So if you dare to go into the dark yourself, this game is for you! There are several ways to get your name on the "high score" list; become the highest-ranking member of one of the rogue's guilds, religious sects, or mage's colleges, or kill the most monsters and get the most treasure. There's a secret to "winning" the entire game. But, naah, we aren't telling. √**INTERNET** →*ftp* monu 1.cc.monash.edu.au→ anonymous→<your email address> →/pub/omega→omega79p 1.zip (for DOS) √**COMPUSERVE**→*go* gamers→Libraries→*Search by file name:* OMEGA.ARC (for DOS) √**GENIE**→*keyword* scorpia→Gamers Libraries→*Download a file:* 934 (for DOS)

Stats
- Difficulty: average
- Competition: personal best
- Number of players: 1
- Interface: ASCII, ANSI
- Platforms: DOS, Amiga, Atari, OS/2, UNIX, Windows

Rogue

Clones of Rogue This is the grandfather of all the roguelike games—well, almost. The original *Rogue* is no longer available, but clones of it are. And while a *Rogue* clone may be less complicated (and less exciting) than the other roguelike offspring now available, it *is* still a good dungeon game. You are a thief character descending into the dungeons in search of

treasures and glory, and the dungeon is populated with monsters looking to make you their next meal. The game uses letters, keyboard symbols, and numbers to draw the map and illustrate the horrors you must kill. √**INTERNET** …→*ftp* ftp.uu.net→anonymous→ <your email address>→/usenet/ comp.sources.games/volume 1→ rogue (for source code) …→*ftp* macbeth.cogsci.ed.ac.uk→anonymous→<your email address> →/pub→rogue.zip (for DOS) √**COMPUSERVE**→*go* gamers→Libraries→*Search by file name:* ROGUE3.ZIP (for DOS) √**GENIE**→*keyword* scorpia→Gamers Libraries→Set Software Library→All Libraries→*Download a file:* 2645 (for DOS)

Stats
- Difficulty: average
- Competition: personal best
- Number of players: 1
- Interface: ASCII
- Platforms: DOS, UNIX

rec.games.roguelike.rogue (ng) It's pretty lonely here, but if you wait long enough, some gray-bearded old warrior—who refused to embrace *Moria*, *Hack*, or the other rogue offspring—will start a discussion. √**USENET**

Support sites

rec.games.roguelike.announce (ng) Here is where the heralds trumpet news of new roguelike games and announce new ports and patches. √**USENET**

rec.games.roguelike.misc (ng) Want hints for the games *Larn*, *BOSS*, and *Omega*? Find your way to this newsgroup for tips and discussion. √**USENET**

Roguelike Games FAQ Confused by the number of roguelike games out there? Want to know if

there's a new version of your favorite game available? This FAQ lists all the common (and some uncommon) roguelike games, along with a few features, related newsgroups, and FTP sites. The FAQ is also posted periodically to the various rec.games.roguelike* newsgroups as well as rec.games. roguelike.moria and rec.games. roguelike.nethack. √**INTERNET** …→*ftp* rtfm.mit.edu→anonymous→ <your email address>→/pub/ usenet-by-group/news.answers/ games→ roguelike …→*ftp* ftp.uu. net→anonymous→<your email address>→/usenet/news.answers/ games→ roguelike.Z

Roguelike Games Files The searches will pull several roguelike games, spell and monster lists, walk-throughs, guides, and modules for use with the many rogues. √**COMPUSERVE**→*go* gamers →Libraries→*Search by keyword:* hack or rogue or moria

> "Choosing this feature at the start of the game will lead you through a series of questions that convert your real-life traits into game characteristics. So if you dare to go into the dark yourself, this game is for you!"

Text adventures

In the age of texture-mapped 3D morphing, playing a text

adventure is the sensory equivalent of reading a book or—try not to lose us on this crazy idea—actually listening to music without watching a video. So give your mind's eye a little exercise with the **Interactive Fiction Archives, The Quest for the Holy Grail**, or the greatest all-time classic of computer gaming, the humbly named **Adventure**.

Fighting the dragon—downloaded from lajkonik.cyf-kr.edu.pl.

On the Net

Analysis

comp.sys.ibm.pc.games.adventure (ng) Discuss adventure games—which originally were text-based exploration and riddle games (named after the original interactive treasure story, *Adventure*) but are now often decorated with graphics and combat sequences. Games that are subjected to heavy analysis include *Hand of Fate*, *Judgment Rites*, and *King's Quest 6*. This newsgroup usually eclipses the related newsgroups comp.sys.ibm.pc.hardware.cd-rom and alt.cd-rom. Do check out the classic newsgroups rec.games.int-fiction and comp.sys.ibm.pc.games.rpg for some heavy role-playing. ✓**USENET**

---

rec.games.int-fiction (ng) Great care has been taken to provide hints without ruining the challenges. The 1992 FAQ has a good history of the text-based adventure games that once ruled the

earth, especially the ones from the defunct Infocom computer-game publisher. The newsgroup's FTP site has MS-DOS, Unix, and Amiga utilities for peeking into the standardized formats of all Infocom games and characters, as well as a strong collection of games and cheat sheets. ✓**USENET** *Archives:* ✓**INTERNET** ...→*ftp* ftp.gmd.de→anonymous→<your email address>→/if-archive ...→*ftp* wuarchive.wustl.edu→anonymous→<your email address>→/mirrors/if-archive

Archives

Interactive Fiction Archives Open up this treasure chest and you'll discover a lot more than just the archives for the interactive-fiction newsgroups—anything having to do with interactive fiction can be found here. The best (and the worst) of the classic shareware text-adventure games, authoring tools, hints, FAQs, newsletters, mapping tools, and gaming solutions are found here. Especially noteworthy are the history of IF

games and the programming manuals found in the /info directory. ✓**INTERNET**→*ftp* ftp.gmd.de→anonymous→<your email address>→/if-archives

Design

rec.arts.int-fiction (ng) "<Open door>" You see a computer lab full of game programmers. They are sitting at their keyboards writing interactive fiction games while carrying on technical conversations. In the corner you hear the fire crackle. "<Listen to programmers>" The programmers are discussing parsers, hypertext, character development, plots, settings, and game design. "<Exit>" The newsgroup is primarily for those who write and program interactive fiction games. To discuss *playing* games, see rec.games.int-fiction. ✓**USENET** *Archives:* ✓**INTERNET**→*ftp* ftp.gmd.de→anonymous→<your email address>→/if-archives

Downloads

Adventure Download the game you pay to play on the commercial services. ✓**INTERNET** ...→*ftp* atari.archive.umich.edu→anonymous→<your email address>→/atari/Games→adventr.arc (for Atari) ...→*ftp* risc.ua.edu→anonymous→<your email address>→/pub/games/colossal→colossal.zip (for DOS) ...→*ftp* wuarchive.wustl.edu→anonymous→<your email address>→/systems/ibm-pc/msdos-games/TextAd→adv350.zip (for DOS)
Stats
• Difficulty: average
• Competition: personal best
• Number of players: 1
• Interface: ASCII
• Platforms: all

Zork The grandaddy of all text adventures. ✓**INTERNET**→*ftp* wuarchive.

wustl.edu→anonymous→<your email address>→/systems/mac/info-mac/game→zork-27m. hqx

Stats
- Difficulty: average
- Competition: personal best
- Number of players: 1
- Interface: ASCII
- Platform: Macintosh

Games

BlackDragon The precursor to all those *Moria/Rogue/Hack* games. The player wanders through a dungeon and monsters drop out of nowhere and attack. The game shows you, in straight ASCII, the portion of the map you're in, but you'll want to maintain a map as you go along. The interface seems primitive—fighting is simply a matter of typing "fight" over and over—but there are more options available than you think. ✓**COMPUSERVE**→*go* gam-590 ✓**GENIE**→*keyword* dragon

Stats
- Difficulty: average
- Competition: personal best
- Number of players: 1
- Interface: ASCII
- Platforms: all

Classic Adventure This is the classic adventure where the magic word is "xyzzy" and the mazes have twisty little passages. But it's also primitive—commands are limited to two-word phrases, and the game's world is a bit disorganized—and you may get lost in a forest or in the underground caves. Really lost. Forever. Sort of the way adventures in RL usually end. ✓**COMPUSERVE**→*go* gam-200 ✓**DELPHI**→*go* ent adv adv ✓**GENIE**→*keyword* adventure

Stats
- Difficulty: average
- Competition: personal best
- Number of players: 1
- Interface: ASCII

- Platforms: all

Dragon's Gate When you enter *Dragon's Gate*, you'll create a character using the online Character Generator. You choose your race (from among 20), your god, your occupation, and all the other aspects your character needs to start off with. New players generally accept the invitation to go to the Training Grounds, an interactive introduction to the game. Head north to reach the Training Square, where you can buy torches from the General Store, weapons from the Armory, and other items you'll want to take on your adventure.

City slum

Heading north, out of the square, you'll hit a crossroads, with three different areas to explore and get a taste for the game: a city slum to the east, a cemetery to the north, and a woodsy area to the west. Back south, toward the Training Square, and east are the Training Guilds, where you'll pass through the Arch to take you into the town of Spur, the center of the actual game. Once you pass through the Arch, however, that's it: you can't go back. In Spur, you'll find other players to talk to or battle with—only don't battle in the Town Square. It's off-limits for combat.

Like-minded religionists

To gain experience, head north for the Guild District, provided you've joined a guild when you created your character, south for the Noble District, where the well-to-do live, east for the temples to hook up with like-minded religionists, or west for the Merchant District, where you can buy more stuff. You'll find other regions to explore—the Poor Quarter to the northwest, the civic Arena east of Town Square for show-offy battles.

You'll even find sewers under the city, but word is they're not for the newbie. Even more game areas exist beyond Spur's boundaries. For a good, condensed explanation of the game and its commands, download the Quick_Start.file from the *Dragon's Gate* Archives on the game's main menu. Or, if you've got the time, the entire *Dragon's Gate* manual (revised) is available either as ManualRev.zip or ManualRev.arc.

DragonFire Chronicles

Also available are ASCII maps, back issues of the game's newsletter, the *DragonFire Chronicles*, and a number of other, more specific manuals for thieving, buying and selling, and even "living and dying." From the game's main menu, you'll also find a link to the Multi-Player Games RoundTable (MP-GRT), with its own bulletin-board topic for *Dragon's Gate* and a file library of more *Dragon's Gate* maps, guides, and newsletter archives. ✓**GENIE**→*keyword* dgate

Stats
- Difficulty: average
- Competition: live
- Number of players: 1+
- Interface: ASCII, ANSI
- Platforms: all

Dungeon The classic adventure that eventually became Infocom's *Zork*. Get yourself an elfish sword (you know, the kind that glows blue when danger is near) and start exploring. Remember to come back home every once in a while to store up your treasures—unless you want the thief to get hold of them. The game has an interface that actually allows for adjectives and prepositions, unlike most early games of this sort. ✓**DELPHI**→*go* ent adv dun

Stats
- Difficulty: average
- Competition: personal best

- Number of players: 1
- Interface: ASCII
- Platforms: all

Enhanced Adventure An enhanced version of *Classic Adventure*. It's larger and more time-consuming, for one thing, and while a lot of the puzzles look similar, some slight variations will keep you on your toes. Commands are also enhanced: You can "examine" things, a helpful feature not found in the original, and you can sometimes use commands of more than two words in case impending doom requires a wordy response. ✓**COMPUSERVE**→*go* gam-201 ✓**GENIE**→*keyword* a550

Stats

- Difficulty: average
- Competition: personal best
- Number of players: 1
- Interface: ASCII
- Platforms: all

Mini-adventures If you need a text-adventure fix, try a quick *Mini-adventure*. You will have to base your decisions more on guessing than on logical reasoning, and a few wrong choices will kill you off, but at least you can choose to return to where you went wrong or restart the game and try again from scratch. Choose from six mini-adventures: *Arena* (for coliseum-style combat), *Dragons Eggs* (search the castle, find the eggs), *Fridenko's Escape* (Stalinist Russia), *Maze of Madness* (find your way through 45 rooms), *The Message* (you, a lowly serf, must get a message to a general), and *Scout Ship Albacore* (space adventure). Each adventure uses multiple-choice questions to obtain your decisions. Some also ask you to roll a die or flip a coin for a random outcome. ✓**DELPHI**→*go* gro gam→Mini-adventures

Stats

- Difficulty: simple

- Competition: personal best
- Number of players: 1
- Interface: ASCII
- Platforms: all

The Quest for the Holy Grail Choose your character, stock up on goods and weapons, and it's off into an unfriendly world. In the beginning all you have to do is stay alive and learn the game. The online help is sketchy, and the monsters seem to know what they're doing. If you're a serious Quester, it'd be best to read the instructions at the top of the game. They scroll by at a startling speed, so keep your buffer open. Oh, and don't be fooled by the small-time look of things: *Quest* has a world well worth mapping. You can easily starve to death, get hopelessly lost, or both. ✓**DELPHI**→*go* ent adv que

Stats

- Difficulty: average
- Competition: personal best
- Number of players: 1
- Interface: ASCII
- Platforms: all

Solutions

The Electronic Gamer A huge archive of computer-game walkthroughs ranging from *BattleTech* to *Pacman* to *Zork*. ✓**COMPUSERVE** →*go* teg

---

Solutions Archive Hints and solutions to hundreds of adventure games. ✓**INTERNET**→*ftp* nic.funet.fi→ anonymous→<your email address> →/pub/doc/games/solutions

Zines

SPAG (j) Tired of winning *Zork*? Does *Witness* leave you listless? Looking for some new action? Read *SPAG*. *SPAG*, short for the Society for the Preservation of Adventure Games, reaches out to fans

of the Infocom games of the '70s and '80s, and keeps you up to date about the interactive fiction games that are now under development. *SPAG* is full of reviews, ads, and news relating to new interactive fiction games available over the Net. ✓**INTERNET**→*email* whizzard @uclink.berkeley.edu ✍ *Write a request Archives:* ✓**INTERNET**→*ftp* ftp.gmd.de→anonymous→<your email address>→/if-archive/SPAG

The Status Line (j) Archives of the Infocom newsletter *The Status Line*, which predominately publishes release announcements for Infocom games. ✓**DELPHI**→*go* gro gam→Infocom Newsletter

---

Part 3

Strategy & Classics

Board games

Computer and human opponents, along with discussion, for centuries-old classics like **Backgammon**, **Checkers**, and **Go** as well as modern standards such as **Bingo**, **Battleship**, and **Stratego** are available in abundance online. And then there are the variations—**Othello**, played with dividing gelatinous cubes called **Boogers**; 3D tic-tac-toe (**SneakATac**); and **Eclectic Avenue Monopoly**, which incorporates—don't ask, it takes too long to explain—virtual dart throwing.

On the Net

Across the board

Board Games Download IBM-compatible versions of classic board games such as *Yahtzee, mah jongg, chess, backgammon,* and *Chinese Checkers.* ✓**COMPUSERVE**→*go* pbsarcade

rec.games.board (ng) Although ostensibly open to discussion of all board games, the conversation is almost exclusively devoted to historical and military strategy games, especially games like *Axis & Allies.* Trading, buying, and selling—although there are separate newsgroups for these activities—account for a significant portion of the traffic. ✓**USENET** *FAQ:* ✓**INTERNET**→*ftp* rtfm.mit. edu→anonymous→<your email address>→/pub/usenet-by-hierarchy/rec/games/board→rec.games.

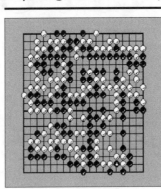

Go *board—downloaded from* http://www.cs.utexas.edu:80/90.

board_FAQ_and_intro

rec.games.board.marketplace (ng) Buy, sell, and trade board-gaming products. ✓**USENET**

Abstract games

rec.games.abstract (ng) Theoretical discussions about games with an abstract or strategy component. ✓**USENET**

Trax An abstract two-player strategy game in the tradition of *chess* and *go* in which players have to place square tiles with black-and-white designs on a board. When you place a tile, the colors at the edge have to match the colors of the neighboring tile. The first player to form a line of eight tiles with a streak or a loop of color wins. Tricky little game. Turns are submitted by email and processed by a computer moderator. The rule book can be found at the archive site. *Info:* ✓**INTERNET** …→*email* munch@soda.berkeley. edu ✍ *Type in subject line:* help …→*ftp* ftp.erg.sri.com→anonymous

→<your email address>→/pub/pbm/trax

Stats
- Difficulty: average
- Competition: turn-based
- Number of players: 2
- Interface: ASCII
- Platforms: all

Backgammon

Backgammon Although there isn't much traffic here, everything's ready for you to play over-the-board (real-time) *backgammon* or speed *backgammon* with someone else, or to leave an invitation for a postal game (one turn every so many days). You'll also find a challenge ladder and a postal tournament to join. After the computer has "rolled a die" to determine who moves first, you're off. ✓**USA TODAY INFORMATION CENTER**→*go* backgammon

Stats
- Difficulty: average
- Competition: live *or* turn-based
- Number of players: 2
- Interface: ASCII
- Platforms: all

Backgammon Roll a pair of electronic dice and remove all your pieces from the board before your opponent gets rid of his. You can also chat with your adversary while you play, or watch another game in progress—unless the players have specified it as a private game. ✓**COMPUSERVE**→*go* ecenter→ Access the Entertainment Center *Interface:* ✓**COMPUSERVE**→*go* ecn-43→Download Game Software **$**

Stats
- Difficulty: average
- Competition: live
- Number of players: 2
- Interface: graphical
- Platform: DOS

Requirements: *EGA graphics or better; 512K RAM; mouse recommended*

Backgammon A *backgammon* game for Windows. ✓**INTERNET**→ *ftp* ftp.cica.indiana.edu→anonymous→<your email address>→ /pub/win3/games→ bg06.zip

Stats
• Platform: Windows

Backgammon Games here are as leisurely or as challenging as you choose them to be. For instance, "Move Verify" allows you to "undo" a move before your choice is sent to your opponent; "Verbose" is a learning tool that guides you through the game, explaining the pros and cons of certain moves. "Double" lets your opponent know you want to double the stake of the game. He or she can either accept and play on for twice the points or decline and forfeit the wager of the game to you. Doubling is limited to 64 games. ✓**THE IMAGINATION NETWORK**→ *select* Clubhouse→Backgammon

Stats
• Difficulty: average
• Competition: live
• Number of players: 2
• Interface: graphical
• Platforms: all

Commands
• To adjust the animation speed of the dice and pieces, select: anim speed
• To record your moves to a text file, select: move log
• To see the points numbered 1–24 for beginners' reference, select: notation

FIBS-First Internet Backgammon Server The *backgammon* boards may be straight ASCII, and thus not very attractive, but the players on this always-active online *backgammon* club are not the least bit hampered by it. Challenge them to matches of limited or infinite length, join in the tournaments, or just watch a couple of highly rated players go at it.

"Who" will tell you who's around and what they're up to ("P" means they're playing, "R" means they're ready to play, a dash means they're incommunicado), and "invite <player>" will pave the way to an online matchup. Internet *backgammon* has one drawback: the board constantly scrolls off the screen due to chat and server messages. To fix this, you'll need a client program. Check the newsgroup for word of the latest software for your platform and where it's being archived. ✓**INTERNET**→*telnet* fraggel65.mdstud.chalmers.se 4321→guest→name <your username>→<your password>→<your password>

Stats
• Difficulty: average
• Competition: live
• Number of players: 2+
• Interface: ASCII
• Platforms: all

Commands
• To get instructions, type: help
• To get a list of players, type: who
• To observe a game, type: observe <player name>
• To invite a player to join a game, type: invite <player name> <"unlimited" or # of parts

rec.games.backgammon (ng) Strategies, tips, rule variants, and lots of analysis. Many regulars are FIBS players, so expect some club-by chat. ✓**USENET** *FAQ:* ✓**INTERNET**→*ftp* rtfm.mit.edu→anonymous→ <your email address>→/pub/ usenet-by-hierarchy/rec/games/ backgammon

Bingo

Bingo *Bingo* and gambling: a dangerous combination. Choose one of the *bingo* parlors to play. Parlors with numbers 1–899 allow you to bet 25 chips, maximum. Braver souls head for parlors 900 or higher, where the maximum bet

is 75 chips. If a game's in progress when you enter the room, either wait for it to end or try another parlor. You'll be given a random *bingo* card to play. If you're superstitious and prefer a different card, select "New Card" until you find one you like. Once the game begins and numbers are getting called, select "Cover" to mark your match. But don't wait to mark your card if you get five in a row. Just select "*Bingo!*" and rack up the chips. ✓**AMERICA ONLINE**→*keyword* casino→Casino Lounge→Play a Game→Play Casino Bingo

Stats
• Difficulty: simple
• Competition: live
• Number of players: 1–23
• Interface: graphical
• Platform: DOS

Commands
• To accept a proffered bingo card, select: register

Checkers

Checkers You may grow old waiting for someone to accept your *checkers* challenge here, but if you do find an opponent, or if you can arrange to meet someone online for a game, you have the option of playing a regular, real-time game or a "postal" (one turn every few days) game. There's also a tournament for *checkers* champs, in two formats: Pro-USAT (which requires a fee and presents prizes in the form of online time) and USAT (no fee, no prizes). ✓**USA TODAY INFORMATION CENTER**→*go* checkers

Stats
• Difficulty: average
• Competition: live *or* turn-based
• Number of players: 2
• Interface: ASCII
• Platforms: all

Checkers Play *checkers* against someone next door or in Europe, and chat it up while you play. If you don't like people lurking over your shoulder and commenting on your moves, select to play a private game. ✓**COMPUSERVE**→*go* ecenter→ Access the Entertainment Center *Interface:* ✓**COMPUSERVE**→*go* ecn-51→Download Game Software **$**

Stats
- Difficulty: average
- Competition: live
- Number of players: 2
- Interface: graphical
- Platform: DOS

Requirements: *EGA or VGA graphics; 512K RAM*

Checkers Deceptively simple, *checkers* can actually involve a great deal of strategy, especially when the "must jump" rule is included, which is the case here. When a capture presents itself, you must take it, regardless of the consequences. If this gets you in over your head, you may "Request Draw," and the game ends with neither winner nor loser...only chickens. ✓**THE IMAGINATION NET-WORK**→*select* Clubhouse→Checkers

Stats
- Difficulty: average
- Competition: live
- Number of players: 2
- Interface: graphical
- Platforms: all

Classic strategy

Battleship An old children's classic that seems to keep coming up in various forms on BBSs everywhere—from real-time head-to-head games to turn-based games. The winner is the last one still afloat. Results of the contest are usually posted in a Top Scores bulletin somewhere on the board. ✓CHECK LOCAL BULLETIN BOARD SYSTEMS FOR THIS OR SIMILAR GAMES

Stats
- Difficulty: simple
- Competition: live *or* turn-based

> "The Net game gives you optional rule variations, including 'Aggressor Advantage,' in which a tied battle goes to the aggressor. Without 'Aggressor Advantage' both flags are blasted off the board in an example of mutually assured destruction.

- Number of players: 2+
- Platforms: all

Eclectic Avenue Monopoly A spin-off on the board game, *Eclectic Avenue Monopoly* adds a few twists like secret squares, trivia questions, gambling, and even dart throwing! Up to eight players can compete against each other. Players get as many turns per day as the Sysop allows. ☎→*dial* 612-566-5532

Stats
- Difficulty: average
- Competition: turn-based
- Number of players: 2+
- Interface: ANSI
- Platforms: all

Stratego Once upon a time, you'd see ads for Milton Bradley's *Stratego* during afternoon reruns of *Gilligan's Island*. But that's about as online as the game got in the analog era. Now kids and adults are playing *Stratego* on INN. As in

the classic board version, you must capture your opponent's flag to win. Unlike the board game, the Net version allows you to save favorite setups for later and gives you optional rule variations, including "Aggressor Advantage," in which a tied battle goes to the aggressor. Without "Aggressor Advantage" both flags are blasted off the board in an example of mutually assured destruction. ✓**THE IMAGINATION NETWORK**→*select* SierraLand→Stratego

Stats
- Difficulty: simple
- Competition: live
- Number of players: 2
- Interface: graphical
- Platforms: all

Go

Go On an 11x11 board, players build territories by alternately placing pieces on the intersections. You can accept a standing challenge, start your own game (either real-time over-the-board games or days-between-moves postal games), play a 15-minute game of "speed" *Go*, or join a postal tournament. ✓**USA TODAY INFORMATION CENTER**→*go* go

Stats
- Difficulty: average
- Competition: live *or* turn-based
- Number of players: 2
- Interface: ASCII
- Platforms: all

Go *Go*'s been played for centuries. Surround territory on the board and try to capture your opponent's "stones." Black moves first, and players with a handicap play black. A game continues until both players "Pass," at which point you mark intersections you consider within your territory. Your opponent may reject your scoring to continue scoring, reject the truce and continue the fight, or bow his or her head. The computer will then count up each player's points. It's as simple as Yalta. ✓**THE IMAGI-NATION NETWORK**→*select* Club-house→Go

Stats
- Difficulty: average
- Competition: live
- Number of players: 2
- Interface: graphical
- Platforms: all

Go Home Page All the *Go* information you could want—and neatly packaged, too—including all the information found in the FAQ, in a more accessible form, access to the *Go* archive, information on proper *Go* etiquette, various gaming clubs, and how to make your own board. You can also jump straight to the *Go* server from here. ✓**INTERNET**→*www* http://bsdserver.ucsf.edu:8000/go/igs

Internet Go Server Novices will enjoy observing games by crack player ManyFaces, the resident *Go* robot. Then they can practice on a 9x9 or 13x13 board with old ManyFaces before taking on a master on a 19x19 board. There are several client programs you can download at the FTP site listed that will make the game easier on the eye. ✓**INTERNET**→*telnet* hellspark.wharton.upenn.edu 6969 *Interface:* ✓**INTERNET**→*ftp* bsdserver. ucsf.edu→anonymous→<your email address>→Go/clients

Stats
- Difficulty: average
- Competition: live
- Number of players: 1 or 2
- Interface: ASCII, ANSI
- Platforms: all

rec.games.go (ng) Analysis of tricky positions and various strategies abound, as well as news from both online *Go* clubs (see below) and real-life ones. The FAQ outlines the rules of the game, of course, but there is also an explanation of the handicapping and ranking systems, a complete bibliography, and a quick list of the vocabulary you need in order to converse with a nine-dan master, even if you can't play like one. ✓**USENET** *FAQ:* ✓**INTERNET**→*ftp* bsdserver. ucsf.edu→anonymous→<your email address>→/GO→FAQ

Gomuko

Gomoku A Japanese version of tic-tac-toe, with a couple of twists. In *Gomoku*, you have to try to get five in a row, instead of three. When you enter the Gomoku Game Room, a choice on the main menu, you may have to wait for an opponent to show up (unless you've planned a match in advance). Before you play, you have to decide what size grid you will play on (standard is 19x19; 13x13 is popular for shorter games), whether you'll use a chess clock, and whether you wish to use any of the optional rule variations.

Variation 1 gives you an additional way to win: by surrounding five pairs of your opponent's pieces with your pairs. Variation 2 specifies that a player may not create two "open 3s" (three in a row with at least one empty square at each end), a position that can develop into "open 4s." Variation 2 thus eliminates a favorite technique for building five in a row. ✓**GENIE**→ *keyword* gomoku

Stats
- Difficulty: simple
- Competition: live
- Number of players: 2
- Interface: ASCII
- Platforms: all

Commands
- To challenge anyone in the Game Room to a match, type: challenge all
- To send a message to another player, type: message <player's number> <message>
- To watch a game in progress, type: watch <game number>

Othello/Reversi

Boogers A gooey variation of *Reversi*. Each player has a colored, gelatinous piece called a booger. Move your booger one square, and it is "cloned"—you now have two boogers on the board. Move your booger two squares, and it will occupy the new space, leaving its former square empty. Any enemy boogers that are sitting on squares bordering your new squares will convert to your boogers' color. "Most boogers on the board" wins the game. Propose a game to a mature friend. ✓**THE IMAGINATION NETWORK**→*select* SierraLand→ Boogers

Stats
- Difficulty: simple
- Competition: live
- Number of players: 2–4
- Interface: graphical
- Platforms: all

Commands
- If your opponent(s) can't move, you may claim the board's unoccupied squares by selecting from the Options menu: claim

Boxes Prodigy's version of the popular game *Othello*. Play solo or against another person. ✓**PRODIGY** →*jump* boxes

Stats
- Difficulty: simple
- Competition: personal best *or* live
- Number of players: 1 or 2
- Interface: graphical
- Platforms: all

FlipFlop As seasoned *Reversi* players know, it can actually be a disadvantage to have a lot of pieces on the board too early—your opponent may turn them all into his own before the end of the game!

This version begins with a virtual coin toss. The winner plays white. If you want to say uncle before the game is over, select "Resign." ✓**THE IMAGINATION NETWORK**→*select* Clubhouse→FlipFlop

Stats
- Difficulty: simple
- Competition: live
- Number of players: 2
- Interface: graphical
- Platforms: all

FlipIt Using Xs and Os, this version of *Othello* lets you play against someone else online or, if no one's around, with the computer. The game uses an 8x8 grid, with columns lettered A–H and rows numbered 1–8, or a 10x10 grid for longer games. ✓**DELPHI**→*go* ent fli

Stats
- Difficulty: simple
- Competition: live
- Number of players: 1 or 2
- Interface: ASCII
- Platforms: all

Commands
- To indicate your move, type: <column letter><row number>
- To play another person, type: play <name>
- To play on a 10x10 board, type: play 10

Internet Othello Server It's *Reversi* on an ASCII server, so players are * and O instead of white and black. No password is necessary if you want to look around (type "who" to see who's around, "games" to see who's playing, and "observe <player name>" to watch the fun). You can even play a game without registering, but if you want to maintain an Othello Rating and compete in tournaments, you need to sign up. Typing "help" isn't particularly helpful; better to ask somone via the "say," "shout," or "whisper" commands to show you the ropes. Then lose

> "Each player has a colored, gelatinous piece called a booger. Move your booger one square, and it is 'cloned.' You now have two boogers on the board. Most boogers on the board wins the game."

yourself in a passionate game of *Reversi*, dive into some hefty game theory, or review the game of the week. ✓**INTERNET**→*telnet* faust.uni-paderborn.de 5000→<your full name>

Stats
- Difficulty: complex
- Competition: live
- Number of players: 2
- Interface: ASCII
- Platforms: all

Othello An 8x8 grid. You challenge the computer. The computer, however, rarely makes a mistake. ✓**DELPHI**→*go* ent boa→Othello

Stats
- Difficulty: simple
- Competition: live
- Number of players: 1
- Interface: ASCII
- Platforms: all

Reversi Surround your opponent's pieces on a 48-square checkerboard in order to reverse them. Play either over-the-board (real-time), "blitz" (in 15 minutes), or postal (days go by be-

tween two moves). There's also a challenge ladder, and there are postal tournaments to compete in. As simple a game as *Reversi* (or *Othello*) is, you'll find articles on strategy in the News, Columns, & Scoresheets area available on the main menu. ✓**USA TODAY INFORMATION CENTER**→*go* reversi

Stats
- Difficulty: average
- Competition: live *or* turn-based
- Number of players: 2
- Interface: ASCII
- Platforms: all

Shogi

Shogi-L (ml) Strategy talk about the game *Shogi*. ✓**INTERNET**→*email* listserv%technion.ac.il@vm.tau.ac.il ✍ *Type in message body:* subscribe shogi-l <your full name>

Tic-tac-toe

SneakATac A 3D version of *tic-tac-toe*, using animated pieces. Using four levels of 4x4 grids, players have to place their pieces in such a way that they connect four boxes vertically, horizontally, or diagonally. Wear your 3D glasses or your opponent will box you in. ✓**THE IMAGINATION NETWORK**→ *select* SierraLand→SneakATac

Stats
- Difficulty: simple
- Competition: live
- Number of players: 2
- Interface: graphical
- Platforms: all

Tic-Tac-Toe A graphical *tic-tac-toe* game. ✓**INTERNET**→*www* http://www.bu.edu/Games/tictactoe

Stats
- Difficulty: simple
- Competition: live
- Number of players: 1
- Platforms: all

Requirements: *A graphical web browser and SLIP connection*

Chess

Movies-on-demand, holodecks, and remote child-rearing
may all remain futuristic hype for some time, but the Net has *chess* covered—no, make that blanketed, captured, checkmated. Play a quick game on the always crowded **Internet Chess Server**; find an email match with **Email Chess Pairing** and report the results to the **Email Chess Ranking Ladder**; or access the formidable game-history archives of the **Internet Chess Library**. Tired of opponents with feelings? Play against the free, master-level GNU program.

On the Net

Across the board

CHESS (echo) The International Chess Echo serves both beginners and experts. Players debate, teach, and learn the subtleties of the game. They also play tournament or one-on-one games of correspondence *chess* through the echo. ✓**FIDONET**

Chess Play blitz games for a quick *chess* fix. Or challenge any comer to a postal or over-the-board game, depending on whether you want to wait days or minutes for your opponent to move. You can also join one of the many ongoing tournaments, or take part in a "simul" (they usually take place on Saturdays). ✓**USA TODAY INFORMATION CENTER**→*go* chess

Elmer Fudd and Bugs Bunny play chess—from chess.uoknor.edu.

Stats
- Difficulty: average
- Competition: live *or* turn-based
- Number of players: 2
- Interface: ASCII
- Platforms: all

Chess Club The club has two message boards that include the Ask the Master folder—featuring chess master Gabriel Sanchez—and a Chess Files area within the PBM & Strategy File libraries. Players gather here for casual games and special tournaments, and engage in USCF-rated competition by making arrangements within the USCF-Rated Play folder on the Chess Club message board and via email to screen name Troon.

Games are played using algebraic notation (there's a file called RULES: Notations within the Chess Files library to explain the notation to chess novices). The Chess Club also arranges Mini-Knights competitions—four-player, double-round-robin tournaments. Send your email entry request to DragoNorth. ✓**AMERICA**

ONLINE→*keyword* chess→The Chess Club

Chess Forum You'll have an edge here if you know *chess*'s algebraic notation. If you don't, download the file Notati.txt from the General/Help library for information on the three forms of notation—short, long, and computer. On the Message board, you'll find sections ranging from Chess Basics and Theory & Analysis to Ask the Masters and Oriental/Variants.

The most popular sections, however, are Casual Games, where actual matches take place; Tourneys (Reserve), in which only members below the 2000 UCSF rating level are eligible to play; and USCF Rated Games, devoted to rated matches and quads played among Chess Forum members. The file library has transcripts of matches, tournament rules, and files for the popular IBM-compatible teaching-and-game database program *ChessBase 3.0*. If all you want is to play a quick game of *chess*, however, head for the conference room Casual Games. ✓**COMPUSERVE**→*go* chess forum

ChessBoard (bbs) Log on for info about the Chicago-area *chess* scene or, if Chicago isn't your town, for *chess* software, game databases of national and international tournaments, and several chess-talk conferences. ☎→*dial* 312-784-3019

The Cleveland Chess SIG Register to find an opponent for PBeM games, record your matches and have your playing skills ranked, or participate in chess discussions in this SIG. Check out the Playing E-Mail Chess—Moves & Rules board for several thorough explanations of PBeM chess. ☎→*dial* 216-368-3888→A visitor→ Explore the system→go chess ✓**IN-**

TERNET→*telnet* freenet-in-a.cwru. edu→A visitor→Explore the system →go chess

Chess servers

Chess Two-player board games like *chess* are often available on BBSs if the BBS has more than one line. Players can compete head to head—in BBS-speak, node to node—usually using an ANSI display (colored ASCII). There are a large number of chess-related BBSs across the country. There is, without any doubt, one near you. Ask around. ✓CHECK LOCAL BULLETIN BOARDS FOR A VARIATION OF THIS GAME

Stats
- Difficulty: average
- Competition: live
- Number of players: 2
- Interface: ANSI
- Platforms: all

Chess The game of kings for two-person play. Chat with your opponent as you wipe his or her pieces off the board. Unless you've selected to play privately, others can watch and comment on your game as well. ✓**COMPUSERVE**→*go* ecenter→Access the Entertainment Center *Interface:* ✓**COMPUSERVE**→ *go* ecn-46→Download Game Software **$**

Stats
- Difficulty: average
- Competition: live
- Number of players: 2
- Interface: graphical
- Platform: DOS

Requirements: *EGA or VGA graphics*

Chess A wide range of options and an attractive graphical interface make this one of the premiere online *chess* games around. The clock allows you to specify how long a game will last (5 minutes to 150 minutes), how many moves in how much time (30 to 60 moves in 30 to 150 minutes, with a

number of variations). Or create your own "custom" clock, especially useful in handicapping an expert player against a novice. When "Verify Moves" is turned on, you'll be asked if your move is okay before it gets sent to your opponent. There's also an option that allows you to load games from other commercial *chess* programs, or save a game in another program's format using algebraic or Forsythe Board Position notation. And because everyone at one time or another has regretted a move, the game even has a Take Back option, which reverts the game to a previous state—provided your opponent agrees. ✓**THE IMAGINATION NETWORK**→*select* Clubhouse→Chess

Stats
- Difficulty: average
- Competition: live
- Number of players: 2
- Interface: graphical
- Platforms: all

Free Internet Chess Server

Another *chess* server on the Internet. Potentially an alternative to the always crowded Internet Chess Server (ICS), this server is a bit buggy and there's rarely anyone on—they're all still on the ICS! ✓**INTERNET**→*telnet* chess.pitt.edu 5000→<your handle> *Register:* ✓**INTERNET**→*email* nash@visus.com ✍ *Email request to register:* fics_ addplayer <your handle> <your full name> <your email address>

Stats
- Difficulty: average
- Competition: live
- Number of players: 2
- Interface: ASCII, graphical
- Platforms: all

Commands
- To get a list of help commands, type: help
- To get a list of ongoing games, type: games
- To observe a game or games, type: observe <game #>

- To get a copy of current game moves emailed to you, type: mailmoves <game # or player's name>
- To get a copy of the moves in a former game, type mailoldmoves <player>
- To quit, type: quit

The Internet Chess Server (ICS) To play real-time *chess* and to connect with the hub of the Internet chess community, check out the ICS. It's often packed with close to 100 players—some having been there for hours and others having just stopped by for a quick game. The server features a system to check the legality of moves, a clock that times moves, the ability to call a game, a widely followed rating system, the option of observing other players' games, a command to save a game to be resumed later, a chat system, and a dozen different board-display options—try changing them with the "style <number>" command to see which one you prefer. Finding an opponent is easy. Just challenge another player. If the player is interested, he'll accept. If not, he'll send a decline message. Everyone can play, chat, and observe, but only registered users can save their games and participate in the rating system. Graphical interfaces are available for most computer platforms (see the Internet Chess Library). √**INTERNET**→*telnet* ics.uoknor.edu 5000→<your handle> *Info:* √**INTERNET**→*ftp* chess.uoknor.edu→anonymous→<your email address>→/pub/chess/ICS_help/→icshlp.zip *Register:* √**INTERNET**→*email* icsregister@ics.uoknor.edu ✍ *Type in subject line:* ICS registration *Type in message body:* Handle: <your handle> Real-Name: <your full name> Sex: <your gender> Age: <your age> *Support:* √**INTERNET**→*email* sleator@cs.cmu.edu ✍ *Email for general questions about*

XBoard *interface—downloaded from* chess.uoknor.edu.

the chess server

Stats
- Difficulty: average
- Competition: live
- Number of players: 2
- Interface: ASCII, graphical
- Platforms: all

Commands
- To begin reading instructions on how to play, type: help intro1 *or* info
- To get a list of online administrators, type: inchannel 0
- To get a list of administrators, type: help admins
- To get a list of the games that are being played on the ICS, type: games
- To observe a game, type: observe <game number *or* player name>
- For instructions on how to initiate, accept, and decline a match, type: help intro5
- To move your piece, type: <the name of the move in extended algebraic notation>
- To get a list of the board display styles, type: help styles

Chess archives

Internet Chess Library Carries *chess*-related material including *chess* programs for several computer platforms, graphical clients for the Internet Chess Server, *chess* images (boards, champions, and ICS

players), and the rec.games. *chess* FAQs.

In the /texts subdirectory, you'll find the FIDE Laws of Chess, a *chess* history, interviews with *chess* champions, and ratings lists. Game databases from the World Championships and master games, stored in a separate subdirectory, are popular draws. With subdirectories for each computer platform, the *chess* files and programs seem almost limitless. Each platform directory has ports of the popular GNU *chess* program as well as unique programs and databases.

In the DOS subdirectory alone, there are more than 30 *chess* programs, an impressive selection of *chess* databases and interfaces, dozens of tools ranging from *chess* lessons to correspondence *chess* managers to C source files for programming, *chess* fonts, and more than a dozen "alternative" *chess* programs. Alternative programs include *checkers, Chinese Chess,* and *laser chess* programs. √**INTERNET** ...→*ftp* chess.uoknor.edu→anonymous→<your email address>→/pub/chess ...→*ftp* ftp.math.uni-hamburg.de→anonymous→<your email address>→/pub/misc/chess *Info:* √**INTERNET**→*www* ftp://chess.uoknor.edu/pub/chess/HTML/home page

Chess replay

Chess Contains results of tournaments from around the world, as well as graphic replays of big moves and matches. The support staff takes a breezy, we're-here-to-have-fun attitude toward the game, especially in the Chess Basics feature for neophytes. The Library has results and replays of other years' matches. In addition, chess enthusiasts compete in Guess-A-Move to guess the next move of a position chosen by a FIDE master from a past match somewhere in the world. Under the menu choice The Latest, the Chess feature also has links to the Games Bulletin Board and its Chess topic. ✓**PRODIGY**→*jump* chess

Chess talk

alt.chess.ics (ng) For chatting about the Internet Chess Server. ✓**USENET**

CHESS (echo) Roundtable for *chess* buffs who seek play-by-email games. ✓**RELAYNET**

Chess-L (ml) A discussion of *chess* for players of all levels. ✓**INTERNET** →*email* listserv@nic.surfnet.nl ✍ *Type in subject line:* subscribe chess-l <your full name>

gnu.chess (ml/ng) Discuss the *GNU Chess* program. Not a very active group. ✓**USENET** ✓**INTERNET**→ *email* info-gnu-chess-request@prep. ai.mit.edu ✍ *Write a request*

rec.games.chess (ml/ng) Looking for an opening move? Interested in rehashing a recent—or historical—championship match? Seeking opinions on a commercial or shareware *chess* program? Both beginners and more experienced players can find discussion threads suited to their own levels.

The newsgroup also carries tournament announcements, requests for people seeking play-by-email opponents, and information about Internet *chess* resources. The Internet Chess Servers are frequently discussed.

The two-part FAQ includes information on chess organizations, ratings and titles, tournaments, playing strategies, mailing lists, FTP sites, and more. A separate gnu.chess FAQ, devoted exclusively to the *GNU chess* program, is also posted periodically. ✓**USENET**

✓**INTERNET**→*email* chessnews-request@tssi.com ✍ *Write a request:* <your email address> *FAQ:* ✓**INTERNET**→*ftp* rtfm.mit.edu→ anonymous→<your email address> →/pub/usenet-by-hierarchy/ games/chess

Scholastic Chess (ml) Discuss scholastic *chess* issues, from elementary-school National Championships to college matches, with a decided emphasis on USCF scholastics. No gaming goes on. It's strictly discussion. The list is often quiet, with periodic bursts of activity. ✓**INTERNET**→*email* scholas tic-chess-request@cis.uab.edu ✍ *Write a request*

Play-by-email

Email Chess Pairing To find an opponent for one-on-one games of play-by-email *chess*, send your name, email address, and level of play, and within a week you should receive the email address of an opponent. Matches are available in seven UCSF rating categories: M (2200+), 1 (2000–2199), 2 (1800–1999), 3 (1600–1799), 4 (1400–1599), 5 (1200–1399), and 6 (1000–1199). William Moxley, who runs the pairing system, is quite willing to answer beginners' questions about email *chess*. ✓**INTERNET**→*email* chess. info@vpnet.chi.il.us ✍ *Type in message body:* <your full name> <your email address> <your level of play: novice, intermediate, *or* expert>
Stats
• Difficulty: average
• Competition: turn-based
• Number of players: 2
• Interface: ASCII
• Platforms: all

Email Chess Ranking Ladder Email Rob Buchner when you begin a match and when the game has been completed—the name of

the person playing the white pieces, the score, the person playing the black pieces, the date completed, the number of moves, and the type of opening. His *chess* ladders are posted once a month to rec.games.chess. ✓**INTERNET**→*email* rainbow@cbnewsc.cb.att.com ✍ *Email with match information*

Play CHESS (echo) Have you just thought of a great new gambit? Come here to try your moves. ✓**WWIVNET**

Team Email Chess Competition Play team *chess* via email. Teams may be from *chess* clubs, scholastic organizations, businesses, agencies, or other organizations. Anyone can play—from beginner to master. Just get four people together. Choose to play every day in the "frantic" category, or as infrequently as ten moves a month. Results are tallied in the rating system. ✓**INTERNET** ...→*email* harvey @marcam.com ✍ *Write a request for information* ...→*email* rpowell @uoguelph.ca ✍ *Write a request*
Stats
• Difficulty: average
• Competition: turn-based
• Number of players: 4
• Interface: ASCII
• Platforms: all

Publications

Chess Chow A bimonthly for-profit publication about *chess* that is distributed via snail mail. You can get information about *Chess Chow* by emailing Mark Ginsburg. ✓**INTERNET**→*email* mginsburg@ raider.stern.nyu.edu ✍ *Email for info*

Shareware

GIICS One of the most popular graphical interfaces to the Internet Chess Server for PC users. ✓**INTER-**

NET→*ftp* chess.uoknor.edu→anonymous→<your email address>→/pub/chess/DOS→giics303.exe

GNU Chess A master-level *chess* program created by the Free Software Foundation. Play against the program, set it to play itself, or use it to analyze games. It comes with a built-in ASCII interface. Features include postscript printouts of games, and game checks for illegal moves and openings. The faster your workstation is, the better the program plays. *GNU Chess* is periodically upgraded and ported to other platforms. Check the Internet Chess Library for a version for your platform. (See XBoard for a graphical interface for *GNU Chess*.) √ **INTERNET** ...→*ftp* prep.ai.mit.edu→anonymous→<your email address>→/pub/gnu→ gnuchess-4.0.pl70. tar.gz ...→*ftp* chess.uoknor.edu→anonymous→<your email address>→/pub/chess/Unix→gnuchess-4.0.pl62.tar.gz

Stats
• Difficulty: complex
• Competition: personal best
• Number of players: 1
• Interface: ASCII
• Platform: UNIX

XBoard A graphical chessboard that is commonly used as an interface to either *GNU Chess* or the Internet Chess Server. It also allows you to track email postal games, review or analyze games that you have saved, observe Net games, and play *chess* against the computer. √ **INTERNET** ...→*ftp* prep.ai.mit.edu→anonymous→<your email address>→/pub/gnu→ xboard-3.0.pl9.tar.gz ...→*ftp* chess.uoknor.edu→anonymous→<your email address>→/pub/chess/X→xboard-3.0.pl9.tar.gz

Stats
• Interface: graphical
• Platform: UNIX

Requirements: *X Windows version X11R4 or higher*

Chinese Chess

Chinese Chess A strong *Chinese Chess* program. √ **INTERNET**→*ftp* chess.uoknor.edu→anonymous→<your email address>→/pub/chess/DOS→cch.zip

Stats
• Platform: DOS

ChineseChessPro1 Pits you against your Macintosh. √ **INTERNET** ...→*ftp* mac.archive.umich.edu→anonymous→<your email address>→/mac/game/board/chinesechesspro→1.01.cpt.hqx ...→*ftp* ifcss.org→anonymous→<your email address>→/software/mac/misc→chinese-chess-pro-101.hqx

Stats
• Competition: personal best
• Number of players: 1
• Interface: graphical
• Platform: Macintosh

Internet Chinese Chess Server A river runs through it. *Chinese Chess* is related to *chess* insofar as you move pieces in order to checkmate the king. The game is played on a 9x9 board (as opposed to 8x8 in *chess*) and that's bisected by a "river." Only certain pieces can cross to the other side. Both halves of the board contain a 3x3 "palace," which houses the king and his guards.

Quarantined king

But whereas a *chess* king has free reign over the board, a *Chinese Chess* king is quarantined to the palace—effective protection of the palace is what separates the winners from the losers. You can take on opponents from around the globe in *Chinese Chess* on the Internet Server. The interface isn't great, but the odds are that you'll find someone friendly enough to

help you out. This is no beginners' forum, though, so understand the rules before you venture in—perhaps it's a good idea to observe a game or two first. While *Jun-Qi*, another board game, is not supported in the *Chinese Chess* server, this is still the place to go to seek out opponents. √ **INTERNET**→*telnet* coolidge.harvard.edu 5555 *Interface:* √ **INTERNET** ...→*ftp* ifcss. org→anonymous→<your email address>→/software/dos/misc→zuvga042. zip (for DOS) ...→*ftp* ifcss.org→anonymous→<your email address>→/software/mac/misc→ICCS.1.0b1. sea.hqx (for Macs)

Stats
• Difficulty: average
• Competition: live
• Number of players: 2+
• Interface: 126
• Platforms: all

Commands
• To get a list of other players, type: who
• To get a list of games being played, type: games
• To observe games, type: observe <game number>

rec.games.chinese-chess (ng) Strategies and variations take up the bulk of the discussion in this newsgroup, although surprisingly active discussions have popped up on game notation and how *Chinese Chess* compares to other strategy games. The extraordinarily detailed FAQ file is posted to the newsgroup every two weeks. It includes the complete rules to the game, a basic look at strategy and game variations, and recommended books and magazines on the subject. √ **USENET** *FAQ:* √ **INTERNET** →*ftp* rtfm.mit.edu→anonymous→<your email address>→/pub/usenet-by-hierarchy/rec/games/chinese-chess→r.g.c-c_A_t_F_A_Q_(F)

Classic cards & casino

The array of card games on the Net is one of the easiest ways of making cyber-converts

out of technophobes. If you like *bridge*, you've got round-the-clock pickup duplicate games on **OKBridge**; if you're a card shark, check out the **Poker Showdown**. Minor classics abound as well, including **Cribbage** and **Hearts**. **BBS Roulette** and other casino games don't pay out real money, but how long can it be before someone sets up a virtual riverboat offshore?

Poker players—downloaded from CompuServe's Archive Photo's Forum.

On the Net

Across the board

Card Games Download shareware card games—*solitaire, poker, gin rummy*, and many more—for play on IBM-compatibles. ✓**COMPUSERVE**→*go* pbsarcade

RabbitJack's Casino The betting is fast and furious here in *RabbitJack's Casino*, where people get 250 chips a day to play *five-card stud poker, blackjack, bingo*, or slot machines. Load the front-end software and your saturday night special, and pick a table. ✓**AMERICA ONLINE**→*keyword* casino *Interface:* ✓**AMERICA ONLINE**→*keyword* download games→Download Casino Software

RSCARDS Play *blackjack, backgammon, checkers, poker, reverse, chess*, or *bridge* in text mode, or download the front-end graphics software. (Mac and Commodore owners can use the terminal set-

ting in the front-end to sign on; other players should run the RSCARDS program within the communications software they use for GEnie.) Compete to be among the top overall scorers on the different scoreboards. You'll find your opponents in the waiting room. ✓**GENIE**→*keyword* rscards *Interface:* ✓**GENIE**→*keyword* rscards→ Software Versions

Stats
- Difficulty: average
- Competition: live
- Number of players: 2+
- Interface: ASCII, graphical
- Platforms: all

Blackjack

Blackjack Step up to the table. It's you against the "house." You'll be given a set amount of "money" to begin with and can play until either you're "broke," you've reached the maximum number of hands allowed per day, or you've run out of your daily allotment of BBS online time. Some *blackjack* doors allow you to accumulate

your winnings over a month; others start you fresh each time. ✓CHECK LOCAL BULLETIN BOARD SYSTEMS FOR A VARIATION OF THIS GAME

Stats
- Difficulty: average
- Competition: high scoring
- Number of players: 1+
- Interface: ASCII, ANSI
- Platforms: all

Blackjack A very popular game that's easy to learn yet difficult to master. First, choose a table: low-stakes tables (1–899) have a 25-chip maximum; high-stakes tables have a maximum of 100, for those eager to lose their shirts fast. The game allows you to make standard *blackjack* decisions: "Hit," "Stand," and if your two cards total 10 or 11, "Double Down." The dealer uses one deck and shuffles only when he has to, so you can benefit from counting cards—something that will certainly get you asked out of most Vegas casinos! ✓**AMERICA ONLINE** →*keyword* casino→ Casino Lounge→Play a Game→ Play Casino Bingo

Stats
- Difficulty: simple
- Competition: live
- Number of players: 1–23
- Interface: graphical
- Platform: DOS

Commands
- To increase your bet, select: +bet
- To decrease your bet, select: -bet
- To bet the maximum, select: max
- To establish your bet with the dealer, select: send

Blackjack A simple *blackjack* game that gives you the usual options: "Insurance" (when the dealer shows an ace), "Double Down" (double your wager and receive one more card), and "Split" (play two cards of equal value as two separate hands). You begin with a fantasy bankroll of 5,000 and try to increase it in 30 hands. A high score gets you on the weekly results sheet, available from the main menu. The game uses four standard decks, so count cards. ✓**USA TODAY INFORMATION CENTER**→*go* blackjack

Stats
- Difficulty: average
- Competition: high scoring
- Number of players: 1+
- Interface: ASCII
- Platforms: all

Blackjack After your CasinoBucks have converted to chips—white is worth one CasinoBuck, red equals five, and blue equals ten—you and up to three other players start betting against the dealer. Get your bet in before the timer expires. When the cards have been dealt, you'll have the following choices: "Hit," "Stand," "Double" (for double down), and "Split." You can continue to "Hit" until you go over 21 or have reached the maximum of five cards. ✓**THE IMAGINATION NETWORK**→*select* CasinoLand→Blackjack

Stats
- Difficulty: simple
- Competition: live
- Number of players: 1–4
- Interface: graphical
- Platforms: all

Commands
- To repeat your previous bet amount, select: same bet

Bridge

Bridge Whoever invites you to a game of *bridge* chooses the scoring variation: NoScore, Rubber, or one of three Chicago variants. In NoScore, you won't see any scoring messages and the game continues until someone leaves.

In Rubber, a rubber lasts until one side fulfills two games by bidding and making contracts that total 100 consecutive points below the line. Chicago uses a four-hand-long chukker. On the first hand, nobody's vulnerable; on the fourth hand, both sides are vulnerable.

Chicago allows the following variations: Duplicate and Authentic (dealer's side vulnerable on second and third hands), Cavendish (dealer's side not vulnerable on second and third hands). Two options allow you to see information on the "last trick" and to display the vulnerability for all scoring variations and the partscores for all partscore variations. In the Bulletin Board area of the Clubhouse, topics such as partnership, lessons, tournaments, bridge events, and bridge columns are discussed. ✓**THE IMAGINATION NETWORK**→ *select* Clubhouse→Bridge

Stats
- Difficulty: average
- Competition: live
- Number of players: 4
- Interface: graphical
- Platforms: all

Bridge Home Page A good

amount of bridge-related material, including access to two bridge clubs with online Web pages (Stanford and the University of Warwick), as well as an introduction to the *OKbridge* FAQ file (complete with a link to the site where the software for playing *OKbridge* is available for downloading). ✓**INTERNET**→*www* http://www.cs.vu.nl/users/staff/sater/bridge/bridge-on-the-web.html

Duplicate Bridge Using a standard 52-card deck, you can play up to 500 hands in *duplicate bridge*, competing for the best score of the week on the leader board. Games start each Monday at noon, EST, and close the following Monday at 8 a.m. All players have to play the same 500 hands. ✓**USA TODAY INFORMATION CENTER**→*go* bridge *Interface:* ✓**USA TODAY INFORMATION CENTER**→store→USA Today Software→USA Today Software→IBM 7.6 $

Stats
- Difficulty: average
- Competition: high scoring
- Number of players: 1+
- Interface: graphical
- Platform: DOS

OKbridge Play *duplicate bridge* on the *OKbridge* server with Internet opponents from all over the world using Delphi's client frontend. A great alternative for people who don't have Unix. ✓**DELPHI**→*go* custom 085

Stats
- Difficulty: complex
- Competition: live
- Number of players: 4
- Interface: ASCII
- Platforms: all

Commands
- To set up an *OKbridge* account, type: /gps on
- To redraw the screen, type: [ctrl]-r

OKbridge Get and set up the

client software, and you're ready to connect to the Global Player Server, where you'll find a round-the-clock duplicate tournament. (That is, after you've screwed up, you can watch others play with the same hand.) There is also a rubber scoring mode in addition to the match point and IMP scoring modes used in duplicate play. If you don't want to do the tournament, join the exhibition games instead, or grab a partner and practice. No need to know the telnet address—the software does everything for you. Just type "ok-bridge." *Interface:* ✓**INTERNET**→*ftp* crash.cts.com→anonymous→<your email address>→/pub/okbridge

Stats
- Difficulty: complex
- Competition: live
- Number of players: 4
- Interface: ASCII
- Platforms: all

Commands
- To practice bidding and discuss the best line of play for a given hand, type: /practice
- To observe a game, type: /observer
- To select a seat for a game, type one of the following: /east or /south or /north or west

---

OKbridge Mailing List (ml) Electronic *bridge* has its own set of problems, and they're all discussed here. Updates to the program are also announced here, as are exhibition matches with the occasional guest celebrity *bridge* expert. ✓**INTERNET**→*email* okbridge-request@cs.ucsd.edu ✍ *Type in message body:* ADD okbridge

---

rec.games.bridge (ng) Bid? Pass? Have an unbeatable system? Here's the place to discuss strategies and systems, unbeatable and less so. The Archive carries a library of FAQ files, from a style guide with the etiquette of posting

> **"'Poker? I hardly know her!' is just the sort of joke you'll hear from a CasinoLand denizen playing five-card draw, five-card stud, six-card stud, or seven-card stud."**

to rec.games.bridge to a discussion and listing of *bridge* clubs and bridge books. ✓**USENET** *Archives:* ✓**INTERNET**→*ftp* arp.anu.edu.au→anonymous→<your email address>→/pub/Bridge/FAQ

Poker

Poker From stud to strip, many variations of *poker* have made their way onto many BBS systems. They're all a bit different in their graphic display (usually color ANSI of some fashion) but the game remains the same. The difference between playing *poker* on a BBS and playing it with a couple of buddies around a table is that on the BBS you'll have to go it alone most of the time—just you against the computer. Your score, though, will probably be logged to a Top Scores bulletin that pits you against the other users on the board who've played *poker* that week. ✓CHECK LOCAL BULLETIN BOARD SYSTEMS FOR A VARIATION OF THIS GAME

Stats
- Difficulty: average
- Competition: high scoring
- Number of players: 1+
- Interface: ASCII, ANSI
- Platforms: all

Poker The name of the game is *five-card stud*, winner takes all. The point of the game is to bluff your way to garnering chips. Each player is dealt one card facing down—the "hole" card—and then four cards facing up, one at a time. Only you can see your hole card. After each up card, you bet against the other players, using standard poker jargon: "Bet," "Check," "Raise," "Call," or "Fold." The house allows three raises in each round. But be warned: The clock ticks, and if you can't decide what to do before time runs out, your hand will be folded if there is a bet, or checked if there is no bet. A round continues until all players still in the hand have been dealt one card down and four up. ✓**AMERICA ONLINE**→*keyword* casino→Casino Lounge→Play a Game →Play Casino Poker

Stats
- Difficulty: simple
- Competition: live
- Number of players: 1–23
- Interface: graphical
- Platform: DOS

Commands
- To see your hole card, select: peek
- To send your bet before the clock runs out, select: send

Poker You're playing five-card draw, 30 hands, either against yourself for high score with very limited options or against an opponent in turn-based play, with up to seven days to play hands. Automatic ante is $2 in fantasy money, each player is limited to three raises per betting round, and you may discard up to three cards. Minimum bet: $1; maximum: $15. ✓**USA TODAY INFORMATION CENTER**→*go* poker

Stats
- Difficulty: simple
- Competition: high scoring
- Number of players: 1+

- Interface: ASCII
- Platforms: all

Poker "Poker? I hardly know her!" is just the sort of joke you'll hear from a CasinoLand denizen playing *five-card draw, five-card stud, six-card stud,* or *seven-card stud.* Choice of game variation rotates around the table—when it's your turn, a window pops up with the four choices for you to select from. Once you're playing, you place bets by selecting your chips on the bottom of the screen. You'll see the pot increase as all the players put in their stake. There are buttons to "Check," "Raise," "Bet," "Call," and "Fold." ✓**THE IMAGINATION NETWORK**→*select* CasinoLand→Poker

Stats
- Difficulty: average
- Competition: live
- Number of players: 2–5
- Interface: graphical
- Platforms: all

Commands
- To begin another round, select: continue

Poker Showdown Play *poker* against the Maxoid Robots—the programmer swears they don't look at your cards—or against humans. You begin with $1,000 in the bank. It's only virtual money, but treat it with respect. Delphi will charge you $2 of real money to get a new bankroll—an exchange rate steep enough to discourage new-money yahoos. Start off by buying 300 or so chips—unless you choose one of the big-money tables, where you'll need more.

Robot Max family

The game is simple to begin: Choose a table; if you're the only one there, you play against Maxelle, Max-Tax, and other members of the robot Max family. If there

are humans at the table, you can exclude the Maxes, or make it a mixed evening of carbon and silicon. Beware: The 'bots know how to use a poker face. Part of the game's appeal is how it helps you keep your cards straight—you're told what your high cards are, what hands you have in the works, and what your betting maximums and minimums are.

Brisk clip

The game moves along at a brisk clip, and you must respond within a few seconds to avoid being folded automatically. You can play *straight poker* (five down, no draw), *five-card stud* (one down, four up, four betting intervals), *five-card draw* (five down, bet, draw three, bet), *seven-card stud* (the favorite: two down, four up, one down, bet five times), and *Texas Hold 'Em* (two down, five in common). Note that in *Texas Hold 'Em* your winning hand must contain at least one of your hole cards. The house remembers your bank between games, so don't bet wantonly—if you leave down by $600, you'll have only $400 the next time. Thursday evenings are for the Poker Tournament, which lasts for one month. You'll only play humans here and you'll get a tournament bank of $1,000 for each week you show up and play at least one game. ✓**DELPHI**→*go* ent pok

Stats
- Difficulty: average
- Competition: live
- Number of players: 1+
- Interface: ASCII
- Platforms: all

Commands
- To choose which kind of game to play, type: go ?
- To get a summary of your cards and the table, type: ?
- To show your hole card(s), type: hole

- To buy ten more chips, type: buy 10
- To visit a new table, type: table < 1st few letters of table name>

Riverboat Poker Sophisticated statistical modeling and a number of *poker* game variations. We're impressed. ✓**INTERNET**→*ftp* ftp.doc. ic.ac.uk→anonymous→<your email address>→/computing/systems/ mac/umich/game/card→river boat1.02.cpt.hqx.gz

Stats
- Difficulty: average
- Competition: personal best
- Number of players: 1
- Interface: graphical
- Platform: Macintosh

Poker 2.2 A rudimentary but capable *poker* game. Bets are automatically set at $100. More chance than skill involved. ✓**INTERNET**→*ftp* ftp.doc.ic.ac.uk→anonymous→<your email address>→ /computing/systems/mac/umich/ game/card→Poker2.2.sit.hqx.gz

Stats
- Difficulty: simple
- Competition: personal best
- Number of players: 1
- Interface: graphical
- Platform: Macintosh

Roulette

BBS Roulette Players compete against each other weekly as well as for the all-time top score. ✓CHECK LOCAL BULLETIN BOARD SYSTEMS FOR THIS OR SIMILAR GAMES ☎→*dial* 904-563-2547

Stats
- Difficulty: average
- Competition: high scoring
- Number of players: 1+
- Interface: ANSI
- Platforms: all

Roulette Convert your CasinoBucks into chips, sit down, take a sip from your brandy, and place your bet (select the field and then click your chips until the Your Bet window reaches the desired amount). *Rien ne va plus!* Stop breathing... ✓**THE IMAGINATION NETWORK**→*select* CasinoLand→ Roulette

Stats
- Difficulty: simple
- Competition: personal best
- Number of players: 1
- Interface: graphical
- Platforms: all

Commands
- To spin the wheel before the timer runs out, select: spin
- For detailed odds of the game, use the "Option" menu to select: odds
- To remove your chips from the board, select: clear all

Slot machines

Slot Machines Grandma's favorite. Slot machines are divided into rows 1–999. Low-stakes machines (1–899) cost one chip to play; high-stakes (900–999) will cost you five. To begin playing, select "+Coin" as many times as you want rows (maximum three). Or select "Play All" to automatically play all three rows. Then spin the reels by selecting "Pull!" ✓**AMERICA ONLINE**→*keyword* casino→Casino Lounge→Play a Game→Play Casino Slot Machines

Stats
- Difficulty: simple
- Competition: personal best
- Number of players: 1
- Interface: graphical
- Platform: DOS

Slots Beat the one-armed bandit! Select a regular machine or a "super" version with five pay lines and start pumping CasinoBucks, up to $5 worth at a time. To place or alter your bet, select the arrows on the machine. Then "pull" the handle. ✓**THE IMAGINATION NET-**

WORK→*select* CasinoLand→Slots

Stats
- Difficulty: simple
- Competition: personal best
- Number of players: 1
- Interface: graphical
- Platforms: all

Commands
- To reveal the payout scheme for a particular machine, select: odds
- For explanation of a payout once you've won, select: last won

Oldies, but...

Cribbage A *cribbage* board used to be part of every family's den or living room. Now you only see them in garage sales. But a new generation of fans has come along to play the game online. Since *cribbage* is traditionally a two-handed game, and the score is constantly updated (hence the use of a pegboard instead of paper and pencil score pads), it's a natural for the Net. Using a standard 52-card deck, this version has no special options, just standard *cribbage* play. Get to 61 points, and you've won yourself a *cribbage* match. Play a seven-game match or one game at a time. ✓**THE IMAGINATION NETWORK**→*select* Clubhouse→Cribbage

Stats
- Difficulty: average
- Competition: live
- Number of players: 2
- Interface: graphical
- Platforms: all

Euchre An old game that is played in partnerships with a reduced deck. Whoever starts a game determines whether it will be played using the common, 24-card deck, using cards 9 through Ace in each suit, or the advanced, 32-card deck, using the cards 7 through Ace. ✓**THE IMAGINATION NET-** WORK→*select* Clubhouse→Euchre

Stats
- Difficulty: average
- Competition: live
- Number of players: 4
- Interface: graphical
- Platforms: all

Commands
- To see who led to the trick, who took the trick, and what cards were in the trick, select: last trick

Hearts Play standard *hearts*, partnership *hearts* (the screen personality "opposite" you is your partner), omnibus *hearts* (10 of diamonds is worth 10 points for the player taking it the trick, and must be gained in order to "shoot the moon") or partnership/omnibus *hearts*, a combination of the latter two. ✓**THE IMAGINATION NETWORK** →*select* Clubhouse→Hearts

Stats
- Difficulty: average
- Competition: live
- Number of players: 4
- Interface: graphical
- Platforms: all

Commands
- To see the score at any time, select: show score
- To see what the cards of the last trick were and who led to the trick, select: last trick

Spades Good training ground for *bridge*. Play *spades* alone or with a partner, with or without the "Sandbags Penalty." If you choose the latter, there's no 100-point penalty for ten overtricks. Grab 'em up. ✓**THE IMAGINATION NETWORK**→*select* Clubhouse→ Spades

Stats
- Difficulty: average
- Competition: live
- Number of players: 4
- Interface: graphical
- Platforms: all

Commands
- To avoid typos in bidding, select: confirm bids

War-gaming & strategy

For when Chess is just a little too dry—or maybe too simple, given the complicated

rules of many of these games—there's the battling computer code of **Core War**, a Net version of the Milton Bradley minor classic **Axis and Allies**, and on-line adaptations of Avalon Hill's multiplayer historical scenarios, including **Republic of Rome**. Games like **Command Decision** use collectible miniature metal figures that have yet to be swallowed by clever screen graphics.

Soldiers—downloaded from Compu-Serve's Graphics Gallery Forum.

On the Net

Support & inspiration

Combat Games (echo) Discuss combat games and meet other fighters. ✓**ICENET**

comp.sys.ibm.pc.games. strategic (ng) Discussion of war games, usually the ones that are modeled on the old Avalon Hill historical scenarios. Many other kinds of strategy-oriented simulations are also covered, including *Civilization, Master of Orion*, and the *V for Victory* games. ✓**USENET**

Strategy and War Games

Discussion about specific game companies, games, game genres (Civil War, WWII), and old games—some for sale, some desperately sought. The Software Library has map and scene editors for *The Perfect General*, play-test shareware games, scenario up-

grades for *Empire Deluxe*, campaign files for *Ancient Art of War*, maps for *Empire*, and much more. ✓**GENIE** ...→*keyword* scorpia→ Games Bulletin Board→set 4 (for messages) ...→*keyword* scorpia→ Gamers Libraries→Set Software Library→War & Strategy Games (for files)

War Games Discuss the lethal battlefield of *Tanks!*, debate the issue of historical or random maps in *The Grandest Fleet*, and rant about the (first) *Perfect General* program's tendency to drop artillery barrages on its own units. The software library has shareware war games, scenarios for *Empire Deluxe* and *Harpoon*, game reviews, and utilities. ✓**COMPU-SERVE**→*go* gamers→Libraries *or* Messages→War Games

War Game SIG Created for war-gamers to talk, trade, and play—currently not much playing. The Officer's Club and Questions for the Cadre are bulletin boards where Avalon Hill games are traded, *Diplomacy* games start-

ed, and *Risk* discussed—and, in theory if not practice, played. ☎→*dial* 216-368-3888→A visitor→ Explore the system→go wargames ✓**INTERNET**→*telnet* freenet-in-a.cwru. edufreenet-in-a.cwru.edu→A visitor →Explore the system→go wargames

Wargaming Club A loose confederation of wargame enthusiasts that holds conferences to discuss such topics as naval games, miniatures, battle games, etc. in the PBM & Strategy Gaming Forum Conference Hall. The Conference Schedule can be found on the Online Gaming Forums window. ✓**AMERICA ONLINE**→*keyword* pbm *Info:* ✓**AMERICA ONLINE**→*email* Ultra42

Core War

Core War *Core War* is a game of warring computer programs that have been written by the players. The object is to have your program—which runs concurrently with the other player's—to be the last to execute a command. The *Core War* programming language is called Redcode, and it's simple. The dozen or so instructions allow players to manipulate values in the host computer's memory. Since the programs reside in the host computer, it is possible—and desirable—to destroy the other player's program by manipulating the portion of memory in which it resides. The ongoing *Core War* games called *King of the Hill* (*KotH*) tournaments require you to submit a commented Redcode program via email. You will receive a reply indicating how well your program did against the current top 20 programs on the "hill." Your program plays 100 battles against each of the 20 other programs; all 21 programs are then ranked from high to low. If you are number 21 you are pushed off the hill; if you are higher than 21 someone else is pushed off. There is a very rigid format for sending in your program—get a copy of the FAQ or the beginner's tutorial (see the archive) for instructions. **√INTERNET** ...→*email* koth@storm king.com ...→*email* pizza@ecst. csuchico.edu

Stats
- Difficulty: difficult
- Competition: turn-based
- Number of players: 21
- Interface: ASCII
- Platforms: DOS, Amiga, Macintosh, UNIX, X Windows

Core War Archive Includes information about playing the game, as well as clients for Amiga, Mac, PC, and X Windows. If you're new to the game, download a set of the official instructions (red-code-icws-88.Z) in the /pub/core-war/documents/standards or the two-part tutorial in the directory /pub/corewar/documents. The quarterly *Core War Newsletter* is also archived here. **√INTERNET**→*ftp* soda.berkeley.edu→anonymous →<your email address>→pub/ corewar/documents/standards→ redcode-icws-88.Z

rec.games.corewar (ml/ng) Learn the rules of *Core War*, post your programs, and get feedback (lots of analysis). **√USENET √INTER-NET**→*email* listproc@stormking.com ✍ *Type in message body:* subscribe corewar-l <your full name> *FAQ:* **√INTERNET** ...→*ftp* rtfm.mit.edu→ anonymous→<your email address> →/pub/usenet/news.answers/ games→corewar-faq.Z ...→*email* pizza@ecst.csuchico.edu ✍ *Type in subject line:* koth faq

Miniatures

Command Decision (ml) Discuss the miniatures tabletop war game commonly referred to as *CD*. The FTP site carries an FAQ, images, playing aids, and archived copies of the mailing list. **√INTER-NET**→*email* cdmailer-request@cwi. com ✍ *Type in subject line:* subscribe <your full name> *Archives:* **√INTERNET**→*ftp* ftp.cwi.com→ anonymous→<your email address> →/cdmailer

Figures (ml) If you are a painter or collector of miniatures (for either war-gaming or relaxation) this mailing list is a fountain of advice on selecting paints, brush techniques, etc. **√INTERNET**→*email* s.hamby@mmu.ac.uk ✍ *Type in subject line:* subscribe figures *Archives:* **√INTERNET**→*ftp* ftp.umd. umich.edu→anonymous→<your email address>→/pub/frp/minia tures

Miniatures Archive Want to go to a miniatures convention in your area? Don't know when or where they are? The /Cons subdirectories, with the U.S. broken down into four regions, store convention notices. And the /pictures subdirectory has images of competition-quality miniatures. **√INTERNET**→*ftp* wais.com→anonymous→<your email address>→/pub/games/ miniatures

Miniatures WWW Archive Links to some of the coolest miniatures-related sites on the Net, complete with photographs of models (if you have a graphical Web browser). *Warhammer Fantasy Battle* and *Warhammer 40K* dominate the sight, but historical games like *Command Decision* are also well represented. **√INTERNET**→ *www* http://www.cis.ufl.edu/ ~thoth/library/recreation.html

rec.games.miniatures (ng) Debate rules, analyze troop tactics, and share painting tips in this active newsgroup. There is a heavy bent toward *Warhammer Fantasy Battle* and *Warhammer 40K*, two of the Games Workshop's more popular (and flamed!) games. Traditional historic games, such as *Napoleon's Battles* and *Command Decision*, are also frequently discussed. If you're new to miniatures painting, you probably have a lot of questions: Which paints should I use? What types of brushes? Should I use white primer or black primer? The painting FAQ is chock-full of useful information on the subject. **√USENET** *FAQ:* **√IN-TERNET** ...→*ftp* biochem.dental. upenn.edu→anonymous→<your email address>→/pub/Miniatures →Painting_Guide+FAQ ...→*www* file://biochem.dental.upenn.edu/ Mosaic/miniatures.html

War simulations

Axis and Allies Milton Bradley's board game of wartime strategy is so popular on the Net that more people may play it online than off. Since a game can last for several hours, and thus rack up a huge bill, most players prefer to play it via message boards—just post your move and log off. **√AMERICA ONLINE**→ *keyword* pbm→PBM and Strategy Messaging→Axis & Allies **√COMPUSERVE**→*go* pbmgames→ Messages→Board Wargames **√PRODIGY**→*jump* games bb→ Choose a Topic→War/Strategy Games

Stats
- Difficulty: average
- Competition: turn-based
- Number of players: 2+
- Interface: ASCII
- Platforms: all

Eagles Cry Newsletter for the game *Delenda Est Carthago*,

"Carthage Must Be Destroyed," a play-by-mail and -email game run by Waveney Games in the UK. The newsletter and game masters' research provide fertile ground for debates on religion, the crusades, the inquisitions, and ecclesial politics. ✓COMPUSERVE→go pbmgames→ Libraries→Role-Playing Games→ Search by keyword: DEL

Operation Market-Garden In September 1944, allied paratroop divisions landed in Holland to wrest conrol of the bridges over the Rhine from occupying Nazi forces. You can play either the Allied or Nazi side (but not the Dutch side) in this online version of the popular board game Operation Market-Garden. The computer handles combat resolution, troop availability, and the masking of enemy troop movements. All you have to do as commanding general is concentrate on strategy: For example (assuming that you're not the Nazi), circumvent antitank fire, drop paratroopers, and take bridges (but don't go too far!). The game's "double-blind" system simulates one of the most terrifying aspects of actual warfare: What the hell is the enemy doing? ✓MPG-NET→go market

Stats
- Difficulty: average
- Competition: live
- Number of players: 2
- Interface: graphical
- Platforms: all

Republic of Rome You're a power-seeking senator in ancient Rome working hard to advance his career and protect Rome from the invading barbarians. If Rome falls, all players (senators) lose, so you'll have to work together to raise and deploy forces and to protect the Empire. Turns include officer elections, force deployment, and political strategies. This PBeM game is based on Avalon Hill's board game by the same name. There are no charges for online play, but players must purchase a copy of the board game for the rules. (Avalon Hill's voice number is 800-999-3222.) *Info:* ✓**INTERNET**→*email* ror@hpeswlw.fc.hp.com ✍ *Type in message body:* help

Stats
- Difficulty: complex
- Competition: turn-based
- Number of players: 2+
- Interface: ASCII
- Platforms: all

Sniper! If you think defeating the Axis powers was difficult, you should play *Sniper*. The glossary alone is 35 pages long. You command a squad of soldiers against an enemy squad. Beginners are encouraged to take on "Patrol Missions," but as you work your way up in rank, you can take on "Infiltrate," "Free/Patrol," "SuperSolo," and "Raid" missions.

No-man's-land

In a Patrol Mission, for example, two opposing squads meet in a no-man's-land between the front lines. Both squads have to get through the area without losing all their men. Your primary goal is to complete the mission, and your overall goal is to advance your military career. You score "hit points" for successful completion of tasks, for casualties you inflict (on the enemy, please), and for other game accomplishments.

There's a file for newbies in the Multiplayer Games Forum Libraries—search by the file name "Recrut.hlp"—as well as a collection of back issues of "In the Trenches" and "Smoke and Rubble," the monthly columns about the game. On the Multiplayer Games Forum Message boards, you'll find discussions about the front-end, as well as questions from bloody new recruits and answers from grizzled old-timers, most of whom are limbless. ✓**COMPUSERVE**→*go* sniper *Interface:* **COMPUSERVE** ...→*go* sniper→ SNIPER Scope for IBM PC (EGA) (for the DOS version) ...→*go* mp games→Libraries→*Search by file name:* WINSCO.ZIP (for Windows)

Stats
- Difficulty: complex
- Competition: live
- Number of players: 1+
- Interface: ASCII
- Platforms: all

Commands
- To join a patrol mission while in the Saloon, type: /mi pa
- To take the tutorial from the Saloon, type: /bootcamp
- To move a unit while in a game, type: mo <unit number> <direction letter> <number of sectors>

"September 1944. All you have to do as commanding general is concentrate on strategy: For example (assuming that you're not the Nazi), circumvent antitank fire, drop paratroopers, and take bridges over the Rhine (but don't go too far!)."

Diplomacy

The email version of Henry's Kissinger's favorite board-
game is also the Net's most
popular play-by-email en-
tertainment, with more
than a hundred separate
many-month games going
on at any one time. The
game takes place in Europe
at the turn of the 19th century, with seven players rep-
resenting one of seven great
European powers (England,
France, Germany, Austria,
Italy, Russia, Turkey).

*Diplomacy map—downloaded from
ftp.netcom.com.*

Online adaptations of the
classic Avalon Hill strategy
boardgame come in many
flavors, from a strict translation of the pre-WWI map
to historical and geographic
variations, like 18th-century
South America, strange
oceanless continental amal-
gamations, and sci-fi Ar-
mageddons. Check out
Variant Diplomacy Maps
for some examples.

Back-stabbing

In the real-life board game,
players negotiate alliances
until the very end—since
no one country is ever
strong enough to stand on
its own—as they try to conquer territory from each
other. Each time-limited
turn is filled with furious
and secretive deal making—

until the army and fleet orders and the back-stabbing
begins. Online, the negotia-
tions and orders take place
through email. A central
computer program, called a
Judge, organizes and coordinates the game, processing
moves and keeping track of
deadlines.

Six-month games

Basic online games have 48-
hour move deadlines, with a
typical game lasting two to
six months, although there
are "warp" versions with
shorter turnaround times.
Electronic versions of the
original rules are considered
to be pirated—you are ex-
pected to buy the Avalon
Hill game rules in print
form (at your local game
store or directly from 1-
800-999-3222 vox)—but
the Judges are loaded with

supporting files that can get
you up to speed.

If you are new, sign on to
a moderated standard game.
Moderated games have a
real-life gamemaster who will
answer your questions. Signing on to a game is a major
commitment. If you don't
intend to play a full game—
usually lasting at least two
months—don't do it.

On the Net

Across the board

Diplomacy Depot One of the
easiest places to get started on
your *Diplomacy* email addiction.
Ongoing games are reported within the folders, and new games are
forming all the time. A loosely organized group of players have
formed the AOL Diplomacy Club
("AOL Dip Club"), which has put
together the "Diplomacy: Online
Kit," a few files that include the
house rules for playing AOL
Diplomacy. *Diplomacy* here dis-
penses with the Judge system and
simply uses a human game master
to collect orders and issue move
reports. Accomplished AOL players will eventually want to swim
out to the deeper waters of Internet competition (starting with
participation in the rec.games.
diplomacy newsgroup). ✓**AMERICA
ONLINE**→*keyword* pbm→PBM &
Strategy Messages→Diplomacy Depot *Info:* ✓**AMERICA ONLINE**→*keyword* pbm →File Library→DIPLO-
MACY: Online Kit

Diplomacy on CompuServe
Browse Libraries and Messages—
each have two *Diplomacy* areas,
one for playing ("Diplomacy

Games") and one for support and discussion ("Diplomacy War Room"). Sometimes it can take a while to gather enough players to begin a game. In the interim, explore the libraries that house the rules for dozens of variants as well as hints, such as suggested strategies for playing Italy (LEPANT. ART). √**COMPUSERVE**→*go* pb-mgames→Libraries *or* Messages →Diplomacy/Games *or* Diplomacy /War Room

Diplomacy on GEnie Dive into *Category 23: Diplomacy*. Local *Diplomacy* flourishes here, with several *Diplomacy* games in progress all the time—each game has its own theme. There is also a topic devoted to the GEnie *Diplomacy* newsletter and one for finding out when new games are starting. The War & Strategy Games Library is packed with *Diplomacy* files—mostly archives of messages, maps, and game rules. For the general rules of *Diplomacy*, download file 157. √**GENIE** ...→*keyword* scorpia→Games Bulletin Board→set 23 (for messages) ...→*keyword* scorpia→Gamers Libraries→War & Strategy Games

Diplomats

Diplomacy Programming Project The future. A project to develop computer programs, called Diplomats, that negotiate and play *Diplomacy* on their own. √**INTERNET**→*email* loeb@geocub. greco-prog.fr ✍ *To get more information, write to Daniel Loeb*

EP Diplomacy

Electronic Protocol's Game Log A list of every standard (EP) game ever played. √**INTERNET**→ *www* ftp://netcom11.netcom.com/ pub/starkey/EP.gamelog

EP Diplomacy Standbys A database of standbys for *Electronic Protocol Diplomacy* games in case a quick replacement is needed. You can register by emailing Eric Klein, the database keeper. Mention the kind of *Diplomacy* you desire, your experience, your name, phone number, address, and country preference. √**INTERNET**→*email* Eric_S_ Klien@cup.portal.com ✍ *To put your name on a standby list, send email with the requested information.*

The EP (Electronic Protocol) House Rules. The standard rules translating *Diplomacy* to email. Half hard-nosed procedures and half commonsense netiquette. You are, for instance, *not* supposed to communicate with other players without going through the Judge in *EP* games. √**INTERNET**→*ftp* nda.com→anonymous→<your email address>→/pub/diplomacy →house.rules

Hall of fame

Nick Fitzpatrick's Diplomacy Hall of Fame A log of every game ever played on any Judge, as well as some non-Judge games. An explanation of the scoring system appears at the top, and a list of the top 100 players is included at the bottom. Learn to look sharp for the likes of such Net *Diplomacy* champs as Aaron Priven and Alan Bick. √**INTERNET**→*ftp* nda.com→ anonymous→<your email address> →/pub/diplomacy→ HallOfFame

Info & instructions

Dip-Advice Conceived as the elite mail list for discussing changes in the house rules and other great issues facing the world of online *Diplomacy*. √**INTER-NET**→*email* majordomo@nda.com ✍ *Type in message body:* subscribe

dip-advice *Archives:* √**INTERNET**→ *ftp* nda.com→anonymous→<your email address>→/pub/diplomacy

Diplomacy A–Z The hefty file boasts more than 1,100 entries covering game terms, organizations, trivia, classic openings, alliances, and strategies. √**INTERNET**→ *ftp* nda.com→anonymous→<your

Diplomacy **Strategy & Classics**

> "Humor, analysis, and, most of all, pure, razor-sharp obsession. Probably one of the most active newsgroups on the Net—despite the utter lack of tired sex, tired ethnic discussions, and tired politics—this is also an excellent forum for precocious newbies..."

email address>→/pub/diplomacy/Documents→AtoZ.tar.Z

Diplomacy Archives Common files include the *Diplomacy* FAQ, lists of opening moves, logs of old online *Diplomacy* games, Nick Fitzpatrick's Hall of Fame, boardmaps, and back issues of the online *Diplomacy* magazines. The main "dippy" archive (nda.com) has interviews with the game's authors, maps, support programs, source code, and e-mags like *EPC2* and *TAP.* Most diplomacy-related files either originate or end up here. ✓ **INTERNET** ...→*ftp* nda. com→anonymous→<your email address>→/pub/diplomacy ...→*ftp* ftp.netcom.com→anonymous→<your email address>→ /pub/diplomacy ...→*ftp* sunburn.uwaterloo.ca→ anonymous→<your email address>→/pub/nick/diplomacy

Diplomacy Gopher Access the *Diplomacy* FAQ, related FTP sites and more. ✓ **INTERNET**→*gopher* philosophy.cwis.uci.edu→Philosophy→Recreation→Games by Wire→Diplomacy

Diplomacy Home Page Links to several *Diplomacy* FTP sites and *Diplomacy* documents—from the FAQ to the Judge Openings List to the *EP* house rules to virtually any other *Diplomacy* document available on the Net. ✓ **INTERNET**→ *www* http://www.hmc.edu/~irilyth/diplomacy/index.html

rec.games.diplomacy (ml/ng) The Internet at its best and the number one clearinghouse for Net *Diplomacy.* Humor, analysis, and, most of all, pure, razor-sharp obsession. Probably one of the most active newsgroups on the Net—despite the utter lack of tired sex, tired ethnic discussions, and tired politics—this is also an excellent forum for precocious newbies to enter the fray without bothering with all those pesky FAQ files. Twice a month the *Internet Diplomacy Journal,* which reviews the games in progress, is posted. The FAQ is a complete overview of *Diplomacy* on the Net. It assumes some familiarity with both (the game and the Net) and includes guides to the current Judges, game variants, FTP sites, *Diplomacy* magazines, and rec.games.diplomacy. A beginner's version is said to be in the works. ✓ **USENET** ✓ **INTERNET**→*email* listserv@mitvma. mit.edu ✍ *Type in message body:* subscribe dip-l <your full name> *FAQ:* ✓ **INTERNET** ...→*ftp* ftp. netcom.com→anonymous→<your email address>→/pub/diplomacy →rec.games.diplomacy.FAQ.1 *and* rec.games.diplomacy.FAQ.2 ...→*email* starkey@netcom.com ✍ *Type in subject line:* FAQ request

Judges

Diplomacy Judges Judges are centralized *Diplomacy* processors on the Internet that communicate through e-mail, registering players for games, dishing up supporting files, receiving game orders, tracking order deadlines, and reporting on moves at the end of a turn. A complete list of Judges is available by FTP. We've listed a few of them. ✓ **INTERNET** ...→*email* judge @morrolan.eff.org ✍ *Type in message body:* help (for the U.S.) ...→ *email* judge@owl.und.ac.za ✍ *Type in message body:* help (for South Africa) ...→*email* judge@ dipvax.dsto.gov.au ✍ *Type in message body:* help (for Australia) ...→ *email* judge@nmt.edu ✍ *Type in message body:* help (for the U.S.) ...→*email* judge@math.utoledo. edu ✍ *Type in message body:* help (for the U.S.) *Info:* ✓ **INTERNET**→*ftp* nda.com→anonymous→<your email address>→/pub/diplomacy →list_of_judges

The Judge Openings List Find a game to join! Updated hourly, this list tells you about new games that are forming and ongoing games that need new players. There's almost always a standard, moderated game, called "New" for beginners, starting up. Read the notes! You don't want to accidentally end up in a Polish- or German-language game. Das ist kein spaß. ✓ **INTERNET** ...→*email* starkey @netcom.com ✍ *Type in subject line:* opening request ...→*ftp* netcom12.netcom.com→anonymous→ <your email address>→/pub/diplomacy/openings ...→*www* ftp:// netcom12.netcom.com/pub/diplomacy/openings.html

Judge Programmers If you thought conquering Europe was tough, try maintaining a Judge. List members are all dealing with the same difficulties. ✓**INTERNET**→*email* majordomo@nda.com ✍ *Type in message body:* subscribe judge-maint

Utilities

Amiga Diplomacy Public domain adjudicator for the Amiga. ✓**INTERNET**→*ftp* nic.funet.fi→anonymous→<your email address>→/pub/amiga/fish/501-600/ff582→Diplomacy.lha

Diplomacy Strategy Map Windows program to map orders and Judge the move report. ✓**INTERNET**→*ftp* nda.com→anonymous→<your email address>→/pub/diplomacy/Sources→ dipstrma.zip

MacDip Macintosh viewer/adjudicator for *Diplomacy* that organizes, stores, and maps Judge files or plain orders. It will also adjudicate non-Judge orders. ✓**INTERNET**→*ftp* cs.unc.edu→anonymous→<your email address>→/pub/vanverth

Mapit Mapit translates Judge game reports into a graphic, showing unit icons and country designations. Most Judges can issue their own maps when requested, but the machine-specific versions tend to be nicer looking and kinder to Judge bandwidth. There are versions for DOS, Windows, Mac, Unix, and NeXT—you just have to be able to compile the code. ✓**INTERNET**→*ftp* nda.com→anonymous→<your email address>→/pub/diplomacy/Sources

Variants

Variant Diplomacy Maps There are dozens of bizarre variations of *Diplomacy* with names like "Necromancer" and "Sudden Death." In fact, some online *Diplomacy* mags discuss nothing

> **"*Britain* is a playing variation with a standard map that gives England six supply centers (good news for Britain) that consist of only armies (bad news for Britain)."**

but strange new games. The FTP site archives several maps for playing variations of *Diplomacy*.

More common maps

The following are some of the more common maps: Standard, a seven-player map of Europe; Gunboat, a version where players remain anonymous; 1898, a standard map, but each player starts with only one supply center; Britain, a standard map that gives England six supply centers (good news for Britain) that consist of only armies (bad news for Britain); Chaos, a standard map, but for 34 players, each beginning in one city; Fleet_Rome, a standard game, except Rome gets a fleet; Loeb9, two new countries, Spain and Norway, make room for up to 9 players; Machiavelli, Avalon Hill's variant, which is also a boardgame, with added complications such as assassination and famine; Pure, with seven players, seven regions that are all interconnected; Youngstown, a map extended to include Asia and up to three additional players.

To get a description of these variations (or others), send a "get info" command followed by the

name of the variant to a judge. ✓**INTERNET** ...→*ftp* ftp.u.washington.edu→anonymous→<your email address>→/public/misc ...→*email* judge@morrolan.eff.org ✍ *To get detailed descriptions of* Diplomacy *variants, type in message body:* get info <variant map name>

Zines

The Abyssinian Prince (j) Begun (and still thriving) in the world of printed paper, and flesh-and-blood mailmen, this zine is also now online and nicely bridges the separate worlds of postal and email *Diplomacy*. Besides the 'zine, which is published every three or four months, you'll get all the message that are sent to "tap@nda.com." ✓**INTERNET**→*email* majordomo@nda.com ✍ *Type in message body:* subscribe tap *Archives:* ✓**INTERNET**→*ftp* nda.com→anonymous→<your email address>→/pub/diplomacy/TAP

Mission from God A biannual, authoritative list of postal *Diplomacy* zines in Britain and beyond, with addresses and reviews. ✓**INTERNET**→*ftp* nda.com→ anonymous→<your email address>→/pub/diplomacy/Magnifique

---

CYBERNOTES

"What bothers me is when two major powers elect a draw. I can understand giving a small but eternally loyal ally a share of the win, but when the two largest powers refuse to attack each other it makes for a silly game."

—from **GEnie's Scorpia RoundTable**

Empire building

Build your silicon castles with noirish crime games like Cartel and Godfather of Crime.

If you prefer the long view of things, **Civilization**'s 2001 journey from tribal life to space travel should settle that nagging question of your leisure time. Other settings for ego-inflating entrepreneurship include the life of a railroad robber baron (**Empire Builder**) and the grandly named **Galactic Overlord**. Don't worry if you get a little absorbed in these games—you'll have plenty of time to ask yourself why after you're done conquering all existence.

Al Capone mugshot—downloaded from CompuServe's Archive Photos Forum.

On the Net

Empire

BSD Empire A cross between *Diplomacy*, *Risk*, and *SimCity*, *BSD Empire* is a simulation game of global economic, political, and military decision making. You control a country that is part of a world made up of hexagonal land and sea sectors.

Babies

Your people dig mines; build roads, schools, hospitals, harbors, and airports; sail ships; fly planes; and they even have babies. You decide on national goals and maneuver your country through diplomatic quagmires. Many of your actions are in real time, with an immediate impact on the game. New variables are added frequent-

ly, depending on the type of game. Blitz games can be updated every ten minutes while other games may be updated every couple of days.

The goal of the game depends on who's playing—do you want to conquer the world or would you rather pursue technological progress? Games can last from one day to several months.

To play you need to acquire a client (get one from the archive) and find a server running the game (look for game announcements on rec.games.empire or on the Blitz list). Blitz games start daily, while long-term games begin about once a month. *Info:* ✓**INTERNET**→*www* http://random. chem.psu.edu/cgi-bin/Empire Check (for a list of Empire games and their status) *FAQ:* ✓**INTERNET** ...→*ftp* ftp.cis.ksu.edu→ anonymous →<your email address>→/pub/ Games/Empire/docs→chainsaw. 3.0.info.tar.Z ...→*ftp* ftp.cis.ksu. edu→anonymous→<your email address>→WhatIsEmpire-FAQ.txt *Interface:* ✓**INTERNET** ...→*ftp* ftp.cis. ksu.edu→anonymous →<your email

address>→/pub/Empire/clients ...→*ftp* ucbvax.berkeley.edu→ anonymous→<your email address> →/pub/games/empire/bsd

Stats
- Difficulty: complex
- Competition: live
- Number of players: 10–80
- Interface: ASCII
- Platforms: DOS, UNIX, Windows, VMS

Commands
- To get instructions, type: info

Blitz List (ml) Announcements about new Blitz games—games of *Empire* that usually last no longer than one real-time session. ✓**INTERNET**→*email* blitz-list-request@bbn. com ✍ *Write a request*

BSD Empire Archives Everything you need (except a server and opponents) to play *Empire*. Includes clients, documentation, source code (in case you want to build a server), the history of past *Empire* games, and utilities. The /documentation subdirectory is filled with hints, FAQs, news, and other *Empire* info. ✓**INTERNET** ...→*ftp* orion.cis.ksu.edu→ anonymous→ <your email address>→ /pub/Games/Empire ...→*ftp* ftp. engg.ksu.edu→anonymous→<your email address>→/pub/Games/ Empire

JunkieFest Games for Newbies (ml) A list announcing when games begin that are oriented toward the newbie—players may ask questions and can stay alive a little longer. ✓**INTERNET**→*email* empire-announce@engg.ksu.edu ✍ *Type in subject line:* subscribe

rec.games.empire (ng) Looking for players? Need someone to take over for you while you're out in the real world for a few days? Want to rehash a game or follow an ongoing one? The newsgroup is a very active forum for discussing the game and meeting prospective opponents. The FAQ covers the *Empire* basics—from compiling your client to connecting to a server to in-game tactics, such as moving civilians and building a ship. The biweekly edition of *Empire News*, which is posted here, is a must-read for *Empire* fans. New games are announced, changes to the game are reported, and anything else of interest to the community is noted. ✓**USENET** *FAQ:* ✓**INTERNET** ...→*ftp* ftp.cis.ksu. edu→anonymous→<your email address>→/pub/Games/Empire ...→*ftp* ftp.engg.ksu.edu→anonymous→<your email address>→/pub /Games/Empire

World Empire Home Page Offers links to the FAQ, the latest version of *Empire News* and a few past issues, a list of current games, the *Empire* FTP archives, and information about server development. ✓**INTERNET**→*www* http:// www.engg.ksu.edu:80//empire/ home.html

TradeWars 2002

TradeWars 2002 Perhaps the granddaddy of all BBS games, *TW 2002* is immensely popular and easy to find on BBSs all over the galaxy. Players buy and sell goods and resources, amass great fortunes and military power, and span the realms of space in search of new frontiers to conquer. There are also many add-on utilities for *TradeWars*, including offline player help, power macro utilities, special graphic terminal programs, and even a five-volume *TradeWars* tip

> "You start as a lieutenant and have to work your way up to Godfather in this well-designed game of 1930s tommy-gun pounding mafia families in New York City."

guide (most likely available at the BBS where you play *TW*). ✓CHECK LOCAL BULLETIN BOARD SYSTEMS FOR THIS OR SIMILAR GAMES ☎→*dial* 215-547-5026/215-332-8514/918-683-2082/501-225-9271/501-330-2845

Stats
* Difficulty: complex
* Competition: turn-based
* Number of players: 2+
* Interface: ANSI
* Platforms: all

The Official TradeWars Sub (echo) More *TradeWars* Talk. ✓**ICENET**

TRADE_WARS (echo) Loaded with tricks, tips, and hints for *TradeWars*. Discussion covers both *Outpost Trader* and *TW2002*. ✓**FI-DONET**

TradeWars Expert Discussion (echo) Where Trade Warriors who've been around the universe a few times, strategize, share tips, and brag about their success. ✓**ICENET** ✓**WWIVNET**

TradeWars from the Driver's Seat (echo) *TradeWars* advice for sysops. ✓**ICENET**

TradeWars Hints, Tricks & News (echo) Get the lowdown on *TradeWars* and meet other players. ✓**ICENET**

TradeWars: The Banned Subjects (echo) Discuss what you can't discuss! ✓**WWIVNET**

Tw2002 "A Players Perspective" (echo) Talk to other *TradeWars* players. ✓**ICENET**

Criminal empires

Cartel As a small-time leader of a minor drug cartel in post-drug-legalized America, your task is to shut down all the rest of the cartels and become the top dog. The first player to earn $1 million is the winner. Here's your opportunity to run guns, hire shady characters, and do "business" with the underside of the drug culture. ✓CHECK LOCAL BULLETIN BOARD SYSTEMS OR SIMILAR GAMES ☎→*dial* 215-443-9434/215-443-7390

Stats
* Difficulty: average
* Competition: high scoring
* Number of players: 1+
* Interface: ANSI
* Platforms: all

Godfather of Crime You start as a lieutenant and have to work your way up to Godfather in this well-designed game of 1930s tommy-gun-pounding mafia families in New York City. Loaded with options like bribery, treachery, robbery, hostage taking, and, of course, family matters. You'd better find a wife quick and hope for a boy if you want to make sure you'll have a successor by the time you're sleeping with the fishes... ✓CHECK LOCAL BULLETIN BOARD SYSTEMS FOR THIS OR SIMILAR GAMES ☎→*dial* 501-741-5699

Stats
* Difficulty: complex

- Competition: turn-based
- Number of players: 2+
- Interface: ANSI
- Platforms: all

Fantasy empires

Olympia *Olympia* is a low-tech fantasy world where players build empires, perfect battle skills, engage in political intrigue, and pursue adventures. Each player controls a group of nobles, who in turn control many commoners. Nobles can study skills, including seven schools of magic, religion, construction, beast-mastery, and combat. Turns are processed once a week and tend to be long and detailed (an average report runs 15 to 25 pages). All players receive periodic copies of *The Olympia Times* for gaming news. There's a fee if you wish to play. *Info:* ✓**INTERNET** ...→*email* info@pbm.com ✍ *Email for automated info* ...→*www* http://www.pbm.com/oly-top.html

Stats
- Difficulty: complex
- Competition: turn-based
- Number of players: 2+
- Interface: ASCII
- Platforms: all

Historical empires

Rise to Power Starting with only a few bushels of wheat, some gold florins, and a small band of knights, you try to unite the ten provinces of 15th-century Germany and rise to its throne. You'll start by building a house and your own barony. Hint: A spouse and children are the key to success for royalty. ✓CHECK LOCAL BULLETIN BOARD SYSTEMS FOR THIS OR SIMILAR GAMES ☎→*dial* 501-741-5699

Stats
- Difficulty: complex
- Competition: turn-based
- Number of players: 2+

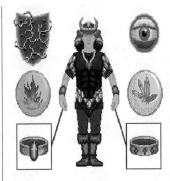

Screenshot from Sid Meier's game Civilization—*from MicroProse.*

- Interface: ANSI
- Platforms: all

Modern day empires

Civilization FAQ *Civilization* is one of the most heavily FAQ'ed personal-computer games on the Net. As the name suggests, the game simulates the development of Western-style "civilization." You start with a tribe that makes scientific discoveries and technological progress, comes into contact with other tribes (friendly and not), and migrates to other continents. The goal, of course, is worldwide dominance and space travel. There are other related files, including civ2.faq and civ.futur.faq. Internet discussion about *Civilization* takes place on the comp.sys.ibm.pc.games.strategic newsgroup, where this FAQ is periodically posted. ✓**INTERNET** ...→*ftp* ftp.uwp.edu→ anonymous→<your email address> →/pub/games/romulus/hints→ civ.faq.Z ...→*www* http://wcl-rs.bham.ac.uk/~djh/civfaq1.html *FAQ:* ✓**INTERNET**→*ftp* ftp.uwp.edu→ anonymous→<your email address> →/pub/msdos/games/romulus/hints→civ.faq

Empire Builder Tycoon that you are, can you be the first to connect five major cities by railroad, run

the railroad, and get a cool $250 million in the bank? By crossing the plains, bridging rivers, and tunneling through mountains, you and your opponents deal ruthlessly with each other while building your empires. You've got $40 million to start with, but railroads can be expensive to build! As soon as you've connected cities, you can start hauling cargo to earn bucks. With your profits, you can buy faster engines. Like any other robber baron, you're going to need a strategy and an eye on the weather. Floods or snowstorms can hamper your progress, and if it's not the weather, then your labor force may strike. In the end, however, a little luck, a lot of planning, and diplomatic aplomb will win the game. ✓**MPG-NET**→*go* empire

Stats
- Difficulty: average
- Competition: live
- Number of players: 2–6
- Interface: graphical
- Platform: DOS

Commands
- To create a game in the Train Station conference room, type: /create
- To invite other players to play, type: /invite
- To join a game someone else has created, type: /join

Global War Popular adaptation of the *Risk* board game—conquer up to 42 nations! If your sysop agrees, this game offers the option to team up with other members of your BBS and challenge members of other alliances. There is a VGA terminal program that works with *Global War* to enhance both graphics and speed, but it is not required. ✓CHECK LOCAL BULLETIN BOARD SYSTEMS FOR THIS OR SIMILAR GAMES ☎→*dial* 206-353-6966/206-353-2494

Stats
- Difficulty: complex

- Competition: turn-based
- Number of players: 2+
- Interface: ANSI, graphical
- Platforms: all

Space empires

Conquest & Destiny Currently played by more than 200 people, this science-fiction role-playing game puts each player at the head of an alien race. Using the particular strengths and weaknesses of your race, you work toward the goal of becoming all-powerful, by working either with other races or against them. The universe consists of 4 billion planets, black holes, wormholes, supernovae, nebulae, and other potential adventure arenas. Three times a week, players mail between 10 and 120 orders to the moderator (a computer program), who processes all orders at once and returns the results via electronic mail. One turn costs between $1 and $7.20, depending on the number of orders. The average cost is around $10 per week. The game is expected to last for many years, and new players are joining all the time. *Info:* ✓**INTERNET**→ *email* p00791@psilink.com ✍ *Email moderator for information* ✓**INTERNET**→*ftp* ftp.erg.sri.com→anonymous→<your email address>→/pub/pbm/conquest_and_destiny

Stats
- Difficulty: complex
- Competition: turn-based
- Number of players: 2+
- Interface: ASCII

Dor Sageth A beginner's introduction to interactive adventure gaming, set aboard the abandoned spaceship *Dor Sageth*. Your goal is to get the ship started again and to head for Earth. You'll die a few times, probably by incinerating into "an isotope quite unknown to Terran scientists," but the game allows you to keep coming back for more. ✓**GENIE**→ *keyword* sageth

Stats
- Difficulty: simple
- Competition: personal best
- Number of players: 1
- Interface: ASCII
- Platforms: all

Galactic Overlord Each player begins with a home planet and ten ships. In daily turns, players attack their opponents or unclaimed planets. All turns are processed simultaneously and only the mightiest overlord survives. ✓CHECK LOCAL BULLETIN BOARD SYSTEMS FOR THIS OR SIMILAR GAMES ☎→*dial* 612-379-8272

Stats
- Difficulty: average
- Competition: turn-based
- Number of players: 2–6
- Interface: ANSI
- Platforms: all

Galaxy Each player controls an empire of planets. The object of the game is to wipe out the other players by capturing their planets and destroying their ships. Technology (allowing ships to fly faster, fight harder, and carry more cargo) is a big factor in the game. Twice each week, a player mails in orders

> "Tycoon that you are, can you be the first to connect five major cities by railroad, run the railroad, and get a cool $250 million in the bank?"

for his ships and planets to the moderator, who processes the orders and mails back the results. The game is free and lasts between 50 and 70 turns. There are usually more than a dozen games simultaneously in progress. *Info:* ✓**INTERNET**→*email* galaxy@acca.nmsu.edu ✍ *To get instructions, type in message body:* help ✓**INTERNET**→*ftp* ftp.erg.sri.com→anonymous→<your email address>→/pub/pbm/galaxy

Stats
- Difficulty: average
- Competition: turn-based
- Number of players: 20–50
- Interface: ASCII
- Platforms: all

Galaxy I Enough of this "earn this" and "buy that" before you can play a game. In *Galaxy I*, you start off with 20 scouts, 20 fighters, 20 missiles, and 2,000 units of fuel. On top of that, your fleet will be near an unowned star system, yours for the taking. The objective in this game is to colonize planets, develop them, destabilize anybody who gets in the way, and thus increase your influence throughout the universe. To master the game's commands, refer to the Command Summary, available from the main menu under Instructions. A front-end is available for the Mac in the Galaxy Archives off the main menu. ✓**GENIE**→ *keyword* galaxy *Interface:* ✓**GENIE**→*keyword* galaxy→The Galaxy Archives→Download a File→31 *and* 32 *and* 33 *and* 34

Stats
- Difficulty: average
- Competition: live
- Number of players: 1+
- Interface: ASCII
- Platforms: all

Geo-Political Warfare Another game of planetary warfare. Your goal is to take control of the galaxy through economic and military imperialism, using your money-management, trading, and urban-planning skills. ✓CHECK LOCAL BULLETIN BOARD SYSTEMS FOR THIS OR SIMILAR GAMES ☎ →*dial* 904-696-9238/904-696-9322

Stats
- Difficulty: complex
- Competition: turn-based
- Number of players: 2+
- Interface: ANSI
- Platforms: all

Hemlock MUSH In the 22nd century, a devastating plague killed virtually the entire human population on Earth, and many humans fled the planet on spaceships. Almost a millennium later, planetary warfare (with distant descendants from the human refugees involved) is common, and as populations grow, imperialism causes new conflicts. A newbie should begin by reading the rather long (ten part) history, followed by descriptions of the families (the different races that are in conflict), and then page members of the families to ask them questions. Enter the Info Area to join a family, then walk through a portal and choose your role (peacekeeper, fighter, politician, etc.). The player base is small, but if you like dark themes, space combat, trade wars, and diplomatic challenges, give it a try. ✓INTERNET→*telnet* pelyco. soar.gsia.cmu.edu 1973→connect Guest Guest *Register:* ✓INTERNET→ *email* kforbes@mentor.cc.purdue. edu ✍ *Email request to register a character:* <your full name> <your email address> <your character's name> <your password>

Stats
- Difficulty: average
- Competition: live
- Number of players: 2+
- Interface: ASCII
- Server: MUSH
- Platforms: all

Commands
- To get information, type: news *or* help
- To get a list of admins, type: +admin
- To find out who is on and taking newbie questions, type: WHO

Iron Ox In the 23rd century, Earth has been stripped of all its natural resources, and new frontiers must be conquered. Only resourceful colonists can survive in this sci-fi-based strategy game. Up to eight players compete on a 5x12 map of an alien world. They cultivate land and harvest with the Iron Ox; they trade, steal, and spy. Several games may be going on at the same time and you can play in more than one. Sysops sometimes offer prizes of free online time. ✓CHECK LOCAL BULLETIN BOARD SYSTEMS FOR THIS OR SIMILAR GAMES ☎ →*dial* 619-462-8406

Stats
- Difficulty: complex
- Competition: turn-based
- Number of players: 2–8
- Interface: ANSI
- Platforms: all

MegaWars I As soon as you choose to play *MegaWars I*, you'll be asked to join either the Coalition or the Empire—at which point you pick a ship and enter the game. Beginners can help their side immediately by capturing neutral planets, marked by "@" on the map. Neutral planets have the pesky habit of firing back, but they're generally easy to subdue if your ship's in shape. Friendly bases are marked by "$$," friendly planets by "++." Beware of the "//" and "--" on the map! Those are enemy bases and planets. They're here for you to destroy. As you earn points, you'll rise in rank and obtain more powerful spaceships. Check out the Multiplayer Games Forum (a link is available from the *Mega-*

Wars I main menu). You'll find a message board there devoted to *MegaWars I*, and a file library with chronicles of battles, help text files, macros, and frontend software for various platforms. ✓COMPUSERVE→*go* mega 1 *Interface:* ✓COMPUSERVE→*go* mpgames →Libraries→*Search in MegaWars I library by keyword:* front end

Stats
- Difficulty: average
- Competition: live
- Number of players: 1–10
- Interface: ASCII
- Platforms: all

Commands
- To move relative to your current position, type: m r <number of x coordinates> <number of y coordinates>
- To see where you are in relation to your teammates and friendly points, type: list coa <or> list emp
- To fire phasers at a coordinate, type: ph <x> <y>
- To fire torpedoes, type: to <number of torpedoes> <x> <y>
- To repeat whatever your last command was: <escape>

MegaWarsIII A version of the Kesmai game *Stellar Emperor* on GEnie. In phase 1, your objective is to battle ships and enemy bases. In phase 2, you develop your colonies to earn the title of Lord Emperor of All the Galaxies. You'll find *MegaWars III* optional frontends for PCs, especially for use on CompuServe, in the Multiplayer Games Forum Library. Also in the library are final scores from past wars, reference texts, and commentary. On the Multiplayer Games Forum Message boards, players discuss the front-end programs, scores, and tactical maneuvers. ✓COMPUSERVE→*go* mega 3 *Interface:* ✓COMPUSERVE→*go* mpgames→Libraries→*Search in MegaWars III library by keyword:*

front end

Stats
- Difficulty: complex
- Competition: live
- Number of players: 1+
- Interface: ASCII
- Platforms: all

Phoenix In the course of about 30 turns (each consisting of up to 200 orders), players compete with each other to take control of at least half the galaxy. Each player controls a space empire and issues orders for his or her ships, factories, and other units. Ally with others or go it alone in this intense game of diplomacy, exploration, and trade. Once a week, a player mails in orders for his or her ships and planets to the moderator ($2.50 per turn), who processes the orders and mails back the results. A graphical interface for the play-by-email game is being developed. *Info:* ✓ **INTERNET**→*email* info@den.com ✉ *Email for automated info*

Stats
- Difficulty: complex
- Competition: turn-based
- Number of players: 2–20
- Interface: ASCII
- Platforms: all

Rebel Space The Interstellar Empire, once benevolent, is crumbling under corruption and a merciless dictatorship. The Emperor sends you out to seek new planets to feed the dying Empire. You accept the mission, though you know that rebellion is rife throughout the stretches of space you'll be traveling.

It's inevitable that you turn your back on the Empire's decay; the only question is, when? And which rebellion will you join: the Environmentalists, the Scientists, the Militarists? Or do you "go Rogue," leaving you with no one to help you or, for that matter,

Queen Elizabeth—screenshot from MPG-Net's Empire Builder.

hinder your progress? Using graphic screens for what is basically a grid-based, play-by-email game, you build an empire of your own, earning points based on civilization levels.

The vastness of space

You have four starships, with different strengths and weaknesses, to search for rich new colonies in the "vastness of space" (for cynics, that's a 15x99 grid.) Build up your planets' civilizations with the TechMods, ameliorate their environment with the EnviroMods, and strengthen your strongholds on them with your DefenseMods.

You'll also engage in a few battles and take over or lose a few planets. You can decide how frequently (two, three, or five turns a week) you want to play—you'll get 25 turns, regardless. If you don't make a move for a week, the game continues each turn with the last orders you issued, and then your empire goes on autopilot, scanning regions, building up colonies, and engaging in warfare. ✓ **PRODIGY**→*jump* rebel space **$**

Stats
- Difficulty: simple
- Competition: play-by-email
- Number of players: 50
- Interface: graphical
- Platforms: all

Commands
- To get instructions, use the command: ?
- To get support, leave a message for Admiral Phineas Fivestarr (Ret.) on the Ask the Admiral topic of the Stargate Cafe

Requirements: *Prodigy membership holder (whose ID ends in "A") must authorize enrollment*

Stellar Conquest A standard space-battle game, in which your goal is to conquer all of the known universe for your team. Explore nearby planets, engage in battle, and work your way up in rank. You earn points for a kill (100) or a planet capture (500). For destroying a planet, you lose 5,000.

At 10,000 points, you get your first promotion: lieutenant. As you increase in rank, you'll be trading goods for "quatloos" (the preferred currency), enlisting armies from friendly planets for battle, and shooting your photon torpedoes and antimatter missiles at enemy ships that get in the way. In the GameSIG Forum, most of the discussion in the *Stellar Conquest* topic is about the optional front-end for IBM-compatibles that's available as shareware in the Databases library. Also in the database are text help files and a user's manual. ✓ **DELPHI**→*go* gro gam→Stellar Conquest *Interface:* ✓ **DELPHI**→*go* gro gam→Databases→Read (and Download)→PASNAZ 3.03 IBM

Stats
- Difficulty: average
- Competition: live
- Number of players: 1+
- Interface: ASCII
- Platforms: all

Commands
- To set a course based on absolute coordinates, type: co <X>,<Y> a
- To see the planets near you, type: l p
- To see the ships in the game and

their coordinates, type: l s
* For a map of your area, type: scan

Stellar Emperor Similar to *Stellar Warrior*, but with a whole new dimension. In addition to ship flight and battle in the first phase of the game, you're also controlling a string of planets in the second phase, trying to achieve the highest level of civilization in your empire by manipulating your bases' economies and populations to greatness. The best colony-builder is named President of the Imperial Senate, while the best warrior is named Lord Emperor of All the Galaxies—not bad for a résumé entry.

Admiral 1.9, the Windows frontend, is optional, but it certainly will help you organize the information you need for effective ship and planet management. You'll find other files in the *Stellar Emperor* category (11) of the MultiPlayer Games RoundTable software library—scores of past games, mostly. The *Stellar Emperor* MPGRT bulletin board topic is full of game talk: proposed enhancements, war stories, and news about the latest skirmishes in the *Stellar Emperor* universe. ✓ **GENIE**→*keyword* emperor *Interface:* ✓ **GENIE**→*keyword* emperor→Download Optional Admiral for Windows Front End

Stats
* Difficulty: complex
* Competition: live
* Number of players: 1+
* Interface: ASCII, graphical
* Platforms: all

Stellar Warrior A live, multiplayer space-combat game set in the 23rd century. The sentient races are divided among four Alliances. Your mission is to blow the guys in the other Alliances away, conquer their planets, and

hold on to your own. Sometimes you'll be acting alone; sometimes you'll be part of an allied operation.

But first you must build a ship: a scout, destroyer, cruiser, battle cruiser, or battleship. Next, take command of your ship. You'll be immediately thrown into the command console, with the ship's computer spitting out what seems like nonsense. It's at this point that most players opt to download the manual—available from the main menu under Instructions.

The game is complex and requires you to take all actions through a specified set of commands. The graphic frontends for the IBM, Atari, and Amiga are available from the MultiPlayer Games RoundTable file library, which will also help make your ship's command console a little easier to understand. Discussions can be found in the MPGRT Bulletin Board under topics 12, 13, and 14. ✓ **GENIE**→*keyword* warrior *Interface:* ✓ **GENIE**→*keyword* mpgrt →Multiplayer Games Software Library→set 12→Download a File→ 186 *or* 187 *or* 189

Stats
* Difficulty: complex
* Competition: live

> "Build up your civilizations with Tech-Mods, ameliorate their environment with EnviroMods, and strengthen your strongholds with DefenseMods."

* Number of players: 1+
* Interface: ASCII, graphical
* Platforms: all

Commands
* To see a map of the universe, type: map
* To move from orbit to impulse power, type: imp
* To travel to a star in hyperspace, type: nav [<target>] [,<warp>]
* For a picture of local starspace, type: pic

Ultimate Universe Well thought-out space-conquest game, with good online help and programmable keyboard macros to make your journey a bit smoother. Also, you can pick up your ship and move it to another BBS! A neat feature if your board isn't challenging enough for you—or, for that matter, if you've been roughed up too often and want to give peace a chance! ✓ CHECK LOCAL BULLETIN BOARD SYSTEMS FOR THIS OR SIMILAR GAMES ☎ →*dial* 508-693-7396

Stats
* Difficulty: complex
* Competition: turn-based
* Number of players: 2+
* Platforms: all

Yankee Trader The future has arrived and the central Earth goverment has found itself unable to maintain law and order through the vastness of space. Trade barons and mercenaries rule the day, and you, with only a small space vessel but great ambitions, are prepared to set out and become one of them. ✓ CHECK LOCAL BULLETIN BOARD SYSTEMS FOR THIS OR SIMILAR GAMES ☎ →*dial* 717-686-3037

Stats
* Difficulty: complex
* Competition: turn-based
* Number of players: 2+
* Interface: ANSI
* Platforms: all

Hundred Years War

How long did the Hundred Years War last? One hundred sixteen years, or as long as six

years on GEnie's simulation of the medieval religious war between France and England. *HYW* is probably one of the most historically rigorous war games yet, and also one of the most detailed. If the play-by-mail strategy game *Diplomacy* is *Risk* without dice, *Hundred Years War* is *Diplomacy* with social history.

Game specifics hew to actual archival documents, right down to the heraldries of landed aristocrats and the territories they held, and to peasant uprisings and the intricacies of court politics. This degree of detail by no means precludes free will, though.

Game variants sometimes break from historical precedent to ponder counter-factual possibilities such as, in one version, "that the strong Kingdoms of France and England never formed, so the powerful magnates of Europe struggle against each other to build their own Kingdoms. There will be Mongol invasions, and the Moorish realm of Cordoba to reckon with as well."

Political maneuvers

HYW produces its own historical record with the help of a bulletin board within the game. This reproduces the great strength of play-by-mail strategy games: Players who never meet in real time ("on the field") can still carry on intricate political maneuvers. Just as in the actual 14th-century war, the role-playing simulation crosses generational lines. You don't play a

Knight on horseback—from Compu-Serve's Living History Forum.

single character. Your first persona ages, marries, raises children, and dies, leaving you to carry out unfinished work through offspring that must marry well.

Herald help

Beginners should avail themselves of the lavish human help within the otherwise daunting *HYW* by seeking the counsel of game staff called Heralds. Most games have at least two Heralds one for the French and one for the English Kings—as well as a few Heralds-at-Large who answer less partial questions. The Heralds "assist the King in ruling the empire and advise the players of that nation." Heralds spend a lot of time in the game hosting roundtables, but they can also be emailed on the GEnie system at HYWH$.

Choosing a game to join

There are always a number of *HYW* games running. Some are long-standing simulations with varying paces (the "Slow Game" updates play only twice a week;

"Game One" has been doing daily, hour-long updates for years), and others are experiments for beginner practice and feature-testing. Beginners will usually want to nose around in a practice run before jumping into the fray of one of the long-running games. ✓**GENIE** →*keyword* hyw

Stats
* Difficulty: complex
* Competition: turn-based
* Number of players: 2+
* Interface: ASCII
* Platforms: all

Hundred Years War Round-Table For *HYW* discussion, attend an "Interactive Court Gathering," where members involved in the same game gather (sometimes weekly). The HYW Bulletin Board (BB) offers more than two dozen separate categories, public and private, that track the unfolding of specific games. And the HYW Real-Time Conference (RTC) offers regularly scheduled meetings on subjects ranging from game techniques to historical topics.

Announcements

Announcements about the RTCs are made in Category 1 in the BB. New players should visit the HYW Help Desk sessions hosted by game Heralds on Saturday afternoons at 3 p.m. EST in Round-Table Conference room 2. Background reading on both the game and medieval times in general is available in the HYW File Library, which also archives highlights from the game bulletin boards. ✓**GENIE**→ *keyword* hywrt

Sports

Fantasy leagues, in which participants assemble teams of real-life players that compete using real-life stats, dominate online sports gaming. Just about every professional team sport is covered in games ranging from from Prodigy's **Baseball Manager** to **NBA** to **USA Today Fantasy Football** to **Grandstand Hockey Leagues**. You haven't truly surfed the Net, though, until you've experienced email **E-Wrestling**.

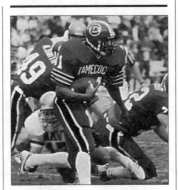

Gaining yards—downloaded from CompuServe's Graphics Gallery Forum.

On the Net

Across the board

Fantasy Sports Manage your dream baseball, football, basketball, or hockey team through the season. First, however, you have to reserve a team by sending an email to "Redcoat" or "Mark_Schey" of Sports Connection Online. You'll get a confirmation upon which you can enter "Fantasy Registration" on the Main Menu and put that team together. You can run a perpetual franchise in a perpetual league—in other words you'll be competing against your friends year after year—or you can try a nonperpetual league. Both carry an annual $10 maintenance fee, and a one-time start-up fee ($10 for perpetual teams, $5 for non-perpetual). Game business and dugout chatter takes place in the Forum, while the Databases carry scores, rosters, and schedules, in addition to rules. ✓**DELPHI**→*go* gro spo **$**

Stats
• Difficulty: average
• Competition: turn-based
• Number of players: 2+
• Interface: ASCII
• Platforms: all

Fantasy Sports League RoundTable When baseball, basketball, football, and hockey are in season, you'll find fantasy leagues taking place here—both official and unofficial. Official leagues are run by the RoundTable staff, unofficial leagues by just about anyone… including you, if you want. The Fantasy Sports Bulletin Board is where the leagues do their business: posting stats, results, lineup choices, etc. Category 15 in the bulletin board allows you to read and post to the Usenet newsgroups related to fantasy leagues. In the Fantasy Sports Software Libraries, fantasists can download rule books, draft rosters, free-agent lists, and box scores. ✓**GENIE**→*keyword* fsl

Stats
• Difficulty: average
• Competition: turn-based

• Number of players: 1+
• Interface: ASCII
• Platforms: all

FANTSPORTS (echo) Fantasy sports games via the message boards. ✓**INTELEC**

Stats
• Difficulty: average
• Competition: turn-based
• Number of players: 2+
• Interface: ASCII
• Platforms: all

Player Track Create a list of 50 players who you follow throughout the baseball season either as a fan or as a fantasy manager. Download stats as often as you like for input into your sport-sim software. The "Customize" option allows you to see players' stats for the week or for the season to date. ✓**PRODIGY**→ *jump* player track

Sports Simulation Forum Besides being a huge repository for sport-sim software support and discussion, this is also a forum where people participate in fantasy-league competition. Official leagues for basketball, baseball, football, golf, auto racing, and hockey are run by the forum's sysops. You'll find all the rules in the Libraries databases—search by the keyword "rules." The last category in the Message and Libraries is reserved for "independent leagues," run by members, and includes all of the aforementioned, plus wrestling. Most of the fantasy leagues use front-end commercial software, such as *Wayne Gretzky III*, *Front Page Sports Football Pro*, or *Pursue the Pennant*. You'll also find discussion of various sport-sim game programs in the Message boards, and patches, upgrades, and scenarios files in the Libraries. ✓**COMPUSERVE**→*go* sprtsims

Stats
• Difficulty: average

- Competition: turn-based
- Number of players: 1+
- Interface: ASCII, graphical
- Platforms: all

Auto Racing

Auto Racing Discuss *Indy Car Racing, Indianapolis 500,* and other racing sims in the Pit Stop. The Auto Racing Library has picture files for *ICR,* program fixes, and more. To compete in the *Indy Car Racing* competition, download the file "Indycar Racing Head2Head" for complete rules. ✓ **AMERICA ON-LINE** ...→*keyword* grandstand→In the Pits Auto Racing→The Pit Stop (for messages) ...→*keyword* grandstand→In the Pits Auto Racing→ Auto Racing Library (for files)

Baseball

Baseball Manager *Baseball Manager*—or *BBM,* as it's often called—is one of Prodigy's hot properties. Players either choose the Classic version for a hefty $125 a season of up to 162 games, or the Lightning version (a sort of "BBM Lite") of 54 games, for around $60 a season. (Prices tend to drop as the season nears its end.) Managers (that's you) first choose which version they want to play, then select "Enroll Now," decide on the American League (with a designated hitter) or the National League (no DH), and sign up for a league by choosing "Next Available" or "Reserved" (if you have friends you want to compete against).

"The Lip"

Name your team, give yourself a nickname ("The Lip" worked for Leo Durocher), and select "Commit." This bills your credit card, but you have seven days to cancel and get a refund. When your team name has been registered with the Commissioner, you enter the Pre-Draft period. This is where you study and rank players available for drafting. During the Draft, each manager in your league picks 28 players for his team, beginning with (first draft) starting pitchers, (second draft) outfielders, (third draft) infielders, and (fourth draft) relief pitchers and catchers. After the draft, you horse- (or pitcher-, catcher-, shortstop-, etc.-) trade. If you can't make a deal for a position you've just gotta have, scramble throught the free-agent lists to find that green-but-promising first baseman to back up your back-injury-prone star. Once your team is set, you'll pick your lineups and pitching rotations.

Roster moves

Now the Season begins. Your team plays every day (except for a three-day break for the All-Stars). Throughout the season, you'll be making roster moves, lineup changes, and pitching rotation adjustments, signing free agents, and trading players. Games are decided based on the daily results of the actual players. If you've got a player in your lineup who didn't play, Prodigy's computers will use an earlier appearance of your player.

Every night, after you've set your pitching starts and batting order (Classic version managers face a few more decisions), the computers whir into action, matching your hamstrung lineup against the opposing team's ace pitcher, your hotshot relievers against their can-of-corn hitters. In the morning, everybody reads the news (displayed in an unforgiving tabloid style) and gets the results to see how they fared—gloats or whines in the Diamond Club. ✓ **PRODIGY**→*jump* bbm **$**

Stats
- Difficulty: average
- Competition: turn-based

- Number of players: 1–10
- Interface: graphical
- Platforms: all

Commands
- To get instructions, use the command: Help
- For more support, leave a message for the Commissioner on the Tryout Club or Diamond Club board

Requirements: *Must be played between noon EST and "curfew" (1 a.m. EST); a Prodigy membership holder (whose I.D. ends in "A") must authorize enrollment; requires 640k RAM; enrollment takes place between real-life baseball's spring training and the end of July*

Baseball Stats Baseball statistics from previous seasons. ✓ **INTERNET** ...→*ftp* eucalyptus.cc.swarthmore.edu→anonymous→<your email address>→/pub/baseball/stats ...→*ftp* wuarchive.wustl.edu→anonymous→<your email address>→/doc/misc/sports/mlb/stats

Fantasy Baseball Download *Fantasy Baseball* software that lets you create a fantasy league for your friends and officemates. Teams are ranked weekly based on point totals. ✓ **PRODIGY**→*jump* fbl→Play Ball! Learn More! Sign On!→Fantasy League Information **$**

Stats
- Difficulty: average
- Competition: turn-based
- Number of players: 2+
- Interface: graphical
- Platform: DOS

Requirements: *IBM 80286 or compatible with graphics card*

Fantasy Baseball Chatter (echo) Managing a *fantasy baseball* team? Stop by for strategizing and trade talk. ✓ **ICENET**

Fantasy Baseball Home Page An attempt to bring together much of the info on *fantasy base-*

ball (and baseball in general) that's scattered over the Internet. There are links to online stat servers (Total Quality Stats is run from here, for instance), team predictions, and a demo of *Windows Fantasy Baseball* software. ✓**INTERNET**→ *www* http://www.cm.cf.ac.uk/ User/Gwyn.Price/fantasy_base ball.html

Grandstand Fantasy Baseball League Classic *fantasy baseball*, with rules based on the book *Rotisserie League Baseball*, by Glen Waggoner (Bantam). Owners draft 23 players from whichever league, AL or NL, they join. A team's performance is based on players' stats in the standard four offensive and four pitching categories: composite BA, total HRs, total RBIs, total SB, composite ERA, total wins, composite ratio of walks-plus-hits to innings-pitched, and total saves. A team's cumulative totals determine its standings in the league.

In the Commissioner's Desk message board, you can ask the *GFBL* commissioner for more details, get rulings, and learn more about the operation of the game. The real meat, however, is on the GFBL League Message Board, where owners brag about their teams, recruit other potential team owners, and talk about games played in their league.

League members download their stats from the GFBL Stats Library. The draft and weekly "league meetings" are held in the Grandstand's Conference Rooms —select "Conference Rooms and Schedules" from the Dugout Baseball menu. Don't miss too many meetings of your league, however. If you miss more than three consecutively, you may get your franchise yanked. ✓**AMERICA ONLINE**→ *keyword* grandstand→Dugout Baseball→Grandstand Fantasy Baseball (GFBL) **$**

Stats
- Difficulty: average
- Competition: live and turn-based
- Number of players: 8–11
- Platforms: all

The Internet Baseball Information Center Join a *fantasy baseball* league or pick up stats for your offline league. ✓**INTERNET**→*www* http://www.gems.com/ ibic/ **$**

Major League Baseball Play *fantasy league baseball* on the Freenet. The forum features a directory of owners, a drafting board, league rosters, game reports, and rules and information. ☎→*dial* 216-368-3888→A visitor→ Explore the system→go games→Pro Status Sports→Major League Baseball ✓**INTERNET**→*telnet* freenet-in-a.cwru.edu→A visitor→Explore the system→go games→Pro Status

> "Every night, after you've set your pitching starts and batting order, the computers whir into action, matching your hamstrung lineup against the opposing team's ace pitcher, your hotshot relievers against their can-of-corn hitters."

Sports→Major League Baseball
Stats
- Difficulty: average
- Competition: turn-based
- Number of players: 2+
- Interface: ASCII
- Platforms: all

rec.sport.baseball.fantasy (ng) Catch-all *Rotisserie-baseball* discussion group for advice on trades, news of injuries, and discussions on those ever-important statistics. ✓**USENET** *FAQ:* ✓**INTERNET**→*ftp* eucalyptus.cc.swarth more.edu→anonymous→<your email address>→/pub/baseball/ fanta-roto

Relaynet Baseball League (echo) Play in an organized *fantasy baseball* league. ✓**RELAYNET**

Rotisserie Baseball Download the diehard fan version of *Fantasy Baseball*. Each week *Rotisserie Baseball* determines rankings of the teams in your league based on their standing in four pitching and four hitting categories, including home runs, stolen bases, runs batted in, wins, saves, and earned run average. A franchise's weekly overall rank is based on the cumulative standings in all eight categories. ✓**PRODIGY**→*jump* fbl→Play Ball! Learn More! Sign On!→Rotisserie League Information **$**
Stats
- Difficulty: average
- Competition: turn-based
- Number of players: 2+
- Interface: graphical
- Platform: DOS
Requirements: *IBM 80286 or compatible, with a graphics card*

Rotisserie Baseball Mailing List (ml) Not a league but an ongoing discussion on the formation of leagues, the trading and auctioning of players, and other issues related to any *fantasy baseball*

leagues. ✓ **INTERNET**→*email* mailserv @uwplatt.edu ✍ *Type in message body:* subscribe roto

Simulation Baseball (GBL) Using the commercial software *APBA Baseball for Windows*, this simulation-league game has each team play three home and three away games. Standings, rules discussions, schedules, and trade talk take place on the GBL League Board. ✓ **AMERICA ONLINE**→*keyword* grandstand→Dugout Baseball→Simulation Baseball (GBL)

Stats
• Difficulty: average
• Competition: turn-based
• Number of players: 10
• Platform: Windows
Requirements: *APBA Baseball for Windows*

Stat Service Downloadable stats for *Fantasy Baseball* or *Rotisserie Baseball* software (to save you the tedium of entering them yourself). ✓ **PRODIGY**→*jump* fbl **$**

USA Today Baseball League With a lineup-per-week, you field nine players (a DH for AL or a utility player for NL makes the ninth) and five pitchers against other *USAT-BL* teams. You win or lose based on performance in eight categories: team BA, total team HRs, total team RBIs, total team SBs, your pitching staff's ERA, the staff's hits-plus-walks-divided-by-innings-pitched ratio, total staff wins, and total staff saves. A game week lasts from Monday through Sunday. There are three seasons: Season I, Season II, and the Playoffs. All teams redraft at the beginning of each season, with F$70 (70 fantasy dollars) to spend. ✓ **USA TODAY INFORMATION CENTER** →*go* fantasy→Fantasy Baseball (USAT-BL)

Stats
• Difficulty: average

Dee Brown—downloaded from wuarchive.wustl.edu.

• Competition: turn-based
• Number of players: 1+
• Interface: ASCII
• Platforms: all

Basketball

Big League Basketball A sports-simulation game running on many BBSs. *BLB* players choose what shot to attempt, what defense to play, etc. There are two eight-minute halves, and as usual, the high scores are posted. If you quit before the game ends, you lose. ✓ CHECK LOCAL BULLETIN BOARD SYSTEMS FOR THIS OR SIMILAR GAMES ☎ →*dial* 205-739-1469

Stats
• Difficulty: average
• Competition: high scoring
• Number of players: 1+
• Interface: ANSI
• Platforms: all

Fantasy/Simulation Hoops Leagues You'll find two kinds of basketball competition here: rotisserie (based on your players' performance in the current series) and simulation leagues, where actual games are computer-simulated, using stats from a previous NBA season. To win in the Grandstand Basketball Association, or GBA, your fantasy team's ten players have to compile the best stats in

11 cumulative categories: minutes played, field-goal percentage, free-throw percentage, three-point field goals made, total points, total rebounds, total assists, least total personal fouls, total steals, least total turnovers, and total blocks. In the Grandstand Basketball Simulation Leagues, there are four games per week (for approximately 15 weeks), decided based on the previous season's stats. Warning: Overplaying a player creates a one-in-ten chance that the player will be "injured." The length of an injury is decided by rolling a die. Injury risk is based on the total number of minutes played last season, so spread 'em out. ✓ **AMERICA ONLINE**→*keyword* grandstand→Off the Glass Basketball→Fantasy/Simulation Hoops Leagues **$**

Stats
• Difficulty: average
• Competition: turn-based
• Number of players: 8–14
• Platforms: all

NBA A basketball fantasy league. Create a team based on real NBA players and follow its progress. The forum features a directory of owners, league rosters and standings, and rules and information. ☎ →*dial* 216-368-3888→A visitor→ Explore the system→go games→Pro Status Sports→NBA ✓ **INTERNET**→ *telnet* freenet-in-a.cwru.edu→A visitor→Explore the system→go games →Pro Status Sports→NBA

Stats
• Difficulty: average
• Competition: turn-based
• Number of players: 2+
• Interface: ASCII
• Platforms: all

Relaynet Basketball (echo) Follow and join basketball play-by-play. ✓ **RELAYNET**

USA Today Basketball League With F$40 (40 fantasy dollars) to blow on Shaq and the guys, you become team president, general manager, and head coach against other weekly players in this online simulation of NBA drafts, lineups, and matchups. You begin the season by drafting ten top players. Then submit your lineup each week for that week's games.

Showers

Nine scoring categories determine whether your team moves ahead in the standings or retreats to the showers in shame: total points scored, total three-point field goals made, total assists, total steals, total blocked shots, total turnovers (keep it low), total rebounds (offensive rebounds count double), total field-goal percentage, and total free-throw percentage.

The highest score obtainable in any game is ten points (includes a bonus point for winning); the lowest is zilch. You'll trade with other teams throughout the season, watch the real-world news for injuries or abysmal performances, and work your way up to a championship season. ✓**USA TODAY INFORMATION CENTER**→*go* fantasy→Fantasy Basketball (USAT-BKL)

Stats
- Difficulty: average
- Competition: turn-based
- Number of players: 1+
- Interface: ASCII
- Platforms: all

Football

Betting Doors-Football Somewhere between plain old gambling and plain old cyberpunk anarchy, you may trip over a BBS that offers sports pools. Football pool "doors" seem to come up frequently on various privately run BBS systems. The prizes offered are up to the system operator. Sometimes you play for real green money, other times for free time online or

> "Somewhere between plain old gambling and plain old cyberpunk anarchy, you may trip over a BBS that offers sports pools."

merely a notice that you were this season's winner. ✓CHECK LOCAL BULLETIN BOARD SYSTEMS FOR THIS OR SIMILAR GAMES

Stats
- Difficulty: simple
- Competition: high scoring
- Number of players: 2+
- Interface: ASCII

Fantasy Football (echo) Play along with others in a *fantasy football* game. ✓**ICENET**

Fantasy Football Download *Fantasy Football* software to run a fantasy NFL league with friends and officemates. ✓**PRODIGY**→*jump* ffl **$**

Stats
- Difficulty: average
- Competition: turn-based
- Number of players: 2+
- Interface: graphical
- Platform: DOS

Requirements: *IBM 80286 or compatible computer with a graphics card*

The Fantasy Football League Create a team of NFL players and pit them against your opponents. Based on the stats of real NFL players, teams compete weekly during the football season. The forum features game reports, mailing lists for each league, a directory of owners, a trading wire, and

rules and information. ☎→*dial* 216-368-3888→A visitor→Explore the system→go ffl ✓**INTERNET**→ *telnet* freenet-in-a.cwru.edu→A visitor→Explore the system→go ffl

Stats
- Difficulty: average
- Competition: turn-based
- Number of players: 2+
- Interface: ASCII
- Platforms: all

Fantasy Football Pool Choose a fantasy team of 16 NFL players with three quarterbacks, two place-kickers, five running backs, and six receivers (wide receivers or tight ends). Contest points are awarded in four categories: touchdown passes, rushing or receiving TDs, real-life extra points after TDs, and field goals. When you've picked your team, you'll be asked to predict how many points it will score. Your prediction will be used only to break a tie. The highest-scoring fantasy team of the week is awarded free online time. ✓**GENIE**→ *keyword* football→Choose this week's Fantasy Team

Stats
- Difficulty: average
- Competition: turn-based
- Number of players: 1+
- Interface: ASCII
- Platforms: all

Football Stats & Stuff A plethora of information—from a list of free agents to a quarterback rating system to statistics files. A fantasy subdirectory at this same sight was rather bare, but stay tuned. ✓**INTERNET**→*ftp* vnet.net→ anonymous→<your email address> →/pub/football/PRO

Grandstand Fantasy Football The premise is simple: If your RL team's players score during the NFL games, your virtual team also scores. Teams play an 18-week schedule. The last two weeks of the NFL schedule are for GFL playoffs. Each participant drafts a 15-player team with at least one quarterback, two running backs, three wide receivers (includes tight ends), and one placekicker. The other eight can be from any of these categories. The draft takes place in the Grandstand Conference Rooms—available from the 50-Yard Line Football menu. Scores are based on your performance in 13 categories. ✓**AMERICA ONLINE**→*keyword* grandstand→50-Yard Line Football→Grandstand Fantasy Football (GFL)

Stats
- Competition: live and turn-based
- Number of players: 8
- Platforms: all

Grandstand Simulation Football Compete against other team owners for the season championship using the commercial software *Front Page Sports Football Pro*. You play only the away games, no home games. ✓**AMERICA ONLINE**→*keyword* grandstand→50-Yard Line Football→GStand Simulation Football (GSFL)

Stats
- Difficulty: average
- Competition: turn-based
- Number of players: 1–28
- Platform: DOS

Requirements: *Front Page Sports Football Pro*

QB1 *QB1* pits your ability to predict the next play against the fortune-telling talent of hundreds or thousands of people nationwide, and not just on GEnie. People in bars and restaurants all over the country are competing against you during televised NCAA and NFL games. Are they going to run the ball outside the left tackle, or pass deep to right? You predict the call and earn points for correct and partially correct consecutive calls (for example, you got the basic

> "*QB1* pits your ability to predict the next play against that of hundreds or thousands of people nationwide. People in bars and restaurants all over the country are competing against you during televised NCAA and NFL games."

play, but were wrong about the direction or distance).

The single most important strategy in winning is to accumulate correct "consecutive calls." If you make an incorrect call, your points are reset to zero. The game also allows you to chat with other GEnie players. Users of the optional front-end software are already in chat mode. Text-only players must type "/cha" to enable chat, then "/sen" followed by a message in order to be heard. ✓**GENIE**→*keyword* qb1 *Interface:* ✓**GENIE**→*keyword* qb1→Download QB1 Front End Software

Stats
- Difficulty: average
- Competition: live
- Number of players: 1+
- Interface: graphical
- Platforms: all

rec.sport.football.fantasy (ng) Not quite as organized as the baseballers, but this newsgroup

compensates for that with discussion of injuries, trades, and the maintenance of Rotisserie football leagues. The FAQ is in progress. ✓**USENET**

Relaynet Football League (echo) Huddle to discuss and pick your teams. ✓**RELAYNET**

USA Today Football League With F$30 (30 fantasy dollars)—imagine each fantasy dollar represents a million RL dollars—to start, you draft an eight-part NFL team: one quarterback, two running backs, two wide receivers, one utility receiver, one placekicker, and a defensive team. Watch your payroll or you'll end up trying to draft your defense with one buck. Submit your lineup each week (or else you're out) and wait for the results. ✓**USA TODAY INFORMATION CENTER**→*go* fantasy→Fantasy Football (USAT-FL)

Stats
- Difficulty: average
- Competition: turn-based
- Number of players: 1–28
- Interface: ASCII
- Platforms: all

Golf

Grandstand's Golf Leagues Compete against other players in several golf leagues. Players upload their turn files from a game to get put on the challenge ladder. You'll need to study the courses for *Links386 Pro* to compete in the most popular contest, the Access Links Pro Tour. Files are uploaded to the Golf Library, and discussion takes place "In the Fairway." ✓**AMERICA ONLINE**→*keyword* grandstand→On the Green Golf

Stats
- Difficulty: average
- Competition: turn-based
- Number of players: 1+
- Interface: graphical

• Platform: DOS

Requirements: *Must own a version of* Links386 Pro

Links Country Club Golf Shoot it out to be in the top five on your favorite BBS in this golf-simulation game. You'll get to choose of either 9 or 18 holes, on a colorful ANSI screen. The hardest part is, just like on the actual links, picking the right club. ✓ CHECK LOCAL BULLETIN BOARDS FOR THIS OR SIMILAR GAMES ☎ →*dial* 815-886-3233/815-886-9381

Stats
• Difficulty: average
• Competition: high scoring
• Number of players: 1+
• Interface: ASCII, ANSI
• Platforms: all

Prodigy Network Golf Tour Download a new course each month and compete against someone else by uploading his or her results. You can view the leader board (with accompanying scorecards), read a hole-by-hole replay (number of strokes per hole), and view key stats: longest drive, closest to the pin, most fairways off tee, most greens, fewest putts, most birdies, most eagles, and fewest bogeys. ✓ **PRODIGY**→*jump* pngt **$**

Stats
• Difficulty: average
• Competition: turn-based
• Number of players: 2+
• Interface: graphical
• Platforms: all

Requirements: Jack Nicklaus Signature Edition

Hockey

Grandstand Hockey Leagues Using various commercial *fantasy-hockey-league* software packages—*NHLPA Hockey, Wayne Gretzky Hockey,* etc.—players form leagues, either as the general manager of an

Soccer player—downloaded from CompuServe's Quick Pictures Forum.

existing NHL team or by drafting favorite players from different teams. Using NHL stats, the teams get matched up against each other and the results are posted on the message boards. ✓ **AMERICA ON-LINE**→*keyword* grandstand→Blue Line Hockey→Fantasy Hockey Leagues **$**

Stats
• Difficulty: average
• Competition: turn-based
• Number of players: 2+
• Platforms: all

Relaynet Hockey League (echo) Pit your hockey team against other Relaynet players (or RIMEers). ✓ **RELAYNET**

Soccer

Electronic Soccer Each player controls a football (or, if you insist on being American, soccer) team. A team roster consists of 11 to 25 players, each of whom has unique skills. Teams make money through ticket sales, and you can spend the revenues paying players, bidding in the draft, and making trades with other teams. The coach trains players and picks the lineup and strategy for each match. The moderation program then determines the result of the match. Each league is divided into divisions,

and has a league championship. The rules are similar for all the leagues (they are based on play-by-postal-mail rules written by Alan Parr in the pre-Net year of 1970). Although the number of participants is limited, the leagues are expanding all the time, and often positions become available in mid-season when coaches disappear. *Info:* ✓ **INTERNET**→*ftp* ftp.erg. sri.com→anonymous→<your email address>→/pub/pbm/eefl

Stats
• Difficulty: average
• Competition: turn-based
• Number of players: 2+
• Interface: ASCII
• Platforms: all

Strategic Postal Australian Rules Football (SPARF) Each gamer controls a team with up to 45 players via email. A player has four types of skills, and grows older (slower and more likely to become injured) as seasons are played. Between matches, team members can be trained, and then the coach picks the lineup for the next match. The moderation program then determines the result of the match, taking into account the strategy and skills of the two teams involved. The results of the match determine not only the team's standing in the league but its popularity, which in turn determines its income, which reflects on a team's ability to pay players' salaries and hire free agents. Enter the trials and tribulations of professional sports. *Info:* ✓ **INTERNET** ...→*email* munch@soda.berkeley. edu ✍ *To get instructions on using the email server, type in subject line:* help ...→*ftp* ftp.erg.sri.com→anonymous→<your email address>→ /pub/pbm/sparf

Stats
• Difficulty: average
• Competition: turn-based
• Number of players: 2+

• Interface: ASCII
• Platforms: all

Wrestling

Cactus Jack Archives Reports on e-wrestling matches across the Net as well as information on real-life wrestling matches. ✓**INTERNET**→*ftp* cactus.jack.health.ufl.edu →anonymous→<your email address>

E-Wrestling Okay, so you're not 300 pounds and covered in steroid-induced muscles, nor is your nickname Gorilla. But now you can pretend all this in the Cyberspace ring of email wrestling. In what is more a work of interactive fiction than a game, players join one of five Federations—or, heck, join them all—and manage their wrestlers through grudge matches, tag teams, and the annual Summit, which brings all the Federations together for an all-star smash-up. Rules vary among Federations, but the gist is the same: Send in your moves electronically to the Fed-head, who then adjudicates to see who lives and who is pile-driven into mush. Results are delivered in the form of a color commentary on the match: "Oooh, I don't think Spider was quite ready for that elbow down his throat!" You get the idea. ✓SEE THE SIDEBAR FOR CONTACTS FROM EACH OF THE FEDERATIONS.

Stats
• Difficulty: simple
• Competition: turn-based
• Number of players: 2+
• Interface: ASCII
• Platforms: all

E-Wrestling WWW Site A small site carrying e-wrestling info, including the newsletter *Ramblin' Round the Ring*, and links to FTP sites with material on some of the E-wrestling's Federations. ✓**INTER-**

Wrestlers—downloaded from Compu-Serve's Graphics Corner Forum.

NET→*www* http://www.cgd.ucar.edu/cas/nexus/ewr

Grandstand Wrestling Association Fantasy role-players have their broadsword-and-spell matches. Now wrestling fans have their own version. Players meet in a chat room, along with a referee, who rolls the online dice to see if, among other things, that "double awesome drop" worked and, with a second roll, if there was any blood. A ton of organizational rules and divisions undergird the GWA. You'll find rules and hints in the Wrestling/Boxing Library off the Squared Circle Boxing/Wrestling main menu. Download the file "GWA Hints from the Pros" for a beginner's how-to. ✓**AMERICA ONLINE**→*keyword* grandstand→Squared Circle Boxing/Wrestling→GStand Wrestling Association (GWA)

Stats
• Difficulty: simple
• Competition: live
• Number of players: 2–4
• Platforms: all

World League Wrestling Professional wrestling in all its charm: fake, but a lot of brute fun! A very quick and simple game where you choose your holds and maneuvers and even your manager may help out with the occasional "chair-over-the-head move." Each BBS

can have only one World Champ, so you'll take a beating from challengers, even when you're not around. The computer will do its best to defend your good (or bad) name. ✓CHECK LOCAL BULLETIN BOARD SYSTEMS FOR THIS OR SIMILAR GAMES ☎→*dial* 304-797-0277

Stats
• Difficulty: simple
• Competition: live
• Number of players: 2+
• Interface: ANSI
• Platforms: all

E-WRESTLING

Join one of these E-Wrestling federations:

Electronic Superstars Wrestling
ap3b+@andrew.cmu.edu
(Aidan Palmer)

Electronic Wrestling Council
beatbox@netcom.com
(Shawn Pearce)

falknemj@cnsvax.uwec.edu
(Mike Falkner)

EWWA
TheMagpie@aol.com

Intercontinental Champions of Electronic Wrestling:
dunhamtim@urvax.urich.edu
(Tim Dunham)

ramosxmrk@urvax.urich.edu
(Mark Ramos)

henry.r.broaddus@dartmouth.edu
(Henry Broaddus)

Pacific Championship Wrestling
bonder@netcom.com
(Bruce Onder)

Part 4

Puzzles, Trivia & Word Games

Mind games

Remember all those games you used to play on car trips?

Well, now you can play them while cruising the Information Superhighway. Compete to **Finish the Phrase** of another player or a famous quote, or explore the countless variations on 20 questions, from **Who Am I?** to the creepy-sounding artificial-intelligence game **Guess the Disease**. Almost every parlor or party game is represented, including clever low-bandwidth adaptations of **Charades** and **Memory Games**, and a heavy-duty **Scavenger Hunt** that tests your Net knowledge.

Albert Einstein—downloaded from ftp.sunet.se.

On the Net

Across the board

Center Stage Game Shows In the Center Stage, hundreds of people can play word or trivia games at the same time. First check the Box Office to see what games are scheduled for the week. Then read the rules—in Game Show Rules. When the day and time arrive for a game you're interested in, choose "Enter Center Stage." The competitors are divided in virtual rows of four to eight people and your entries are visible only to the players in your row—a class cutup's dream. To respond to the game-show host's questions, who's on the "stage" so everyone can see him, use the "Ask a Ques-

tion" feature. Depending on the game and your answer, the host will determine whether to broadcast your input to the auditorium audience. Prizes are in the form of free connect time. Many of the AOL games listed on the following pages are played in the Center Stage. ✓ **AMERICA ONLINE**→*keyword* center stage

Games Parlor Conversation, jokes, and "hugs" have a higher priority in these word and trivia games than winning. But despite the laid-back attitude, there's an official game master and play can become rather intense. New players will find the games easy to join and learn. In fact, there are usually one or two helpers who'll zap you the rules upon request—while you're playing.

Or you can read one of the Game Rules folders from the Game Parlor window before beginning. An evening of parlor games generally starts between 7 p.m. and 8 p.m. EST in the People Connection public rooms Game Parlor and Game Parlor

Too, and each game lasts for about an hour. Check the Game Schedule from the Game Parlor window for the date and time of your favorite games. Also available from the Game Parlor window: Gamer's Gazette and Parlor Ponderables message boards, and the Parlor Antics library of downloadable sounds for use in the Game Parlor rooms. ✓ **AMERICA ONLINE**→*keyword* pc→Rooms→Game Parlor or Game Parlor Too

Puzzle Box A hodgepodge hour's worth of games, made up of three parlor games of the host's choosing. ✓ **AMERICA ONLINE**→*keyword* pc→Rooms→Game Parlor or Game Parlor Too

Stats
• Difficulty: simple
• Competition: live
• Number of players: 2–23
• Interface: ASCII
• Platforms: all
Requirements: *Played only at scheduled times*

Finish the phrase

Danglers The host provides a few words (e.g., "My favorite place is..."). You have 15 seconds (after the host says "Enter!") to finish the sentence. If your answer matches another player's, you earn a point. ✓ **AMERICA ONLINE**→*keyword* pc→Rooms→Game Parlor or Game Parlor Too

Stats
• Difficulty: simple
• Competition: live
• Number of players: 2–23
• Interface: ASCII
• Platforms: all
Requirements: *Played only at scheduled times*

Ditto Similar to *Danglers* in that you earn points for finishing a sentence with exactly the same word or phrase as another player. Often, however, the host will use a phrase, movie line, or song lyric with a twist. E.g., "Love the one you're with—unless you're with...." ✓**AMERICA ONLINE**→*keyword* pc→Rooms→Game Parlor *or* Game Parlor Too

Stats
- Difficulty: simple
- Competition: live
- Number of players: 2–23
- Interface: ASCII
- Platforms: all

Requirements: *Played only at scheduled times*

Quotables A game like *Dictionary*, except that it uses incomplete quotations from famous people. Players must come up with a plausible or a bogus completion of the quote. One player posts the actual full quote, and all players vote for the most likely one. Voting for the right quote earns a point. Making others vote for your nonsense quote earns a point as well. ✓**AMERICA ONLINE**→*keyword* pc→Rooms→Game Parlor *or* Game Parlor Too

Stats
- Difficulty: simple
- Competition: live
- Number of players: 2–23
- Interface: ASCII
- Platforms: all

Requirements: *Played only at scheduled times*

Guessing games

Borderlines The host sends a question via private "Instant Message" to one player (e.g., "Which did you enjoy more, high school or college?") Other players try to guess how he or she answered. ✓**AMERICA ONLINE**→*keyword* pc→Rooms→Game Parlor *or* Game Parlor Too

Stats
- Difficulty: simple
- Competition: live

> **"Storytelling gets silly when kids are asked to supply nouns, verbs, adjectives, adverbs, and exclamations, from which a twisted tale develops."**

- Number of players: 2–23
- Interface: ASCII
- Platforms: all

Requirements: *Played only at scheduled times*

Charades The host sends the charade in a real-time message to a player, then announces the category (e.g., "Desserts") and the number of words in the charade to the other players. The first player gives clues (e.g., "Second word: sounds like fellow"), and the other players try to guess the answer. If they think they know the whole charade, they send an "Instant Message" to the host. ✓**AMERICA ONLINE**→*keyword* pc→Rooms→Game Parlor *or* Game Parlor Too

Stats
- Difficulty: simple
- Competition: live
- Number of players: 2–23
- Interface: ASCII
- Platforms: all

Requirements: *Played only at scheduled times*

Guess the Disease Think of a disease. The game will ask you a couple of questions and try to deduce your illness. If you have a Web browser that supports "forms," you can teach it new diseases. Fun, fun, fun. ✓**INTERNET**→

www http://www.reed.edu/cgi-bin/karl-animal?intro

Stats
- Difficulty: simple
- Competition: personal best
- Number of players: 1
- Interface: graphical
- Platforms: all

Requirements: *A Web browser*

Lasagna Mastermind for Italian-food lovers? Guess a three-digit number that the computer has chosen. "Cheese" means you've chosen the right number in the right position, "meatballs" means you've chosen the right number but in the wrong position, and "noodles" means you're outta luck. The game is timed, so work quickly. Buon appetito! ✓CHECK LOCAL BULLETIN BOARD SYSTEMS FOR THIS OR SIMILAR GAMES ☎→*dial* 416-498-5259/416-498-5962

Stats
- Difficulty: simple
- Competition: high scoring
- Number of players: 1
- Interface: ANSI
- Platforms: all

Parts Is Parts The host sends a word, like "school," via "Instant Message" to one player, who then slowly lists that item's component parts, such as "pencils," "bubblegum," and "bells," until the other players guess the word. ✓**AMERICA ONLINE**→*keyword* pc→Rooms→Game Parlor *or* Game Parlor Too

Stats
- Difficulty: simple
- Competition: live
- Number of players: 2–23
- Interface: ASCII
- Platforms: all

Requirements: *Played only at scheduled times*

People, Places and Things Players "on stage" ask the emcee yes-or-no questions ("Are you still alive?" "Have you written a book?"); audience members try to guess the identity of the person, place, or thing the emcee is portraying. ✓ **AMERICA ONLINE**→*keyword* center stage

Stats
- Difficulty: average
- Competition: live
- Number of players: 2+
- Interface: ASCII
- Platforms: all

Requirements: *Played only at scheduled times*

Poll Position Using the "Interact" feature when you're in the Center Stage, you cast a vote in a poll (e.g., "Which is the best book? 1–*David Copperfield*, 2–*War and Peace*, 3–*Scruples*"). Then, using the "Ask a Question" feature, you predict which item will win the most votes and by what percentage. Best guess wins the round. ✓ **AMERICA ONLINE**→*keyword* center stage

Stats
- Difficulty: average
- Competition: live
- Number of players: 2+
- Interface: ASCII
- Platforms: all

Requirements: *Played only at scheduled times*

Treasure Hunt The host sends an "Instant Message" to a player, making that player the "treasure bearer." The treasure consists of two words, depicting either a thing (e.g., "steering wheel"), a person ("private detective"), or an idea ("common currency"). Players must first guess who has the treasure and then guess what the treasure is. ✓ **AMERICA ONLINE**→*keyword* pc→Rooms→Game Parlor *or* Game Parlor Too

Stats
- Difficulty: simple
- Competition: live
- Number of players: 2–23
- Interface: ASCII

- Platforms: all

Requirements: *Played only at scheduled times*

Twenty Questions Guess the host's identity in five rounds of four questions. ✓ **AMERICA ONLINE**→*keyword* pc→Rooms→Game Parlor *or* Game Parlor Too

Stats
- Difficulty: simple
- Competition: live
- Number of players: 2–23
- Interface: ASCII
- Platforms: all

Requirements: *Played only at scheduled times*

Who Am I? Guess who or what the host is depicting, with the help of a maximum of five clues. The fewer clues you need, the higher your score. ✓ **AMERICA ONLINE**→*keyword* pc→Rooms→Game Parlor *or* Game Parlor Too

Stats
- Difficulty: simple
- Competition: live
- Number of players: 2–23
- Interface: ASCII
- Platforms: all

Requirements: *Played only at scheduled times*

Who Sings Me? A variation on *Who Am I?* Players guess musicians' or bands' names from the clues given. ✓ **AMERICA ONLINE**→*keyword* pc→Rooms→Game Parlor *or* Game Parlor Too

Stats
- Difficulty: simple
- Competition: live
- Number of players: 2–23
- Interface: ASCII
- Platforms: all

Requirements: *Played only at scheduled times*

Humor

Punchlines Inspired by the spirit of Carnac, the host provides the

punch line and you come up with a matching joke. For the punch line "To get to the other side," possible jokes might be "What's a summary of Manifest Destiny?" and "What seems to be my girlfriend's goal in bed?" ✓ **AMERICA ONLINE**→*keyword* pc→Rooms→Game Parlor *or* Game Parlor Too

Stats
- Difficulty: simple
- Competition: live
- Number of players: 2–23
- Interface: ASCII
- Platforms: all

Silly Fill-ins Kids supply nouns, verbs, adjectives, numbers, and other grammatical elements, which get turned into a story. Sometimes the story makes sense, sometimes it doesn't, but they're guaranteed a giggle. ✓ **COMPUSERVE**→*go* tmc-26→Silly Fill-ins

Stats
- Difficulty: 8 & under
- Competition: personal best
- Number of players: 1
- Interface: ASCII
- Platforms: all

Twisted Tales Storytelling gets silly when kids are asked to supply nouns, verbs, adjectives, adverbs, and exclamations, from which a twisted tale develops. ✓ **PRODIGY**→*jump* twisted tales

Stats
- Difficulty: 8 & under
- Competition: personal best
- Number of players: 1 or 2
- Interface: graphical
- Platforms: all

Commands
- From the game's main menu, select: How to Play
- From the game's main menu, select: Help with Words

Math games

Square Off Add, subtract, multiply, and divide to get to the target number in Phase 1. You have four minutes. In Phase 2 of the game, fill in the missing number or operand to complete the equation. You have two minutes. (Phase 2 features a bonus—as you choose different fields to finish the equations, you reveal a picture.) But first, choose your Challenge Level. Level 1 involves numbers from 0 to 30, up to four numbers in an equation, and operators + and −. Levels 2 and 3 involve numbers from 0 to 99, and operators +, −, x, and /. Equations are most difficult in Level 3. You can play only once a day, but if you're on one of the three weekly high-score lists, you'll receive a free *Square Off* T-shirt. ✓**PRODIGY**→*jump* square off

Stats
- Difficulty: 12 & over
- Competition: high scoring
- Number of players: 1
- Interface: graphical
- Platforms: all

RocketQuiz Using addition, subtraction, multiplication, and division, you try to type the answer to a math problem on the blackboard faster than your opponent, and thus move your rocket toward the finish line. You can choose the level you wish to play—the "arrgghh" level is exceptionally difficult. You've been warned. ✓**THE IMAGINATION NETWORK**→*select* Sierra-Land→RocketQuiz

Stats
- Difficulty: all ages
- Competition: live
- Number of players: 2–3
- Interface: graphical
- Platforms: all

Memory games

Match-it An interactive version of the old *Memory* game. The computer and you take turns revealing pairs of words under 16 colored

tiles. Most matches wins. Difficulty level allows you to determine how much the computer will remember. ✓**PRODIGY**→*jump* match-it

Stats
- Difficulty: 8 & under
- Competition: personal best
- Number of players: 1
- Interface: graphical
- Platforms: all

Commands
- From the main menu, select: How to Play

Police Artist It's more fun to create goofy faces than to actually match the villain's face in this game for very young kids. If you play by the (few) rules, however, you see a villain's face, chosen randomly by Prodigy's computers; on the next screen, try to remember what the face looked like by choosing different eyes, noses, mouths, chins, and hairstyles. If you forget what the villain looked like, select "See the villain" for a reminder. ✓**PRODIGY**→*jump* police artist

Stats
- Difficulty: 8 & under
- Competition: personal best
- Number of players: 1
- Interface: graphical
- Platforms: all

Total Amnesia Door A version of the memory game *Concentration* for BBSs. ✓CHECK LOCAL BULLETIN BOARD SYSTEMS FOR THIS OR SIMILAR GAMES ☎→*dial* 508-765-9387

Stats
- Difficulty: simple
- Competition: high scoring
- Number of players: 1+
- Interface: ANSI
- Platforms: all

Scavenger hunt

Internet Hunt (ng) Search the vast resources of the Net in a monthly scavenger hunt against

other savvy Netters. The archived questions and answers are great sources of information about the Net. ✓**INTERNET** …→*gopher* gopher.cni.org→The Internet Hunt …→*ftp* ftp.cic.net→anonymous→<your email address>→/pub/hunt ✓**USENET**→ alt.internet.services

Stats
- Difficulty: complex
- Competition: the Net
- Number of players: 1+
- Interface: ASCII
- Platforms: all

WWW Addict's Pop-Culture Scavenger Hunt How well do you know the Web? Questions about specific Web sites come in four different categories, from easy to impossible. Hunt for answers and, if you find them, add your name to a victors list. ✓**INTERNET**→*www* http://www.galcit.caltech.edu/~ta/wwwhunt.html

Stats
- Difficulty: complex
- Competition: high scoring
- Number of players: 1+
- Interface: graphical
- Platforms: all

> "Guess a three-digit number. 'Cheese' means you've chosen the right number in the right position; 'meatballs' means right number, wrong position; and 'noodles' means you're outta luck."

Mazes

The Net is one big maze of its own, but maybe you'd care for something marginally more manageable—how about the hundred levels of **Wizard Maze 3D**, the caves of Wumpus (hunt the creature with your crooked arrow), or even a maze based on puzzle clues scattered across the Internet's World Wide Web (**Prazer Maze 5**)?

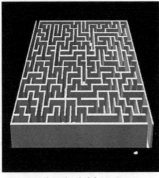

A maze—downloaded from Compu-Serve's Graphics Support Forum.

On the Net

AJ Dakota Having already found (and stolen) the Orb of Kings—the game begins with all that drudgery out of the way—you've got to escape alive. To do so, you travel square by square (using the [Tab] key, arrow keys, or mouse) from the bottom corner of the room to the upper right. Easy enough, except that some of the 90 squares on the floor of the room contain traps that, when "stepped on," bring the ceiling crashing in on you.

Safe tiles

You can determine which tiles are safe by the number on the tile you're standing on. The first square says 0, which means that none of the three tiles surrounding it hold traps. But with the next step you might end up on a tile with the number 2, which means that two tiles surrounding your tile are trapped; you just don't know which ones (unless you've managed to figure it out from other tiles you've been on).

If you suspect that a particular tile is trapped, you can [Tab] to the "Mark" button, which turns off the "stepping" feature and allows you to put an X on the suspect tile(s). (Be sure you turn "Mark" off again before you proceed.)

So what happens if, despite your best efforts, you step on a trapped tile? You get two chances —think of them as poles that allow you to prop up the collapsing ceiling—before it caves in and you're a goner. You can even pick up additional poles along the route. You also might end up squashed like a bug. ✓**PRODIGY**→ *jump aj dakota*

Stats
- Difficulty: 12 & over
- Competition: personal best
- Number of players: 1
- Interface: graphical
- Platforms: all

The HTML Maze The object is to reach the F. You move through rows of X's by clicking one of the numbers that surround the X you land on. The number on top of the X describes how many spaces you will move north if you click it. The number below the X indicates the steps you will go south, etc. You can reach the F only if the last number you click moves you straight towards the F over the

right number of spaces. A little tricky. ✓**INTERNET**→*www* http://spider.navsses.navy.mil/www/mazeintro.html

Stats
- Difficulty: average
- Competition: personal best
- Number of players: 1
- Interface: graphical
- Platforms: all

Requirements: *A graphical Web client that highlights the targeted text (Mosaic for the Mac works) and a SLIP connection*

The Labyrinth Door An online maze game in which you have to not only get out of the maze but do so in the fewest moves possible (often there is a preset number of moves and a maximum time allowed per turn). You'll get colored chalk to mark where you've been, but be warned: Other players may erase your marks or leave marks to confuse you. ✓CHECK LOCAL BULLETIN BOARD SYSTEMS FOR THIS OR A SIMILAR GAME ☎→*dial* 314-328-1532

Stats
- Difficulty: average
- Competition: turn-based
- Number of players: 2+
- Interface: ASCII, ANSI
- Platforms: all

Murder Mansion There's been a murder and you must roam about in search of clues to unmask the killer. But be careful—the killer is also stalking you. If you take too long to bust him, you'll be his next victim. ✓CHECK LOCAL BULLETIN BOARD SYSTEMS FOR THIS OR A SIMILAR GAME ☎→*dial* 206-871-9539/206-871-9340

Stats
- Difficulty: simple
- Competition: high scoring
- Number of players: 1+
- Interface: ANSI
- Platforms: all

Prazer Maze 5 Follow the

URLs (that's Net-speak for Web link addresses), solve puzzles, talk to creatures buried in the Web, and advance through a maze that reveals itself as you solve more riddles. Here's how the puzzle begins: "This is the center, apparently. The planes of existence stretch out around you; some open and beckoning, some blocked to your spirit. Most are esoteric and of little importance to you, but you are drawn to several [the following are your choices]: the physical, or literal plane; the plane of structure; the plane of shape; and the plane of essence. This place seems to revolve around a multi-dimensional object, a monolith which seems to continue through all the planes. Your sight cannot penetrate it." ✓ **INTERNET**→*www* http://orac. andrew.cmu.edu:5823/pra5

Stats
- Difficulty: complex
- Competition: personal best
- Number of players: 1
- Interface: graphical
- Platforms: all

Requirements: *A graphical Web client supporting the "forms" extensions to HTML, such as NCSA Mosaic 2.0., and a SLIP connection*

Wizard Maze 3D You're a wizard's apprentice and have prematurely challenged the wizard, Thargo. As recourse you've been tossed into the bottom of a 100-level 3D maze—all this before the game even begins. As you attempt to escape, finding your way through each level with only a few spells and a compass at your side, the chamber begins to fill up with sleeping gas. If you can't reach the exit quickly enough, you will "fall asleep" and be carried back down a level. Make it all the way out, though, and you'll become the new wizard! ✓ CHECK LOCAL BULLETIN BOARD SYSTEMS FOR THIS OR A SIMILAR GAME ☎→*dial* 703-963-3878

Stats
- Difficulty: average
- Competition: high scoring
- Number of players: 1+
- Interface: ANSI
- Platforms: all

Sokoban

Sokoban Shareware A game of maneuvering objects through a maze to specific destinations by "pushing" them. It was this simple concept that undoubtedly inspired the arcade classic *Boulderdash*. The rules are simple; the solutions are surprisingly difficult. ✓ **INTERNET** ...→*ftp* faui43.informatik.uni-erlangen.de→anonymous→<your email address>→/mounts/epix/public/pub/amiga/aminet/game/misc→ASokoban 1.1.lha (for Amiga) ...→*ftp* mrcnext.cso.uiuc.edu→anonymous→<your email address>→/pub/info-mac/game→mac-sokoban-21.hqx (for Macintosh) ...*ftp*→anonymous→<your email address>→/mirror/atari/Games→sokoban.arc (for Atari) ...→*ftp* pion.lcs.mit.edu→anonymous→<your email address>→/pub/xsokoban→xsokoban-3.2d.tar.Z (for XWindows)

Stats
- Difficulty: average
- Competition: personal best
- Number of players: 1
- Interface: graphical
- Platforms: all

XSokoban Home Page Provides a quick jump to the source-code archives, access to the "global score list," and links to the installation notes, update logs, and manual pages for "the spiffiest version of *Sokoban* around." ✓ **INTERNET**→*www* http://clef.lcs.mit.edu/~andru/xsokoban.html

Wumpus

Wumpus The Wumpus lives in a cave of 20 rooms. He's asleep 70 percent of the time. You're job is to figure out which rooms are connected to which rooms (the map doesn't help much), find the Wumpus, and shoot your "crooked arrow" through up to five rooms in one shot, hoping to hit the ugly creature. When you're one room away from the Wumpus, you'll get a warning that you're about to bump into the Wumpus. Warnings are also issued in case you're approaching a hazard—a swarm of bats, for instance, or a flock of crooked-arrow-eating "tumaeros." ✓ **DELPHI**→*go* ent boa→Wumpus

Stats
- Difficulty: average
- Competition: personal best
- Number of players: 1
- Interface: ASCII
- Platforms: all

Super Wumpus Like regular *Wumpus*, except that the number of rooms in the cave changes from game to game. Each room has two to five tunnels leading to other rooms. To make your Wumpus hunt more challenging, the cave is "transfinite": Just because a tunnel leads from Room A to Room B doesn't mean you can use that same tunnel to get from Room B to Room A. In addition, the Wumpus is on the move, and sometimes the entire transfinite universe just breaks down. When that happens, either you'll find yourself in a completely new room in a new cave with new connecting tunnels or you're dead. There's less logic and more chance involved in this super version of *Wumpus*. ✓ **DELPHI**→*go* ent boa→Super Wumpus

Stats
- Difficulty: average
- Competition: personal best
- Number of players: 1
- Interface: ASCII
- Platforms: all

Puzzles

Where to go on the Net for puzzles? Well, what are you looking for? The Web offers the wow factor—graphics, puzzle playing, and impressive programming. See the **4x4 Puzzle with Image**. The crowd from **rec.puzzles** on Usenet takes thoroughness and intensity to new heights—there's even a commitee, the **Puzzle Oracle**, to field questions. And the **Cube Lovers** list? Hint: it's been up for 14 years.

On the Net

Across the board

Logic Puzzles and Brain Teasers (echo) Puzzle people challenge each other. ✓**ICENET**

Puzzle Oracle Looking for a puzzle solution? Query the puzzle oracle and a group of rec.puzzle regulars will search the rec.puzzle archives to see if it's there. They promise a response in two days. ✓**INTERNET**→*email* puzzle-oracle@ questrel.com ✍ *Write for help & support*

rec.puzzles (ng) From ancient chestnuts to brand-new stumpers. Check out the FAQ, which claims to "assist readers in determining if their nifty new puzzle is not quite so nifty or new after all." The rec.puzzle archive has more than 500 puzzle solutions. ✓**USENET** *Archives:* ✓**INTERNET** ...→*email* archive-request@questrel.com ✍ *To get an index of the archive, type in message body:* return_address

Thinker—*screenshot from Prodigy's children's game.*

<your email address> send index ...→*ftp* ftp.cs.ruu.nl→anonymous→ <your email address>→/pub/ NEWS.ANSWERS *FAQ:* ✓**INTERNET**→*ftp* rtfm.mit.edu→anonymous →<your email address>→/pub/ usenet/news.answers/puzzles→faq *Support:* ✓**INTERNET**→*email* archive -comment@questrel.com ✍ *To send corrections or ask questions, send email*

Assorted

Cube Lovers (ml) The *Rubik's Cube* list may be slow at times, but then it's been around for 14 years and counting. ✓**INTERNET**→*email* cube-lovers-request@life.ai.mit.edu ✍ *Write a request Archives:* ✓**INTERNET**→*ftp* rtfm.mit.edu→anonymous→<your email address>→ /pub/cube-lovers

Emporium While many BBS doors are takeoffs on board games, *Emporium* offers a truly new and original strategy/puzzle game. Collect the proper colors of tokens to purchase cards in the *Emporium* bin. ✓CHECK LOCAL BULLETIN BOARD SYSTEMS FOR THIS OR A SIMILAR GAME ☎→*dial* 314-328-1532 **Stats**
- Difficulty: average
- Competition: high scoring
- Number of players: 1+
- Interface: ANSI
- Platforms: all

Oxyd Solve subtle puzzles with a marble you roll through the brightly illustrated game levels. The stages (there are more than 100 of them) get increasingly difficult and the solutions require a certain elegance (or at least a steady hand on the mouse). Believe it or not, but with two players over a local network or modem connection, each marble seems to take on the personality of the person controlling it. ✓**INTERNET** ...→*ftp* archive.umich.edu→anonymous→<your email address>→ /mac/game/demo→oxyd3.5.cpt. hqx (for Macs) ...→*ftp* archive. umich.edu→anonymous→<your email address>→atari/Games→

> "Believe it or not, but with two players over a local network or modem connection, each marble seems to take on the personality of the person controlling it."

oxydcolor.zip <or> oxyd2.lzh (for Atari) ...→*ftp* wuarchive.wustl. edu→anonymous→<your email address>→/systems/amiga/aminet/ game/think→oxyd.lha (for Amigas) ...→*ftp* archive.umich.edu→ anonymous→<your email address> →/msdos/games→oxydv39.zip (for DOS) ✓**COMPUSERVE**→*go* gamers→Libraries→*Search by keyword:* oxyd (for Amiga, Atari, DOS, and Mac versions)

Stats
- Difficulty: average
- Competition: live (network) *or* personal best
- Number of players: 1 or 2
- Interface: graphical
- Platforms: DOS, Amiga, Atari, Macintosh ,NeXT

PD-Games (ml) Interested in game theory from an academic perspective? With a focus on *Prisoner Dilemma*–type puzzles, this list discusses game theory, paying attention to the technical and philosophical aspects—"the nature of social cooperation," for example. ✓**INTERNET**→*email* pd-games-request@ math.uio.no ✎ *Write a request*

Peg Game Your pieces are the blue squares and the computer's pieces are the red triangles. Green circles are neutral. Take more of your pieces off the board than the computer does. To remove a piece, it must be adjacent to a piece previously removed by the opponent. Continue until no further moves are possible. If you are forced to take a red triangle on your move, then the piece counts for the computer and vice versa. ✓**INTERNET**→*www* http://www.bu.edu/ htbin/pegs

Stats
- Difficulty: simple
- Competition: live
- Number of players: 1
- Interface: graphical

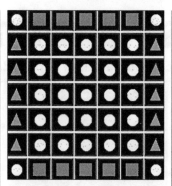

Screenshot of Peg Game—http://www. bu.edu/htbin/pegs.

- Platforms: all

Requirements: *A graphical Web browser and a SLIP connection*

Children

Reverse The game will present you with a string of numbers, 1 through 9, in a random order. Your goal is to get them in numerical order by reversing a set each turn. Try to use as few moves as possible. ✓**DELPHI**→*go* ent boa→Reverse

Stats
- Difficulty: 8–12 years
- Competition: live
- Number of players: 1
- Interface: ASCII
- Platforms: all

Thinker Determine what colors are used in the four-box pattern, and in what order they're used. The game allows you ten turns to figure it out. ✓**PRODIGY**→*jump* thinker

Stats
- Difficulty: 12 & over
- Competition: personal best
- Number of players: 1
- Interface: graphical
- Platforms: all

Commands
- From the main menu, select How to Play
- To enter your guess, select DONE

Requirements: *Color monitor to view colors (monochrome monitors see colors as letters A–H)*

Sliding-tile puzzles

3x3 Puzzle Move the numbered tiles in *3x3 Puzzle* around to match the image in the example— tiles number 1 through 8 should be in order. ✓**INTERNET**→*www* http://www.cm.cf.ac.uk/htbin/ AndrewW/Puzzle/puzzle.p

Stats
- Difficulty: simple
- Competition: live
- Number of players: 1
- Interface: graphical
- Platforms: all

Requirements: *A graphical Web browser and a SLIP connection*

4x4 Puzzle Move the virtual tiles around so that they are in order. ✓**INTERNET**→*www* http://www. cm.cf.ac.uk/htbin/AndrewW/ Puzzle/puzzle4x4.p

Stats
- Difficulty: simple
- Competition: live
- Number of players: 1
- Interface: graphical
- Platforms: all

Requirements: *A graphical Web browser and a SLIP connection*

4x4 Puzzle with Image Another 4x4 sliding-tile puzzle. This time the puzzle is an image (it has several different images, so you can play more than once). ✓**INTERNET**→*www* http://www.cm.cf.ac. uk/htbin/AndrewW/Puzzle/puzzle 4x4image

Stats
- Difficulty: average
- Competition: live
- Number of players: 1
- Interface: graphical
- Platforms: all

Requirements: *A graphical Web browser and a SLIP connection*

"Serious" gaming

No, this is not the psychedelic section, although BayMoo does recreate a virtual Haight

Ashbury. We're talking the spiritual landscape and discourse of the **Divination Web II**, stock-market games like **Bulls and Bears** that won't cost you any principal, educational hits like **Carmen Sandiego**, and the hard-core political simulation **The Next President** (TNP), in which you get to role-play a United States senator—an experience that may in fact cost you your principles.

On the Net

Finance

Bulls and Bears Think how nice it would be if someone gave you $100,000, tax-free, to invest in the stock market. That's the basic premise behind this stocks-and-options simulation game. Your goal is to increase your portfolio as much as you can. The game's creators stress that all orders are merely simulations—you aren't actually buying stock, even though it may look like you are.

You receive dividends and interest on any cash balance in your portfolio, and the game has a few conventions and controls to ensure a realistic market feel, such as "The maximum number of shares traded must be less than 10 percent of the volume of stock sold that day in the real market." The game includes a list of "helpful definitions" for the financial neo-

Screenshot from Prodigy's Where in the World is Carmen Sandiego?

phyte and a list of the menus you'll use most often to study the market and make trades. ✓ **AMERICA ONLINE**→ *keyword* bulls and bears ✓ **COMPUSERVE**→ *go* etgame

Stats
- Difficulty: average
- Competition: personal best
- Number of players: 1+
- Interface: ASCII
- Platforms: all

Geography

Where in the World is Carmen Sandiego? To play, first read the dossiers on Carmen's gang, the Villains' League of Evil (VILE). Along the way, your clues will point to one of these bad guys. When that happens, select "start" from the main menu, and you'll be at the scene of a crime, with a cute weekly introduction to the world of gumshoe detectives.

Notre Dame

Then, with the game's story set, you start to travel. You might go to Paris and visit the Notre Dame, the Champs Elysee and L'Opera.

Or you might go to Brazil and the Planalto Palace, the Supreme Court, and the Yacht Club. At each stop, you'll be given a clue to the culprit's identity and where he or she is headed next. You've got to know your geography, however, because a clue might read, "I just saw someone leaving with a large box on a freighter headed for the Adriatic!"

Chief

You'll be given three choices of countries to travel to next, but if you dawdle in gathering clues, the chief will jump in and tell you to move on. Finally, you either run out of time or identify enough features of the crook to make a match with the crook-catching computer. Another crime solved! You can play as often as you like, but only your first attempt each week will count for the Winners Hall of Fame. ✓ **PRODIGY**→ *jump* carmen

Stats
- Difficulty: 12 & over
- Competition: personal best
- Number of players: 1
- Interface: graphical
- Platforms: all

Politics & culture

OceanaMUSE Help create your own island-state. Develop the state's culture, install a government (democratic, aristocratic, etc.), deal with the young nation's economic and ecological growing pains, and pursue technological progress. Travel to other islands for a state visit by ferry or submarine, or explore the oceans. Oceana may sound like Utopia, but it's not. There are many issues to deal with, and as such it's a great—don't take this wrong—"learning environment." Above all, it's a lot of fun. ✓**INTERNET**→*telnet* k12.cnidr.org 4201→connect stow away *Info:* ✓**INTERNET**→*ftp* k12.cnidr.org→anonymous→<your email address>→/pub/VirtualReality/Oceana *Register:* ✓**INTERNET**→*email* oceana@k12.cnidr.org ✍ *Write a request:* <your full name> <your email address> <your character's name> <your characters on other MUDs>

Stats
- Difficulty: 12 & over
- Competition: live
- Number of players: 1+
- Interface: ASCII
- Server: MUSE
- Platforms: all

Commands
- To get information, type: help *or* news
- To get help, type: !help <message to officials>

TNP *TNP* began as an election-year game called *The Next President*, where players—"campaign managers"—got to manage a fictional presidential campaign. Apparently, so many people enjoyed the discussions that ensued that the game lives on as discussion-only.

Every player is a U.S. senator, and the only goal seems to be to live out your C-Span/*Crossfire* fantasies. Members debate real and imagined legislation, discuss political philosophy, and refer to each other as, for example, "the distinguished gentlewoman from the great state of Iowa." Libertarians are well represented, unlike the real-world Senate. The *TNP* Senate Floor topic reads like the *Congressional Record*, as do some of the committee hearing subjects. ✓**PRODIGY**→*jump* games bb→Bulletin Board→Prodigy Games topic→TNP*

> "Every player is a U.S. senator, and the only goal seems to be to live out your C-Span/*Crossfire* fantasies. Members debate real and imagined legislation, discuss political philosophy, and refer to each other as, for example, 'the distinguished gentlewoman from the great state of Iowa.'"

Stats
- Difficulty: simple
- Competition: n/a
- Number of players: 1+
- Interface: ASCII
- Platforms: all

Religion

Divination Web II People with an interest in mystical, occult, or religious philosophies share knowledge and insights. The landscape of the MUD is being developed to reflect the spirituality theme, and you can post your ideas for the MUD on the Idea Board when you log in.

The Café is the public meeting area; the OMNet Node offers information about the Occult and Mystical Network (OMNet). ✓**INTERNET**→*telnet* bill.math.uconn.edu 9393→create <your character name> <your password> *Support:* ✓**INTERNET**→*email* jtraub@zso.dec.com

Stats
- Difficulty: average
- Competition: live
- Number of players: 1+
- Interface: ASCII
- Server: MUCK
- Platforms: all

Commands
- To get a list of help topics and commands, type: help

San Francisco

BayMOO Take a virtual trip to San Francisco and the Bay Area. Get residency here and add your own twist to the MOO—building is encouraged! Besides a gopher hole for Internet information searches, there's a a Parisian square with a café and a bookstore; Ohlone Village, where the language of the San Francisco Native Americans is being revived; Zot's Improv Palace of the Poor, where you can play games (type "gl" in this room for a list of choices); the Hotel California, where each room's a different experience; and many restaurants and bars where you might just bump into Gertrude Stein.

Hippie Haight

The MOO has three separate areas: the Bay Area, Netspace, and Other Worlds. In the Bay Area, you can explore subsections devoted to contemporary issues, to eras past (the Gold Rush or Hippie Haight), and increasingly to specific counties. Other Worlds offers Neptune, Paris, a Retrogarden coffee bar, and more. And then

> ## "Make a clone of Robbie the Robot, and program it to say what you like."

there's Netspace, where you can start a programming career on *BayMOO*. You can make a clone of Robbie the robotic clerk and program your robot to say what you want (see the BayMOO TV Studio).

Objects to be cloned

In Davey Jones' Locker, there are tons of objects and rooms to be cloned and customized. Just take some. Once connected to *Bay-MOO*, newbies should take two tours: the Word Room Tour is a three-minute look at *BayMOO* from a language perspective (more amusing than it sounds); the WarpTour is a five-minute excursion through the three sections of *BayMOO*.

After that, you can start your own explorations and, perhaps, do some virtual building. ✓**INTERNET** →*telnet* mud.crl.com 8888→con nect guest *Register:* ✓**INTERNET**→ *email* blast@crl.com ✍ *Email request to register a character:* <your full name> <two choices for a character name> <your research interests> <your email address>

Stats
- Difficulty: average
- Competition: live
- Number of players: 1+
- Interface: ASCII
- Server: MOO
- Platforms: all

Commands
- To get a description of the MOO, at the connect screen type: theme
- To go to a player anywhere on the MOO, type: @join <player>

- To teleport an object, type: @move <object> to <room>

The future

EON Virtual School Notice the large rocklike structure floating in space. It's been left by aliens for others (that means you) to use— and perhaps to be led to higher realms. *EON* is devoted to learning, and you must register to "become a learner." Your first task on the MOO is to find your way to the EON Immigration Center, where you'll be asked to apply for membership and describe your research interests. ✓**INTERNET**→*telnet* mcmuse.mc.maricopa.edu 8888 *Support:* ✓**INTERNET**→*email* eon@ mc.maricopa.edu ✍ *Email for help & support*

Stats
- Difficulty: average
- Competition: live
- Number of players: 1+
- Interface: ASCII
- Server: MOO
- Platforms: all

Commands
- Go to the Help Desk in the Receiving Room for New Immigrants
- To get help, type: page help=<your message>

MicroMUSE (Cyberion City)

Introducing kids (and adults as well) to the wonders of Cyberspace is the raison d'être of this MUSE. Any mention of MUDs in the popular press usually includes a reference to *Cyberion City*, a simulated 24th-century space colony. In fact, the attention has brought a rush of new users that the site has been unable to handle. So for the time being, it's not accepting guest connections. The admins are currently developing new procedures for registering characters. Telnet to the site and read the announcements for more informa-

tion. ✓**INTERNET**→*telnet* chezmoto. ai.mit.edu 4201

Stats
- Difficulty: average
- Competition: 12 & over
- Number of players: 1+
- Interface: ASCII
- Server: MUSE
- Platforms: all

CYBERNOTES

"And now for a backward glance at the past of the future, here is MARINETTI'S RETROGARDEN.

The RetroGarden [caffeinated]: A coffee bar, carved out of the rock, way down here over the edge of the continental shelf. It is decorated in flotsam, jetsam, the debris of plane crashes, locomotive wrecks... The walls are draped in what appears to be the charred outer canvas of a dirigible.

Obvious exits: north to Sargasso Terminal

Wyndham_Lewis is sitting at the bar. Andre Breton and Karen Eliot are sitting at Andre's table. Ezra Pound and Monty Cantsin are sitting at Ezra's table. Boccioni is sitting on a stool behind the bar. Grinch is standing here."

—from **BayMOO**

Trivia games

It's a little perverse, when you think about it, to use computers to play trivia games.

Aren't *they* supposed to organize and retrieve data for us? Well, anyway, put the info back in information age with trivia games that span advertising slogans, show biz, and a database of questions from the *College Bowl*. Correctly answering the question is always the point, but enjoy the spurious premise of **2151**, in which correct answers elect you president of the U.S.A., and other would-be TV quiz shows like **Super Brain Challenge** and **On Your Toes**.

Screenshot from Prodigy's Frantic Guts.

On the Net

Across the board

Blankety Blanks Fill in the blanks using the context of the phrase: e.g., "Little Buddy" _____ played Gilligan. (Answer: Bob Denver.) ✓**AMERICA ONLINE**→*keyword* pc→Rooms→Game Parlor *or* Game Parlor Too

Stats
* Difficulty: simple
* Competition: live
* Number of players: 2–23
* Interface: ASCII
* Platforms: all
Requirements: *Played only at scheduled times*

Categorically Trivial Choose your category—the Bible, sports, American history, firsts, movies, music, or musicals—and stand

back. This test will throw random questions at you until you've missed five. At that point, you can either try to boost your score in that same category or choose another category. A sample question from the Bible category: "Who was Peter's host in Acts while he was staying at Joppa?" ✓**COMPUSERVE**→ *go* tmc-66→Categorically Trivial

Stats
* Difficulty: average
* Competition: personal best
* Number of players: 1
* Interface: ASCII
* Platforms: all

College Bowl Trivia Site Hundreds of trivia-question packets straight from *College Bowl* competition. ✓**INTERNET**→*ftp* oddjob. uchicago.edu→/pub/college_bowl

Double Dare *Jeopardy*-inspired ("Phrase your answer in the form of a question"). The host types the category, its point value, and the answer. Players must type the correct question within five seconds. Each round has a "do-you-dare," where a player who chooses the

category and value gets to wager points on the answer. ✓**AMERICA ONLINE**→*keyword* pc→Rooms→Game Parlor *or* Game Parlor Too

Stats
* Difficulty: simple
* Competition: live
* Number of players: 2–23
* Interface: ASCII
* Platforms: all
Requirements: *Played only at scheduled times*

Frantic Guts Perhaps the fastest way to blow four bits, *Frantic Guts* is for die-hard trivia fans only. Although similar to Prodigy's *Guts*, *Frantic Guts* will cost you 50 cents a game, and you don't have the option of "holding" once you've started. Choose either Regular (for questions at all seven levels of difficulty) or Expert (for questions from only levels four through seven). Answer as many questions correctly as possible in seven minutes. As in an arcade game where you're pumping quarters (which, in fact, you are), the game's high scorers show up at the end of the game. Why anyone who hasn't memorized the *World Almanac*, the *Encyclopaedia Britannica*, and the average annual rainfall of all 50 states would want to pay to play this game is beyond us. ✓**PRODIGY** →*jump* frantic guts **$**

Stats
- Difficulty: complex
- Competition: high scoring
- Number of players: 1+
- Interface: graphical
- Platforms: all

The Grolier Whiz Quiz Based on *Grolier's Academic American Encyclopedia*, the *Whiz Quiz* asks multiple-choice questions in a category of your choice. Play alone or with a group of friends at your computer. ✓**COMPUSERVE**→*go* whiz

Stats
- Difficulty: average
- Competition: live
- Number of players: 1–4
- Interface: ASCII
- Platforms: all

Guts You've got seven minutes to answer seven questions every week for seven weeks. Answer correctly and you go on to the next, more difficult question. Answer a question incorrectly, however, and your score for the whole game (not just the week's turn) is set back at zero. To be declared the overall winner, you have to have the highest score after seven weeks. It can be frustrating to get through three or four levels and then miss a question.

Even more frustrating, however, is that once you've zeroed out (or answered all seven questions correctly, if you're that trivia-smart), you have to wait until the following Wednesday morning to continue competing. The ultimate frustration, however? You're not told the correct answer when you miss a question, so you don't have an "in" if you get that question again in the next round or in an-

> "The classic game show meets chaos theory. Anyone can jump into the IRC's never-ending, auto-mated *Jeopardy* game at any time, play a few rounds, and jump back out again."

other game—which is not unlikely, as the questions are randomly generated. ✓**PRODIGY** →*jump* guts

Stats
- Difficulty: complex
- Competition: high scoring
- Number of players: 1+
- Interface: graphical
- Platforms: all

Hands Up Trivia poker. Each question represents a playing card. By correctly answering the questions, you amass up to five cards for your "hand." The player who holds the high hand at the end of the round wins. ✓**AMERICA ON-LINE**→*keyword* center stage

Stats
- Difficulty: average
- Competition: live
- Number of players: 2+
- Interface: ASCII
- Platforms: all

Requirements: *Played only at scheduled times*

#jeopardy The classic game show meets chaos theory. Anyone can jump into the IRC's never-ending, automated *Jeopardy* game at any time, play a few rounds,

and jump back out again. Consequently, there are generally close to 30 people playing at any given moment, unlike in television's more controlled three-player version. And there's no buzzer to hit, either: It's the fastest typist who gets the points. Helpful tip: Set up a macro for the important word "alex," which must precede every answer in order for the robot host "Alexbot" to recognize it. ✓**INTER-NET**→*irc* /channel #jeopardy

Stats
- Difficulty: average
- Competition: live
- Number of players: 3+
- Interface: ASCII
- Platforms: all

Liam's Web Quiz A weekly list of questions. ✓**INTERNET**→*www* http://altair.herts.ac.uk:8000/html/ WebQuiz.html

Stats
- Difficulty: average
- Competition: high scoring
- Number of players: 1+
- Interface: ASCII, graphical
- Platforms: all

NTN Trivia With this game of 15-minute trivia contests, you're competing not only against other people on GEnie but with men and women across North America in bars, restaurants, and hotels that are part of the NTN Interactive Television Network. The GEnie players often take high score, however.

There are three clues for each question. Each clue narrows the possible answers further down until the answer is practically given away. So think fast to get the most points out of your reply! You'll need to download the front-end software (IBM, Amiga, or Mac) to play, but once you do, not only can you compete, but you can also "chat" live with your fellow GEnie players.

People who get to know each other chatting often continue their conversation on the Multiplayers Games RoundTable bulletin board, in a special category for *NTN Trivia* buffs. ✓ **GENIE**→*keyword* trivia *Interface:* ✓ **GENIE**→*keyword* trivia→Download NTN Trivia Front End Software

Stats
• Difficulty: simple
• Competition: live
• Number of players: 2+
• Interface: ASCII
• Platforms: all

NTN Trivia Messages After you've met fellow gamers playing *NTN Trivia*, you may want to continue the conversation here on the message boards. Talk about the game, find out more about your competitors, and gloat, congratulate, or whine over your last match. ✓ **GENIE**→*keyword* mpgrt→Multiplayer Games Bulletin Board→set 30

On Your Toes A trivia game show wherein the player who wins the "toss-up" question is invited "on the stage" to answer four questions within 30 seconds. If he or she can't answer correctly, the audience is allowed to compete for the prize. The audience member who first correctly answers the contestant's missed question becomes the next contestant on stage. ✓ **AMERICA ONLINE**→*keyword* center stage

Stats
• Difficulty: average
• Competition: live
• Number of players: 2+
• Interface: ASCII
• Platforms: all
Requirements: *Played only at scheduled times*

Query Quest Another *Jeopardy*-inspired "Phrase your answer in the form of a question" game.

✓ **AMERICA ONLINE**→*keyword* pc→Rooms→Game Parlor *or* Game Parlor Too

Stats
• Difficulty: simple
• Competition: live
• Number of players: 2–23
• Interface: ASCII
• Platforms: all
Requirements: *Played only at scheduled times*

Roll 'Em Rolling a ten-sided die, the host determines from which of the show's ten categories the question will come and how many points the answer is worth. Be the first to answer correctly. ✓ **AMERICA ONLINE**→*keyword* center stage

Stats
• Difficulty: average
• Competition: live
• Number of players: 2+
• Interface: ASCII
• Platforms: all
Requirements: *Played only at scheduled times*

Stage II Trivia Although you could play alone, you'll have more fun with a group of friends, each of whom will be assigned a number. One person should act as typist and judge. The game will ask you six trivia questions, the answers to which have a theme in common. If you're playing alone, just type in the answer. If you're playing in a group, type in the answer, a comma, and the number of the person who came up with it. You can guess the theme at any time during a round. The earlier you guess it, the more points you'll rack up. ✓ **COMPUSERVE**→*go* tmc-80

Stats
• Difficulty: average
• Competition: live
• Number of players: 1+
• Interface: ASCII
• Platforms: all
Commands
• To guess the theme at any time,

hit: esc *or* /t
• To review the answers for a round, type: /r
• To display the question again, type: /q
• To end the game and tally the score, type: /e

Super Brain Challenge Designed to separate the geniuses from the merely bright, this test has four challenges for you to overcome, each consisting of 25 questions: *Whiz-Kid's Waterloo*, *The Questor's Quiz*, *The Brain Boggler*, and *The Championship Challenge*. The questions are difficult and the time to answer is limited. The test's authors don't want to scare anyone off, but they do state that this is not for the timid. ✓ **COMPUSERVE**→*go* tmc-99→Super Brain Challenge

Stats
• Difficulty: complex
• Competition: personal best
• Number of players: 1
• Interface: ASCII
• Platforms: all

3-In-A-Row *Tic-tac-toe*, except that you have to answer questions to get an X or an O. And it doesn't matter which you get; you only need to get three in a row of either letter to win. ✓ **AMERICA ONLINE**→*keyword* center stage

Stats
• Difficulty: average
• Competition: live
• Number of players: 2+
• Interface: ASCII
• Platforms: all
Requirements: *Played only at scheduled times*

Three Ring Circus A general knowledge trivia game in which the host provides an opener question, along with a clue to the answer—a list, an anagram, a lyric, etc. (e.g., "Author of 'Annabel Lee.' Anagram: OGDERALAELEPN."

Answer: Edgar Allen Poe.) The host then asks a series of knowledge questions based on the opener. The questions get increasingly difficult as they're worth more and more points. ✓**AMERICA ONLINE**→ *keyword* pc→Rooms→Game Parlor *or* Game Parlor Too

Stats
- Difficulty: simple
- Competition: live
- Number of players: 2–23
- Interface: ASCII
- Platforms: all

Requirements: *Played only at scheduled times*

TQ Trivia Bet your points! After the category has been given, you can wager 25 to 75 percent of your total points. When the answers are in, you can see how the other players did and how players in previous games answered the question—often a consolation if you've bombed. A feature close to any trivia fan's heart: Each question is followed by interesting information on the topic. ✓**DELPHI**→ *go* ent tq

Stats
- Difficulty: average
- Competition: live
- Number of players: 1+
- Interface: ASCII
- Platforms: all

Trivia Extremely popular on BBS systems, *trivia* games exist in all shapes and sizes. Themes for these games (called doors on BBSs) can be as specific as *Gilligan's Island*, Hawaiian language, Emergency Medical Services, and sexual knowledge. Chances are you'll vie against the rest of the users on the board for rights to the trivia throne. ✓CHECK LOCAL BULLETIN BOARD SYSTEMS FOR A VARIATION OF THIS GAME

Stats
- Difficulty: average
- Competition: high scoring
- Number of players: 1+

- Interface: ASCII, ANSI
- Platforms: all

Trivia Archive DOS programs for general, children's, movie, sports, world, science, television, and United States trivia. ✓**INTERNET**→*ftp* wuarchive.wustl.edu→ anonymous→<your email address> →/systems/ibmpc/msdos-games/ Trivia

Trivia Club Created as a Delphi refuge for AOL "triviots," the Trivia Club has a conference room for *trivia* games—usually after 8 p.m. EST—a forum for score results and chat, and a database of files, where triviots leave bios, GIFs of themselves, game schedules, and useful utilities. Games last between an hour and an hour and a half, and good humor and sportsmanship are valued much more than ability at trivial things like *trivia*. The evening's game schedule is displayed in the conference room. ✓**DELPHI**→*go* ent tri

Trivia Time A weekly list of trivia questions followed by the answers to last week's questions and the names of those who won. ✓**INTERNET**→*finger* cyndiw@magnus1.com

Stats
- Difficulty: average
- Competition: high scoring
- Number of players: 1+
- Interface: ASCII
- Platforms: all

Trivia Unlimited Running the gamut from TV to history, the test gives you a "warm-up" option to try a range of questions, but if you live, you can head straight for the sudden-death test, in which you continue to answer new questions until you've missed five. Even when you get a question right, the game gives you a little factoid about the subject. ✓**COMPUSERVE**→ *go* tmc-66→Trivia Unlimited

Stats
- Difficulty: average
- Competition: high scoring
- Number of players: 1+
- Interface: ASCII
- Platforms: all

Trivial Pursuits (echo) Talk with others about the trivial, and match your wits with the best. ✓**ICENET**

2151 The year is 2151 and the American political system has undergone profound change. Presidency by popular vote is no more—now the most qualified candidate gets the job. In this glorified trivia contest, players answer questions from five tough categories. The person with the highest score becomes president. You get one play a day to try to hold the office as long as possible. ✓CHECK LOCAL BULLETIN BOARD SYSTEMS FOR THIS OR SIMILAR GAMES ☎→*dial* 609-628-4311

Stats
- Difficulty: simple
- Competition: high scoring

> "Bob Illuminati's jokes are horrible, and the questions can sometimes be tough, but players develop a rapport with each other, probably because Bob allows you to chat freely at half-time."

- Number of players: 1+
- Interface: ANSI
- Platforms: all

You Guessed It An odd, computerized mix of *Trivial Pursuit* and *Family Feud*. Your host, Bob Illuminati, is a smart-ass computer program. Once they're in the game area, prospective contestants line up in the Lobby and type "/PLAY". If you prefer to watch a game, type "/VIEW". As a viewer, you get to "answer," too, and your answers gets tallied into the poll of the top three answers for use in future games. Bob Illuminati's jokes are horrible, and the questions can sometimes be tough, but players develop a rapport with each other, probably because Bob allows you to chat freely at halftime. ✓ **COMPUSERVE**→*go* ygi

Stats
- Difficulty: average
- Competition: live
- Number of players: 2–6
- Interface: ASCII
- Platforms: all

Advertisements

Madvertising The host will display a slogan or jingle or other advertising from television, radio, billboards, and magazines. The first person to identify the advertiser wins 100 points. If there is a tie, players are invited "on stage" to defend their position. ✓ **AMERICA ONLINE**→*keyword* center stage

Stats
- Difficulty: average
- Competition: live
- Number of players: 2+
- Interface: ASCII
- Platforms: all

Requirements: *Played only at scheduled times*

Slogans Couch potatoes score big as they identify the advertiser whose slogan the host provides—

e.g., "The best part of waking up." Answer: Folger's (in your cup). ✓ **AMERICA ONLINE**→*keyword* pc→Rooms→Game Parlor *or* Game Parlor Too

Stats
- Difficulty: simple
- Competition: live
- Number of players: 2–23
- Interface: ASCII
- Platforms: all

Requirements: *Played only at scheduled times*

Slogans for Sale If you'd type "Winston tastes good AS a cigarette should," you'd be grammatically correct, but you'd lose this game of sometimes dated jingles and slogans. Your task: Complete ten well-known TV slogans by adding the missing word or words (in option 1). Or (in option 2) keep on guessing until you miss five. The higher your score, the better your chances of being added to the list of Madison Avenue Masters. ✓ **COMPUSERVE**→*go* tmc-26→Slogans For Sale

Stats
- Difficulty: simple

> **"Why anyone who hasn't memorized the *World Almanac*, the *Encyclopaedia Britannica*, and the average annual rainfall of all 50 states would want to pay to play this game is beyond us."**

- Competition: high scoring
- Number of players: 1+
- Interface: ASCII
- Platforms: all

Children

SmartKids Quiz With a different focus each week, *SmartKids Quiz* asks children a series of eight questions with three possible answers each. Getting the correct answer on the first or second try increases your score. The right answer also gives you more information about the question's topic. Every week a top scorer is named the SmartKids Quiz Genuine Genius. ✓ **PRODIGY**→*jump* smartkids quiz

Stats
- Difficulty: 8–12 years
- Competition: live
- Number of players: 1
- Interface: graphical
- Platforms: all

State Your Capitals An amusing and effective way for kids to learn the state capitals. Each multiple-choice question has a silly sentence about someone who lives in a state's capital. The player's job is to pick the correct town. ✓ **COMPUSERVE**→*go* tmc-66→State Your Capitals

Stats
- Difficulty: 8–12 years
- Competition: live
- Number of players: 1
- Interface: ASCII
- Platforms: all

Trivia for Kids Kids can choose from three categories: Folk and Fairy Tales, Animal Facts, and Science and Nature. Answer questions until you've missed five of them. If you think you can score higher, the game lets you play again or pick another category. ✓ **COMPUSERVE**→*go* tmc-1→Trivia for Kids

Stats
- Difficulty: 8–12 years
- Competition: live
- Number of players: 1
- Interface: ASCII
- Platforms: all

Trivia for Teens If you've paid attention in school, you may do pretty well here. If you haven't, select the first choice, which is a ten-question practice quiz. The sudden-death test lets you answer questions until you've missed three. High score will get you listed on the Honor Roll. Here's an interesting spoiler: What's the automobile on the back of the $10 bill? A Hupmobile. ✓COMPU-SERVE→*go* tmc-11→Trivia for Teens

Stats
- Difficulty: average
- Competition: high scoring
- Number of players: 1+
- Interface: ASCII
- Platforms: all

History

I Remember That...! Guess the year that a particular event occurred (all events took place between 1950 and 1993). You have the option of "betting" a range of years from one to seven. The shorter the range, the more points you win. ✓CHECK LOCAL BULLETIN BOARD SYSTEMS FOR THIS OR SIMILAR GAMES ☎→*dial* 804-587-4382/ 804-587-4289

Stats
- Difficulty: simple
- Competition: high scoring
- Number of players: 1+
- Interface: ANSI
- Platforms: all

Time Warp The host picks one player to choose a category from a list (e.g., science, politics, music, wars, movies). The host will then ask a time-line question based on that category. Players must answer

with the exact year to get five points, or within a year for three points. ✓AMERICA ONLINE→*keyword* pc→Rooms→Game Parlor *or* Game Parlor Too

Stats
- Difficulty: simple
- Competition: live
- Number of players: 2–23
- Interface: ASCII
- Platforms: all

Requirements: *Played only at scheduled times*

Movies

Academy Awards Trivia So many Hollywood careers have been affected by the Oscars that we can now answer a whole ream of questions regarding Oscar-winning performances, acceptance speeches, also-rans, backstage banter, scripts, and more. ✓GENIE→ *keyword* sbq→Academy Awards Trivia→The Oscars

Stats
- Difficulty: average
- Competition: personal best
- Number of players: 1
- Interface: ASCII
- Platforms: all

Celebrity Trivia Games Did you know that Joseph P. Kennedy and Gloria Swanson had a thing for each other? Or that Jerry Lewis was born as Joseph Levitch? You may not score big here, but you'll be able to bone up on celebrity gossip. There are nine categories to choose from, including Judy Garland, Frank Sinatra, the Three Stooges, and Alfred Hitchcock. ✓GENIE→*keyword* sbq→Celebrity Trivia Games

Stats
- Difficulty: average
- Competition: personal best
- Number of players: 1
- Platforms: all

Mixed Trivia Games For a

hodgepodge of entertainment trivia, take a look at these nine games. With questions from all categories in the *Showbiz Quiz* area, you never know what they'll be asking next. ✓GENIE→*keyword* sbq→ SHOWBIZQUIZ→Mixed Trivia Games

Stats
- Difficulty: average
- Competition: personal best
- Number of players: 1
- Interface: ASCII
- Platforms: all

Motion Picture Trivia Games If you really know your movies and your movie history, you'll shine in these quizzes. Subjects range from silent films and MGM musicals to biblical films and cult movies. There are also quizzes just about the *Star Wars* trilogy, *The Wizard of Oz, Gone with the Wind*, and *Casablanca*. Many questions are about plots and characters; others cover the shooting of the film, the backstage squabbles, and news related to the movies. Here's

> "Did you know that Joseph P. Kennedy and Gloria Swanson had a thing for each other? Or that Jerry Lewis was born as Joseph Levitch? You may not score big here, but you'll be able to bone up on celebrity gossip."

a sample: "In the *Star Wars* trilogy, what was the name of the bounty hunter who delivered Han Solo to Jabba the Hut?" Answer: Boba Fett. Who loves the smell of Napalm in the morning? ✓ **GENIE**→*keyword* sbq→Motion Picture Trivia Games

Stats

- Difficulty: average
- Competition: personal best
- Number of players: 1
- Interface: ASCII
- Platforms: all

Movie Star Trivia Games

Quizzes that test your knowledge on nine different screen legends: Fred Astaire, Bette Davis, Paul Newman, Greta Garbo, Dustin Hoffman, John Wayne, Clint Eastwood, Marilyn Monroe, and W. C. Fields. For example, did you know that Dustin Hoffman really was a "marathon man"? He ran marathons in high school for the Los Angeles High School track team. ✓ **GENIE**→*keyword* sbq→ Movie Star Trivia Games

Stats

- Difficulty: average
- Competition: personal best
- Number of players: 1
- Interface: ASCII
- Platforms: all

ShowBizQuiz

With approximately 50 questions to answer in 76 categories covering the whole range of entertainment—"Frank Sinatra Challenge," "Hot Rocks—The Rolling Stones," "TV Detective Puzzle," "Cult Films"—your goal is to be named an Entertainment Ph.D. ✓ **COMPUSERVE**→*go* gam-57

Stats

- Difficulty: average
- Competition: high scoring
- Number of players: 1+
- Interface: ASCII
- Platforms: all

ShowbizQuiz

Find all the sin-gle-player entertainment-trivia games on GEnie through this menu. Whether you're an expert on film's silent era, English pop music, or the Academy Awards, there's a quiz sure to stump you. ✓ **GENIE**→*keyword* sbq

---

TV Show Trivia Games

Couch potatoes will score high on these seven multiple-choice quizzes, covering such diverse boob-tube subjects as *Star Trek*, *Leave It to Beaver*, Rod Serling's *Twilight Zone*, and Hanna Barbera cartoons. For example, in the "*Flintstones* and *Jetsons*" quiz, you might find this question: "In the premiere *Flintstones* episode, what was the name of the gadget that Barney built?" Answer: the Flintstone Flyer. ✓ **GENIE**→*keyword* sbq→TV Show Trivia Games

Stats

- Difficulty: average
- Competition: personal best
- Number of players: 1
- Interface: ASCII
- Platforms: all

Music

Harmony

The host gives a word (e.g., "moon") as a song cue and players think of a song lyric using the cue (e.g., "Moonlight in Vermont…"; "It's a marvelous night for a moon dance…"; "Moonlight becomes you…"). ✓ **AMERICA ONLINE**→*keyword* pc→Rooms→Game Parlor *or* Game Parlor Too

Stats

- Difficulty: simple
- Competition: live
- Number of players: 2–23
- Interface: ASCII
- Platforms: all

Requirements: *Played only at scheduled times*

Music Trivia Games

If you're the kind of person who knows that *Oklahoma* premiered at the

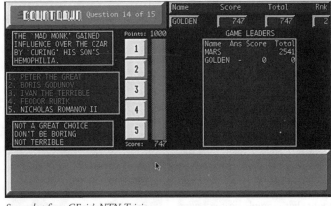

Screenshot from GEnie's NTN Trivia.

St. James Theater in New York, or that the Stones video *Undercover of the Night* was banned from British television, you'll find a quiz in here to test your wits. There are puzzles about big bands, the Beatles, Stephen Sondheim, and pop and rock music. ✓**GENIE**→*keyword* sbq→Music Trivia Games

Stats
- Difficulty: complex
- Competition: personal best
- Number of players: 1
- Platforms: all

Musical Circus The host gives openers (e.g., "Name the artist and the song in which this lyric appears: 'I met her in a Kingstown bar/ I feel in love, I knew it had to end.'" Answer: Bruce Springsteen, "Hungry Heart") followed by questions based on the opener (e.g., "Who plays saxophone for the E-Street Band?" Answer: Clarence Clemons). Follow-up questions get increasingly difficult and earn more and more points. ✓**AMERICA ONLINE**→*keyword* pc→ Rooms→ Game Parlor *or* Game Parlor Too

Stats
- Difficulty: simple
- Competition: live
- Number of players: 2–23
- Interface: ASCII

- Platforms: all
Requirements: *Played only at scheduled times*

Musical Madness A fill-in-the-blank game based on music titles, song lyrics, or song "plots" (e.g., "Name the song with this plot: Girl wants her wayward boyfriend to consider how well she's treated him before he cheats again." Answer: "Stop! In the Name of Love"). ✓**AMERICA ONLINE**→*keyword* pc→ Rooms→Game Parlor *or* Game Parlor Too

Stats
- Difficulty: simple
- Competition: live
- Number of players: 2–23
- Interface: ASCII
- Platforms: all
Requirements: *Played only at scheduled times*

Name that Tune Another twist on the standard trivia games, this one gives you the first line of a song (the lyrics, not the tune) and you have three chances to guess the title. ✓CHECK LOCAL BULLETIN BOARD SYSTEMS FOR THIS OR SIMILAR GAMES ☎→*dial* 609-235-5297

Stats
- Difficulty: simple
- Competition: high scoring
- Number of players: 1+

- Interface: ASCII
- Platforms: all

Sing Out "Name that tune" from portions of song lyrics, rather than notes. ✓**AMERICA ONLINE**→*keyword* pc→Rooms→Game Parlor *or* Game Parlor Too

Stats
- Difficulty: simple
- Competition: live
- Number of players: 2–23
- Interface: ASCII
- Platforms: all
Requirements: *Played only at scheduled times*

Quotations

Classic Quotes Choose either the first quiz, to complete ten famous quotes, or the second, in which you'll to complete as many quotes and authors' names as you can until you've tried five times. Top three scorers get their name on the Classic Quotes Master list. ✓**COMPUSERVE**→*go* tmc-45

Stats
- Difficulty: average
- Competition: high scoring
- Number of players: 1+
- Interface: ASCII
- Platforms: all

Science

Science Trivia Quiz Test your knowledge of biology, chemistry, and physics. The quiz questions match the style and the complexity of the College Board's Achievement and Advanced Placement Tests. Top scorers are entered into the Hall of Fame. ✓**COMPUSERVE** →*go* gam-53

Stats
- Difficulty: complex
- Competition: high scoring
- Number of players: 1+
- Interface: ASCII
- Platforms: all

> **"Think you're such a sports buff, do you? Okay, here's one for you: If there are men on first and third base, on what base or bases is a force-out possible?"**

Sports

Sports Trivia Think you're such a sports buff, do you? Okay, here's one for you: If there are men on first and third base, on what base or bases is a force-out possible? That's just one of the sample questions you'll find in this trivia game that tests your knowledge in the sports category of your choosing: basketball, baseball, football, soccer, tennis, or all sports. ✓**COMPUSERVE**→*go* tmc-66→Sports Trivia

Stats
- Difficulty: average
- Competition: personal best
- Number of players: 1
- Interface: ASCII
- Platforms: all

Tests

Board of Regents The New York State Board of Regents administers a test to all high-school graduates before they can get their diplomas. Based on the actual test, this game asks you 50 questions in your choice of five categories: math, biology, chemistry, social studies, and physics. If you score in the top percentiles, your name will be added to the Honor Roll. ✓**COMPUSERVE**→*go* tmc-55

Stats

- Difficulty: average
- Competition: high scoring
- Number of players: 1+
- Interface: ASCII
- Platforms: all

IQ Challenge This test isn't meant to be an actual IQ test, but it functions pretty much like one. The instructions say that "the results should give you a fair estimate of how smart you are." Your score is based both on the number of correct answers you give and on the time it takes you to give them. The faster you finish the test correctly, the better your score. Here's a sample: What are the two missing numbers: 2 5 10 13 26 x y? ✓**COMPUSERVE**→*go* tmc-99→IQ Challenge

Stats
- Difficulty: average
- Competition: personal best
- Number of players: 1
- Interface: ASCII
- Platforms: all

TMC Analogies If you want to go to graduate school, you'll have to take the Miller Analogies Test. But for practice, or just for fun, you'll want to give these "bicycle is to orange as Karl Marx is to..."-type questions a try. The first option is a practice test of 25 analogies. Option 2 is a 50-minute timed test of 100 analogies, for which you'll be scored. ✓**COMPUSERVE**→*go* tmc-51→TMC Analogies

Stats
- Difficulty: average
- Competition: personal best
- Number of players: 1
- Interface: ASCII
- Platforms: all

TMC Intelligence Test Another intelligence test, covering general knowledge as well as logical reasoning. You have a 20-second time limit to answer each of the 26 questions. If you answer within 12 seconds, you get a better score. ✓**COMPUSERVE**→*go* tmc-99→TMC Intelligence Test

Stats
- Difficulty: average
- Competition: personal best
- Number of players: 1
- Interface: ASCII
- Platforms: all

CYBERNOTES

"Speaking of the Superfriends, does anyone remember the two kids and their dog who were on the show before the WonderTwins? Her name was Wendy. I think his was Marvin. I also remember there being a bit of sexual tension between Wendy and Robin, actually between Wonder Woman and Aquaman, too. Does anyone else recall this or is it my warped childhood mind?"

"Well, Christy...if your mind is warped, then so is mine because when I saw the name Wendy, bells started going off in my head! Weren't they ALWAYS getting into trouble and having to be bailed out by one of the Superfriends? I think the entire show was filled with sexual tension, yes, but I thought it was between Batman and Robin? (wink) :+_)

—from **rec.games.trivia**

Word games

Franny Doodly hates *Anagrams* but she loves *Scrabble*.

She can't stand **Rhymes**, but she adores **Shuffle**; she loathes **Jumbled Words**, but she loves **Scrambled Eggs**. For her, **Word Builders** is tired, but **Hellzapoppin** is wired. **Jotto** is hot; **sKrAm-BIE** is not. **Hinky Pinky** is an absolute bore, **WWW Hangman** rules supreme. So what's her deal, anyway?

On the Net

Acronyms

Acronyms After the host has provided an acronym you have 30 seconds to come up with the most creative use of the letters you can. As soon as the host says "Go," type your acronym definition (e.g., "SLICK: Sam Left In Carrie's K-car, Science Lessons Infect Catatonic Kindergarteners"). ✓ **AMERICA ONLINE**→*keyword* pc→ Rooms→Game Parlor *or* Game Parlor Too

Stats
* Difficulty: simple
* Competition: live
* Number of players: 2–23
* Interface: ASCII
* Platforms: all

Requirements: *Played only at scheduled times*

Anagrams

alt.anagrams (ng) The place to find out that I, ROSS PEROT anagrams into POSTERIORS. Palindromes also discussed herein. ✓ **USENET**

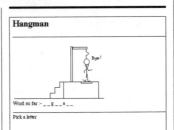

Hangman

Word so far :- _ _ g _ _ a _ _

Pick a letter

b c d e h i j l m ,

n p q r s t u v w x z ,

A hanging—from http://www.cm.cf.ac. uk/htbin/robh/hangman?go.

Crossword puzzles

Compass Clues Similar to a live crossword puzzle. The host posts five horizontal clues and five vertical clues (e.g., a six-letter word meaning "ugly"; answer: "homely"). Points are awarded for correct answers and for guessing the theme. Send you answer via "Instant Message." ✓ **AMERICA ONLINE**→ *keyword* pc→Rooms→ Game Parlor *or* Game Parlor Too

Stats
* Difficulty: simple
* Competition: live
* Number of players: 2–23
* Interface: ASCII
* Platforms: all

Requirements: *Played only at scheduled times*

Crossword Games (ml) For discussion of *Scrabble* and other crosswordlike games. ✓ **INTERNET**→ *email* saint@mit.edu ✍ *Write a request*

Crossword Games Pro (ml) *Scrabble* discussion for tournament players with an NSA rating. ✓ **IN-**TERNET→*email* saint@mit.edu *Write a request*

---

rec.puzzles.crosswords (ng) Discussions of major daily crosswords, cryptic-clue contests, news on tournaments, and general crossword passion. The group also puts out a three-part FAQ. ✓ **USENET** *FAQ:* ✓ **INTERNET**→*ftp* rtfm.mit.edu→anonymous→<your email address>→/pub/usenet-by-group/news.answers/crossword-faq

Fill in the blanks

Drawkcab "A man, a plan, a canal—Panama." The player gets two fill-in-the-blank phrases (e.g., "___perate; ___iment"), which you must fill in using the same letters, but reversed in the second clue ("des; sed"). ✓ **AMERICA ONLINE**→ *keyword* pc→Rooms→Game Parlor *or* Game Parlor Too

Stats
* Difficulty: simple
* Competition: live
* Number of players: 2–23
* Interface: ASCII
* Platforms: all

Requirements: *Played only at scheduled times*

Three to One After the host has given three fill-in-the-blank phrases, players must find one word that fits in all three blanks; e.g., "Out ____; ____ Bank; Go ____, young man." Answer: "West." ✓ **AMERICA ONLINE**→*keyword* pc→ Rooms→Game Parlor *or* Game Parlor Too

Stats
* Difficulty: simple
* Competition: live
* Number of players: 2–23
* Interface: ASCII
* Platforms: all

Requirements: *Played only at scheduled times*

Grids

Grids The host will give you a grid of four letters by four letters. You form words from letters that adjoin each other in the grid, whether horizontally, vertically, or diagonally. Consonants are valued at ten points, vowels at five. ✓**AMERICA ONLINE**→*keyword* center stage

Stats
- Difficulty: average
- Competition: live
- Number of players: 2+
- Interface: ASCII
- Platforms: all

Requirements: *Played only at scheduled times*

Super Grids Like the game *Grids*, but here the grid is made of 36 letters rather than 16, and the host determines on which side of the grid your letter formations must begin. In the regular rounds you have to create words of at least six letters. Bonus rounds require seven. ✓**AMERICA ONLINE**→*keyword* center stage

Stats
- Difficulty: average
- Competition: live
- Number of players: 2+
- Interface: ASCII
- Platforms: all

Requirements: *Played only at scheduled times*

Hangman

Alphabet Soup A variation on *Hangman*, where three players guess letters for the blank spaces in the host's words or phrase. Then all the players try to guess the word or phrase before the buzzer. ✓**AMERICA ONLINE**→*keyword* pc→ Rooms→Game Parlor *or* Game Parlor Too

Stats
- Difficulty: simple
- Competition: live
- Number of players: 2–23

> "If you have a graphical Web browser (such as Mosaic), you can watch your stick man climb the scaffold, stick his head in the noose, and go bye-bye—all because you didn't guess the correct letters."

- Interface: ASCII
- Platforms: all

Requirements: *Played only at scheduled times*

FITB A twist on *Hangman*, pronounced "Fit-bee." You can play alone or with a group of friends around your computer. Select Easy, Hard, or Goofy clues and categories. After you've guessed the clues in standard *Hangman* style, you're given an opportunity to guess which category they fall under. "Goofy" can actually be difficult, because the clues may be puns or plays on words. ✓**PRODIGY**→*jump* fitb

Stats
- Difficulty: average
- Competition: live
- Number of players: 1–4
- Interface: graphical
- Platforms: all

Hangman Guess the word before you're at the end of your rope. ✓**INTERNET**→*ftp* athene.uni-pader

born.de→anonymous→<your email address>→/news/comp.binaries. ibm.pc/volume 17

Stats
- Difficulty: simple
- Competition: personal best
- Number of players: 1
- Interface: ASCII
- Platform: DOS

Hangman Among the many word games found on bulletin board systems, *Hangman* and its variations are traditional favorites. It's you against the computer, although your "score" is often ranked against those of other BBS players—perhaps even posted in a BBS bulletin! ✓CHECK LOCAL BULLETIN BOARD SYSTEMS FOR A VARIATION OF THIS GAME

Stats
- Difficulty: simple
- Competition: high scoring
- Number of players: 1+
- Interface: ASCII, ANSI
- Platforms: all

Hangman You can get a hint at the beginning, but it'll cost you a head. Even without a hint, seven wrong letters will leave you dangling. But if you guess five more words right than wrong, you're eligible for the Hall of Fame. ✓**COMPUSERVE**→*go* hangman

Stats
- Difficulty: simple
- Competition: personal best
- Number of players: 1
- Interface: ASCII
- Platforms: all

MasterWord A multiplayer, graphic version of the *Hangman* classic, in which correctly guessed letters "explode" across the screen. You choose a word that the other players must guess, and you must find their words. To do so, you select letters from the "letter machine" at the top of the screen. The letter falls down the chute, "explodes," and falls into place in the words in which it appears. While chatting with other players, you can compare notes, and use one opponent to help you defeat another. ✓ **AMERICA ONLINE**→*keyword* masterword→Enter the Word Library *Interface:* ✓ **AMERICA ONLINE**→*keyword* download games→ Download MasterWord Software

Stats
- Difficulty: average
- Competition: live
- Number of players: 2+
- Interface: graphical
- Platforms: all

Commands
- To guess a word, use the letter machine to select: ?
- To submit a guessed letter or word, select: ctrl-return

WWW Hangman If you have a graphical Web browser (such as Mosaic), you can watch your stick man climb the scaffold, stick his head in the noose, and go bye-bye—all because you didn't guess the correct letters. ✓ **INTERNET**→ *www* http://www.cm.cf.ac.uk/ htbin/RobH/hangman?go

Stats
- Difficulty: simple
- Competition: live
- Number of players: 1
- Interface: graphical
- Platforms: all

Requirements: *A graphical Web browser and a SLIP connection*

Humor

alt.humor.puns (ng) Some of these are so bad, your computer might spontaneously shut off. Definitely requires a high groaning tolerance. ✓ **USENET**

Laugh Lines Using a letter the host provides, players compete to come up with the longest alliterative sentence (e.g., "D: Dastardly Detectives Dish Dirt Daily Dur-

ing Daytime Games.") ✓ **AMERICA ONLINE**→*keyword* pc→Rooms→ Game Parlor *or* Game Parlor Too

Stats
- Difficulty: simple
- Competition: live
- Number of players: 2–23
- Interface: ASCII
- Platforms: all

Requirements: *Played only at scheduled times*

Initials

#initgame The "other" (beside *Jeopardy*) nonstop IRC game, assisted by an IRC "bot," but actually run by the players themselves. One player becomes the host by changing his nickname to something like BC_MAAR. BC are the initials of a famous person; the other four letters give pertinent information, as follows: the first letter is either M or F, for male or female; the second, A or N, for American or not; the third, A or D, for alive or dead; the fourth, R or F, for real or fictional. So BC would be a real, living American male. Players then ask yes-or-no

> "It is quick, polished, and the computer hardly ever loses. Comes complete with a large dictionary. The program is equipped to suggest moves to the bewildered human."

questions in order to further deduce the identity of the person. The first player to guess that BC is Bill Clinton becomes the new host and a new round begins; thus, the game is never-ending as long as there are quick-thinking gamers around to play it. ✓ **INTERNET**→*irc* /channel #initgame

Stats
- Difficulty: simple
- Competition: live
- Number of players: 3+
- Interface: ASCII
- Platforms: all

Commands
- To review all the information gleaned so far, type: /recap

Initials The host gives initials (e.g., "TPS"), followed by a clue every few seconds (e.g., "Movie." "Spy." "Hepburn." "1939." "Tracy Lord.") The fewer clues it takes you to guess the answer (*The Philadelphia Story*), the higher your score. ✓ **AMERICA ONLINE**→ *keyword* pc→Rooms→Game Parlor *or* Game Parlor Too

Stats
- Difficulty: simple
- Competition: live
- Number of players: 2–23
- Interface: ASCII
- Platforms: all

Requirements: *Played only at scheduled times*

Nutty Notes Using the opening sentence to a letter and an acronym provided by the host (e.g., "Dear Boss, I won't be in today because...IQUIT"), players finish the correspondence using the acronym letters in order ("Initial Queries Unanswered Indicate Termination"). ✓ **AMERICA ONLINE**→*keyword* pc→Rooms→Game Parlor *or* Game Parlor Too

Stats
- Difficulty: simple
- Competition: live
- Number of players: 2–23

- Interface: ASCII
- Platforms: all

Requirements: *Played only at scheduled times*

Rhymes

Hinky Pinky A rhyming game. Answer the question with two words that rhyme and have the same number of syllables. For example, "What's Hemingway's incisor?" Answer: writer biter. ✓**AMERICA ONLINE**→*keyword* pc→Rooms→Game Parlor *or* Game Parlor Too

Stats
- Difficulty: simple
- Competition: live
- Number of players: 2–23
- Interface: ASCII
- Platforms: all

Requirements: *Played only at scheduled times*

Rhymes For closet poets. In the main rounds, you're asked to supply a word that rhymes with the given word, or to provide the next line of a couplet. If no one else matches your rhyme, you earn double points. In bonus rounds, players have to create a couplet based on a theme. ✓**AMERICA ONLINE**→*keyword* pc→Rooms→Game Parlor *or* Game Parlor Too

Stats
- Difficulty: simple
- Competition: live
- Number of players: 2–23
- Interface: ASCII
- Platforms: all

Requirements: *Played only at scheduled times*

Scrabble

Brainstorm The host will name a category, list some letters, and assign a point value to each letter. Your job is to come up with the word that has the most point value for the letters you use. For exam-

ple, if you're given G-F-O-D-C-H-R, with points 2-4-1-2-5-3-3, respectively, and the category is Animals, your answer might be "FROG," for 10 points. ✓**AMERICA ONLINE**→*keyword* center stage

Stats
- Difficulty: average
- Competition: live
- Number of players: 2+
- Interface: ASCII
- Platforms: all

Requirements: *Played only at scheduled times*

Crab A single-player *Scrabble* game for the Macintosh. It is quick, polished, and the computer hardly ever loses. Comes complete with a large dictionary. The program is equipped to suggest moves to the bewildered human. ✓**INTERNET**→*ftp* plaza.aarnet.edu.au→anonymous→<your email address>→/micros/mac/info-mac/game→crab.hqx

Stats
- Difficulty: average
- Competition: personal best
- Number of players: 1
- Interface: graphical
- Platform: Macintosh

#scrabble No one's ever here, but if they were, they'd be talking about *Scrabble.* ✓**INTERNET**→*irc* /channel #scrabble

---

Scrabble There is almost certainly a *Scrabble* game running on a BBS near you. *Scrabble* games are very popular. Usually they allow you to make one move a day. Some of them automatically send email to let you know it's your turn. If you think you'll get off easy without someone to verify your words for accuracy, think again. These games often come with huge online dictionaries that may or may not accept your entry.

Stats
- Difficulty: simple

- Competition: turn-based
- Number of players: 2+
- Interface: ASCII, ANSI
- Platforms: all

WisDOoM Despite the somewhat vague opening description, everyone here does one thing and one thing only—play *Scrabble.* Tournaments are always on the horizon. Games can be either timed or not, at your option. *The Official Scrabble Players Dictionary* is available online (for challenges only! You can't just look up any word that pops into your mind), and the server supports official *Scrabble* ratings—wear it like an electronic badge when you challenge other players to a game. Purists may balk, but you can also take your board—everyone carries one around—to the "workshop" and customize it to your liking. If you don't feel much like playing, you can sit in on the other games and kibitz. When you register, you have to wait for a day or so before your password is validated, but don't let that put you off. ✓**INTERNET**→*telnet* next7.cas.muohio.edu 8888

Stats
- Difficulty: average
- Competition: live
- Number of players: 2+
- Interface: ASCII
- Platforms: all

Commands
- To get a list of basic help topics, type: help
- To register, type: request <your handle> <your email address> <your full name>
- To get a map of WisDOoM, type: map1
- To begin *Scrabble* instructions, type: help play1
- To meet another player to discuss starting a game or to observe a game already in progress, type: join <player name>

Scrambled words

Jumbled Words Some people can look at a scrambled word and unscramble it instantly. If you're one of them, go immediately to the Expert category and leave the rest of us sweatin' in Easy, working our way up to Medium. In Easy, the words have four or five letters, they're well-known, and even children should be able to solve them. As you move up, the words get longer and more and more obscure. ✓**COMPUSERVE**→*go* tmc-26→Jumbled Words

Stats
- Difficulty: average
- Competition: personal best
- Number of players: 1
- Interface: ASCII
- Platforms: all

Mad Scramble The host will give you a point value for the *Mad Scramble*, a "mad clue" (e.g., "Sound investment advice"), a subject ("phrase, 4 words"), and the scramble ("YELLOWBUSH-LIGH"). The object is to discover the answer ("BUY LOW SELL HIGH") and earn big points. ✓**AMERICA ONLINE**→*keyword* center stage

Stats
- Difficulty: average
- Competition: live
- Number of players: 2+
- Platforms: all

Requirements: *Played only at scheduled times*

Scramble The Ulcer Maker. As soon as one player types "Go," the countdown begins. You're given 16 letters in a 4x4 grid. You have 90 seconds to make as many words as you can with the letters, using each of them only once. (If "a" appears three times in the letters you've chosen, you're still only using each "a" once.) The more letters you use, the higher your score

(long-winded words will be displayed for all to admire at the end of the game). Just when you think you've found the perfect six- or seven-letter word, the game will invariably tell you that some other player has already used it. So fast-paced and addicting that players don't chat in between games, because they're biting their nails waiting to play again. ✓**DELPHI**→*go* ent scr

Stats
- Difficulty: complex
- Competition: live
- Number of players: 2+
- Interface: ASCII
- Platforms: all

Commands
- To indicate you're ready for the next round, type: rd

Scrambled Eggs Another scrambled-word game. The words get progressively harder, and the two highest-scoring audience members are called on stage to do unscrambling battle in the championship round. ✓**AMERICA ONLINE**→*keyword* center stage

Stats
- Difficulty: average
- Competition: live
- Number of players: 2+
- Interface: ASCII
- Platforms: all

Requirements: *Played only at scheduled times*

Shuffle It's a two-part game. The host gives a scrambled word; you must unscramble it. Each time a word is unscrambled, the host will put some of the letters into a *Hangman*-style puzzle. As soon as you guess the puzzle, send an "Instant Message" to the host. ✓**AMERICA ONLINE**→*keyword* pc→Rooms→ Game Parlor *or* Game Parlor Too

Stats
- Difficulty: simple
- Competition: live
- Number of players: 2–23

- Interface: ASCII
- Platforms: all

Requirements: *Played only at scheduled times*

---

sKrAmBlE Be the first to unscramble the word or create a new word with the letters or do both. ✓**AMERICA ONLINE**→*keyword* center stage

Stats
- Difficulty: average
- Competition: live
- Number of players: 2+
- Interface: ASCII
- Platforms: all

Requirements: *Played only at scheduled times*

Untanglers You have 25 seconds to solve the host's *Untangler* (e.g., "CnHiIxNoAn" is "Nixon in China." ✓**AMERICA ONLINE**→*keyword* pc→Rooms→Game Parlor *or* Game Parlor Too

Stats
- Difficulty: simple
- Competition: live
- Number of players: 2–23
- Interface: ASCII
- Platforms: all

Requirements: *Played only at scheduled times*

Word association

Cryptic Titles Using purple prose (e.g., "brightly colored aquatic vessel"), the host puts forth clues for which players find the correct movie, song, or book title (e.g., "Yellow Submarine"). ✓**AMERICA ONLINE**→*keyword* pc→Rooms→ Game Parlor *or* Game Parlor Too

Stats
- Difficulty: simple
- Competition: live
- Number of players: 2–23
- Interface: ASCII
- Platforms: all

Requirements: *Played only at scheduled times*

InCommon Players determine the relationship between items. Using the game's own example, the host might list "Swiss, Jack, sharp...." If all the players answer "words related to cheese," the host might continue: "yataghan, pointed, cutting tool, Bowie." The answer turns out to be "words related to knives." ✓**AMERICA ONLINE**→*keyword* pc→Rooms→Game Parlor *or* Game Parlor Too

Stats
- Difficulty: average
- Competition: live
- Number of players: 2–23
- Interface: ASCII
- Platforms: all

Requirements: *Played only at scheduled times*

Name It The host gives a *Name It* category (e.g., "Name a religious holiday.") The players come up with answers ("Christmas," "Hanukkah," "Ramadan.") Original answers get double points. ✓**AMERICA ONLINE**→*keyword* pc→Rooms→Game Parlor *or* Game Parlor Too

Stats
- Difficulty: simple
- Competition: live
- Number of players: 2–23
- Platforms: all

Requirements: *Played only at scheduled times*

Name That Theme The host determines how many "keywords" (not be confused with AOL's navigation keywords) will be found in the clues. For instance, in the clue "Days of Wine and Roses," the keyword might be "roses." Based on that clue and others, players guess the theme—"Valentine's Day." ✓**AMERICA ONLINE**→*keyword* pc→Rooms→Game Parlor *or* Game Parlor Too

Stats
- Difficulty: simple
- Competition: live

> "Purists may balk, but you can take your *Scrabble* board —everyone carries one around —to the 'workshop' and customize it."

- Number of players: 2–23
- Interface: ASCII
- Platforms: all

Requirements: *Played only at scheduled times*

Shout It Out "On-stage" contestants and audience members vie for the most word associations— e.g., "things that fly"—they can muster. ✓**AMERICA ONLINE**→*keyword* center stage

Stats
- Difficulty: average
- Competition: live
- Number of players: 2+
- Interface: ASCII
- Platforms: all

Requirements: *Played only at scheduled times*

Assorted games

Dictionary A popular game adapted to the chat rooms. Find the correct definition for a word, or try to fool others with a phony definition. One player posts the correct answer. The others put forth the most believable definition they can. Then everybody votes for the most likely answer. Players earn a point if they select the correct definition and a point if they've fooled a competitor. ✓**AMERICA ONLINE**→*keyword* pc→Rooms→Game Parlor *or* Game Parlor Too

Stats
- Difficulty: simple
- Competition: live
- Number of players: 2–23
- Interface: ASCII
- Platforms: all

Requirements: *Played only at scheduled times*

Fender Bender A game to test your vanity-plate-reading abilities. Using the example from the online rules, the host will post the puzzle (e.g., "QRESFLO") and a clue ("inquisitive guy"). Players have ten seconds to guess the answer ("curious fellow"). ✓**AMERICA ONLINE**→*keyword* pc→Rooms→Game Parlor *or* Game Parlor Too

Stats
- Difficulty: simple
- Competition: live
- Number of players: 2–23
- Interface: ASCII
- Platforms: all

Requirements: *Played only at scheduled times*

Hellzapoppin A virtually rule-free word game, in which the host posts a question or challenge (e.g., "Name all the states that include the letter K," "List as many characters as you can from *The Wizard of Oz* before the buzzer.") ✓**AMERICA ONLINE**→*keyword* pc→Rooms→Game Parlor *or* Game Parlor Too

Stats
- Difficulty: simple
- Competition: live
- Number of players: 2-23
- Platforms: all

Requirements: *Played only at scheduled times*

Jotto Guess the computer's five-letter word before the computer guesses yours. ✓**INTERNET**→*ftp* walton.maths.tcd.ic→anonymous→<your email address>→/news/games/volume 11

Stats
- Difficulty: simple

- Competition: personal best
- Number of players: 1
- Interface: ASCII
- Platforms: all

Lucky 7 By rolling the Center Stage dice, the host generates seven letters. Players submit words formed with those letters, earning points based on the number of letters they use: 4 letters earn 10 points, 5 letters earn 15, 6 earn 20, and using all 7 earns bonus points. ✓**AMERICA ONLINE**→*keyword* center stage

Stats
- Difficulty: average
- Competition: live
- Number of players: 2+
- Interface: ASCII
- Platforms: all

Requirements: *Played only at scheduled times*

Mixups Players form words of five or more letters based on the host's randomly selected letters, plus one letter of each player's own choosing, excluding "s" for plurals (unless "s" is one of the randomly selected letters). The longest word wins 100 points per letter. ✓**AMERICA ONLINE**→*keyword* center stage

Stats
- Difficulty: average
- Competition: live
- Number of players: 2+
- Platforms: all

Requirements: *Played only at scheduled times*

Wheel of Fortune Perhaps because it's an easy game to jump into and get started without much "basic training," *Wheel of Fortune* and its ilk can be found on many BBSs. In most cases you'll play against the computer. Your score is matched against those of other board members. ✓CHECK LOCAL BULLETIN BOARD SYSTEMS FOR A VARIATION OF THIS GAME

Stats
- Difficulty: simple

- Competition: high scoring
- Number of players: 1+
- Interface: ASCII, ANSI
- Platforms: all

Word Builders Players build words based on at least three letters provided by the host. The letters must be used in order, but not necessarily together—e.g., "FRST." Possible answers might be "first," "frost," "forest," "frustration," and "farthest." ✓**AMERICA ONLINE**→*keyword* pc→Rooms→Game Parlor *or* Game Parlor Too

Stats
- Difficulty: simple
- Competition: live
- Number of players: 2–23
- Interface: ASCII
- Platforms: all

Requirements: *Played only at scheduled times*

Word Chains Using relatively free association, players try to guess words in a chain. Once a word in the chain has been discovered, it becomes the clue for the next word. ✓**AMERICA ONLINE**→ *keyword* pc→Rooms→Game Parlor *or* Game Parlor Too

Stats
- Difficulty: simple
- Competition: live
- Number of players: 2–23
- Interface: ASCII
- Platforms: all

Requirements: *Played only at scheduled times*

Word Hunt The host gives a word, and players have 20 seconds to come up with as many other

> "Test your vanity-plate-reading talents: e.g., QRESFLO."

words as possible that can be formed using some or all of the same letters. Each letter can be used only once, and the new words must be at least three letters long—e.g., "bachelor" might yield "cab, bore, arc, bale, lob, orb, crab, roach, breach." ✓**AMERICA ONLINE**→*keyword* pc→Rooms→Game Parlor *or* Game Parlor Too

Stats
- Difficulty: simple
- Competition: live
- Number of players: 2–23
- Interface: ASCII
- Platforms: all

Requirements: *Played only at scheduled times*

Word Play A mishmash of questions with guidelines that vary by question. Only for the mentally nimble. ✓**AMERICA ONLINE**→*keyword* pc→Rooms→Game Parlor *or* Game Parlor Too

Stats
- Difficulty: complex
- Competition: live
- Number of players: 2–23
- Interface: ASCII
- Platforms: all

Requirements: *Played only at scheduled times*

Word Revenge The host requests a secret word—e.g., a famous person, or a well-known landmark—from a particular player, who responds via "Instant Message." The host then gives clues to the other players in the form of a sentence that is, at least tangentially, related to the word. ✓**AMERICA ONLINE**→*keyword* pc→Rooms→ Game Parlor *or* Game Parlor Too

Stats
- Difficulty: simple
- Competition: live
- Number of players: 2–23
- Interface: ASCII
- Platforms: all

Requirements: *Played only at scheduled times*

Part 5

Personal Computer & Video Games

Acorn, Tandy, TI & Unix

There's no such thing as an orphan in Cyberspace, thanks to the depth of file archives

and machine users. Any expert will tell you that a machine is cutting-edge as long as it runs the programs you use—by this standard, the Tandy Color Computer (CoCo) using *Fenix* may as well be a gazillion–gigahertz RISC speedster. Net daddy UNIX is also included here.

On the Net

Acorn

comp.sys.acorn.games (ng) The Acorn is dead, long live the Acorn! Even though the old 8-bit machine can't compete with today's multimedia powerhouses, you can still play *Space Invaders* and *Brick Out*—and discuss them with other loyal Acorn users. ✓**USENET**

Tandy

OS9 Games For OS9 users, the operating system for Tandy color computers, a.k.a. "CoCo," there's game talk in the OS9 Forum in the Games and Graphics topic. In the Database, you'll find some of the latest GNU *Chess* software, *Shanghai* (a *majongg* game), and updates to software handed out at nationwide CoCoFests. ✓**DELPHI** ...→*go* com os9→Forum→clear *→ set games (for messages) ...→ *go* com os9→Databases→Games (for files)

Tandy Color Computer Games Discuss games for the CoCo (including *Chawks3 Football*, *Vortex*

Factor, and *Dragons of Dagorath*). Shareware includes some classics from *Rainbow Magazine* dating back to 1985. ✓**DELPHI** ...→*go* com col→Forum→clear *→games (for messages) ...→*go* com col→Databases→Games (for files)

Tandy Games Although the number of games uploaded has dropped in the last three years or so, you'll still be able to find games here for the TRS-80 and other Tandy computers. Most are arcade-style, although the two most popular downloads are *Sopwith*, a WWI flight simulation, and *Solitair*, a graphic card game. ✓**GENIE**→ *keyword* tandy→Tandy Software Libraries→Set Software Library→All Libraries→*Search by search string:* game

Tandy 100 Games Discuss and download games for the Tandy Model 100 and other Tandy models. Discussion is somewhat sparse (except in the General/Help and For Sale areas), and the games are pretty basic. Among the more popular downloads: *Fenix.SJS*, an arcade-style game, similar to *Demon Attack*; *Micro-Starfighter*, space shoot-'em-up; and a little number called *SEXFUN.100*. ✓**COMPUSERVE**→*go* tandylaptop→Libraries *or* Messages

Texas Instruments

TI Games Texas Instruments stock soared when the company discontinued its PC, but archives never die. You'll find a small collection of games for the TI to download, including one dating back to 1985 called *Visit the Psy-*

chiatrist. ✓**DELPHI** ...→*go* com ti→Forum→clear *→set games (for messages) ...→ *go* com ti→Databases→Games (for files)

Unix

comp.sources.games (ng) Discussion and announcements regarding the source code for Net-authored computer games. The archive site has the source code for many games. Dominated by Unix programs. ✓**USENET** ✓**INTERNET**→*ftp* ftp.uu.net→anonymous→<your email address>→/usenet/comp.sources. games

Unix Games An archive of Unix games, including *Space War* (complete with a game master and weapons), *Empire*, *Tetris*, and *XAsteroids*. ✓**GENIE**→ *keyword* unix→ UNIX Software Libraries→Set Software Library→All Libraries→*Search by search string:* game

Orphans

Games for Orphaned Computers The sun'll come out tomorrow. The library holds a number of (mostly arcade-style) games for computers that nobody loves anymore, especially the TI series. These include, among the more popular choices, *Honey Hunt*, based on the Milton Bradley game of the same name; *Karate*, chop action for the TI-99/4a; *Spacestation Pheta*, wherein you conquer each level of the space station; and *Tetris*, for the Geneve and 99/4a. ✓**GENIE**→ *keyword* ti→TI Software Libraries→ *Search by search string:* game

Amiga games

Who cares if the Amiga's parent, Commodore, declared itself belly-up in April 1994?

It's only brought the on-line Amiga community closer together. Hyperactive newsgroups, massive archives, and blistering head-to-head action all await online. The Amiga lives!

On the Net

Amiga Arts Gaming Message board for discussing games on the Amiga—especially for artists who like to play a game when they're taking a break. Download games for the Amiga from the Games library (*Rings of Zon* is popular, as is the *Monopoly* freeware game). The Game Hints/Scenerio [*sic*] library has patches, utilities, cheats, and hints. The Game Demos library has sometimes-playable demos of soon-to-be or recently released Amiga games. ✓**COMPUSERVE** ...→*go* amigaarts→Messages→CD32/Games (for messages) ...→*go* amigaarts→Libraries→Games <or> Game Hints <or> Game Demos (for files)

Amiga Games In the Holodeck category of GEnie's Amiga Starship, you'll find discussions about a number of games, including *Gunship 2000*, *The Settlers*, *Elite II: Frontier*, and *Hired Guns*. In the library, a ton of Amiga games are there for the grabbing. Popular choices include: *Pac91*, a *PacMan* clone that boasts of its similarity to the original; *Pacman87*, a variation on *PacMan* with mazes, traps, and more; and *Lode*, a *Lode Runner* clone for the Amiga with 50 levels. ✓**GENIE** ...→*keyword* amiga

→Amiga Bulletin Board→set 6 (for messages) ...→*keyword* amiga→Amiga Software Libraries→Set Software Library→All Libraries→*Search by search string:* game (for files)

AMIGAGAMES (echo) Discuss gaming software for the Amiga. ✓**FIDONET**

Amiga SIG Games See the forum for Amiga gaming discussions, and download shareware games, as well as game cheats, map editors, and more from the Databases. One download is called *Cow Wars*—you fire bovine-type animals at your opponent. ✓**DELPHI** ...→*go* com ami→Forum→clear *→set games (for messages) ...→*go* com ami→Databases→Games (for files)

Aminet Gaming Archive A seemingly endless collection of Amiga shareware, freeware, and demo versions of games. ✓**INTERNET** ...→*ftp* wuarchive.wustl.edu→anonymous→<your email address>→/systems/amiga/aminet/game ...→*ftp* ftp.doc.ic.ac.uk→anonymous→<your email address>→/aminet/game ...→*ftp* ftp.luth.se→anonymous→<your email address>→/pub/aminet/game

comp.sys.amiga.games (ng) Discussion of games for the Commodore Amiga with some nose-thumbing in the direction of far more successful and expensive home computer systems that are not as well suited to graphical action. Also see the related newsgroup for CD-ROM users, comp.sys.amiga.cd32. ✓**USENET**

Commodore

Commodore Art/Games Forum Gaming discussion is virtually nonexistent, but the libraries carry many games for the Commodore. *Pinball* or *Terminator II*, anyone? ✓**COMPUSERVE**→*go* cbmart

Commodore Games Download games for the Commodore 64 or 128. Among the most popular choices: *Damsels*, an adult adventure game; *Eagle Empire*, similar to the arcade game *Phoenix*; and *Wheel of Fortune*, with an accompanying puzzle maker so you can stump your friends. ✓**GENIE**→*keyword* commodore→Commodore Software Libraries→Set Software Library→All Libraries→*Search by search string:* game

Commodore Games Talk and download games for the C-64 and C-128. The Database has shareware files, including *Strip Poker* with Samantha Fox as your opponent (rated PG). ✓**DELPHI** ...→*go* com com→Forum→clear *→set fun (for messages) ... →*go* com com→Databases→Fun (for files)

Utilities

Amiga Archivers Amiga programs to compress or extract files. ✓**COMPUSERVE**→*go* amigauser→Libraries→Archivers/Crunchers ✓**INTERNET**→*ftp* wuarchive.wustl.edu→anonymous→<your email address>→/systems/amiga/aminet/util/arc ...→*ftp* ftp.doc.ic.ac.uk→anonymous→<your email address>→/aminet/util/arc ...→*ftp* ftp.luth.se→anonymous→<your email address>→/pub/aminet/util/arc

Apple][games

No, Apple did not invent the personal computer, but it did make the first PC worth writing freaky software for. We're talking low-res color-and-sound games like *Lemonade, Little Brick Out,* and *Deathstar,* and high-res masterpieces of memory efficiency and ingenuity like *Viper, Sneakers,* and *Karateka.* The Apple][is where many of today's celebrated video-game entrepreneurs and programmers first cut their game-design chops. Swing by **comp.sources.apple2** for insights into game programming, or download the work of others from the formidable **Apple][(8-bit games) Archives.**

On the Net

Apple][(8-bit) Games Archives Archives of public-domain freeware and shareware games for the old Apple][. Find out what all those elementary and secondary schools ended up using their computers for. Highlights include *Apple Trek,* an adaptation of the arcade blockbuster *Defender,* a *Wheel of Fortune* clone, and a slew of EAMON text adventures. ✓ **INTERNET** ...→*ftp* apple2.archive. umich.edu→anonymous→<your email address>→/archive/apple2/ 8bit/games ...→*ftp* wuarchive. wustl.edu→anonymous→<your email address>→/systems/apple2/games ...→*ftp* grind.isca. uiowa.edu→anonymous→<your

email address>→/pub/apple2/ games

Apple II Games A huge forum for Apple II gamers: two message boards, several software libraries, and its own conference hall. Among the more popular games that are discussed (or that have related files in the libraries): *Sub Battle Simulator, Zany Golf, Mean 18, Alien Mind,* and *Task Force.* ✓ **AMERICA ONLINE**→*keyword* a2 games

Apple II Games On the Bulletin board a number of discussions flourish, including games for classic Apples, IIgs-specific games, and *Dungeon* (*Zork*) for the IIgs. In the software library, find fantasy and adventure games galore, *pinball, backgammon,* and more. Among the more popular files: *Tetrotrix,* a French clone of *Tetris; Pangea* (space shoot-'em-up); and *Space Harrier* (a demo that allows you to shoot but not die). ✓ **GENIE** ...→ *keyword* a2→A2 Bulletin Board→ set 6 (for messages) ...→*keyword* a2→A2 Software Libraries→Set Software Library→All Libraries →*Search by search string:* game (for files)

Apple II Games Apple II (8-bit and 16-bit GS) games are discussed in the Forum, while shareware games are found in the Database: dungeon-this, wizard-that, shoot-this, blast-that, and a game called *PlasmaLab* (and its update, *Plasma Lab* v2.7), which has computer-generated colonies growing and multiplying. ✓ **DELPHI** ...→*go* com app→Forum→clear *→set entertainment *or* set miscellaneous

(for messages) ...→*go* com app→ Databases→Entertainment (for files)

Apple II Games/Entertainment Not very busy, but there's some discussion on the message boards and there are several downloadable arcade and combat games in the library. ✓ **COMPUSERVE**→*go* appuser→Libraries *or* Messages →Games/Entertainment

comp.binaries.apple2 (ng) Public-domain programs and graphic images, often relating to games, are posted here. The source code (that is, the programmer's recipe) is sometimes cross-posted to comp.sources.apple2. In the archive the games that are posted to the newsgroup are, well, archived. ✓ **USENET** *Archives:* ✓ **INTERNET**→*ftp* wuarchive.wustl.edu→ anonymous→<your email address> →/usenet/comp.binaries.apple2/ Game

comp.sources.apple2 (ng) Source code for public-domain Apple][programs, posted by programmers. Dissecting someone else's quirky little game is how most great programmers learn the trade. ✓ **USENET**

GS (16-bit) Games Archive Games that run only on the souped-up GS machines and put the Sega and Nintendo 16-bit software to shame, thanks to the fancy GS sound and graphics chips they hold. Worthy archive contents include a shoot-'em-up *Tetris* variant, a *Sim City*–type (build your own city) diversion called *Cyber War,* and a color version of the minor classic *Lunar Lander.* ✓ **INTERNET**→ *ftp* wuarchive. wustl.edu→anonymous→<your email address>→/systems/apple2/gs/game

Atari games

Atari created the first video games and a discontinued
line of PCs that were the quintessential games machines. Were? Take a look at the tremendous caches of free game software available from archives on the Internet, independent BBSs, and commercial services. See the **Atari Gaming Archive** for perhaps the most impressive example. Online discussions and electronic magazines—especially in **comp.sys.atari.st** and on CompuServe and GEnie—function as extended user-group lifelines for owners of the Atari PCs. So get online before you even consider abandoning your old ST.

Atari 520ST—downloaded from GEnie's Atari ST RoundTable.

bits to 64. Atari gaming is widely covered here. Typical issues bulge at more than 200K. ✓**COMPUSERVE** →*go* gamers→Libraries→Game Magazines ✓**GENIE**→*keyword* st→ Atari ST RT Libraries→Set Software Library→Atari Explorer - ST Format ✓**INTERNET**→*email* stzmagazine-request@virginia.edu ✍ *Type in subject line:* subscribe ...→*ftp* rahul.net→anonymous→<your email address>→/pub/wilsont/AEO ...→*ftp* atari.archive.umich.edu→ anonymous→<your email address> →/atari/magazines

On the Net

Across the board

Atari Computer Games The Games & Entertainment topic holds most of the gaming discussions, though you're apt to find others elsewhere in this Forum. The Database holds a number of games ranging from *NetHack* to patches and maps for *Tower*. ✓**DELPHI** ...→*go* com ata→Forum→clear *→set games (for messages) ...→ *go* com ata→Databases→Games (for files)

Atari Explorer Online Magazine (j) Complete, if not always critical, biweekly coverage of the Atari computing world, from 8

Atari Gaming Archive Most Atari-related information on the Net either originates at this mammoth FTP site or filters back into it. There are always large numbers of freeware or shareware games to download—*Scrabble* to *Larn* to *Breakout* to *GNU Chess*. Start by downloading the index (0index). ✓**INTERNET**→*ftp* atari.archive. umich.edu→anonymous→<your email address>→/atari/Games *Info:* ✓**INTERNET**→*email* atari@ atari.archive.umich.edu ✍ *To get instructions on how to access files via email, type in message body:* help

Atari Gaming Forum Discussion is sparse, but the libraries carry hundreds of games for Atari

users—from *NetHack* to *Oxyd* to a *Ms. Pacman* clone. Also includes home-video-system topics. ✓**COMPUSERVE**→*go* atarigaming

Atari 8-bit

Atari 8-bit Games The Games! category of the bulletin board hosts discussions of *Alternate Reality*, the Atari 7800 ProSystem, multiplayer computer games, and *Maze of AGDAgon*. The software library is filled with adventure, arcade, and other games, including such popular downloads as *Xevious*, a version of the popular Atari arcade game by the same name; *The Empire Strikes Back*, a version of the Atari 2600 game; *Tetrix*, which claims to be better than the original *Tetris*; and *WarGames86*, a global-conflict game about the futility of war. ✓**GENIE** ...→*keyword* atari8→Atari Bulletin Board→set 4 (for messages) ...→*keyword* atari8→Atari Software Libraries→Set Software Library→*Search by search string:* game (for files)

Atari-ST

Atari ST Games Use the message board to discuss everything from *Towers* to *Oxyd* to *Amberstar*. In the libraries, you'll find Atari-related files and hundreds and hundreds of games for the Atari ST. Among the most popular: *Space Wars v.3*, a color version; *ROCM*, a "graphic adventure science fiction arcade action game" requiring joystick and color monitor; and *Galactic Warriors*, the complete game with different levels and the ability to earn extra men. ✓**GENIE** ...→*keyword* st→Atari ST Bulletin Board→set 9 (for messages) ...→*keyword* st→Atari ST RT Libraries→*Search by search string:* game (for files)

Macintosh games

Fervent bulletin-board, newsgroup, and forum discussions of Mac games dot the Net,

while the commercial services and the Monster Macintosh Gaming Archives maintain freeware and shareware game archives that are oceanic in their proportions. If you can swing a fancy Internet connection that takes advantage of the Mac's built-in network capabilities, you're in for some of the best personal-computer gaming on the Net (chalk it up to Apple's heavy influence on those hotbeds of game development called college campuses).

Inside MacGames *cover—from AOL's Macintosh Games Forum.*

On the Net

comp.sys.mac.games (ng) Discuss gaming on the Mac— from winning defensive strategies in *Spectre* tank battles to manipulating bond issues in *Sim City 2000.* Very lively. ✓ USENET *FAQ:* ✓ **INTERNET** ...→*ftp* rtfm.mit.edu→ anonymous→<your email address> →/pub/usenet-by-group/comp.sys. mac.games→comp.sys.mac.games_ FAQ ...→*www* http://www.cis. ohio-state.edu/hypertext/faq/ usenet/macintosh/games-faq/ faq.html

MAC-GAMES (echo) For any and all Mac gaming discussion. ✓ FI-DONET

Macintosh Games CompuServe's overall area for discussing games played on the Macintosh. Includes message boards

with such areas as *PML Football Field* (to debate what makes one game better than another), Fun on Power Macs (to discuss this nascent gaming world), Adventure Games, Flight Simulation, and Arcade/Action Games. Downloadable game files and tons of sound files from TV shows and movies are in the libraries. ✓ **COMPU-SERVE**→*go* macfun

Macintosh Games Discuss Mac games on the message boards, participate in live conferences on Friday nights at 10 p.m. EST, and download a number of games from the extensive Software Libraries (or the News Files library). Among the more popular games: *Quagmire,* a robot-to-the-rescue arcade game with six inter-level movies; *Zero-G Pinball,* a gravity-free pinball game; *Macman Classic Pro,* a PacMan variation; *Ultra Tank; Tron (Kerrigan),* based on the arcade game/movie; *Monopoly; Risk (II and III); Klondike 5.1,* the Mac version of the popular soli-

taire game; and an '80s classic called *Mac vs. IBM,* in which you, controlling the Mac at the bottom of the screen, try to destroy the IBM at the top. ✓ **AMERICA ONLINE** →*keyword* mgm

Macintosh Games Carries a number of Topics on which are discussed *Falcon, Hornet,* Favorite All-Time Games, CD-ROM games, *Myst,* and *Hellcats Over the Pacific.* The Software Libraries have a staggering number of shareware/freeware games and upgrades, hints, and tips, some as recent as yesterday, others dating back to the mid-1980s. Among the more popular downloads of the last decade: *Bowl-A-Rama,* a bowling game for the Mac; *Crystal Raiders,* a joystick action game from England; and *BMX—The Racing Game,* a bike-through-obstacle-course arcade game. ✓ **GENIE** ...→*keyword* mac→Macintosh Bulletin Board→set 5 (for messages) ...→*keyword* mac→Macintosh Software Libraries→Set Software Li-

> "In an '80s classic called *Mac vs. IBM,* in which you, controlling the Mac at the bottom of the screen, try to destroy the IBM at the top."

brary→All Libraries *Search by search string:* game (for files)

Macintosh ICONtact Games

Games get discussed in the Entertainment topics while the database has arcade games, action/adventure games, board/word/puzzle games, card games, and related files, sounds, graphics, and demos. *Siege of Darkwood* (in the Action/Adventure topic), a fantasy role-playing game continuing the saga of Darkwood and the exploits of Derek, once a peasant, now Captain of the Guard. Popular hits in the arcade section include *Oxyd* and *Tetris Max* (which get an honorable mention in the 1993 MacUser Shareware Awards). ✓**DELPHI** ...→*go com mac*→Forum→clear *→set entertainment (for messages) ...→*go com mac*→Entertainment SIG→Databases (for files)

Monster Macintosh Gaming Archives

More than 100 shareware and public-domain games from *Sokoban* to *Hangman* to *Star Trek* to *Oxyd.* ✓**INTERNET** ...→*ftp* wuarchive. wustl.edu→ anonymous →<your email address>→/systems/mac/info-mac/game ...→*ftp* sumex-aim.stanford.edu→anonymous→<your email address>→/info-mac/game ...→*ftp* mac. archive.umich.edu→anonymous→ <your email address>→/mac/game

News & reviews

Inside Mac Games Reviews and previews of Macintosh games fill this monthly electronic magazine. The online demos—about half of each edition—are free, but if you want the full edition, you'll have to subscribe. Information on how to subscribe is included. ✓**INTERNET** ...→*ftp* sumex-aim.stanford.edu→ anonymous→<your email address> →/info-mac/per/ingam ...→*ftp*

wuarchive.wustl.edu→anonymous→ <your email address>→/systems/ mac/info-mac/per/ingam ✓**AMERICA ONLINE**→*keyword* mgm→Software Libraries→Publications

Macintosh Games Publications

Uploads of popular magazines, little-known publications, and now-defunct 'zines related to gaming on the Mac. Includes back issues of *Inside Mac Games, Home & School Mac, MacGames Digest, Anti-Matter E-Magazine,* and others. Some reviews of individual games (*Spaceship Warlock, Iron Helix,* etc.) can be found here as well. ✓**AMERICA ONLINE**→*keyword* mgm→Software Libraries→Publications

Utilities

The Macintosh Communications Forum For all your Macintosh utility needs—compressing, extracting, image viewing, and communicating. Find dozens of the shareware programs that are needed for trips on the data highway. ✓**AMERICA ONLINE**→*keyword* mcm

Macintosh Compression Utilities Download programs for all your Macintosh compressing and extracting needs. ✓**INTERNET** ...→*ftp* wuarchive.wustl.edu→ anonymous→<your email address> →/systems/mac/info-mac/cmp ...→*ftp* sumex-aim.stanford.edu→ anonymous→<your email address> →/info-mac/cmp ...→*ftp* mac. archive.umich.edu→anonymous→ <your email address>→/mac/ util/compression ✓**GENIE**→*keyword* mac→Macintosh Software Libraries →Utilities, Tools & DA's *Search by search string:* compress ✓**COMPUSERVE**→*go* macff→Access File Finder→*Search by keyword:* compress *or* extract

PC games

Seems like every game is made for the IBM (and compati-
bles). On the Internet alone, general discussion of PC games is divided into no less than seven separate **comp.sys.ibm.pc.games*** newsgroups, not counting the separate newsgroups for megahits like the Net-friendly *Doom*. Commercial and Internet archives burst with thousands of public-domain and shareware games. Some of the slickest electronic magazines available on any subject—don't miss **Game Bytes**, monthly megabytes devoted to nothing but reviewing and mastering the latest commercial PC game releases. And this is supposed to be the serious business computer.

Screenshot of a cover of the electronic gaming magazine Game Bytes.

On the Net

Across the board

comp.sys.ibm.pc.games.announce (ng) Bottom line: Scan as a backup in case you miss something on the other newsgroups, but don't rely on it for first word of new toys. Regular postings include the PC Games FAQ (twice a month) and a patches list for customizing and cheating at popular games (see FTP Sites for Game Editors and Updates). The two-part PC Games FAQ-Guide to the Gaming World—with info on an abundance of Internet resources—is the real gem here and recom-mended background reading before posting to the comp.sys.ibm. pc.games newsgroups. **✓USENET** *FAQ:* **✓INTERNET**→*ftp* rtfm.mit.edu→anonymous→<your email address> →/pub/usenet-by-hierarchy/comp /sys/ibm/pc/games/announce

comp.sys.ibm.pc.games.misc (ng) Spill-over topics that don't fit the specialized newsgroups dedicated to gaming on the PC. Usually not very lively, except as the unofficial location for discussing sports and puzzle games. Until there's a sports subgroup, come here for games like *Links 386 Pro* and *Formula 1 Grand Prix.* **✓USENET**

Discussion of IBM games (echo) IBM gamers compare notes. **✓WWIVNET**

Games for New IBM Users Find popular shareware (as well as add-ons and patches to commercialware) for IBM-playable games in the Adventures library, the Gen Fun & Games library, the Word & Card Games library, and the Sports & Chance library. **✓COMPUSERVE**→*go* ibmnew→Libraries

Gaming (echo) Hints and cheats fill the International Personal Computer Gaming Conference. Discuss all types of PC games and share tips about the gaming market. **✓FIDONET**

IBM Computer Games (echo) Gamers with an IBM-compatible share hints and frustrations. **✓WWIVNET**

IBM Computer Games (echo) Get hints and reviews, and join in on the general discussion about IBM computer games. **✓ICENET**

IBM PC Games Very large bulletin board with active discussions about *Wolfenstein 3D*, *Commander Keen*, IBM vs. Amiga games, soundcards, joysticks, and many other topics. In the RoundTable library, find a wide range of shareware games for IBM PCs and compatibles, including these popular downloads: *#1 Galaxy*, an arcade game; *Lab3D*, a 3D action game with a variety of art and original music at each level; and *ModSS*, a virtual-reality adventure game in which you solve puzzles and shoot bad guys. **✓GENIE** ...→*keyword* ibmpc→IBM PC RoundTable Bulletin Board→set 7 (for messages) ...→*keyword* ibmpc →IBM Software Libraries→ Set Software Library→All Libraries→*Search by search string:* game (for files)

PC-Compatible Games Find discussions about the hottest games for the PC in the Forum. *Doom* files reside in the Database, along with aircraft (antique, military, etc.) to fly in Microsoft's *Flight Simulator*, and a ton of fantasy adventure games, arcade games, and shoot-'em-up space games. **✓DELPHI** ...→*go* com pc→ Forum→clear* →set games (for messages) ...→*go* com pc→Databases→Games (for files)

PC Games Forum A major hub

for discussing games played on the PC, including those for BASIC, DOS, and Windows. File libraries have downloadable shareware games, game add-ons, and game cheats and editors. ✓**AMERICA ON-LINE**→*keyword* pc games

Genres

comp.sys.ibm.pc.games. action (ng) Discuss MS-DOS action and arcade games, classified as such by their fast-paced emphasis on hand-eye reflexes. Stay on the lookout for breakaway newsgroups devoted to the most popular games, such as alt.games.doom and alt.games.mk2. ✓**USENET**

comp.sys.ibm.pc.games. adventure (ng) Discuss adventure games, which originally were text-based exploration and riddle games (the game category is named, in part, for the original interactive treasure story, *Adventure*) but are now often decorated with graphics and combat sequences. Popular games subjected to heavy analysis include *Hand of Fate*, *Judgment Rites*, and *King's Quest 6*. This newsgroup usually eclipses the related newsgroups comp.sys. ibm.pc.hardware.cd-rom and alt. cd-rom. Do check out the classic newsgroups rec.games.int-fiction and comp.sys.ibm.pc.games.rpg for some heavy role-playing. ✓**USENET**

comp.sys.ibm.pc.games.flight -sim (ng) An unmoderated group to discuss air- and space-flight simulation games. Heavy-duty *X-Wing* discourse, not to mention other hits like *Aces Over Europe*, *Air Warrior*, *Falcon 3.0*, and the venerable Microsoft's *Flight Simulator*. ✓**USENET**

comp.sys.ibm.pc.games.rpg (ng) Discussion of role-playing

games (RPG) that have descended the board game *Dungeons & Dragons* and the text-based computer game *Adventure*. Popular examples include *Dark Sun*, *Shattered Lands*; *Lands of Lore*; and *Ultima VII Part 2*. For related topics see the often more lively newsgroup comp.sys. ibm.pc.games.adventure. ✓**USENET**

comp.sys.ibm.pc.games.strat egic (ng) Discussion of mostly war games that are modeled on the old Avalon Hill historical scenarios and other kinds of strategy-oriented simulations. Popular games that are well covered include *Civilization*, *Master of Orion*, and the *V for Victory* episodes. ✓**USENET**

Hardware

comp.sys.ibm.pc.hardware* (ng) A collection of PC hardware newsgroups that carry smart discussions on game-related issues, including comp.sys.ibm.pc.hardware.cd-rom, comp.sys.ibm.pc. hardware.chips, comp.sys.ibm.pc. hardware.storage, comp.sys.ibm. pc.hardware.systems, and comp. sys.ibm.pc.hardware.video. ✓**USENET** *FAQ:* ✓**INTERNET**→*ftp* rtfm.mit.edu→anonymous→<your email address>→/pub/usenet-by-hierarchy/comp/sys/ibm/pc/hard ware

comp.sys.ibm.pc.soundcard (ng) Great resource if you're shopping for a soundcard for the PC. If you already have one, stop here for expert discussion on how to get the most out of it with your specific game software. The PC Soundcard FAQ includes a lot of technical detail on soundcards and contact information for numerous manufacturers from Activision to Voyetra and further Cyberspace points of PC soundcard interest such as mailing lists for musicians

and programmers. ✓**USENET** *FAQ:*
✓**INTERNET**→*ftp* rtfm.mit.edu→
anonymous→<your email address>
→/pub/usenet-by-hierarchy/
comp/sys/ibm/pc/soundcard→
comp.sys.ibm.pc.soundcard_FAQ

Hints & cheats

PC Gamers HintNet (echo)
Meet other PC gamers and get
them to give you their secrets.
✓**ICENET**

**PC Game Hints and Cheats
Archives** Subtle suggestions and
straight-out solutions for most of
your favorite games. ✓**INTERNET**
…→*ftp* ftp.uwp.edu→anonymous→
<your email address>→/pub/ms-
dos/asa …→*ftp* ftp.funet.fi→anony-
mous→<your email address>→
/pub/doc/games/solutions …→*ftp*
risc.ua.edu→anonymous→<your
email address>→/pub/games/so
lutions

Romulus FTP Site One of the
richest motherlodes of cheats,
hints, cracks, and FAQs for PC
games. ✓**INTERNET** …→*ftp* ftp.uwp.
edu→anonymous→<your email ad-
dress>→/pub/msdos/games/
romulus …→*ftp* nctuccca.edu.tw→
anonymous→<your email address>
→/PC/uwp/romulus

Multimedia

Multimedia PC Discuss games
played on PC CD-ROM systems.
Library has a number of sound-
(WAV, MIDI) and soundcard-re-
lated files. ✓**COMPUSERVE**→*go*
gamers→Libraries *or* Messages→
Multimedia PC

News & reviews

Game Bytes (j) Exhaustive, devoted coverage of MS-DOS computer games from one of the finest
free electronic magazines on the
Net. Reviews, reports, and interviews usually include screenshots
from the games themselves. Published as a DOS application in
two separate versions, with and
without megabytes of graphics.
Available from many locations.
✓**INTERNET** …→*gopher* gopher.cic.
net→Electronic Serials→Alphabetic
List→G→Game Bytes …→*ftp* ftp.
cic.net→anonymous→<your email
address>→/pub/e-serials/alpha
betic/g/game-bytes …→*ftp* ftp.
uml.edu→anonymous→<your email
address>→/msdos/Games/Game
_Bytes ✓**COMPUSERVE**→*go* gamers
→Libraries→Game Magazines
✓**AMERICA ONLINE**→*keyword* pc
games→Software Library→*Search
by keyword:* gamebyte

The Net PC Games Top 100 (j)
A weekly "best-of" chart for PC
games, compiled from a week's
worth of votes sent in by email,
and posted to all the comp.sys.
ibm.pc.games* groups. Voting,
open to all those with email, is explained in each issue. Those who
vote are temporarily added to a
mailing list, and receive the chart
automatically via email. See the
FAQ for instructions on the syntax for voting. ✓**INTERNET** …→
email jojo@hacktic.nl ✍ *To vote,*

> "Download editors
> and patches to bend
> the rules in your
> favor, and then see
> how that frustrating
> game does once you
> come back at it with
> infinite lives."

type in subject line: vote …→*ftp*
rtfm.mit.edu→anonymous→<your
email address>→/pub/usenet-by-
hierarchy/comp/sys/ibm/pc/
games/announce

OS/2

OS/2 Games Skimpy amount of
game talk in the Games category
on the bulletin board, although
you'll find other, sporadic discussions in categories such as Other
Applications and Multimedia. In
the software library, the games fall
into the board-, card-, and arcade-
game categories. Popular choices
include *Greed*, an OS/2 version of
the UNIX classic, and *PMbots11*,
an "addictive" avoid-the-robots
game. ✓**GENIE** …→*keyword* os/2→
OS/2 Bulletin Board→set 35 (for
messages) …→*keyword* os/2→
OS/2 Software Library→Set Software Library→All Libraries *Search
by search string:* game (for files)

Shareware plus

PC Game Demo Archives A
much better way to choose games
than the pretty ads and packaging
in the mail-order catalogs and
software stores. ✓**INTERNET** …→*ftp*
ftp.uml.edu→anonymous→<your
email address>→/msdos/Games/
Demos …→*ftp* ftp.uwp.edu→
anonymous→<your email address>
→/pub/msdos/demos …→*ftp*
wuarchive.wustl.edu→anonymous→
<your email address>→/systems/
ibmpc/msdos-games/demos …→
ftp ftp.funet.fi→anonymous→<your
email address>→/pub/msdos/
games/gamedemos

**PC Game Editors & Patches
Archives** Download editors and
patches to customize scenarios or
simply and crudely bend the rules
in your favor (check comp.sys.
ibm.pc.games.announce for a regularly posted list of patches). Let's

see how that frustrating game does once you come back at it with infinite lives.... Also, archives for shareware and commercial upgrades, and—ahem—de-copy-protected "cracks" of commercial software (ostensibly for those who already have legal copies). ✓ **INTERNET** ...→*ftp* ftp.uml.edu→anonymous→ <your email address>→/msdos/ Games/Editors ...→*ftp* ftp.uml.edu →anonymous→<your email address>→/msdos/Games/Patches ...→*ftp* wuarchive.wustl.edu→ anonymous→<your email address> →/pub/MSDOS_UPLOADS/games /Patches ...→*ftp* wuarchive.wustl. edu→anonymous→<your email address>→/systems/ibmpc/msdos-games/Patches...→*ftp* ftp.funet. fi→anonymous→<your email address>→ /pub/msdos/games/ editors ...→*ftp* wuarchive.wustl. edu→anonymous→<your email address>→/systems/ibmpc/msdos-games ...→*ftp* ftp.funet.fi →anonymous→<your email address>→ /pub/msdos/games/patches

PC Games FTP Sites One of the reasons you got on the Net in the first place—free games! These sites include hundreds of shareware games ranging from *Castle Wolfenstein 3D* to the satirical *Toxic the Groundhog* ✓ **INTERNET** ...→*ftp* ftp.uml.edu→anonymous→<your email address>→/msdos/Games ...→*ftp* msdos.archive.umich.edu→ anonymous→<your email address> →/msdos/ games ...→*ftp* ftp.funet. fi→anonymous→<your email address>→/pub/msdos/games ...→*ftp* ftp.funet.fi→anonymous→ <your email address>→/pub/ms dos/windows/games ...→*ftp* wuarchive.wustl.edu→anonymous →<your email address>→/pub/ MSDOS_ UPLOADS/games

Software companies

APOGEE (echo) *Apogee* players can talk strategy and describe their experiences here. ✓ **INTELEC**

Apogee/Software Creations Support Board (echo) Talk to others who play and make *Apogee* games. ✓ **ICENET**

id FTP Site Unofficial archive of id games in their shareware/demo form, including *Keen 4* (*Goodbye Galaxy*), *Wolfenstein 3D*, *Aliens Ate My Baby Sitter*, *Keen 1* (*Invasion of the Vorticons*), *Doom*, and *Spear of Destiny*. The home-brew subdirectory contains several related FAQs and screenshots. ✓ **INTERNET**→*ftp* ftp.uwp.edu→anonymous→<your email address>→/pub/msdos/ games/id

Special needs

Games for Special Needs IBM Users Basic, classic games, as well as various educational and motor-skill-developing games. ✓ **COMPUSERVE**→*go* ibmspec→Libraries→Recreation & Games

Utilities

PC Archive Utilities Before enjoying the FTP riches, you may need to find the program tools for decompressing DOS files; fairly complete collections of these tools can be found at these FTP sites. ✓ **INTERNET** ...→*ftp* ftp.uml.edu→ anonymous→<your email address> →/msdos/Archivers ...→*ftp* ftp. uwp.edu→anonymous→<your email address>→/pub/msdos/arcers ...→*ftp* ftp.funet.fi→anonymous→ <your email address>→/pub/ msdos/packing ...→*ftp* msdos. archive.umich.edu→anonymous→ <your email address>→/msdos/ compression

The PC Telecommunications Forum Find everything from communications shareware to compression utilities for DOS and Windows. ✓ **AMERICA ONLINE**→*keyword* ptc

Windows

Games for Windows Downloadable games to play in Windows. The most popular files include *Backgammon V.06*; *Chomp* for Windows 3.0, a *PacMan*-like game; *Blitzer*, a helicopter shoot-'em-up; *Risk* for Windows; *MJWIN*, *Mah Jongg* for Windows; *Lander*, a simulation of a *Lunar Excursion* Module; *TetWin*, *Tetris* for Windows; *Winpool*, *Windows Billiards*; *WSLAM*, based on *Air Hockey*; and *KillBarn*, where you hunt down Barney, the infamous purple dinosaur, and burn him to death. ✓ **AMERICA ONLINE**→*keyword* pc games→Browse Individual Libraries→ Other→Windows Games

Windows Games To discuss and download files for games played in Windows. ✓ **COMPUSERVE**→*go* winfun→Libraries *or* Messages→Other Games/Fun

Windows Games Arcade and adventure games for Windows and Windows NT, including, among the more popular choices *Break-Thru*, a 3D breakout game; *Empire*, in which you build piping to lead flowing water from one place to another; and *Funicons*, game-oriented icons of what the author describes as "cute chicks." ✓ **GENIE** →*keyword* windows→Windows Software Library→Set Software Library→All Libraries *Search by search string:* game

Windows NT

Windows NT Games/Fun Discuss and download games for Windows NT. ✓ **COMPUSERVE**→*go* winfun→Libraries *or* Messages→ Win NT Games/Fun

Video games

Arcade-game addicts grew up (or did they?) to be Net

jockeys, so it shouldn't be a surprise to find an embarrassment of riches for the video-game junkie on the Net. The FAQs and discussion newsgroups, like those in the **rec.games.video*** group, on the Internet are vital institutions of video-game culture—thick with historical memory for obsolete formats and early-'80s classics, frenetic with word of novel puzzles and innovative technologies. Everything's here: cheat sheets, code lists, adventure strategies, cartridge pirating, screen shots, high scores, paranoid speculation, used machines, hot-wiring how-to's, and every so often a passionate tribute to millions of years of human evolution, which has climaxed amid the fantastic, proliferating, accelerating world of video games not even two decades old.

On the Net

Across the board

Andy Eddy (GamePro Magazine) FTP Site for Arcade and Videogame FAQs Master library of FAQs for popular games and the machines that run them. Besides specific video-game news-

Pacman—*downloaded from America Online's Video Games Forum.*

groups, this is currently the best video-game resource on Internet. ✓**INTERNET**→*ftp* ftp.netcom.com→ anonymous→<your email address> →/pub/vidgames/faqs

rec.games.video.misc (ng) Spillover discussions from the other rec.games.video* groups. General discussion of video-game systems such as Sega and Nintendo that take cartridges and are intended for home use. Discussions on system-specific newsgroups tend to be more informative, but this is a good starting place. ✓**USENET**

Super Power (echo) Discuss Super Nintendo and Sega Disc games. ✓**WWIVNET**

Video Games A general forum for discussing video games and virtual reality. Hints and game codes, especially for *NBA Jam* and *Mortal Kombat II*, are in the Hints, Tips, Pics & Cheats library. Press releases for games and gaming systems can be found in the News/Product Information section of the main window. ✓**AMERICA ONLINE**→*keyword* video games

Video Games Two spots on Prodigy to discuss your favorite video games are the Video Games topic and the Video Games Clubs. The clubs, organized around specific games, have officers and a core group of loyal followers—most of whom are kids and young teens. ✓**PRODIGY**→*jump* games bb→Choose a Topic→video games *or* video game clubs

Video Games (echo) Discuss home console video games, including Sega, Super Nintendo, 3DO, and others. ✓**WWIVNET**

Video Games Forum The place to find message boards, file libraries, and chat rooms for the major cartridge games, as well as resources related to coin-op games and game design. ✓**COMPUSERVE**→ *go* vidgam

Video Game SIG One of the best gaming forums on the Cleveland FreeNet, this special interest group has game news ("What's the latest word on Sega?"), game reviews (the Atari Lynx area is especially impressive), bulletin boards with general video-game talk, a

> "Committed to Sega and infuriated at the thought of someone equally fond of Nintendo? Try to keep it here. This is the newsgroup equivalent of 'Let's step outside.'"

hints-and-tips area where codes and passwords are posted, and a Q&A section. ☎→*dial* 216-368-3888→A visitor→Explore the system→go vgames ✓**INTERNET** →*telnet* freenet-in-a.cwru.edu→A visitor→ Explore the system→go vgame

#vidgames Real-time discussions all over the place—high-score braggadocio, puzzles to solve in new games, hidden "Easter eggs" to find in old games, and, of course, virtual reality just over the artificial horizon. ✓**INTERNET**→*irc* /channel #vidgames

World of Video Games This site offers virtually everything a video gamer could want: a classified ad section for games, cartridges, home gaming systems, a conference room to discuss video gaming, a forum for messages, and an Internet Gopher just for video games. The database has files related to Sega, Sega Genesis, Turbo-Grafx, Atari, photos of game screens, and more. ✓**DELPHI**→*go* gro wor→Databases *or* Forum

Cheats

The Video Game Folklore List Programmers call them "Easter eggs"—hidden screens and features that are activated by a command or an event, and this list explains several popular ones—although it could use some additions. ✓**INTERNET** ...→*ftp* wiretap. spies.com→anonymous→<your email address>→/game_archive/ info→NostalgaList ...→*gopher* wire tap.spies.com→Video Game Archive →info→NostalgaList

Classics

alt.games.video.classic (ng) Video-game nostalgia?!? Discuss the classics of video games, from *Space Invaders* to *Pacman*. ✓**USENET**

> **"Nostalgia? Discuss the classics—from *Space Invaders* to *Pacman*."**

Lists

Anime Video Games Exhaustive list of video games (on all platforms) that incorporate the distinctive style and story lines of animated Japanese action comics. Maintained by Steve Pearl. ✓**INTERNET**→*ftp* romulus.rutgers.edu→ anonymous→<your email address> →/pub/anime/misc→anime-games.Z

Cardiff's Video Game Database Browser Links to the powerhouses of video-game information on the Net, including Nintendo and Sega FTP sites, the video-game FAQs, archives of video-game newsgroups, online video-game 'zines, and a searchable list of video-game titles with detailed playing info and cheat options. ✓**INTERNET**→*www* http:// www.cm.cf.ac.uk/Games/

The Good, The Bad, and The Awesome An exhaustive, if subjective, list (with ratings) of all the major cartridge games available for Genesis, Sega CD, Super Nintendo, TurboGrafx, and TurboGrafx CD. ✓**COMPUSERVE**→*go* vidgam→Libraries→General/Help→ GBA.ZIP

News and reviews

Game Master Journal (j) Free electronic magazine. Compares itself to the commercial magazines on the newsstand that cover arcade and home video games, but this weekly easily bests them in lead time and energy—if not edit-

ing. GMJ is cross-posted to most of the videogame-related newsgroups, but also available through e-mail. ✓**INTERNET** ...→*email* shu bert@usc.edu ✉ *To get the latest issue of GMJ, type in subject line:* send GMJ new ...→*email* shubert @usc.edu ✉ *To receive all future issues, type in the subject line:* add GMJ

rec.games.video.advocacy (ng) If you're committed to Sega and infuriated at the thought of someone equally fond of Nintendo, try to keep it here. This is the newsgroup equivalent of "Let's step outside." ✓**USENET**

CYBERNOTES

"What is 'Blast Processing'?
"Sega hype. The phrase means exactly nothing. Sega later tried to explain it by claiming it describes the methods used by Sega to get characters like Sonic moving on the screen very fast. (Which still means nothing, of course.) Sega again explained that this is because characters can be drawn on the screen while a different screen is being displayed (which is known as page flipping and isn't new) and that background processing is ignored so sprites can be moved really fast (which isn't new either)."

—from the **rec.games. video** FAQ

Home gaming systems

Eventually everyone will play the latest video games over the Net, *Mortal Kombat*ing

opponents down the street and halfway around the world. For now, though, make do with the lively sectarian game and game-machine discussions, which cover nearly every game product, whether obsolete (e.g., **alt.atari.2600**) or in development (Project Reality in **rec.game.video.nintendo**). You'll soon discover that those magazines and books full of game secrets and cheats are cribbed from the public-spirited, collective work of Internet game mavens.

Sega's Sonic the Hedgehog and Tails–from http://thrall.cm.cf.ac.uk/Games/console/sega.

On the Net

Across the board

Classic Game Systems Bulletin Board Pong, Mattel Intellivision, ColecoVision, and Atari 2600 haven't died—they live on in the hearts and minds of these diehard fans. ✓ **GENIE**→*keyword* videogames→Video Games Bulletin Board→set 10

News on major Vid game systems (echo) Get the news about Sega, Nintendo, 3DO, Jaguar, etc. ✓ **ICENET**

Portables Discuss portable video-game players, especially the Nintendo Game Boy, the Atari Lynx, and the Sega Game Gear. ✓ **COMPUSERVE**→*go* vidgam→Libraries *or* Messages

3DO

rec.games.video.3do (ng) Discuss your mondo toy 3DO (pronounced three-dee-oh) with other early adapters in this newsgroup dedicated to the most expensive, hyped, and, yes, powerful home game system ever. Regular topics range from the games that exist to the games that are supposed to, but there's also a techie flavor with practical advice for software developers and imaginative speculation about "1-Way ISDN connections" and "MPEG movies on CD-ROM"—the future-talk must warm the leveraged cockles of 3DO founder Trip Hawkins. No FAQ as of this writing, but one should emerge soon—check for a file name, something like 3do.faq—at Andy Eddy's site for arcade-game FAQs. ✓ **USENET**

3DO Discussion While the Forum's favorite topic is "just-how-great 3DO actually is," *John Madden 3DO* and *Total Eclipse* are also quite popular—each has its own folder! ✓ **AMERICA ONLINE**→*keyword* video games→ Let's Discuss→3DO Discussion

3DO Interactive Multiplayer Bulletin Board *Total Eclipse, The Horde, Crash 'N Burn,* and *John Madden Football* discussions are the big draws here. ✓ **GENIE**→ *keyword* videogames→Video Games Bulletin Board→set 5

3DO Multiplayer A place to post questions, retrieve files of press releases and reviews, and chat about games played on the 3DO Interactive Multiplayer, including *Stellar 7, Total Eclipse* and *John Madden Football.* ✓ **COMPUSERVE**→*go* vidgam→Libraries *or* Messages→3DO Multiplayer

Amiga CD32

rec.games.video.cd32 (ng) Gaming talk and information about the Amiga CD32. ✓**USENET**

Atari/Jaguar/Lynx

alt.atari.2600 (ng) Newsgroup discussion devoted not just to the first mass-market video-game system for the home, but to the whole chunky, low-res way of life when video games didn't get by on pretty looks alone. ✓**USENET**

alt.games.lynx (ng) Discuss games and gadgets for the Lynx, trade *Electrocop* for *Slime World*, or learn the password for *Blue Lightning's* night mission. The FAQ provides a nice history of the Lynx's development (it was originally called Handy), lists of games, pointers to other on- and off-line resources, basic developer information, and practical advice for the Lynx owner on subjects like cleaning scratches off the screen or how to store game wafers that are not in use (in plastic baseball-card sleeves.) ✓**USENET** *FAQ:* ✓**INTERNET**→*ftp* ftp.netcom.com→anonymous→<your email address>→pub/vidgames/faqs→lynx.faq

Atari/Atari Jaguar Bulletin Board Sporadic discussion about video games for Atari, particularly for the Atari Lynx. ✓**GENIE**→*keyword* videogames→Video Games Bulletin Board→set 4

Atari Gaming Forum Discussion and file libraries related to gaming on the Atari 8-Bit, Jaguar, and Lynx systems. ✓**COMPUSERVE**→ *go* atarigaming

Atari Jaguar Discuss games for the Atari Jaguar system, including Tempest 2000 and Cybermorph. The library is essentially a reposi-

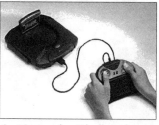

Atari Jaguar—http://thrall.cm.cf.ac.uk/ Games/console/atari.

tory of press releases and game announcements. ✓**COMPUSERVE**→*go* vidgam→Libraries *or* Messages→ Atari Jaguar

Atari SIG The Jaguar and Lynx areas offer hints and cheats, reviews, access to the rec.games. video.atari Usenet newsgroup, game summaries (direct from the Atari Corp.) and local discussion. ☎→*dial* 216-368-3888→A visitor →Explore the system→go lynx→ Lynx Support Area *or* Jaguar Support Area ✓**INTERNET**→*telnet* freenet-in-a.cwru.edu→A visitor→Explore the system→go lynx→Lynx Support Area *or* Jaguar Support Area

Jaguar Archive A meager but likely-to-grow archive of game screen shots. ✓**INTERNET**→*ftp* atari. archive.umich.edu→anonymous→ <your email address>→/pub/ atari/Jaguar

Jaguar Discussion Talk about several Atari systems, including the Jaguar, the Lynx, vintage Atari systems (5200 and 2600) as well as Atari games, such as *Tempest 2000*, and *Aliens Vs. Predators*. ✓**AMERICA ONLINE**→*keyword* video games→Let's Discuss→Jaguar Discussion

Jaguar FAQ Information about Jaguar, Atari's low-cost answer to 3DO (which is actually manufactured by IBM). Provides a list of existing and vaporware games, a

comprehensive technical overview of the 64-bit machine, instructions for pumping up the video quality at little cost (bypass the cheap RF modulator), and interesting background material about the development tools for writing Jaguar games. *FAQ:* ✓**INTERNET**→ *ftp* ftp.netcom.com→anonymous→ <your email address>→/pub/ vidgames/faqs→jaguar.faq

Jaguar-L (ml) As with any new platform, discussion on this list centers on the ostensibly imminent arrival of new programs to run on your bleeding-edge machine. ✓**INTERNET**→*email* listserv@ ctrc.idde.saci.org ✍ *Type in message body:* subscribe jaguar-l <your full name>

Lynx FTP Site A hack to boost the speed of the Lynx I; a walk through *Bill & Ted's Excellent Adventure;* a list of cheats, passwords, and other stuff; notes on *Chip's Challenge;* the Lynx FAQ; Robert Jung's reviews of Lynx games, and more. ✓**INTERNET**→*ftp* atari.archive. umich.edu→anonymous→<your email address>→/pub/atari/Lynx

Game Genie

Game Genie and Gold Finger Code Server A database of hundreds of patch codes organized by game name and available through a mail server. ✓**INTERNET** ...→*email* game-genie-serv%nvcc.uucp@grou-cho.sonoma.edu ✍ *To get instructions on how to use the mail server, type:* help ...→*email* gold-finger-serv%nvcc.uucp@groucho.sono ma.edu ✍ *To get instructions on how to use the mail server, type:* help

Game Genie Archive Need codes for your Game Genie (a piece of equipment fitted between a game cartridge and game machine that lets you cheat, most commonly by granting you infinite lives instead of the usual three)? A large collection of the codes you feed your Game Genie is available for gamers with cheating hearts. ✓**INTERNET**→*ftp* ftp. netcom.com→anonymous→<your email address>→/pub/vidgames/ gamegenie

Game Genie codes for all systems (echo) Literally learn the inside stuff about Game Genie. ✓**ICENET**

Neo-Geo

Neo-Geo's Samurai Shodown! (echo) Feeling courageous? Come on down to the *Shodown!* ✓**WWIVNET**

Neo-Geo's Samurai Shodown! (echo) Get the lowdown on the *Shodown* by meeting people who know. ✓**ICENET**

SNK Neo-Geo Bulletin Board Not much traffic, but a few fans of *Samurai Shodown* tend to post messages here. ✓**GENIE**→*keyword* videogames→Video Games Bulletin Board→set 6

Nintendo

Nintendo Share inside tips on *Super Metroid* and those nutty Mario guys, download Game Genie codes, and chat with other Nintendo players. ✓**COMPUSERVE**→ *go* vidgam→Libraries *or* Messages →Nintendo

NINTENDO (echo) The latest scoops on the popular systems and games. ✓**RELAYNET**

Nintendo Discussion Discussions of *Super Metroid, NBA Jam, Project Reality,* and other games and systems for the Nintendo, in-

Super Mario—downloaded from America Online's Video Game Forum.

cluding Game Boy. ✓**AMERICA ON-LINE**→*keyword* video games→Let's Discuss→Nintendo Discussion

Nintendo GameBoy (ml) Wide-ranging discussions cover the strategies for beating—and the codes for cheating—games like *Final Fantasy Adventure, Zelda,* and *Faceball 2000.* Quality technical advice for the wirehead also abounds. ✓**INTERNET**→*email* game boy@mentor.cc.purdue.edu ✐ *Type in subject line:* subscribe *Archives:* ✓**INTERNET**→*email* gameboy@ mentor.cc.purdue.edu ✐ *To get a list of files, type in subect line:* archive *Type in message body:* help *Info:* ✓**INTERNET**→*finger* game boy@mentor.cc.purdue.edu

Nintendo Game Boy FAQ Find an introduction to the toy; game reviews, cheats, strategies, and piracy; Game Genie coverage; and detailed technical advice for fiddling with the GB (connect it to your home computer). *FAQ:* ✓**INTERNET**→*ftp* ftp.netcom.com→ anonymous→<your email address> →/pub/vidgames/faqs

Nintendo Power (echo) News for Nintendo players. ✓**WWIVNET**

Nintendo Power (echo) Talk with others on how to get the

most out of your Nintendo. ✓**ICENET**

Nintendo/Super Nintendo Bulletin Board Discuss *Street Fighter II, Final Fantasy II, Super Mario World,* and *Shadowrun.* ✓**GENIE**→*keyword* videogames→ Video Games Bulletin Board→set 2

rec.games.video.nintendo (ng) Active discussions ranging from the original NES home game cartridge system to the current Super NES to future speculation like "Project Reality." Most talk is advice on playing games, peppered with expressions of preference for Nintendo machines over the rival Sega Genesis, and techniques for illicitly pirating cartridges. ✓**USENET**

SNES (ml) How do you kill the last boss in *Super Bomberman,* anyway? Subscribe and your mailbox will never again want for the answers to such urgent questions. ✓**INTERNET**→*email* snes-request@ spcvxa.spc.edu ✐ *Type in subject line:* subscribe

SNES Review List Cut-to-the-bone reviews of game cartridges. ✓**INTERNET**→*ftp* brownvm.brown.

> "How do you kill the last boss in Super Bomberman, anyway? Subscribe and your mailbox will never again want for the answers to such urgent questions."

edu→anonymous→<your email ad-dress>→/james.394

Philips CD-I

Philips CD-I Post messages and download press releases and FAQs for Philips CD-I games, such as *Dark Castle, Escape From Cyber-City,* and *Laser Lords.* ✓**COM-PUSERVE**→*go* vidgam→Libraries *or* Messages→Philips CD-I

Philips CD-I Bulletin Board Conversation about games for the Philips CD-I player. ✓**GENIE**→*key-word* videogames→Video Games Bulletin Board→set 7

Sega

alt.sega.genesis (ng) Less philosophical than rec.games. video.sega, this is where you find out how to remove lint out of a joystick or how to start from any level in *Bio Hazard Battle.* ✓**USENET**

Game Gear FAQ Special atten-tion for the smaller sibling of the Genesis, the handheld color portable. Game reviews, hints, and cheats (includes Action Replay and Game Genie coverage), span-ning every creature from Sonic the Hedgehog to Stimpy the Chi-huahua. *FAQ:* ✓**INTERNET**→*ftp* ftp.netcom.com→anonymous→<your email address>→/pub/vidgames/faq

Genesis Secrets FAQ Detailed instructions for those A-B button combinations for every game from *Afterburner II* to *Zoom!!* Updates posted to alt.sega.genesis and rec.games.video.sega newsgroups. *FAQ:* ✓**INTERNET**→*ftp* rtfm.mit.edu→ anonymous→<your email address> →/pub/usenet/news.answers/gam es/video-games/sega

Genesis Technical FTP Find all

the technical details, including a programmer's FAQ, Genesis joy-stick pinouts, and Genesis hard-ware internals. ✓**INTERNET**→*ftp* ftp.spd.louisville.edu→anonymous→ <your email address>→/pub/sega

rec.games.video.sega (ng) Sega talk with lots of practical in-formation on Genesis games and hardware, but with additional ap-petite for discussions about ar-cade hits and next-generation topics like virtual-reality "ride-films," the 64-bit Saturn, the coming cable delivery system for Sega games, and multiplayer net-works. ✓**USENET**

Sega Message board and files re-garding Sega games, including walk-throughs, demos, and codes for specific games and Game Ge-nie. ✓**COMPUSERVE**→*go* vidgam→Li-braries *or* Messages→Sega

Sega Bulletin Board Discus-sions of *Mortal Kombat, Sonic the Hedgehog, NBA Jam, Landstalker,* and other Sega games. ✓**GENIE**→ *keyword* videogames→Video Games Bulletin Board→set 3

Sega CD Secrets FAQ There's a trick for every disc: access mania

> "There's a trick for every disc: access mania mode, take unlimited shurikens, or peek at the hid-den footage in the infamous *Night Trap.*"

mode, take unlimited shurikens, or peek at the hidden footage in the infamous *Night Trap.* Updates posted to alt.sega.genesis and rec.games.video.sega newsgroups. *FAQ:* ✓**INTERNET**→*ftp* rtfm.mit.edu→ anonymous→<your email address> →/pub/usenet/news.answers/ games/video-games/sega

Sega Discussion *NBA Jam* talk; discussion about the *Mortal Kom-bat* CD, *Sonic the Hedgehog 3,* Sega CD, Sega Saturn, and Game Gear; and actual, rumored, planned, and won't-see-the-light-of-day Sega games and systems. ✓**AMERICA ONLINE**→*keyword* video games→Let's Discuss→Sega Discus-sion

TurboGraphx

TG-16 Mailing List (ml) Can get extremely lively, a consideration if you don't like your mailbox clogged with 15 *Super Metroid* messages a day. *Neo Nectaris, Mili-tary Madness,* group discounts on game cartridges, and plenty of info on Japanese games for the Turbo-Grafx-16. ✓**INTERNET**→*email* turbo-list-request@cpac.washington.edu ✍ *Type in subject line:* subscribe

TTI Bulletin Board While these gamers like the sound on the Duo and they're willing to share tips on games like *Galaga 90* and *Bonk's Adventure,* most of the talk here centers on the dearth of support for the TurboGrafx-16 and Turbo Duo. ✓**GENIE**→*keyword* video-games→Video Games Bulletin Board→set 8

Vectrex

rec.games.vectrex (ng) Buy or trade cartridges and machines for the defunct Vectrex gaming sys-tem. ✓**USENET**

Arcade games

The hottest arcade games reverberate throughout the Usenet newsgroups, with separate

discussions surrounding each version for each machine. If a game goes supernova, as *Street Fighter* and *Mortal Kombat* both did in the last three years, look for a discussion group devoted to it in the **alt.games*** area of Usenet. With or without a newsgroup, exhaustive FAQs are almost a guarantee for the big games like *NBA Jam*. And, hey, pinball's still kicking on the Net—check out **The Pinball Archives**.

NBA Jam *screenshot—downloaded from GEnie's Scorpia RoundTable.*

On the Net

Across the board

ARCADE (echo) Covers a variety of arcade games and their home console conversions. Includes reviews and hints. ✓**FIDONET**

Arcade Games (echo) For lovers of arcade games only—no computer-game talk here! ✓**WWIVNET**

Coin Ops A Poppin'—The Killer List of Video Games (KLOV) The best, most complete list of arcade video games ever compiled, with more than 1,000 entries. ✓**INTERNET** …→*ftp* wiretap.spies.com→anonymous→<your email address>→/game_archive/info/klovdb→KLOV …→*gopher* wiretap.spies.com→Video Game Archive→info→klovdb→KLOV …→*ftp* ftp.netcom.com→anonymous→<your email address>→

/pub/vidgames/faqs→klov.all …→*email* musjndx@gsusgi2.gsu.edu ✍ *Type in subject line:* send klov *Type in message body:* Mail-to: <your email address>

Coin-Op Arcade Games Find discussions on several arcade games here—*Mortal Kombat* and *NBA Jam* are the big draws. ✓**PRODIGY**→*jump* games bb→Choose a Topic→coin-op arcade games

Coin-Op Video Games Bulletin Board For discussions of quarter-eating *Super Street Fighter II* games, *NBA Jam*, *Virtua Fighters*, and *Mortal Kombat II*. ✓**GENIE** →*keyword* videogames→Video Games Bulletin Board→set 9

Coin-Ops Discuss popular coin-operated video games, especially *Mortal Kombat II* and *NBA Jam*. The library has lists of moves for *MK2* and an *NBA Jam* FAQ. ✓**COMPUSERVE**→*go* vidgam→Libraries *or* Messages→Coin-Ops

Insert Coin Here (echo) Discuss video-game coin-ops—from *Space Invaders* to *Mortal Kombat II*. ✓**WWIVNET**

List of Arcade Game Manufacturers Arcade-game manufacturers, with fairly complete contact information. ✓**INTERNET** …→*ftp* wiretap.spies.com→anonymous→<your email address>→ /game_archive/info→FAQ.addresses …→*gopher* wiretap.spies.com→Video Game Archive→info→FAQ.addresses …→*email* rgva@gisatl.fidonet.org ✍ *Type in subject line:* request manufacturer *Type in message body:* mail-to: <your email address>

rec.games.video.arcade (ng) Ground zero for discussion of coin-operated and home-system video games, ranging from the practical (cheat sheets) to the technical (maintenance, retrofitting, and pirating) to the philosophical (are you addicted? What are the best games of all time?). Most useful information is quickly incorporated into FAQs that are posted on the newsgroup (coverage of hot new games is practically simultaneous with their release) and archived. In the archive, check out the cheat sheet (cheatList), Killer List Of Videogames (gameList), repair hints (repairHints), and hint sheets for almost every game. ✓ USENET *Archives:* ✓ INTERNET→*ftp* wiretap.spies.com→anonymous→ <your email address>→/game_ archive *FAQ:* ✓ INTERNET→*ftp* rtfm.mit.edu→anonymous→<your email address>→/pub/usenet-by-hierarchy/rec/games/video/ arcade

rec.games.video.arcade.collecting (ng) Probably the most extensive clearinghouse for video-game-machine collecting. Includes technical discussions about collecting, fixing, and maintaining arcade video games. ✓ USENET

NBA Jam

NBA JAM! (echo) Get the inside scoop on how to play in the *Jam*. ✓ ICENET

NBA Jam Codes and Strategies Guides to playing and winning *NBA Jam*. Both sites carry the *NBA Jam* FAQ with cheats, strategies, and game history. The AOL site is full of *Jam* codes. ✓ INTERNET→*ftp* ftp.netcom.com→ anonymous→<your email address> →/pub/vidgames/faqs ✓ AMERICA ONLINE →*keyword* video games→ Hints, Tips, Pics & Cheats

Pinball

Eric Pinball Arcade-style pinball. Control the flippers with the shift keys, and then shoot with the space bar. ✓ COMPUSERVE→*go* zenith→Libraries→*Search by file name:* PIN-

BAL.ZIP ✓ GENIE→*keyword* scorpia→ Gamers Libraries→Set Library Category→Gravis Ultrasound Files→ *Download a file:* 6840 or 7875 (the second file is a new version)
Stats
* Competition: personal best
* Number of players: 1
* Interface: graphical
* Platform: DOS
Requirements: *VGA graphics*

The Pinball Archives Obsessed with pinball? The archive has an extensive collection of files on pinball, including FAQs, lists of pinball games, opinion polls about pinball, descriptions and game rule sheets, tips, images, and technical and maintenance information. ✓ INTERNET ...→*ftp* ftp.rahul. net→anonymous→<your email address>→/pub/sigma/pinball ...→*ftp* ftp.funet.fi→anonymous→ <your email address>→/pub/ misc/pinball ...→*www* ftp://ftp. rahul.net/pub/sigma/pinball/Pin ball.html *Support:* ✓ INTERNET→ email sigma@rahul.net ✍ *Email to receive a copy of the archive list twice a week*

rec.games.pinball (ng) Pinball discussions. The newsgroup carries a monthly post called PAPs that lists pinball machines and their hobbyist owners. The newsgroup's two-part FAQ is oriented more around the hobbyist than the player—from how to buy a new or used machine to detailed maintenance tips. ✓ USENET *FAQ:* ✓ INTERNET→*ftp* ftp.rahul.net→anonymous →<your email address>→/pub/ sigma/pinball/Info→faq*

Pinouts and cheats

The Pinouts Archive for Video Games Video-game schematics lovingly reproduced in ASCII graphics. ✓ INTERNET ...→*ftp* wiretap.spies.com→anonymous→

<your email address>→/game_ archive/boardPinouts ...→*gopher* wiretap.spies.com→game_archive →boardPinouts ...→*email* rgva@ gisatl.fidonet.org ✍ *Type in subject line:* request pinouts *Type in message body:* mail-to: <your email address>

The Video Game Cheat Sheet Make the most of game bugs, loopholes, and back doors and get high scores with low effort for dozens of arcade games. ✓ INTERNET ...→*ftp* wiretap.spies.com→anonymous→<your email address>→ /game_archive/cheatList ...→*gopher* wiretap.spies.com→Video Game Archive→cheatList

Wiretap Video Game Archives A huge archive of video arcade information and pinouts. Includes lists of arcade-game parts, a guide to video-game-machine auctions, and an archive on configuring old video-game machines. Pinouts range from *Pacman* to *Donkey Kong*. ✓ INTERNET ...→*ftp* wiretap.spies.com→anonymous→ <your email address>→/game_ archive ...→*gopher* wiretap.spies. com→Video Game Archive

Part 6

Sex, Hubs, MUDs & More

Adult gaming

Some people have trouble talking about sex, but they're
not the ones who're playing **Studs!**, an adventure in which you—a gigolo—work to please your client (don't worry, there's a sister version, **Studettes!**). They're also not the ones who take the raunchy **Sexquiz** or pour their *Penthouse Forum* fantasies into the **Story-Book Writer**.

On the Net

Bordello! A favorite on just about any BBS, *Bordello* allows you to run your own house of ill repute. You'll need to hire girls based on their attributes and see to it that they don't catch any diseases or get roughed up by opposing players. You'll have to slug it out with your enemies and plan your strategies for sabotaging their houses, breaking into their vault and other such chicanery. Great fun and a quick and easy play! ✓CHECK LOCAL BULLETIN BOARD SYSTEMS FOR THIS OR SIMILAR GAMES ☎→*dial* 717-325-9481

Stats
- Difficulty: average
- Competition: turn-based
- Number of players: 2+
- Interface: ANSI
- Platforms: all

Endless Story A variation on the story-writer-type game found on many BBSs. In this incarnation, each user adds a single line. In others, users may add as much to the story as they like. Beware, the result usually merges the absurd

Warrior women—downloaded from wuarchive.wustl.edu

with the pornographic. ✓CHECK LO-CAL BULLETIN BOARD SYSTEMS FOR THIS OR SIMILAR GAMES ☎→*dial* 302-436-4780

Stats
- Difficulty: simple
- Competition: turn-based
- Number of players: 2+
- Interface: ASCII, ANSI
- Platforms: all

Enrich Your Sexual Word Power What do you know about sex? Here's the ten-question test. Ten points for the correct answer on the first try; seven points on the second try; four points on the third try. ✓**COMPUSERVE**→*go* human →Interactive Programs→Enrich Your Sexual Word Power

Stats
- Difficulty: simple
- Competition: personal best
- Number of players: 1
- Interface: ASCII
- Platforms: all

Fantasy Land Perhaps one of the more bizarre combinations of

sex and combat that we've come across in a game. *Fantasy Land* offers randomly selected sexual encounters and situations (that range from tame to X-rated depending on the upbringing of your BBS sysop).

In each of the encounters you may use "items" to achieve your goal—to have sex with an "opponent" and have it more often than other players on the BBS. You'll roam through rooms looking for either offensive or defensive items to aid you in your quests. Try the "numbness spell" to fight off the "leather whip"—works almost every time. Ouch! ✓CHECK LOCAL BULLETIN BOARD SYSTEMS FOR THIS OR SIMILAR GAMES ☎→*dial* 612-566-5532

Stats
- Difficulty: average
- Competition: high scoring
- Number of players: 1+

> **"In the encounters you may use 'items' to achieve your goal—to have sex with an 'opponent' and have it more often than other players on the BBS. Try the 'numbness spell' to fight off the 'leather whip'—works almost every time. Ouch!"**

- Interface: ASCII, ANSI
- Platforms: all

Fiction Therapy Group Add a line to ongoing, usually twisted, stories. ✓INTERNET→*www* http://www.galcit.caltech.edu/~ta/fiction/fiction.html

Stats
- Difficulty: simple
- Competition: turn-based
- Number of players: 1+
- Interface: ASCII, graphical
- Platforms: all

How Self Conscious Are You? Martha and Howard (your robotic hosts) introduce you to dozens of people (don't worry, they're not real—no one's watching you.) Then, based on how closely you match the feelings expressed by those you're introduced to, you're given a thorough psychoanalysis. ✓**COMPUSERVE**→*go* human→Interactive Programs→How Self Conscious Are You?

Stats
- Difficulty: simple
- Competition: personal best
- Number of players: 1
- Interface: ASCII
- Platforms: all

Sexquiz Trivia questions of a sexual nature—candlelight to S&M. There's something to play with for everybody... ✓CHECK LOCAL BULLETIN BOARD SYSTEMS FOR THIS OR SIMILAR GAMES ☎→*dial* 609-235-5297

Stats
- Difficulty: simple
- Competition: high scoring
- Number of players: 1+
- Interface: ASCII
- Platforms: all

Storybook Writer For a change of pace from the rock'em-sock'em world of death and destruction in many games, try *Storybook Writer* for more literary—if not always more high-minded—fun. Each

Fantasy couple—downloaded from wuarchive.wustl.edu.

user picks up the story where the last person left off and adds whatever he or she likes to the tale at hand. This can lead to some uproariously funny episodes, mayhem, or erotica. ✓CHECK LOCAL BULLETIN BOARD SYSTEMS FOR THIS OR SIMILAR GAMES ☎→*dial* 805-541-2106

Stats
- Difficulty: simple
- Competition: turn-based
- Number of players: 2+
- Interface: ASCII, ANSI
- Platforms: all

Studettes! A sister game to *Studs*. In this version, the players are female prostitutes trying to keep their "clients" happy. ✓CHECK LOCAL BULLETIN BOARD SYSTEMS FOR THIS OR SIMILAR GAMES ☎→*dial* 717-325-9481

Stats
- Difficulty: average
- Competition: high scoring
- Number of players: 1+
- Interface: ANSI
- Platforms: all

Studs! Perhaps the raunchiest game we've seen come down the Information Superhighway, *Studs!* places you in the role of a male prostitute on the prowl for a few good tricks. The main "trick" is to

please your "client" as much as possible. Don't be early. Don't be late. And by all means, use protection or you're asking for trouble. Definitely not for the politically correct. ✓CHECK LOCAL BULLETIN BOARD SYSTEMS FOR THIS OR SIMILAR GAMES ☎→*dial* 717-325-9481

Stats
- Difficulty: average
- Competition: high scoring
- Number of players: 1+
- Interface: ANSI
- Platforms: all

Truth or Die The author warns that players may stumble upon some "pretty rude and nasty questions that might offend some people." Sounds like fun to us. Players are asked personal questions, and they must answer truthfully. Players also submit their own questions. The rub is that they may be asked their own questions! ✓CHECK LOCAL BULLETIN BOARD SYSTEMS FOR THIS OR SIMILAR GAMES ☎→*dial* 410-860-0212

Stats
- Difficulty: simple
- Competition: high scoring
- Number of players: 2+
- Interface: ASCII
- Platforms: all

Witty Write-ins The stories can get a little racy in this adult version of Mad Libs (though rarely past PG-13). You're asked to supply parts of speech or more specific words, like "part-of-body," which then get used in a story. Generally, the results read like nonsense, but it's interesting to see how your grammatical contributions find bad company. ✓**COMPUSERVE**→*go* tmc-26→Witty Write-Ins

Stats
- Difficulty: simple
- Competition: personal best
- Number of players: 1
- Interface: ASCII
- Platforms: all

Social MUDs

Like "new innovation," Social MUD may be redundant,
since all MUDs are at heart heavily decorated chat rooms, but follow the extra emphasis to the bottom of the ocean in **DeepSeas**, the surreal drug chatter of **TrippyMush**, or the pits of the MUD from hell, (**Evil!**) **Mud**. Devout minimalists should visit the stripped-bare, no-theme, just-talk **QuartzPARADISE**.

Anthropomorphic bunny—from AOL's Mac Graphics & CAD Forum.

On the Net

MUDs

CaveMUCK The cave through which you enter this virtual world is dark and cold. If you enjoy exploring or building and want to be part of a smaller (somewhat cliquish) community with several "old time" MUDders, then don't be scared off. There's a lot to see here.

On the other hand, if you're looking for role-playing, adventures, a large crowd, or newbie help, this is not the place for you. The caves and tunnels lead to small lodges, hotels (with working elevators) that rent rooms, and lots of hidden areas. In the underground Games Complex, you can challenge other players to *hearts*, *Othello*, *chess*, *Seawar*, or *Shogi*. A robot will deal your *hearts* game.

Anime region

An anime region was created by several Japanese animation buffs. Exploring the region might bring you face-to-face with a villain from an anime series or might get you a lunch date with Kotobuki C-ko. A few years ago during the big building frenzy on *CaveMUCK*, some areas were created that were definitely not cavelike. To get there, you'll have to come above ground—perhaps through a crack in some rocks. The "map" or "exit" command, which is also used on other MUCKs, is a real treat. Instead of just listing available exits, it diagrams the surrounding areas. ✓**INTERNET**→*telnet* cave.tcp.com 2283→connect guest guest *Register:* ✓**INTERNET**→*email* jingoro@ cave.tcp.com ✍ *Email request to register a character* <your character's name> <your password> *Support:* ✓**INTERNET**→*email* wizards@ cave.tcp.com

Stats
- Difficulty: average
- Competition: live
- Number of players: 1+
- Interface: ASCII
- Server: MUCK
- Platforms: all

Commands
- To get a list of wizards, type: wizards
- To get a list of fun global (use anywhere) commands, type: global
- To get a diagram of the surrounding area, type: map

DeepSeas Connect to *DeepSeas* and you'll find yourself at the bottom of an Ocean in a beer garden called SnnnOCTOPUS's. The beer garden is a comfortable place and, like most places in this underwater world, contains enough savvy coding to distract you from its raison d'être—socializing. The players are a little older, with quite a few Ph.D.s floating around, and discussions range from computer programming to the latest episode of *Babylon 5*. Day and early-evening hours are busiest.

Navigating

Navigating the ocean is a bit tricky—it's a three-dimensional layout and an "experiment in dynamic spaces." Wherever you are in *DeepSeas*, you'll have an x, y, and z coordinate, and you can move only a single coordinate at a time. Rooms often do not seem to exist until you move into them. So don't be afraid to try to enter an object, such as the submarine—even if it is not listed as an exit. In contrast to the always-hopping beer garden (0,0,0), the Pink Oyster Club (0,1,20) is an on-again, off-again hangout (though you might even be asked to perform a song or two).

Yellow submarines

Builders on this MUSH have a quirky sense of humor and they've created yellow submarines, underwater wormholes, sunken spaceships, slot machines, magic eight-balls for fortune telling, dangerous whirlpools, and lots of other underwater surprises. As on most MUSHes, to find out what you can do with an object, use the "look <object>" command. ✓**IN-TERNET**→*telnet* muds.okstate.edu 6250→connect guest guest *Register:* ✓**INTERNET**→*email* deepseas-request@muds.okstate.edu ✍ *Send a request to register your character:* <your character's name> <your password>

Stats

- Difficulty: average
- Competition: live
- Number of players: 1+
- Interface: ASCII
- Server: MUSH
- Platforms: all

Commands

- To get more information, type: news
- To move into an object, type: enter <object>
- To move out of an object without exits, type: out

(Evil!) Mud From the belching lava pits in the Town Square to the Taxicab of Death in "West Corner of the Swamp" (all resemblances to *FurryMUCK* are intentional) to the abortion clinics and miniature-golf courses, black humor is the theme of the day on *(EVIL!) Mud*. There is quite a lot to explore—get a map by typing "help map." *(EVIL!) Mud* does not have a huge player population, but on occasion, when a MUD with many of the same players goes down, *(EVIL!) Mud* comes to life.

Jesus, the robot

Even on a regular day, you will always find Xibo (head wizard) and his friends accompanied by Jesus, the MUD's Maas-Neotek robot, chatting in the square, at MUD-dom's equivalent of the Algonquin Round Table of the 1920s. For information about the MUD, visit the kiosk in the Evil Town Square. To send mail, page Jesus and tell him to pass on your message. This is one of the grand old dinosaurs of MUDdom. It runs obsolete

code, but at the same time it supports a truly marvelous, yet insane, database. (P.S. Next time you're in Evil Town Square, type "turtle".) Note: If you do not give yourself a description before you log off, your character will be automatically recycled and will not be there the next time you log in. ✓**INTERNET**→*telnet* intac.com 4201→create <your character's name> <your password>

Stats

- Difficulty: average
- Competition: live
- Number of players: 2+
- Interface: ASCII
- Server: TeenyMUD
- Platforms: all

FurryMUCK While *Lambda-MOO* gets all the press, *Furry* is both the most famous and the most infamous among people who actually play MUDs. A large and devoted clientele enjoy its theme of anthropomorphic animals—"furries."

Tinysex

On a typical afternoon on *Furry-MUCK* you will find cartoon mice, humanoid foxes, noble unicorns, and sleek, sexy pantherettes all chatting amiably with each other. On a typical evening you will find hundreds of MUDders en-

> **"The wizards frequently have to scold people who have wandered into G-rated West Corner of the Park on sex-based escapades."**

gaging in the activity for which *FurryMUCK* is universally known: tinysex. Tinysex, loosely defined as simulated text-based sexual activity between two or more MUD characters, has a strong appeal for many *FurryMUCK*ers.

You may simply wish to hang out or role-play the character of, say, a space ranger in the Fox Space Forces, but you can't get away from the sex forever. At one time or another, you'll probably experience a come-on or be fondled. The wizards frequently have to scold people who have wandered into G-rated West Corner of the Park on sex-based escapades. The MUCK rarely crashes, and it has a well-built landscape and a large, stable community. Often there are close to 200 players connected for most of the day and night.

Taxi stands

You can spend days exploring the landscape, from Pounce's River to the far-off North Pole, and still not see everything. To aid in your exploration, there are taxi stands and stepdisks all over. To use a stepdisk, simply enter the room where it is found and type "nn", "ss", "ee", or "ww".

For a tutorial on building on TinyMUD-style MUDs, go to the Town Hall south from the Park on Furry Avenue. There are a few restrictions on building on *Furry-MUCK*. The MUD has been up since September 1990, and the database is very large—approaching 100,000 items—the reason why you will find yourself restricted via quota in the number of rooms and items you can add to the database. (Especially good builders will receive larger quotas.) ✓**INTERNET**→*telnet* sncils.snc.edu 8888→connect guest guest *Register:* ✓**INTERNET**→*email* fmadmin@sncils.snc.edu ✍ *Email request to register a character:* <your character's name> <your

Social MUDs Sex, Hubs, MUDs & More

password>

Stats
- Difficulty: average
- Competition: live
- Number of players: 1+
- Interface: ASCII
- Server: MUCK
- Platforms: all

Commands
- To get a list of active wizards, type: wizzes
- To get a list of players who can help you, type: helpstaff

LambdaMOO It would probably be easiest to list all the things XeroxPARC's *LambdaMOO* doesn't have. Definitely the leading candidate for the title of largest MOO (more than 8,000 residents), *Lambda* is a veritable universe, centering on a cavernous mansion, with dozens of people chatting in the living room and several exploring the dining room, where games (*Ghost*, *Set*, a *Rubik's Cube*, *Scrabble*, *Upwords*) are served.

Want to get out into the world? Just leave through the kitchen door, wave to the people soaking in the hot tub, and watch out or you'll stumble across the helipad, complete with helicopters ready to fly you around. (You can sky-dive from them, too.) There are sections where role-playing gamers do their stuff.

MOO-Hell

There's a casino, a theater, a MOO-Heaven and MOO-Hell. (Hell is filled with mystery novels, all with the last page missing.) *Lambda* is actually so large it has its own government, really, complete with issues you can vote on. The XeroxPARC admins recently curtailed the number of new users they accept. So you may have to join a hundred or so others on a waiting list and exist as a "guest" for a month or so, at least until the MOO's popularity decreases a

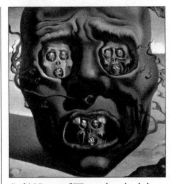

Dali's Visage of War—*downloaded from wuarchive.wustl.edu.*

---

bit. But it'll be worth the wait! (Lots of users create roses to give to other MOO residents.) ✓**INTERNET**→*telnet* lambda.parc.xerox.com 8888→help *Info:* ✓**INTERNET**→*ftp* ftp.parc.xerox.com→anonymous→ <your email address>→/pub/ MOO

Stats
- Difficulty: average
- Competition: live
- Number of players: 1+
- Interface: ASCII
- Server: MOO
- Platforms: all

Commands
- To get a list of help topics, type: help
- To page someone who has volunteered to help, type: page help <your question>
- To get a list of wizards, type: help wizard-list
- To take the general MOO tutorial, type: @tutorial
- To add your name to the waiting list for character creation, type: @request <your character name> for <your email address>

QuartzPARADISE There's no theme, building, or role-playing. Just people chatting. ✓**INTERNET**→ *telnet* quartz.rutgers.edu 9999 *Register:* ✓**INTERNET**→*email* bbs@ quartz.rutgers.edu ✍ *Email to register a character*

Stats
- Difficulty: simple
- Competition: live
- Number of players: 2+
- Interface: ASCII
- Server: MUCK
- Platforms: all

TinyTIM "It's NOT just a game....It's a really, really BIG game!" is its slogan. False advertisement is not an issue here. The world features, among other things, a city, a church, forests, ski slopes, a hotel, adventures, space thingies, and an incredible clock that responds to 200 commands. You can visit the Hall of Parties, where events and conversations at real-life *TinyTIM* parties (yes, MUDders get together face-to-face sometimes) are immortalized , take a room at the Grand Hotel, or attend a dragon hatching. And *TIM* is the oldest MUSH still running.

Humor

But *TIM* is best known for its sense of humor and, might we say, hipness. Where else can you find a help command for tinysex? The 2,000 people who belong to this community don't come here to exclusively role-play vampires or pretend to be a furry animal; they get together without an enforced theme (not that you can't role-play here; it's just that you don't have to). The Main Area Place, or the Nexus, is probably the most popular hangout. And when people aren't socializing there, they're probably building.

Online Frisbee

Sketch the Cow, the upbeat admin at *TinyTIM* has created such additions as Online Karaoke, an Online Lava Lamp that generates '70s lyrics, and, of course, an Online Dunk Tank. Another player created an Online Frisbee that gets tossed between players on the MUSH. And another built a world that imitates XTC and They Might Be Giants lyrics. "We consider these two musical groups to be the unofficial 'house' bands," says Sketch. Although you may be tempted to jump right in, we highly recommend that you choose "NEW" at the first exit. The overview of *TIM* that follows is not only full of interesting information but also well written and amusing. An excellent introduction to MUSHing in general. ✓**INTERNET**→*telnet* yay.tim.org 5440→ create <your character's name>→ <your password> *Info:* ✓**INTERNET** …→*www* http://yay.tim.org …→ *ftp* yay.tim.org→anonymous→ <your email address>

TooMUSH]I[Says *TooMUSH]I[* creator Edmond Meinfelder, "*TooMUSH* was to be the *Cheers* of the MUSHes, a place where everybody knows your name. However, I made it a bit more than that. I extended the invitation to players whose servers are down to come to *TooMUSH* and build their own area. In both capacities it has been successful. We have hosted people from *Amber, PernMUSH, SouCon, Garou, Narnia, Two Moons,* and other MUDs that went down.

Notables

Also, this has become a gathering place of the many notables in the MUSH (and MUD) community." So from its origins as a refugee camp, *TooMUSH* has become something of a hangout for Dinos (people who've been around the virtual MUD block a few times).

There's no real official theme and most people are here to kibitz in one of the two main hangouts: the Main Bar of the Abyss (#150) and the Sphere (#645). The first is predominantly inhabited by Pern

people; the second, by *AmberMUSH* players. There are a lot of neat and unique commands built into this MUSH, including the global command "+theme <your idea>," which allows a player to set the theme of an area to whatever he or she wants—not everyone will play along though.

MUD history

What to see while you're here? There's a Magic Eightball and a *Star Trek* plot generator. If you're into MUD history, some wizards have left histories of their MUDding careers—type "news wizards." Beware, though, that this is a competitive place where people are very critical of each other's MUD accomplishments. And if you're not a somebody in the MUD world, well, who are you and what are you doing here?

On the other hand, for newbies who can endure the abuse, this is a sure entrance into the clue elite, and a Valhalla of refreshing debate on the state of MUDding, religion, alternate lifestyles, and more. Ahh, and stay tuned for Too4— the next edition in the *TooMUSH* saga. ✓**INTERNET**→*telnet* lodestar.gb. nrao.edu 7070→connect guest guest *Info:* ✓**INTERNET**→*www* http://bunda.gb. nrao.edu/

Stats
- Difficulty: average
- Competition: live
- Number of players: 1+
- Interface: ASCII
- Server: MUSH
- Platforms: all

Commands
- To find out what wizards are online, type: +wizards

TrippyMush If bizarre psychedelic hallucinations are your thing, then this MUSH is for you. New to MUSHing? Head for the Gnu Players' Locker for newbie info. There are five main areas, or

"planes of insanity."

MUSHsphere II is the most central area. From there you can get to the Sea of Holes, which is the gateway to dozens of strange adventures, including Dante's Inferno. (Log in as Dante Dante to explore the circles of hell.) Or slide down to SubTrippy, a subterranean urban environment complete with a mall and an IHOM (International House of Mollusks). Or you may explore the Asylum, where you can set up your own place.

Dali painting

At TrippyMUSH Towers you can take care of administrative needs, including leaving suggestions to the Admin. But other than that, there is no way to tell where you'll end up on this MUSH. You may enter a Dali painting or a bathtub only to end up in a geriatrics ward or a set from *Star Trek*. Or you may fly over the rainbow and end up in the Geraldo Rivera Memorial Waiting Room, about to be operated on by a mad scientist.

Many of the descriptions are grotesque or decidedly not PC, so if you are easily offended (e.g., dwarf-tossing goes on here), you may want to skip this one. (Note: Site may change. If it does, try "trippy.org 7567".) ✓**INTERNET**→ *telnet* newton.sos.clarkson.edu 7567→create <your character> <your password>

Stats
- Difficulty: average
- Competition: live
- Number of players: 1+
- Interface: ASCII
- Server: MUSH
- Platforms: all

Commands
- To get information, go to the Gnu Players' Locker
- To get a list of wizards, type: wizzes

MUDs

You'll shake hands with other players when you're intro-

duced. You'll sit down for a chat with a MUD friend. You'll smile at, wave at, and hug the characters you gather with each night. And if you meet the right someone, you may even MUD-marry. (To get a look at your MUD spouse, download his or her GIF from the **MUD Clients and GIF Archive**.)

Some MUDs give players free rein to build—learn a little programming while you play. They'll carry programming manuals and tutorials to get you started. But if programming isn't your thing, there are plenty of mysteries to be solved, monsters to be killed, and scenes to be role-played.

Who's playing

While the majority of the MUDs that come and go on the Net have themes—from Tolkien to *Star Trek*—story lines, combat systems, and other gamelike features, the success and appeal of a particular MUD depends on who's playing. In these virtual worlds, entirely dependent on the text descriptions and text-talk that scroll across computer screens, interesting MUD companions are essential.

MUD dino couple Jennifer (Moira) and Russ (Random) Smith—downloaded from ftp.math.okstate.edu.

To begin MUDding, you'll have to learn the jargon, master a few commands, and devote some time to finding the "right community."

MUD lists

Read the **rec.games. mud*** newsgroups to follow the comings and goings of MUDs. And check out **Doran's** or one of the other MUD lists for more MUD options than you'll ever use.

On the Net

Across the board

Brother Sean's MUD Guide Lots of MUD information! Includes links to the MUD FAQs, MUD Lists, and other MUD-related Web and FTP sites. ✓ **INTERNET**→*www* http://www.cec.wustl.

edu/~sad2/MUD/index.html

The Internet Games MUD-List (ml) Keep your finger on the pulse of the MUD community—MUDders share impressions and the all-important addresses! ✓ **INTERNET**→ *email* jwisdom@gnu.ai.mit.edu ✍ *Type in subject line:* mud list

Monster MUD Archive A MUD archive with servers, clients, and numerous MUD-related documents. Includes general manuals for using MUSH sites as well as MUD-specific manuals for *Pern-MUSH*, *TinyTim*, and others. ✓ **INTERNET**→*ftp* caisr2.caisr.cwru. edu→anonymous→<your email address>→/pub

MUD Archives Large MUD archives storing clients, servers, robots, and MUD documents (including MUD lists and the MUD FAQs). Both archives will carry some of the same files but will each have original files as well. ✓ **INTERNET** ...→*ftp* ftp.tcp.com →anonymous→<your email address>→/pub/mud ...→*ftp* ftp.ccs. neu.edu→anonymous→<your email address>→/pub/mud

rec.games.mud.admin (ng) Discussion for administrators and programmers of MUDs. Share tips and info on building MUDs. ✓ **USENET**

rec.games.mud.announce (ng) Announcements about new MUDs, lamentations for deceased MUDs, updates on site changes, and regular postings of the multi-part MUD FAQ.

If your favorite MUD is down for a long period of time, check here for an announcement about why, and when (or if) it's expected back up. The MUD FAQ is perhaps the best source of information for the new MUDder. Includes an introduction to the basic vocabulary of the MUD world, hints on how to start (what to do and what not to do), an extensive list of clients detailing features and where to download them from, and an explanation of the MUD Remote WHO Servers. ✓USENET ✓INTERNET→*email* rgm-announce-request@glia.biostr.washington.edu ✍ *Write a request FAQ:* ✓INTERNET ...→*ftp* rtfm.mit.edu→anonymous→ <your email address>→/pub/ usenet-by-hierarchy/rec/games/ mud/announce ...→*ftp* ftp.math.ok-state.edu→anonymous→<your email address>→/pub/muds/ misc/mud-faq

---

rec.games.mud.misc (ng) Discussion of MUDs in general, announcements, and whatever doesn't fit into the other MUD newsgroups. ✓USENET

Clients & GIFs

MUD Clients and GIF Archive Carries MUD servers and a huge selection of clients and documents for MUSHes, MUDs, MUCKs, and other servers. Also includes an online "photo album" with more than 200 images of active MUDers in GIF, TIFF, and JPG files. ✓INTERNET→*ftp* ftp.math.okstate. edu→anonymous→<your email address>→/pub/muds

Education

CBNVEE (ml) A list for those interested in the ideas of the Coalition for Building Networked Virtual Educational Environments. Discussion focuses on how to use MOO, MUSE, or MUSH software to create learning environments. ✓INTERNET→*email* listserv@mcmuse.mc.maricopa.edu ✍ *Type in message body:* subscribe cbnvee <your full name>

History

MUD History Archive Lauren Burka's MUD Archive traces the history of MUDs from Richard Bartle's first MUD to the innovations of the present. Site carries Burka's chronology of MUDs as well as documents, MUD logs, and postings from newgroups and mailing lists highlighting MUD achievements and issues. There are even logs of Julia, an intelligent

MUD robot that responds to human MUDders. Also features links to other noteworthy MUD info on the Net. ✓INTERNET→*www* http://www.ccs.neu.edu/USER/lpb /muddex.html

Links

The Experimental MUD WWW Page Links to several interesting MUDs and WWW pages. ✓INTERNET→*www* http://

MUD JARGON	
bot	a program imitating a human being that can deliver messages and pass on other info
dino	a longtime MUDder
equip	the items you are currently using
exits	your options for leaving an area
furry	an anthropomorphic intelligent animal
god or immort	the person who owns the MUD database
IC	in character, meaning you are acting in your MUD character's persona, *not* your own
haven	a flag that indicates a no-killing area
hit points	a numeric representation of, essentially, a character's life (lose too many points in combat and you're dead)
inv	your on-hand possessions
log	a record—screen capture—of MUDding activities
mana	a numeric representation of the amount of energy a character has available to cast spells
maving	using the wrong commands and making conversations confusing
mob or mobile	a monster in the game
movement	a numeric representation of the amount of movement a player has available
newbie	a player who is new to the game
OOC	out of character, meaning you are acting as yourself, *not* as your MUD character
PK/PKing	player killer/player killing
RL	real life
spamming	saying too much at once, and having a lot of text scroll on to other players' screens
stats/score	numeric evaluation of your character's progress, "health", and/or strengths
tinysex	using MUD commands or "descriptive prowess" to imitate having sex
wiz	to "win" the game and be appointed wizard
wizards	players who have either "won" the game or been appointed by gods to help run it

math.okstate.edu/russ/mud.html

MUD Gopher Organizes MUDs by server and offers direct connections to many of them. Also features a link to the Virtual Spaces Gopher at the University of Texas. √**INTERNET**→*gopher* gopher.micro. umn.edu→Fun & Games→Games→ MUDs

Virtual Spaces Offers articles about MUDding, lists of FTP-site files, descriptions and direct links to many MUDs, announcements of new MUDs and those looking for new sites, old MUD lists, and the MUD FAQs (not always the latest, though!). √**INTERNET**→*gopher* actlab.rtf.utexas.edu→Virtual Spaces: MUD/

Lists

Automatic MUD List An online MUD database searchable by the name (or part of a name) of a MUD. A search returns the names of relevant MUDs, their Net addresses, server types, and status (up or down). The status may not always be current. You can also download the list from the FTP site. √**INTERNET** ...→*telnet* moe.coe. uga.edu 4801 ...→*ftp* moe.coe.uga. edu→anonymous→<your email address>→/pub/mud→ mudlist.auto

Commands
• To get a list of MUDS (and their addresses) that begin with a specific letter(s), type: @mudlist <letter(s)>
• To get a list of MUDS (and their addresses) that fall within a specified alphabetical range, type: @mudlist < 1st letter(s)>*<2nd letter(s)>
• To get a list of MUDS (and their addresses) that include a specific set of letters in no particular position, type: @mudlist *<set of letters>*
• To get instructions, type: help

• To quit, type: QUIT

Cardiff's MUD Page Primarily a source of MUD lists, including Doran's and the Automatic MUD List. Also offers links to other MUD Web pages. √**INTERNET**→ *www* http://www.cm.cf.ac.uk/ User/Andrew.Wilson/MUDlist

Doran's Mudlist A periodically published list of almost 500 active MUDs and their addresses by server type. The list is quite extensive but not comprehensive, as MUD administrators may request to be left off it and new MUDs may have opened since it was verified. It is frequently posted to rec.games.mud.announce. √**INTER-NET**→*email* awozniak@joule.calpoly. edu ✍ *Type in subject line:* SUBSCRIBE

Programmers

Programmer's MUD Archive An archive of technical documents and utilities related to MUD programming with separate directories for TeenyMUDs, TinyMUCKs, and Über- and UnterMUDs. √**INTERNET**→*ftp* ftp.white. toronto.edu→anonymous→<your email address>→/pub/muds

Remote WHO server

MUD RWHO Server Want to know which MUDs your friends are on? Telnet to a RWHO server to get lists of players on participating MUDs. The second site is a European RWHO server. √**INTER-NET** ...→*telnet* riemann.math.ok state.edu 6889 ...→*telnet* nova.tat. physik.uni-tuebingen.de 6889

Diku

DikuMUD Server For those interested in setting up their own DikuMUD, you can download a

copy of the DikuMUD server. √**INTERNET**→*ftp* coyote.cs.wmich. edu→anonymous→<your email address>→/pub/Games/DikuMUD→ dikumud.tar.Z

rec.games.mud.diku (ng) Covers everything about DikuMUDs from administrative and technical matters to new site announcements to loud boasting and flaming. This is perhaps the most abrasive of the MUD groups, with "my MUD's better than yours" dominating the discussion. The FAQ covers general information about DikuMUDs, issues related to starting a MUD or building an area in an existing MUD, site openings and closings, and where to find Diku utilities, patches, and source code. The Unofficial List of DikuMUDs is periodically here as well. √**USENET** *FAQ:* √**INTERNET**→ *ftp* rtfm.mit.edu→anonymous→ <your email address>→/pub/ usenet-by-hierarchy/rec/games/ mud/diku

CYBERNOTES

"MUDs are places where you can explore, achieve, chat, and role-play; where you can create, where you can live, where you can die; where you can be whoever or whatever you want to be. They use the language of the mind, not the language of the senses: the images they convey are more vivid than graphics could ever be. Experience them while you can."

—from **Richard Bartle** (richard@spuddy.uucp)

The Unofficial List of Diku-MUDs A list of DikuMUDs, their addresses and other MUD stats: number of levels, number of classes, number of areas, and whether player killing is allowed. The list also prints brief "notes" about the MUD if the list owner is sent any other information. ✓**INTERNET** ...→*www* http://www.cis.ohio-state.edu/hypertext/faq/usenet/games/mud/diku/faq2/faq.html ...→*ftp* rtfm.mit.edu→anonymous→ <your email address>→/pub/usenet-by-hierarchy/rec/games/mud/diku→The_Totally_Unofficial_List_of_Internet_Muds ...→*email* mondays@bsu-cs.bsu.edu ✍ *Email with MUD submissions or corrections*

LPMud

LPMud Archive Includes LP-Mud clients, utilities, and MUD Libs. ✓**INTERNET**→*ftp* ftp.lysator.liu.se→anonymous→<your email address>→/lpmud

---

rec.games.mud.lp (ng) Detailed discussions of players' favorite LPMuds, announcements of new MUDs, and smatterings of player braggadocio. ✓**USENET** *FAQ:* ✓**INTERNET**→*ftp* actlab.rtf.utexas.edu→anonymous→<your email address>→/MUD/LPmud/FAQ

MOO

Cardiff MOO Page Programmer-level information on MOOs and MOO-net (a network of MOOs). Nonprogrammers might be interested in the "netwho" search: Click on a MOO name, and a list of players connected to that MOO will be displayed. ✓**INTERNET**→*www* http://www.cm.cf.ac.uk/User/Andrew.Wilson/CardiffMOO

MOO Archive An archive for MOO programmers and players. Features a MOO programmers manual and tutorials, the LambaMOO server, and MOO code. Hint: Don't overlook the "/contrib" subdirectory—lots of articles and papers about MOOs. ✓**INTERNET**→*ftp* ftp.parc.xerox.com→anonymous→<your email address>→/pub/MOO

MOOcows (ml) Thinking of starting a MOO? Interested in incorporating WWW features into your MOO? Discuss MOO innovations and new releases of the *LambdaMOO* core. Pavel Curtis, the man who designed the MOO, is an active contributor. ✓**INTERNET**→*email* moo-cows-request@parc.xerox.com ✍ *Write a request*

MUSE

MUSE Archive An archive specializing in MUSE-related material, including the MUSE manual, general information, guides to specific MUSEs, charters, and other info. ✓**INTERNET**→*ftp* chezmoto.ai.mit.edu→anonymous→<your email address>→/muse

MUSH

MUSH Hacks (ml) Discussion for those interested in programming their own MUSH server. ✓**INTERNET**→*email* mushhacks-request@caisr2.caisr.cwru.edu ✍ *Write a request*

MUSH Manual Everything you need to know to play on a MUSH. Commands are well described with examples. ✓**INTERNET**→*ftp* nic.funet.fi→anonymous→<your email address>→/pub/doc/games/mud→mushman-2.007.tar.gz

---

TinyMUSH Programmers (ml) Covers technical discussions relat-

ed to MUSH programming. Share tricks and learn new techniques. ✓**INTERNET**→*email* tinymush-programmers-request@cygnus.com ✍ *Write a request*

Tiny

Introduction to MU*s Site Provides links to several documents written about MU* design, programming, and management. There are also links to many of the other MUD Web sites. ✓**INTERNET**→*www* http://www.vuw.ac.nz/who/Jamie.Norrish/mud.html

---

rec.games.mud.tiny (ng) Active group with the latest news and discussion in the Tiny MU* world, including MUSHes, MUCKs, MUSEs and others. ✓**USENET**

Modem-to-modem

With active directories like Macintosh Modem Players, network utilities such as Inter-

net Head to Head (IHHD), and on-line forums like **Modem-to-Modem Gaming Lobby**, you'll never want for human companionship again, or at least not for live cannon fodder. M2M games are the very definition of action and strategy Net games as far as we're concerned—we're talking the hottest stuff, *Falcon* dogfights, *Doom* blast-a-thons, *Battle Chess* dismemberment—elevating soulless competition between man and machine into a nerve-racking tit for tat among members of the same species. We don't want to get just responses. We want to smell fear.

On the Net

The Head-to-Head Connection (echo) For those who enjoy head-to-head competition, here's where to meet your next victim. ✓**WWIVNET**

IHHD (ml) Learn more about IHHD, help develop the software, and share a virtual beer after a head-to-head competition. ✓**INTERNET**→*email* listserv@cactus.org ✍ *Type in message body:* subscribe ihhd <your full name>

Internet Head-to-Head Daemon (IHHD) For head-to-head Internet play, you'll definitely

Screenshot from Tom Landry's Strategy Football.

want to get your hands on IHHD. Used in conjunction with compatible (often commercial) software, IHHD makes head-to-head gaming over the Internet possible. Games like *Doom*, *Air Warrior*, *Battle Chess*, and *Empire Deluxe* already have an IHHD following. In other words, as long as you're willing to configure it, you can play against your Net friends without the long-distance charges! ✓**INTERNET**→*ftp* rex.pfc.mit.edu→anonymous→<your email address>→/pub /IHHD/src→dialer1.6.4.shar *Info:* ✓**INTERNET**→*ftp* cactus.org→anonymous→<your email address>→ /pub/IHHD→HowTo
Requirements: *Internet provider must be running Unix and you must be able to compile the program on the Unix machine.*

Internet Modem Players Listing (ml) A relatively new weekly mailing of Internet gamers interested in head-to-head gaming, using either the good old phone lines or the IHHD. The list provides modem numbers, maximum baud rates, type of computer sys-

tem, games of interest, and email addresses. The list also attempts to track how many people played certain games. *Doom*, for instance, led the pack in the summer of '94. The list is regularly posted to many of the gaming newsgroups on Usenet. Look for this list to take off. ✓**INTERNET** ...→*email* pawcamp@u.cc.utah.edu ✍ *Type in subject line:* request impl ...→ *www* http://chemotaxis.biology. utah.edu/IMPL/IMPL.html

Macintosh Modem Players Server A server listing Macintosh gamers interested in playing modem-to-modem games. Players are listed by area code, email address, and the modem games in which they're interested. The email server allows players to add their name, search for other players, or get help. ✓**INTERNET** ...→*email* area code@chemotaxis.biology.utah.edu ✍ *To get a list of commands for using the Macintosh, type in subject* *line:* help …→*www* http://chemo taxis.biology.utah.edu/AreaCode Files/AreaCodeFiles.html

Modem Games Forum Where people meet and discuss their favorite games (particularly those with modem-to-modem capability). Explore the forum's libraries for files—patches, scenery, instructions—related to games played in CompuServe's Modem-to-Modem Gaming Lobby. Many gamers also transform the libraries into a gaming field. They upload game turns, which their opponents can then download and run. This "turn exchange" continues until someone wins. Big-name games such as *VGA Planets* and *Empire Deluxe* offer upload-download play. And the biggest draw on the message boards? Modern air combat, especially *Falcon 3.0* and *MiG-29*. The results of "tournaments" played in the lobby are often on the forum's message boards—there's always a new tournament being announced. ✓**COMPUSERVE**→*go* modemgames

Modem-to-Modem Challenge Board A directory of CompuServe gamers looking for opponents. Search by game title, phone number, or name. Players may choose to connect via the MTM Gaming Lobby or to call each other directly. ✓**COMPUSERVE**→*go* mtm-challenge

Commands
• To return to previous menu, type: M
• To go back a page, type: B

Modem-to-Modem Gaming Play real-time against people from anywhere in the country for the cost of a Delphi connection. Gamers meet either on the forum's message board or in the Game Room. Actual playing takes place in the Game Room. Favorite modem-to-modem games that you can download free from Delphi's Database are *Doom* (level one), a *Risk*-like game called *Conquest, The Perfect General* (demo), a variation of *Go* called *Telego*, a card-game program called *Telecards* for playing *Gin Rummy, Cribbage,* and *Crazy Eights.* All database games are DOS- or Windows-compatible. You can also bring your own store-bought game— and many people do. *Conquered Kingdoms, Empire Deluxe, Falcon 3.0,* and *Global Conquest* are consistent hits. ✓**DELPHI**→*go* ent mod

Commands
• For a list of commands /help
• To get a list of available opponents /who

Modem-to-Modem Gaming Lobby All your favorite PC game lacks is a living opponent. *Tom Landry Strategy Football* and *Empire Deluxe* are much more fun when the enemy is of flesh and blood. If the game—commercial or shareware—has modem-to-modem capabilities, CompuServe is the place to look for opponents. Who cares where your opponent lives as long as he or she likes— and owns—the same game. Once you and your opponent are connected, exit your communications program (probably Information Manager) and run the game. (Set up the game as if you were connected directly, rather than via modem, as the connection is already established!) Reduced rates are in effect and support is available in the evening hours. ✓**COMPUSERVE**→*go* mtmlobby

Commands
• For help on commands, type: /help
• To see who else is in the Lobby, type: /who
• To challenge a player, type: /challenge <user number> *or* /challenge <user number>

<game title>
• To accept a challenge, type: /accept <user number>
• To see a list of user numbers, type: /users

Play-by-(e)mail

Just as the novelty, ease, and near-instantaneous gratifi-cation of email has revived letter-writing for many people, it has also spawned a geometric increase in play-by-email games—so much so that the online fervor also bolsters postal-mail games. Board games like *chess* and *Diplomacy*, sci-fi and fantasy games such as *Feudal Lords* and *Celestial Empire*, and sports games—from the *Electronic Football League* to *Ultra Cricket*—all run over email routes. **The PBeM Magazine** keeps tabs on Net games, so get a copy to find out what's playing today. Some PBeMs play out in a few days (especially with "warp mode" 12 hour turns); others, with typical two-to-four-day turns, can last for months. Companies like **Adventures by Mail** and the **Gamer's Den** have a vested interest in keeping you hooked. No word—yet—on the longest continuous PBeM game!

On the Net

de.alt.games.pbem (ng) The Germans dominate PBeM on the Net—they organize and participate in many of the PBeM games. It should therefore come as no surprise that they've organized their own newsgroup. *Sprechen Sie*

Map for Axis and Allies—*from AOL's PBM and Strategy Gaming Forum.*

Deutsch? Then here's a good place to find a PBeM game to join. ✓**USENET**

PBEM Magazine Back issues of Greg Lindahl's definitive *Play-By-Email Magazine,* a fabulous source of information on the PBeM scene. ✓**COMPUSERVE**→*go* pbm games→Libraries→PBM Magazines →*Search by keyword:* pbem ✓**INTER-NET**→*ftp* ftp.erg.sri.com→anonymous→<your email address>→/pub/pbm/PBEM-Fanzine

PBM and Strategy Gaming Forum For the discussion and playing of strategy games. Many different types of games—sci-fi, historical, fantasy, political, strategy, board, and others—are played on the message boards and in email. The PBM and Strategy Messaging Board has posts discussing the rules, scenarios, and the forming of matches, as well as postings of actual turns. Also included is some collaborative fiction based on the games.

The File Library holds rules for PBM play for various games,

maps, character generators, and more. Real-time gaming and out-of-game discussion takes place in the Conference Hall. Among the more popular of the hundreds of games played by mail here (there may be any number of matches or tournaments going on for a particular game): *VGA Planets, Axis and Allies, Diplomacy,* and *Suzerainty.* Expect some of this forum's energy to transfer into the Usenet newsgroups now that they are available to AOL users. ✓**AMERICA ONLINE**→ *keyword* pbm

PBM Archives General play-by-mail information with subdirectories of rules and related material for individual games. Download the huge PBM List for info on commercial and non commercial games, including descriptions, costs, and addresses. The PBM FAQ and back issues of the PBeM

> "Every message that's ever been posted to the play-by-mail board is available for browsing—making the GEnie PBM board, one of the single best Net sources for brushing up on the phenomenon's explosive development."

zine, as well as the rules for games such as *Arena*, *Atlantis*, *Galaxy*, and the *Republic of Rome*, are also stored here. ✓**INTERNET** ...→*ftp* ftp. erg.sri.com→anonymous→<your email address>→/pub/pbm ...→ *ftp* ftp.cp.tn.tudelft.nl→anonymous→ <your email address>→/pub/pbm

PBM WWW Home Page Offers links to the the PBM FAQ, the PBeM fanzine, the PBM FTP site, and a list of PBM and PBeM games. ✓**INTERNET**→*www* ftp://ftp. erg.sri.com/pub/pbm/pbm.html

Play-By-Mail Games As with all GEnie discussion groups, every message that's ever been posted to the play-by-mail board is available for browsing—making the GEnie PBM board by default, one of the single best Net sources for brushing up on the phenomenon's explosive development. Oh, yeah, it's also a great place to find a game to join. *Diplomacy*, the king of PBM gaming, even has its own separate discussion group in the Games RoundTable. The library carries introductory and instructional files for specific play-by-mail games as well as maps and utilities. ✓**GENIE** ...→*keyword* scorpia→ Games Bulletin Board→set 19 (for messages) ...→*keyword* scorpia→ Gamers Libraries→Set Software Library→Play-By-Mail Games (for files)

Play-By-Mail Games Forum For discussion and game playing (via message boards) in a number of categories: science fiction, roleplaying, fantasy, *Diplomacy*, board war games, and others. The library has player lists, character generators, rule variants for *Diplomacy*, uploaded turns, and results of games. ✓**COMPUSERVE**→*go* pbm-games

rec.games.pbm (ng) Searching for a PBeM game? How about *Monster Island* or *Atlantis*? The newsgroup is full of players and PBM businesses looking for people to join new or ongoing games. Both email and postal-mail games are covered. Players are usually more than willing to offer hints or explain the history of their favorite game. The FAQ provides an overview of the PBeM scene. ✓**USENET** *FAQ:* ✓**INTERNET** ...→*ftp* ftp.erg.sri.com→anonymous→<your email address>→/pub/pbm→rec_ games_pbm.faq.Z ...→*ftp* ftp.uu. net→anonymous→<your email address>→/usenet/news.answers/ games→play-by-mail.Z

Companies

Adventures by Mail A play-by-mail company offering two games to play via AOL: *Quest* and *Monster Island*. (See the Fantasy section for specific game descriptions.) Takes the game-master drudgery out of organizing and processing games—for a fee. ✓**AMERICA ON-LINE**→*keyword* pbm→Adventures By Mail ✓**INTERNET**→*email* bob@abm. com ✉ *Write for info*

Gamer's Den This for-profit company organizes and processes PBeM games like *VGA Planets*. Think of it as a kind of gamers' dating service. ✓**INTERNET** ...→ *email* info@den.com ✉ *Email for automated info* ...→*email* support @den.com ✉ *Write for help and support*

PBeM Server

Richard's PBeM Server Moderates play-by-email strategy games. The server is fairly new and games are added periodically. Send for the instructions and a list of the games. *Info:* ✓**INTERNET**→ *email* pbmserv@netcom.com ✉ *Type in subject line:* help

Gaming hubs

Welcome to gaming central! Need a video-game spoiler, quick trivia fix, or, perhaps, "something different" in your day-to-day gaming life? Stop by the hubs of gaming activity on the Net—from Prodigy's **Game Center** to the Internet's **Games and Recreation Web** Site. Don't expect them to be comprehensive. Do expect them to offer easy access to Net games you didn't even know existed. The more general gaming talk on the Internet's **Games-L** mailing list may be "the place" for referrals to more specific discussion boards or may be—in their all-encompassing, no-game-too-old-or-insignificant coverage—just what you're looking for.

On the Net

Across the board

COMMA Fun and Games The page features direct links to the sliding-tile puzzle games, *Hangman*, solutions to the *Lemmings II*, the Videogame Database Home Page, and the *Crossfire Page*. ✓**INTERNET**→*www* http://www.cm.cf.ac.uk/Fun/

Entertainment & Games Connections to adventure games, board and logic games, word games, trivia games, and more.

Screenshot from Prodigy's Game Center.

✓**DELPHI**→*go* ent

The Entertainment Center To play or watch graphical-interface games *StarSprint* (space combat), *backgammon*, *chess*, and *checkers*. ✓**COMPUSERVE**→*go* ecenter *Interface:* ✓**COMPUSERVE**→*go* ecenter→ Download Games **Requirements:** *DOS and EGA graphics or better to play or watch games in the center*

Game Center Hosted by the editors at *Computer Gaming World*, the Game Center is the top-level menu for all of Prodigy's game-related activities. Features five daily news items from *CGW*, new game hints each month, and a weekly poll about your favorite games. ✓**PRODIGY**→*jump* game center

Game Room A main menu for GEnie gaming. If you don't know what you wanna play, start here. There are links to the Games RoundTable, the Multi-Player Games menu (featuring games like *Cyberstrike*, *Air Warrior*, and *Hundred Years War*), the Multi-Player Games RoundTable, Computer Game Design RoundTable, TSR Online RoundTable, a menu of Classic Games (adventure and pop-culture trivia), and the Software Games Club (a vendor of shareware and commercial games

to download). ✓**GENIE**→*keyword* games

The Gamers' Forum Messages, files, and conferences for computer gaming. Find tips, hints, reviews, and instructions from other players. The hottest topics in the message boards are usually Adventure Games (*7th Guest* and *King's Quest*, especially), Action Games (and *Doom* in particular), and Computer RPG's (especially *Arena* and *Ultima 8*). Popular files for downloading are new *Doom* levels and WAD files, available in the Action Game Aids section of the Library. ✓**COMPUSERVE**→*go* gamers

The Games and Recreation Web Site This site not only offers links to *backgammon*, *bridge*, and *Go* servers, but also guides to *Othello*, *Sokoban* info, links to other Web gaming pages (*Play by Mail*, *Bolo*, *Paradise Netrek*, *Empire*, *XPilot* and *Crossfire*), and a direct connection to the *chess* archives. New to Net gaming? Start here. ✓**INTERNET**→*www* http://www.cis.ufl.edu/~thoth/library/recreation.html

Games BB Discuss all manner of games—modem-to-modem, video games, arcade games, paper RPGs, CD-ROM games, *Dungeons & Dragons*, fantasy, text adventures, chess, and *Star Trek, Star Trek, Star Trek*. ✓**PRODIGY**→*jump* games bb

GameSIG For general game talk or for discussion and files related to role-playing games, computer RPGs, message-based RPGs, adventure games, *Diplomacy*, *Quest*, *Stellar Conquest*, and more. The GameSIG also has adventure-game hints (e.g., *Bard's Tale I* and *II*, *Hitchhiker's Guide to the Galaxy*, *Leather Goddesses of Phobos*, *Lurking Horror*, etc.), and a conference area for live chat and live gaming. To try a few simple, interactive text adventures, select the Mini-Adventures choice, but be sure to have a coin or a pair of dice on hand; outcomes in the Mini-Adventures are often determined by a flip or a roll. ✓**DELPHI**→*go* gro gam

---

Games RoundTable Hosted by Scorpia, GEnie's game maven, the Games RT hosts a forum and databases for players of computer games of any sort: adventure, action/arcade, sports, strategy/war, RPG, and board games. In addition, the forum hosts discussion categories like play-by-mail (snail or email), *Diplomacy*, game magazines and newsletters, message-based role-playing, as well as support categories from a number of game publishers (e.g., MicroProse, Spectrum Holobyte, New World Computing, and Avalon Hill). The RT's database has shareware, patches, hints, cheats, and editing programs for games in all categories; a category just for *Doom*, with new levels and new sounds; DMSmiley.zip, a program that attaches yellow smiley buttons to the chests of *Doom* bad guys. ✓**GENIE**→*keyword* scorpia

Gaming Information Exchange A forum for the general discussion of gaming, game philosophies, rule variations, and player experiences (what works, what doesn't). Includes a calendar of upcoming game conventions; excerpts from the Internet's Live-Action Role-Playing (LARP) list; a message board for comments, opinions, speculations, and questions; another message board for game-industry news and rumors; a Gamer's Registry, allowing you to search by state or game system; a library of downloadable files for gamers' reference and enjoyment

---

> **"Get the program that attaches smileys to the chest of *Doom* bad guys."**

(including an article by a Methodist minister on the role of religion in *AD&D*); and an entire section of hints and tips for online live and message-based role-playing and game mastering. ✓**AMERICA ONLINE**→*keyword* gix

Online Gaming Forums The top menu for most of AOL's game-related message boards, libraries, conferences, professional-game-designer areas, and a few role-playing and play-by-mail games. Includes places to ask general questions, issue gaming challenges, and go to other gaming areas on AOL. ✓**AMERICA ONLINE**→*keyword* ogf

---

Zarf's List of Interactive Games on the Web A page full of games—several puzzles and *Mad Lib* games, a pop culture scavenger hunt, *Othello*, tic tac toe, and more—that are played via the Web. ✓**INTERNET**→*www* http://www.cs.cmu.edu:8001/afs/cs.cmu.edu/user/zarf/www/games.html

Big boards

Games Plus (bbs) Play the big-name BBS games like *Trade Wars 2002* and *Forbidden Lands* or the classics like *Yahtzee* and *Sea Battle*. All games, and there are dozens, come with instructions. For most of them, the player has the option to play head-to-head with another player or to challenge the computer. ☎→*dial* 608-822-2000

Steve Jackson's Board/The Il-

---

luminati Online (bbs) Game designer Steve Jackson is a legend in the gaming world, and if you're looking for serious game discussions, his board offers some of the best out there—particularly for role-players. Conferences range from FASA's *BattleTech* to Steve Jackson's *GURPs* to White Wolf's *Werewolf: The Apocalypse*. The dial-up BBS offers game play as well. ☎→*dial* 512-448-8950 ✓**INTERNET**→*telnet* io.com→new

Game talk

The Best game would have.... (echo) Read and post messages about what online players want in their "perfect game." ✓**WWIVNET**

Gamer's Consortium (echo) Gather here with other gamers. ✓**WWIVNET**

GAMES! (echo) Discuss anything and everything about computer games. Includes Nintendo, SuperNES, Sega, Atari, Gameboy, IBM PC, and Mac games. ✓**WWIVNET**

Games (echo) Discuss all types of computer games, but particularly those played on BBSs. ✓**SMARTNET**

GAMES (echo) Discuss, boost, bash: commercial, shareware, video and computer games, game doors, and game boards. ✓**RELAYNET**

Games: Help & Hints (echo) Join a general forum to discuss all kinds of games: online, computer, and video. ✓**ICENET**

Games-L (ml/ng) As broad a coverage of gaming topics as you're likely to find on the Net—everything from *Zork* to head-to-head *Doom* competition on the Internet. ✓**INTERNET**→*email* listserv@

brown.brown.edu ✍ *Type in subject line:* subscribe games-l ✓**USENET**→ bit.listserv.games-l

GamesWorkshop (echo) Advice on all kinds of games. ✓**WWIVNET**

On-Line Game Chat (echo) Talk about your favorite online games. ✓**WWIVNET**

Online Game Discussion (echo) Meet other online game players, and find out who's playing what, where, and why. ✓**ICENET**

rec.games.misc (ng) If the game you're interested in doesn't have a newsgroup and you don't mind the baggage carried over from other gaming newsgroups (lots of FAQs), start a discussion here. ✓**USENET**

Multiplayer gaming

Multi-Player Games A menu to take you to the gaming powerhouses on GEnie—the multiplayer games. Featured games include the award-winning *Cyberstrike*, *Air Warrior*, *Hundred Years War*, *Dragon's Gate*, *Federation II*, *Galaxy I*, *GemStone III*, *Multi-Player BattleTech*, *NTN Trivia*, *Orb Wars*, *QB1*, *RSCards*, *Stellar Emperor*, *Stellar Warrior*, and *Island of Kesmai*. ✓**GENIE**→*keyword* mpgames

Multi-Player Games Forum Looking for help with *Island of Kesmai* or *MegaWars*? Fellow gamers, designers, and CompuServe staffers are here to share their gaming secrets. There are messages and files related to *MegaWars I*, *MegaWars III*, *Island of Kesmai*, *British Legends*, *You Guessed It*, *Sniper*, and the Entertainment Center. ✓**COMPUSERVE**→*go* mpgames

Multiplayer Games Round-Table Support, discussion, and files related to GEnie's multiplayer games: *Cyberstrike*, *Air Warrior*, *Hundred Years War*, etc. ✓**GENIE**→*keyword* mpgrt

News & reviews

Computer Game Review (echo) Check out what others think about the latest computer game releases. Includes playing hints. ✓**WWIVNET**

Computer Game Review + Hints HQ (echo) Add to the review collection. ✓**ICENET**

The Electronic Gamer A huge archive of computer-game walkthroughs, ranging from *BattleTech* to *Pacman* to *Zork*. ✓**COMPUSERVE** →*go* teg

The Game Hints and Cheat Hotline (echo) Learn the cheats on your favorite games. ✓**ICENET**

Game Review (echo) Read or post about your favorite games and rip apart the ones you hate. ✓**WWIVNET**

> "Game designer Steve Jackson is a legend in the gaming world, and if you're looking for serious game discussions, his board offers some of the best out there."

Games FAQs and Things A burgeoning Web site with links to game-related Usenet FAQs, independent FAQs, home pages (*Battle*, *Crossfire*, etc.), and FTP sites. ✓**INTERNET**→*www* http://wcl-rs. bham.ac.uk/~djh/index.html

Inside Games Update Back issues of this multi-platform, bi-weekly gaming newsletter. ✓**AMERICA ONLINE**→*keyword* pc games→ Browse Individual Libraries→Other →Game Hints & Fixes

Intelligent Gamer (j) Aren't we all! Useful information, spanning video games from closet-size coin-ops to handheld battery-ops. Published as a DOS program. ✓**INTERNET**→*ftp* busop.cit.wayne.edu→ anonymous→<your email address> →/pub/pselect/intgmr ✓**COMPUSERVE**→*go* gamers→Libraries→ Game Magazines

Newsletters and Magazines Back issues of the *Games Round-Table Newsletter* and other gaming newsletters and magazines. ✓**GENIE** →*keyword* scorpia→Gamers Libraries→Set Software Library→All Libraries→*Search by search string:* newsletter *or* magazine

Share & Software

Computers & Software Talk computer games. Most of the chatter centers on sports sims and fantasy-league software, although there are a few silicon-based chess- and war-gaming discussions going on as well. ✓**USA TODAY INFORMATION CENTER**→*go* forum→Gamer Forum→Computers & Software

Shareware Gaming (echo) Discuss your favorite shareware games with other gamers and find out what's worth trying or buying. ✓**ICENET**

Game design & co.'s

The Net hums with peer support for new and expert game creators and, increasingly,

product support from game publishers. Free-speech cyber-victor Steve Jackson (io.games.design) and Avalon Hill, creators of *Diplomacy*, both maintain an exemplary online presence. Maybe playing all those games will inspire you to write your own game, as Richard Garriott (photo) did.

On the Net

Design

Computer Game Designers Forum Discuss the design and development of computer games on the message board. Also includes a small library of downloadable files related to the creation and enhancement of computer games. ✓**AMERICA ONLINE**→*keyword* game design

Computer Games Design RoundTable What's the best way to get started as a game designer? What to do about piracy? These are some of the issues that get discussed in the CGDRT. It's also the national communications center for members of the *Journal of Computer Game Design*. On the Bulletin Board, designers discuss programming techniques, game design theory, game genres, computer technology, and the politics of "da bizness." In the Software Libraries, you'll find archives of important board posts and utilities useful to designers, including sound and graphics editors. ✓**GE-**

Game designer Richard Garriott with his game—from wuarchive.wustl.edu.

NIE→*keyword* cgd

GAME DESIGN (echo) Discuss game design. ✓**RELAYNET**

Game Design Check here for MIDI music, a computer artist who can help you complete your great shareware idea, or the ins and outs of hex files. ✓**PRODIGY**→*jump* games bb→Choose a Topic →Game Design

Game Designers Forum On the Game Design Messaging board, professionals discuss game-design mechanics for role-playing, board games, and other non computer games. The Game Design File Exchange and Archive holds useful downloadable files for game designers', including information and bylaws about the Independent Game Designers' Association. ✓**AMERICA ONLINE**→*keyword* game design

io.games.design Dedicated to the creators of both role-playing and board games. Various designers from Steve Jackson Games,

FASA, and other gaming companies are here to talk about the philosophy of game design, the best sources for components (dice, boards, etc.), and the legalities of making and selling your own games. If you want to create your own game, come here and find out how! ☎→*dial* 512-448-8950→ <your login>→<your password>→ <choose a newsreader like "tin">→ io.games.design ✓**INTERNET**→*telnet* illuminati.io.com→<your login>→ <your password>→<select a newsgroup reader like "tin">→io.games. design
Requirements: *Must have an account.*

rec.games.design (ng) A crowded place. Discussions about computer games, RPG games, board games, and what-have-you are all housed under this one roof. ✓**USENET** *FAQ:* ✓**INTERNET**→*ftp* ftp.uu.net→anonymous→<your email address>→/usenet/news. answers/games→design-FAQ.Z

rec.games.programmer (ng) The group is specifically about adventure-game programming, says the newsgroup description header, but odds are that if you've got a game in the works, adventure or not, and you've got a question, this is the place to go. ✓**USENET** *FAQ:* ✓**INTERNET**→*ftp* rtfm.mit.edu→ anonymous→<your email address> →/pub/usenet-by-hierarchy/rec/ games/programmer→FAQ:_3-D_Information_for_the_Programmer

V_RPG (echo) Designers discuss role-playing games and their designs. ✓**FIDONET**

Companies

GameBase Product and Company Database
Submit reviews of game products, find profiles of game companies, get news about upcoming and recent releases, and read general overviews of popular games and related materials. ✓**AMERICA ONLINE**→*keyword* game-base

Commands
- To find articles within GameBase, select: Search GameBase

Game Company Support
Leave messages for and read posts from editors of game-industry and gamer-oriented magazines and newsletters in the Publications choice; download game rules, updates of game manuals, character sheets, newsletters, and journals in the GCS File Library; retrieve company catalogs from the GCS Catalogs and Boards; and write to representatives of several game companies (e.g., Atlas Games, FASA Corporation, Mayfair Games, Ragnarok Enterprises, White Wolf Game Studio, and World Building Magazine) in the Gaming Support Messaging area for access to the Gaming Playtest Center, where these companies run play tests of their still-unreleased products. ✓**AMERICA ONLINE** →*keyword* gcs

---

Game Publishers
Use these bulletin-board categories and software libraries to find support, hints, files, and upgrades from commercial game-software publishers. Included in the mix are FASA, Bethesda Softworks, MicroProse, Interplay, id Software, Maxis, Origin Systems, West End Games, Spectrum HoloByte, GDW, Avalon Hill, Sierra On-Line/Dynamix, SSI, LucasArts, Sir-Tech, New World Computing, Omnitrend, Virgin Games/Westwood

Studios, Hero Games/Hero Software, and White Wolf Games. ✓**GENIE**→*keyword* scorpia→Games Bulletin Board *or* Gamers Libraries

---

Game Publishers A
Topics in both the Messages and Libraries include support, discussion, files, patches, and upgrades for the following game publishers: Accolade, Bethesda Softworks, Cyberdreams, Electronic Arts, LucasArts Entertainment, Merit Software, Origin, Sierra On-Line, Strategic Simulations, Inc., SubLogic, and Three-Sixty Pacific. ✓**COMPUSERVE**→*go* gamapub

---

Game Publishers B
Support, discussion, files, and more for the following game publishers: Access, Activision/Infocom, Disney/Buena Vista, GameTek, Impressions, Interplay, Konami/Ultra, MacPlay, Mallard, Maxis, MicroProse, Sir-Tech Software, Spectrum Holo-Byte, and Westwood Studios. ✓**COMPUSERVE**→*go* gambpub

---

Game Publishers C
Still more discussion, help, upgrades, scenarios, and the like for the following game publishers: Avalon Hill, Cactus Development, Changeling Software, Diamond Dreams, Dynamix, Humongous Entertainment, Inline Software, Intergalactic Development, Legend Entertainment, Masque Publishing, Mindcraft, Omnitrend, Papyrus Software, Quantum Quality Productions, and Tsunami Media. ✓**COMPUSERVE**→*go* gamcpub

---

Game Publishers D
Even more game company-related talk, hints, utilities, and patches. Includes the following companies: Crystal Dynamics, New World Computing, Software Sorcery, Strategic Studies Group, ThrustMaster, and Trilobyte Software. ✓**COMPUSERVE** →*go* gamdpub

Email & BBS support

Access Software
✓**INTERNET**→ *email* linkspro_1@aol.com ✍ *Email with general correspondence*

Accolade
(bbs) ☎→*dial* 408-296-8800 ✓**INTERNET** ...→*email* accolade@aol.com ✍ *Email with general correspondence* ...→*email* 76004.2132@compuserve.com ✍ *Email with general correspondence*

Activision
✓**INTERNET**→*email* support@activision.com ✍ *Email with general correspondence*

Apogee
(bbs) ☎→*dial* 508-368-4137/508-365-2359/508-368-7036 ✓**INTERNET**→*email* apogee@ delphi.com ✍ *Email with general correspondence*

Avalon Hill
✓**INTERNET** ...→*email* ahgames2@aol.com ✍ *Email with general correspondence* ...→*email* 72662.1207@compuserve ✍ *Email with general correspondence* ...→ *email* avalon.hill@genie.geis.com ✍ *Email with general correspondence*

Bethesda Softworks
(bbs) ☎→*dial* 301-990-7552 ✓**INTERNET** ...→*email* bethesda01@aol.com ✍ *Email with general correspondence* ...→*email* 71333.234@compuserve. com ✍ *Email with general correspondence*

Broderbund
(bbs) ☎→*dial* 415-883-5889

Disney Software
(bbs) ☎→*dial* 818-567-4027 ✓**INTERNET** ...→ *email* disneysoft@aol.com ✍ *Email with general correspondence* ...→ *email* 71333.14@compuserve.com ✍ *Email with general correspondence* ...→*email* disneysoft@delphi. com ✍ *Email with general correspondence* ...→*email* jvnx63a@ prodigy.com ✍ *Email with general*

correspondence

Dragon's Eye Productions
✓**INTERNET**→*email* cat@bga.com ✍
Email with general correspondence

Dynamix (bbs) ☎→*dial* 209-683-4463 ✓**INTERNET**→*email* sierras @aol.com ✍ *Email with general correspondence*

Epic MegaGames (bbs) ☎→*dial* 414-789-4360 ✓**INTERNET** →*email* 70007.1631@compuserve. com ✍ *Email with general correspondence*

id Software (bbs) ☎→*dial* 508-365-2359/508-368-4137 ✓**INTER-NET**→*email* help@idsoftware.com ✍ *Email with general correspondence*

Intergalactic Development, Inc. ✓**INTERNET**→*email* 76356. 2172@compuserve.com ✍ *Email with general correspondence*

Interplay Productions (bbs) ☎→*dial* 714-252-2822 ✓**INTER-NET**→*email* 76702.1342@compu serve.com ✍ *Email with general correspondence*

Looking Glass Technologies, Inc. ✓**INTERNET**→*email* nedl@lglass. mhs.compuserve.com ✍ *Email with general correspondence*

LucasArts (bbs) ☎→*dial* 415-257-3070

Maxis (bbs) ☎→*dial* 510-254-3869 ✓**INTERNET**→*email* support@ maxis.com ✍ *Email with general correspondence*

Microprose (bbs) ☎→*dial* 410-785-1841 ✓**INTERNET** ...→*email* 76004.2223@compuserve.com ✍ *Email with general correspondence* ...→*email* microprose@genie.geis. com ✍ *Email with general corre-*

spondence ...→*email* xhfk15d@ prodigy.com ✍ *Email with general correspondence*

Papyrus Design Group (bbs) ☎→*dial* 617-576-7472 ✓**INTERNET** ...→*email* 72662.2150@compu serve.com ✍ *Email with general correspondence* ...→*email* papyrus @world.std.com ✍ *Email with general correspondence*

Quantum Quality Produc-tions ✓**INTERNET** ...→*email* 75300. 3223@compuserve.com ✍ *Email with general correspondence* ...→*email* qqp@delphi.com ✍ *Email with general correspondence*

Shadowsoft Inc. ✓**INTERNET**→ *email* 76056.1537@compuserve. com ✍ *Email with general correspondence*

Silicon Knights ✓**INTERNET**→ *email* denis@spartan.ac.BrockU.CA ✍ *Email with general correspondence*

Sir-Tech ✓**INTERNET** ...→*email* 76711.33@compuserve.com ✍ *Email with general correspondence* ...→*email* sirtech@northnet.org ✍ *Email with general correspondence*

Spectrum HoloByte (bbs) ☎→*dial* 510-522-8909 ✓**INTERNET** ...→*email* sholobyte@aol.com ✍ *Email with general correspondence* ...→*email* 76004.2144@compu serve.com ...→*email* holobyte@ genie.geis.com ✍ *Email with general correspondence* ...→*email* tknj33a@prodigy.com ✍ *Email with general correspondence*

Strategic Simulations, Inc. (bbs) ☎→*dial* 408-739-6137/408-739-6623 ✓**INTERNET** ...→*email* stratsim@aol.com ✍ *Email with general correspondence* ...→*email* 76711.250@compuserve.com ✍ *Email with general correspondence*

Three-Sixty Pacific ✓**INTERNET** ...→*email* threesixty@aol.com ✍ *Email with general correspondence* ...→*email* 76711.240@compuserve. com ✍ *Email with general correspondence*

Appendices

Netted!

A selection of the hottest and most addictive game sites in Cyberspace

Absolutely do not miss

Cardiff's Video Game Database Browser ✓INTERNET→*www* http://www.cm.cf.ac.uk/Games/

The Internet Chess Server (ICS) ✓INTERNET→*telnet* ics.uoknor. edu 5000→<your handle>

LambdaMOO ✓INTERNET→*telnet* lambda.parc.xerox.com 8888→ help

Netrek Home Pages ✓INTERNET ...→*www* http://obsidian.math.ari zona.edu:8080/netrek.html ...→ *www* http://www.cs.cmu.edu: 8001/afs/cs/user/jch/netrek/ README.html ...→ *www* http:// www.cis.ufl.edu:80/~thoth/par adise/ (for Paradise Netrek)

Shadow of Yserbius ✓THE IMAGINATION NETWORK→*select* Me-dievaLand

Best shoot-'em-up

Air Warrior ✓GENIE→*keyword* air

CyberStrike ✓GENIE→*keyword* cyberstrike

Stellar Conquest ✓DELPHI→*go* gro gam

Best sports simulation

Baseball Manager ✓PRODIGY →*jump* bbm $

Best game FAQ

"Official Doom FAQ" ✓INTER-NET ...→*ftp* ap641@cleveland. freenet.edu→anonymous→<your email address> ✍ *Type in subject line:* DOOM FAQ Request ...→*ftp* ftp.uwp.edu→anonymous→<your email address>→/pub/msdos/ games/id/home-brew/doom

Best place to meet head-to-head

Modem-to-Modem Gaming Lobby ✓COMPUSERVE→*go* mtmlob-by

Best cheat sites

Andy Eddy (GamePro Maga-zine) FTP Site for Arcade and Videogame FAQs ✓INTERNET→ *ftp* ftp.netcom.com→anonymous→ <your email address>→/pub/ vidgames/faqs

Game Genie Archive ✓INTER-NET→*ftp* ftp.netcom.com→anony-mous→<your email address>→ /pub/vidgames/gamegenie

Best gaming zine

Game Bytes (j) ✓INTERNET ...→ *gopher* gopher.cic.net→Electronic Serials→Alphabetic List→G→Game Bytes ✓COMPUSERVE→*go* gamers →Libraries→Game Magazines ✓AMERICA ONLINE→*keyword* pc games→Software Library→*Search by keyword:* gamebyte

Best place to flirt

Federation II ✓GENIE→*keyword* fed

FurryMUCK ✓INTERNET→*telnet* sncils.snc.edu 8888→connect guest guest

Kender's Kove ✓INTERNET→*tel-net* harvey.esu.edu 6715→<your character's name>→<y or n>→ <your password>→<your pass-word>

You Guessed It ✓COMPUSERVE →*go* ygi

Best MUD combat

Btech 3056 ✓INTERNET→*telnet* mccool.cbi.msstate.edu 3056→ create <your character> <pass-word>

Genocide ✓**INTERNET**→*telnet* pip. shsu.edu 2222→<your character's name>→<y or n>→<your password>→<your password>

Most "serious" game

TNP (The Next President) ✓**PRODIGY**→*jump* games bb→Bulletin Board→Prodigy Games topic →TNP

Toughest word game

sKrAmBlE ✓**AMERICA ONLINE**→ *keyword* center stage

Games to crash the office network

Bolo ✓**INTERNET** …→*ftp* fpm. uchicago.edu→anonymous→<your email address>→Bolo992package. sit.hqx ✓**AMERICA ONLINE**→*keyword* mgm→Software Libraries→*Search by keyword:* bolo v.0.99.2 ✓**COMPUSERVE**→*go* mac fun→Libraries→ *Search by file name:* BOLO.CPT

Doom ✓**INTERNET** …→*ftp* infant2. sphs.indiana.edu→anonymous→ <your email address>→/pub/doom

Strongest computer opponent

Crab ✓**INTERNET**→*ftp* plaza.aar net.edu.au→anonymous→<your email address>→/micros/mac/ info-mac/game→crab.hqx

Better than Alex and Vanna

#jeopardy ✓**INTERNET**→*irc* /chan nel #jeopardy

Wheel of Fortune ✓CHECK YOUR LOCAL BULLETIN BOARD SYSTEM FOR A VARIATION OF THIS GAME

The raunchiest

Studs! ✓CHECK LOCAL BULLETIN

BOARD SYSTEMS FOR THIS OR SIMILAR GAMES ☎→*dial* 717-325-9481

Hottest game flame wars

rec.games.mud.diku (ng) ✓**USENET**

rec.games.video.advocacy (ng) ✓**USENET**

The most exclusive games

GarouMUSH ✓**INTERNET**→*telnet* party.apple.com 7000→connect guest guest

MicroMUSE (Cyberion City) ✓**INTERNET**→*telnet* chezmoto.ai.mit. edu 4201

The quietest

Zen MOO ✓**INTERNET**→*telnet* cheshire.oxy.edu 7777→create <your meditation name>→<your meditation password>

The most crowded

LambdaMOO ✓**INTERNET**→*telnet* lambda.parc.xerox.com 8888→ help

You saw the movie, now play the game

Star Wars ✓**INTERNET**→*telnet* techno.stanford.edu 4402→connect guest

Ten Forward Lounge *Star Trek.* ✓**AMERICA ONLINE**→*keyword* pc→ Member Rooms→Ten Forward Lounge

ToonMUSH II *Who Framed Roger Rabbit?* ✓**INTERNET**→*telnet* merlin. mit.edu 1941→connect guest guest

Tron ✓**INTERNET**→*telnet* 141.241.84. 65 4000→guest→[return]

You played the game, now read the book

Discworld Terry Pratchett's *Discworld* series. ✓**INTERNET**→*telnet* mud.compulink.co.uk 4242→<your character's name>→<y or n>→ <your password>→<your password>→<male or female>→[return]

DuneMUSH Frank Herbert's *Dune* series. ✓**INTERNET**→*telnet* mellers1.psych.berkeley.edu 4201→ connect guest guest

MUME IV J. R. R. Tolkien's *Lord of the Rings.* ✓**INTERNET**→*telnet* 128.178.77.5 4242→<your character's name>→<y or n>→<your password>→<your password>→<f or m>→<your race>→<your class>→ <your alignment>

NarniaMush C. S. Lewis's *Narnia Chronicles.* ✓**INTERNET**→*telnet* argo.unm.edu 6250→connect Guest Guest

PernMUSH Ann McCaffrey's *Dragonriders of Pern.* ✓**INTERNET**→ *telnet* cesium.clock.org 4201→ create <your character's name> <your password>

Realms of the Dragon (RotD) Robert Jordan's *Wheel of Time* series. ✓**INTERNET**→*telnet* 141.215.69.7 3000→guest

Super shareware sites

Aminet Gaming Archive Especially *Air Traffic Controller, Amigoids, AmyChess, Blaster, Cross Circuit,* and *Fighting Warriors.* ✓**INTERNET** …→*ftp* wuarchive. wustl.edu→anonymous→<your email address>→/systems/amiga/ aminet/game

Apple][(8-bit) Games Archives Especially the *EAMON*

text adventures, the *Defender* clone, *Wheel of Fortune*, *Star Trek TNG*, and the *Ultima* clone. ✓**INTERNET** …→*ftp* apple2.archive. umich.edu→anonymous→<your email address>→/archive/apple2/ 8bit/games

Atari Gaming Archive Especially *Arena Earth*, *Bartman*, *Berserk!*, *Bugs*, *Caves of Madness*, *Centipede* (better than the arcade version!), *Moria*, *Tetris*, and *Battle*. ✓**INTERNET**→*ftp* atari.archive. umich.edu→anonymous→<your email address>→/atari/Games

Monster Macintosh Gaming Archives Especially *Bolo*, *Bouncing Balls*, *Curse of Vengeance*, *Daleks*, *Donkey Kong*, *Maelstrom*, *Oids*, and *Oxyd*. ✓**INTERNET**→*ftp* mac.archive.umich.edu→anonymous→<your email address>→ /mac/game

---

PC Games FTP Sites Especially *Doom*, the *Commander Keen* games, *Castle Wolfenstein 3D*, *Solar Hockey League*, *Epic Pinball*, and *Xargon*. ✓**INTERNET** …→*ftp* ftp.uml.edu→anonymous→<your email address>→/msdos/Games …→*ftp* msdos.archive.umich.edu →anonymous→<your email address>→/msdos/games

Tandy Games Especially *Beer*, *Control of the Anthill*, *Escape from Mars*, *Lunar Lander*, *Secret Agent*, *Sopwith*, *Turbo*, and *Solitair*. ✓**GENIE**→*keyword* tandy→Tandy Software Libraries→Set Software Library→ALL Libraries→*Search by search string:* game

Unix Games Especially *Netrek*, *Empire*, *BlastApp*, *CoreWars*, *XPilot*, and *Star Castle*. ✓**GENIE**→*keyword* unix→UNIX Software Libraries→Set Software Library→ALL Libraries →*Search by search string:* game

---

The ultimate treasure hunt

Gemstone III Annual treasure hunts—for real gems! ✓**GENIE**→ *keyword* gemstone

Programmers Award

Jim Knutson (IHHD)

Kevin Smith and Scott Silvey (Netrek)

Richard Bartle and Roy Trubshaw (the first MUD)

Stuart Cheshire (Bolo)

The more things change…

Tic Tac Toe ✓**INTERNET**→*www* http://www.bu.edu/Games/tictac toe

WWW Hangman ✓**INTERNET**→ *www* http://www.cm.cf.ac.uk/ht bin/RobH/hangman?go

Game magazines' Deep Throat

rec.games.video.arcade (ng) ✓**USENET**

The most game hype

News on major Vid game systems (echo) ✓**ICENET**

The online classic

Adventure Download the game. ✓**INTERNET** …→*ftp* atari.archive. umich.edu→anonymous→<your email address>→/atari/Games→ adventr.arc (for Atari) …→*ftp* risc. ua.edu→anonymous→<your email address>→/pub/games/colossal→ colossal.zip (for DOS)

Classic Adventure Play it online. ✓**COMPUSERVE**→*go* gam-200

✓**DELPHI**→*go* ent adv adv ✓**GENIE**→ *keyword* adventure

Longest running game discussion

Cube Lovers (ml) ✓**INTERNET**→ *email* cube-lovers-request@life.ai. mit.edu ✍ *Write a request*

Longest running online game

Hundred Years War ✓**GENIE**→ *keyword* hyw

Best name for an online team

L.A. Will Riot for Food (Intercollegiate Netrek League) ✓**INTERNET**→*ftp* soda.berkeley.edu →anonymous→<your email address>→/pub/netrek/INL

Most helpful MUD administrator

Sketch the Cow from TinyTIM ✓**INTERNET**→*telnet* yay.tim.org 5440→create <your character's name>→<your password>

You must be joking!

E-Wrestling WWW Site ✓**INTERNET**→*www* http://www.cgd. ucar.edu/cas/nexus/ewr

Guess the Disease ✓**INTERNET** →*www* http://www.reed.edu/cgi-bin/karl-animal?intro

Slot Machines ✓**AMERICA ONLINE** →*keyword* casino→Casino Lounge →Play a Game→Play Casino Slot Machines

Elizabeth's picks: best children's games

Thinker ✓**PRODIGY**→*jump* thinker

Where in the World is Carmen Sandiego? ✓PRODIGY→ *jump* carmen

"The DAMNED" ✓INTERNET→*telnet* janus.library.cmu.edu 6250→ connect guest guest

Nathaniel's Top 3

CyberStrike ✓GENIE→*keyword* cyberstrike

Diplomacy Home Page ✓INTERNET→*www* http://www.hmc.edu/~irilyth/diplomacy/index.html

Virtua Fighters Especially the Virtua Fighter FAQ (to kick butt at the arcade). ✓INTERNET→*ftp* ftp.netcom.com→anonymous→<your email address>→/pub/vidgames/faqs

---

Derek's moral ruin

Free-Form Gaming Forum Especially The Red Dragon Inn. ✓AMERICA ONLINE→*keyword* ffgf

Poker Showdown ✓DELPHI→*go* ent pok

Game boards

by area code

201

Blackstar!
335-6132
Cheers Online
624-1375
Chessboard
605-1292
Deredain's Realm BBS
703-1219
Get A life!
677-3040
Jezebel's Parlour
927-2932
New Jersey Intelligence Agency
669-9857
Remote Host BBS
729-7046
The cave of Wonders
387-0640
The Eagle's Nest
939-2695
The Game's Afoot BBS
487-7556
The Silver Bullet BBS
812-9352
The Starship Enterprise
283-1806

203

Applause BBS
754-9598
Bruce's Bar & Grill
236-3761
Endeavor! BBS
763-0016
GameMasters Refuge
645-0128
HH Info-Net
738-0342
Homebase
668-2343
Joe's Garage
635-6569
Mystic Software Network
536-9549

Our House BBS
599-3970
Shorelines
931-1853
The Candle Light
777-0168
The Conniption Fit BBS
448-6668
The Continuum BBS
759-5853
The Shotgun BBS
969-0825
The Vampire Connection BBS
269-8313
Windsor Manor
688-4973
Wizzard's Cave
284-3374

204

Aerospace
837-3214
Twilight Exchange
878-9614

205

Computer Works
671-0092
Dateline BBS
747-4194
FastBytes BBS
774-9946
Genesis Online
620-4150
Harvey's Home of the Lazy DOG
586-0216
KickAxis BBS
733-0253
Lumby's Palace BBS
520-0041
Mystery Island BBS
926-3943
SFE Systems USA
650-0107

StarBase 12
647-7184
The Crenshaw County BBS
335-3968
The Edge BBS
891-3403
The Southern Alliance
753-6620
VisionQuest BBS
926-6100

206

2001 InfoNeet
524-5638
Big Daddy's
259-0587
Cameron's Railroad
659-2132
Capital City On-Line!
956-1123
Electric Lasagna
867-5299
Fritz's BBS
792-3379
PC Pulse BBS
377-8508
Ski So Soft BBS
459-5094
Techno-Care BBS
459-4703
The Dark Masters' BBS
846-8312
The Gaming Connection
742-4044
The Happy Hunting ground
367-9131
The Pony Express!
367-9131
The Sceptic Tank
754-4878
We Be Games BBS
475-0708

207

Celebration Station
374-5161

Circular Logic BBS
873-4981

Maine Line BBS
499-2999

Schoodic Computer BBS
963-5809

The Plain Brown Wrapper BBS
324-1902

The ScuttleButt E.E.S
363-2660

208

After Hours BBS
345-6121

Idaho Interactive BBS
345-4987

Indigo BBS
734-6592

Lake's Lodge
476-5427

Night Flight
529-4248

V&K After Hours
237-5707

209

Fresno Public Access
277-3008

Shadow Lands BBS
452-1158

The Code-3 BBS
686-3575

The Game Palace
858-4652

The Haunted Castle BBS
826-1900

The Hot Rod Shop VBBS
891-0435

The Tin Continuum
877-4921

The Wizards Palace VBBS
798-2092

Vipers Nest
583-9657

210

Gamer's Edge
623-1516

Gamers Inc
667-9354

Heart of the Hills BBS
257-6290

Neon Jungle
656-0109

Ranger Station
672-2219

Terminus BBS
490-2359

The Games BBS
633-3311

Tri-Com Data Network
725-5398

212

Access New York
580-6473

FPX2
627-0531

Game Line
541-5596

Mindvox
989-1550

213

Southside Info Exchange
778-6450

The Westside
933-4050

214

Black Gold BBS
783-6893

Chess Board
641-1136

Chrysalis
690-9295

DFW Programmer's Exch
398-3112

Hogard Software Solution
641-6292

Interface America
235-4015

Lost In Time
642-6095

Serial Port!
625-4528

THe GaRBaGe DuMP
644-6060

215

Black Magic Kingdom BBS
559-1415

Channel Surfer
257-7888

ClockWork BBS
546-7088

DSC
443-9434

Entertainment Technologies
335-9850

Game Power Headquarters
969-6916

LOGON: Philadelphia
572-8240

Mechanix Choice BBS
887-0171

Middle Earth Online
921-8836

Punch Into The Future BBS
352-0413

The Chatterbox BBS
536-0892

The Computer Shop BBS
395-9823

The Cosmic Forge
926-1213

The Gateway to the End of Time
454-9862

The Hotline BBS
393-8594

The Keep BBS
855-0401

The Legend! BBS
759-2961

The Naked City
535-2135

The Twilight Connection BBS
944-0532

Tradewars 2 BBS
547-5026

Viking Tradewars BBS
332-8514

216

Arcadia BBS
567-9629

Christian Network #1
741-6244

Game Boards

Data Station #1
782-1289
Night Heat BBS
779-7914
Online BBS
949-5581
PC Ohio
381-3320
Rusty & Edies
726-0737
The Arena BBS
673-1950
The Sports Connection
741-4105
Willie's World BBS
322-1095

217

Computer Corner BBS
422-2585
PDC BBS
347-0280
Suburbia BBS
337-6312
The Polish Hideout
857-6370
The Ultimate BBS
792-3663

218

Northern Light BBS
828-9302

219

Crystal CaveModem
778-4281
Dune Master
879-9570
Matabele BBS
662-8035
River Bottom
273-0936
The BoatHouse
223-8879

301

11th Hour BBS
299-3292

Advanced Data Services
695-9116
Altered Reality BBS
431-0239
C'mon Inn BBS
990-7565
Castles gate
490-8679
Infinetwork
498-6183
Kerbside Software
698-0704
LexiCom
983-9856
Moonshadow
630-6948
Pandemonium
371-9105
Sandy's Castle
753-8230
The Gameboard Plus
627-4787
The Ultimate Domain
870-0689
Tim's House of Fun BBS
705-7115

302

Dark Tower
629-4780
Delaware Gamer's BBS
479-5482
Inner World BBS
239-7242
Second Reality BBS
284-0570
The Krystal Palace
762-9245

303

Adventure Quest I
280-0205
Assassins Guild
722-6881
Cougar's Castle
781-8990
DLS InfoNet
347-2921
Evil Ed's
766-5815

Gates of Delirium
751-3883
Kaya BBS
678-0393
Nix*Pix
375-1263
North Street BBS
884-1391
The Berean Connection
693-9263
The Colorado Connection
423-9775
The Forum
226-4218
The Horizon
766-3104

304

Boot Camp BBS
872-6029
Seneca Station
636-9592
Starbase 90 BBS
252-6390
The Red-Eye
846-6339
WildCat! West Virginia
636-9097

305

A Midnight Rave
270-6780
Fun Connection
583-7808
Phoenix Software Library
791-9574
Priority One BBS
783-2111
Ray's Place BBS
977-3099
Switzerland BBS
266-8468
The Hobby Line BBS
966-2677
The Honey Drpper
220-0369
The Library BBS
581-5162
The Phoenix BBS
572-6086

Ups And Downs
434-8403
Wild Palms BBS
472-4431

306

Martensville Tradewars
242-8812
The Games Room BBS I
786-6253
The Games Room BBS II
786-6252
The Missing Link
775-1512
The Pool Hall
586-8490

307

Fascinations
382-6851
Runamuck BBS
265-3022
Wass Up
382-6245

308

Towne Crier Systems
487-5390

309

Future Link Computing BBS
676-0387
Le Roy Acres BBS
963-2273
Rod's Place BBS
836-1432

310

Bad Connection
325-6961
Illusions
804-3224
Market / Net Online
763-6888
Miller's Party Board
815-0117
Pacific Coast Outlaw BBS
589-9135

The Link BBS
459-1264
West Coast Access
573-3750

312

CEBBS
902-3599
Chicago MegaPhile BBS
283-4035
Home Again
665-7319
Sharks's Den
922-2839
Stygian Abyss BBS
384-6250
The Chess Board BBS
784-3019
The Power Palace
594-0643
The Round Table BBS
777-9480

313

Army of the Southern Cross
769-5859
Bruce's Place BBS
562-0051
Gateway Online
291-5571
Margaritaville BBS
891-4313
SliPPED DiSK
546-5950
Solaris: Somewhere Online
942-4447
The Danger Zone
782-4524
The Forbidden Zone BBS
971-5130
The Hardrive Cafe
885-6663
The Olympic BBS
946-5931
The Red Eye BBS
728-0213
The Ultimate Connection PCBoard
232-1905
UnStoppable Dragons BBS
697-0609

314

Cyborg BBS
443-1420
Maggie's Place
642-7144
The L&S BBS
248-1951
The Tornado Room
386-5136

315

Dreamscape
458-3482
T.O.I.L. BBS
331-1556
The Second Foundation
393-6504
ZOO Station
597-1160

316

ChessPlayer's Forum
386-7054
Dutchmen's
683-2143
Flying Microchip
241-4139
Game Room
669-0100
New World Info Service BBS
262-1829
Phone Cops Donut Shop BBS
364-8584
Synergy
522-6240
The Game Den
522-7062
The Landing Zone!
729-7944
The MotherLode
441-0047
Z-Link
744-2831
Zippy's Balloon
231-2249

317

Absolute Connection
861-9333

Game Boards

Bill And Ted's Excellent BBS
883-4510
Brian's Board BBS
342-4320
New Ross BBS
723-1510
Pandaemonium
580-1531
The Wheel
298-0798
Traders' Connection
359-5199
Wayward Son BBS
362-9075
Workplace Connection
742-2680

318

Home-Port
994-2764
The Crypt BBS
226-9126

319

Allnighter BBS
296-3836
Goodee's BBS
235-3099
Rush Hour
568--6370
The Electric Nightline BBS
337-0674
The MNissing Link
235-0772

401

Information Resource System (IRS) BBS
783-7559
Meeting House BBS
848-2200
Milliways
943-2581
Remote Control Access
658-2574

402

GreasePalace BBS
451-4085

Late Nite
291-6164
MCS Software Development
293-0984
The Graveyard BBS
339-9474
The Last Frontier
572-4013
The Mages Inn
734-4748

403

Absolute Entertainment
272-9410
Boonies Bar & Grill
935-4382
BorderQuest
262-5095
C.R.I.S.I.S.H.Q
686-0449
Chromehenge
225-2221
Electric Birdmen BBS
251-4278
Games'R' Us
437-2787
GSL! Games BBS
874-2023
Hardwired
434-7996
Little Dog on a Pillow
287-2258
Magic's BBS
569-2882
Much Too Much James BBS
258-0634
Pandora's Box BBS
282-7616
Squornshellous Zeta
273-7025
T-8000 Info System
246-4487
The Time System VBBS
276-4592

404

Access Alpha
475-0980
Dragons Lair BBS
287-9400

Faster-Than-Light
292-8761
Paradise BBS
925-8980
PC Atlanta
395-6327
Pretenders
451-3753
Prime Time Online
667-3084
Quanah's revenge
968-0220
System Level Information Media Exchange
447-5619
The Chess Club
944-6865
The Neutral Zone
944-3639
The Vortex
971-7730

405

Cyber City BBS
737-4177
PC-Oklahoma
243-3200
Sword's Point BBS
682-1628
The Boarding House
377-8561
The Cutting Edge BBS
793-1919
The GameRoom BBS
391-4713
World Games Network
447-4098

406

Game Connection
761-3850
Midnight BBS
587-8163
The Cultural Wasteland BBS
782-7941
The No-Name BBS
348-2006
The Zoo
251-4487
Valley Light BBS
273-6399

WestNet BBS
458-9379

407

America 1st BBS
690-1267
EatsSide System
337-1274
GameMaster
823-9460
Infinite Space Online Network
856-0021
My Cozy Kitchen
687-9355
Osceola Express BBS
348-5295
Planet GS
264-2528
Politically Incorrect BBS
632-7549
Sensible Software
298-5830
Starship Enterprise
383-9820
The Black Hole
639-1822
The Eagle's Hideout
547-4233
Trade Wars Haven
359-7815
Windchimes
881-9025

408

Atlantis BBS
377-8510
Gnome's Guesthouse
249-9230
Monterey Gaming System
655-5555
Shakala BBS
734-2289
The Checkered Demon BBS
264-9018

409

The Blackhole BBS
982-8864

The Warp Zone
886-4175

410

AACyberNet
674-5427
Chess Etcetera BBS
674-6835
Forces Unknown
644-5100
Greg's Corner
781-6735
Hotline BBS
882-6191
Pixels & Chips BBS
398-6256
Tech Noir
859-0974
The Core
840-9356
The Games and Graphics BBS
672-5360
The Whiplash Fantasy
836-3072
Tilt
521-4808
VBARNET BBS
761-3406

412

AmeriBoard II--The Eagle
479-0548
Freddies Play-House
226-3129
MetroPitt
487-9223
Milliways
766-1086
The Doberman Gang BBS
767-7068

413

G-Comm BBS
436-7638
Hidden Fortress
731-8166
Springfield Public Access
536-4365

414

Games Galore and More BBS
453-7813
Madame's Play House
486-2400
Mister Dude's Wild Ride!
289-0708
Online Data Systems
761-5120
Spatula City BBS
459-9052
The Crystal Barrier
457-8399

415

California Online
331-4081
Outland Games Network
325-9904
The Cutting Edge
931-0583
The Gamer
255-0732

416

The WAR Board
486-6546

417

The Computer Matrix
862-8910

418

Comm-85 BBS
248-6890

419

Easy Access BBS
385-2188
OU812 BBS
427-1900
Roundtable BBS
693-8503
The Fortress
524-6528

Game Boards

501

CIA Amiga BBS
851-7418
Cindy & Eddie's BBS
942-4147
Cybertek
758-4229
Ferret BBS
791-0275
IVIE-LINK BBS
665=2580
Rare Moment BBS
568-5233
The Cat's Meow BBS
225-9271
The Chicken Coop
273-2442
The Cutting Edge
663-3343
The Gameing BBS
932-7355
The Moonman BBS
565-6868
The Moreland Beacon BBS
641-2007
The Tower of High Sorcery
329-7508
Wye Mtn.BBS
330-2845

502

Cyber Punk City
753-1015
Dance of Shiva
899-7872
Great Scott!
732-8554
The Barbarian's Hut
352-2169
The Homefront BBS
942-0089

503

A Byte Of Aloha
591-7542
Electronic Pub Svc
681-0907
Heaven
829-7117

Magnetic Inx the Machine BBS
476-0729
Noha's Kitchen
289-4945
Play Tradeward Online BBS
287-5829
The Advanced System BBS
657-3359
The File Dump BBS
369-2271
The Inferno
637-3178
The Last Frontier
883-1239

504

Computer Associates of Louisiana BBS
851-4230
DataCom BBS
275-2605
Fishing Hole
888-8243
The Black Rainbow
769-4575
The Laboratory
837-0155
The Point BBS
391-2122

505

MDC Computer BBS
434-0258
Scooter's Place
784-5471
The Albuquerque ROS
296-3000
The Cajun Clickers BBS
756-9659
The GaRBaGe DuMP BBS
294-5675
The Tech Source
255-0697

506

The Gamers Board BBS
652-8943

507

Lost Gonzo BBS
625-8321
PC-MONITOR
373-1100

508

Auto Exec BBS
833-0508
Consumer's ShowCase BBS
583-7693
Crystal Mountain BBS
249-2156
Dark Realms
695-3420
Dystopia
533-5266
GCS Bulletin Board System
370-4293
Pure Coincidence BBS
677-2472
Stealth BBS of New Belford
997-4982
The CooKoo's Nest
744-8824
The Gamemasters' Sanctum
852-4641
The "Q" Continuum
640-1470
The Studio BBS
872-5865
Total Access BBS
342-2200

509

Bob's Interplanetary BBS
487-3734
Columbia Basin BBS;
766-2867
Extensions BBS
886-0306
Fudd BBS
633-1535
Hunter/Killer BBS
662-8239
Prowler's Domain
327-8922
Quicksilver BBS
762-6845

Starwest-BBS
758-6248
Wally World Wacky Hackers! BBS
529-3726
We Be Games 'n' Stuff
545-4249

510

Aardwolf Express
797-8700
Night Creature
481-9774
The Tri-Valley PC Place
551-5320
VIPER 1 PREMIUM BBS
535-0231

512

Abyss BBS
282-2605
Accolade
388-1100
Apollo Zone
323-2713
City Limits Adult BBS
837-1271
Entropy Tango
451-3512
Funsmut Hotel South
447-2151
Gas Pipe
836-5644
Image Processor
331-7447
Infinity
835-7777
Suburbia Station
836-8633
The Armada
328-5082

513

Smoke Signals
984-5786
Sunset Strip
339-3957
The Cottage by the Stream
235-2605

TradeZone BBS
367-1727
Type Too! Basement
451-8990

514

Quebec Online
525-6090
THE GAMEMASTER
875-6650
Zone Infernale;
799-1516

515

I Can "C" Clearly Now
472-3651
The Other Side BBS
232-0969

516

Around Town--Islip Terrace
859-0703
East Coast Connection
742-1923
Harbinger BBS
472-1036
Kesco
679-0023
Modem Gamers Forum
661-4145
PenDragon's Lair
374-0551
Stages
823-0732
The Game Paddler BBS
493-0785
The Hard Disk Cafe
796-7686
Tower of Power
981-8372

517

Live-On-Line
789-9826
Micro Assets BBS
356-3478
Sound Power System
792-4680

518

First data Resources
762-0388
Minas Morgul BBS
436-0052
Non-Sequitur BBS
359-7887
Speedy's Trading Post
762-2640
WaveForm BBS
381-4417

519

...and Justice for All
570-3159
Electic Knights Chess
442-6449
New Edge Data Systems BBS
371-8383
The Edge BBS
974-4603

601

After Hrs BBS
371-0423
DaRK Ph!Ber
924-6890
Gameboard Plus II
892-5915
Hacker's Heaven
388-3745
Looney Bin
455-9073

602

City Lights
233-0560
Computer Sickbay
757-1981
Empty Pockets BBS
831-7979
Flatland Center
649-7438
Foothills BBS
460-5352
Millie's Madness
432-7854

Game Boards

NTSBC/CompuSult BBS
836-8575
Pinnacle
951-8379
Quantum Leap
937-1356
RaceBBS
669-9225
Run-Time BBS
525-3711
Saguaro Station
846-2318
Sunwise
584-7395
The Danish Tower
459-6514
The Rock Garden
220-0001
Windows in Time
253-1946

603

Botnay Bay
431-7090
Brickyard BBS
332-0419
Computer Castle
382-6938
Exile's Gate
644-5724
Icehouse BBS
863-3537
Snowbound! BBS
253-4256
Solutions BBS
642-7343
The Cosmopolitan BBS
666-0108
The Starship BBS
595-9677

604

AIS Multiline
489-4206
Computer Patch
668-6129
Double Exposure BBS
939-9540
Information Overload
475-3441

Nighthawk BBS
299-7067
Yak Shak
724-3200

605

Capitol View BBS
224-0982
The Computer Palace
229-4535
What Is It
692-1537

606

Cincidel
282-9803
Club Meg
474-3496
Magic$oft BBS
371-6337
Playland BBS
268-0776
The Empire
833-5696
The Niche BBS
885-4757

607

Pax Tharkas
749-3689
Sugar Mountain
732-4565
The Forum BBS
272-1371

608

Delta One Systems
356-6569
Game plus
822-2000
Screaming Demon
257-1852
The Connecting Line BBS
365-2302

609

Alpha Omega BBS
692-1502

BB's BBS
768-6585
Cheers Online
443-9008
Lil' Red's Weird World
723-6730
MegaByte BBS
835-1090
Poindexter Online
486-1983
The Amiga Zone
953-8159
The Black Forest BBS
386-1274
The Wall BBS
758-1991

610

Buckwheat BBS
534-4446
Rick's Cafe Americain
740-9886
Ship of Fools BBS
644-4629
Starship BBS
284-6428
The Elite BBS
666-0480
The Web BBS
352-4172
Time Out BBS
857-2648

612

Elk River pcBBS
441-6579
Infiniti
861-7460
P.C. MegaMall System
488-5112
Smart Stuff
926-9811
The Dark Side of the Moon
231-1726
The Other Place
783-0266

613

1000 Island Game Exchange
382-2734

Gamers Realm
841-6583
Games 'R' Us
526-1891
Legion of the Damned
237-4592

614

Doug's Place BBS
759-7018
Down Under BBS
262-9927
NightOwl Online
855-7101
Outer Limits
363-4228
PC Warehouse BBS
374-5254
Protean!II BBS
862-6574
Software Solutions BBS
594-2265
The Vault BBS
387-2762
The Wizard's Gate
224-1635

615

Anomalous BBS
952-5638
Bill's BBS
482-2097
C Delight
573-1357
Coles Kingdom
657-5708
Data-Link BBS
569-5842
On Line Gamer's Clinic
754-0473
The Fellowship Board
263-1046
The Game Board
744-9523
The Heart of Tennessee (HOT) BBS
890-8715
The Northern Lights BBS
831-9284
The Other World BBS
577-9342

The Sounds of Silence
865-5817
The TeePee!
378-8488

616

Files Galore
365-0659
Full Moon Cafe
685-8719
Late Night
664-6074
Macatawa Multiline
399-1141
Magnetic Mountain
637-6965
Phoenix BBS Systems
392-8175
Repeat Offender
429-8765
The Cat's Eye
375-5013
The Evans BBS
754-6180
The Gameroom
273-1371
The Taz's BBS
373-4231
The The Jungle BBS
392-3477
Windows++ VBBS
892-4692

617

Crossroads
623-6345
Donna Dee's Dungeon
894-3090
The Data Express BBS
247-3383
The Outpost BBS
871-2683

618

Dragon Realms
483-6900
Hard Disk Cafe
684-3990
Phantasmagoria BBS
867-2394

The Garage BBS
344-8466
The Omega Line
392-4607
World Horizon Network
482-5239

619

Adventure Games of America
566-4076
D.J.M. BBS
588-6941
DNIS
864-1468
Rendezvous BBS
689-8550
Sin*City
528-0322
The SHC Editor's BBS
563-1598

701

Node Dakota BBS
224-1431
The Dakota Central Telenet BBS
674-8115

702

AmigaBoard
423-8352
Eagle's Nest BBS
853-4703
Gravity Well
256-8514
Lisa
452-8309
MegaSystem BBS
849-2207
Superboard
423-6675
The Guardian of Darkness BBS
738-4364
Vega$ Online
222-0409
Wizzard's Alley
738-2378

Game Boards

703

Crystall Quill
241-7100
Digital Dreams
885-0980
Pleasure Palace
669-7335
Tellurian Base BBS
381-4037
The ESCape Zone BBS
730-0127
The Fishin' Hole
729-4231
The MBT
552-8767
Wildcat's Den
491-5726
YOUR BBS
659-6448

704

AlphaTech BBS
697-1447
Digital Dreams/2
254-0345
onal Touch BBS
545-1380
Private Investigators Exchange BBS
563-5480
The Basement BBS
628-9908
The Game Room
392-7607
The Shadow Dragon
546-5250

706

LANworks
549-2772
Populus
569-0773
The Imperial Palace BBS
592-1344

707

Color Galaxy Milky Way
585-8246

708

Cesspool BBS
352-9231
Charles Parker
260-8818
Chicago Area Computer Center
739-0201
Chicago Syslink
795-4442
Creative Thoughts BBS
382-3904
Cue Ball Online
782-0948
Cyber Comm Networks
697-9572
Great Northern BBS
634-9368
Left Side of Normal
949-9898
Maranatha!
628-0330
Scandal's BBS
356-5633
The File Sponge BBS
548-6103
The House of Games
918-8421
The Wild Onion
993-0461
Tigers Claw
223-2820

712

Midwest Connection BBS
276-6534
Transportation Plus BBS
255-0784

713

A Shot In The Dark
864-9553
Altair IV BBS
947-2253
Attic Light BBS
488-7760
Back To Basic
470-8844
Houston Game Designer
955-8920

Land of the Yohons
474-3753
MacEndeavour
640-1298
New Ware Club
558-9420
Software Expressions
541-3910
The Game Board
353-2706
The Pachyderm Pwr & Police BBS
464-7429
The Wooden Shoe
474-9657
Toon Town BBS II
332-0809
Town Square
477-2681

714

4Next GT BBS
956-4698
CA Sel Help BBS
525-1706
Eden- The Electronic Garden
548-1900
Happy Trails BBS
547-0749
Mystic Fortress
739-8125
Real Estate Online
969-9624
Sleepless Knights
523-8838
The Big Blue Mac
493-4779
The Kandy Shack
636-2667
The Liberty BBS
996-7777
The Locker room
542-5917
The Safety Net BBS
457-8066
The Solar System BBS
837-9677

715

E-Sports
848-2508

The Byte Shop
832-7961
The Byte Stops Here
341-9723
The Twilight Zone
652-2758

716

Blue Moon Online System
874-8941
Buffalo Data Systems
895-1146
Medina Online
798-5549
Meng's Madhouse
964-8323
RAM Enterprises BBS
892-8428
The All American BBS!
652-8438
The Dark Star BBS
668-6596
The Krystal Doorway
589-1669
The Panic Zone
473-0252
The Viper's Lair
787-1155

717

Bitt's Place
387-1725
C.W.'s Playroom
898-2941
Cyberia--The Final Stop in Cyberspace
840-1444
Ike's Place BBS
538-3009
Megabyte BBS
296-6377
Merchantmen BBS
225-5586
Network 24
652-0874
Pennsylvania Online!
657-8699
Potens Draco BBS
272-4310
Sawbuck's
632-2788

The Cat in the Hat
420-1942
The Northeast File Bank
876-0152
The Third Floor BBS
321-8457

718

Dimension Z
381-1643
Expressways BBS
636-3081
Haven! BBS
293-3768
HTBBS Network Services
380-8003
Innovations BBS
575-2914
LCS International BBS
225-9568
Mind Matters BBS
951-6652
Sherwood ForeST
522-0768
Spark*Net Online Systems
447-5544
Spectrum BBS
253-8110
The Glendale Tower BBS
417-8601
The Northern World BBS
987-8786

719

Dragon's Den
598-6746
The Bargain Basement
630-1104
The Wizards Liar
598-7680

801

48 Files BBS
756-0905
Rocky Mountain Software BBS
963-8721
The Cedar Chest BBS
586-8751

The Chess Board
966-1168
The Realm of Magic RBBS
299-1419

802

AutoByte BBS
285-6846
Peak BBS
388-1558
Shock! BBS
868-5274

803

Bedrock Cafe
899-6940
Confused Fools BBS
796-7612
Dazed and Confused BBS
873-5797
Direct Access
365-1657
The Arcs and Sparks BBS
824-0070
The Cosmic Connection BBS
862-7789
The Interstate BBS
871-7477

804

Club PC BBS
357-0357
Games Master BBS
474-4761
Joe's Place
520-0536
Joe's Room
887-2569
The Genesys BBS
499-9101
The Midnite Express
862-4663
The Music BBS
739-7289
The Zoo BBS
431-9363
Valhalla BBS
560-0701

Game Boards

Yellow Branch BBS
821-5906

805

Mad Greek's BBS
942-0702
Tehachapi Mountain
822-6587
The FunZone
988-0549
The Seaside
964-4766
TWH Game Master BBS
272-9455
Ventura County's Information Network
485-8982

806

Philosopher's Stone
358-0342

808

Hawaii OnLine
246-8887
Hawaiian Oasis
935-3148
One Step Beyond BBS
695-8352
TBird's BBS
423-3152
The Aloha Network
621-8845
The Country Cupboard
488-0617
The Crow's Nest
423-9788
The Game Hub II
682-5183

810

Battle Zone
949-8839
Electronic Lucidity
680-8861
The Carnival BBS
235-0158
The Space BBS
234-9242

812

Bufkin Ridge Ranch
838-9053
DataCom USA
949-4904
Taco Hell
333-9721
The Star Fire BBS
235-9254

813

BBShare
758-3223
Beach Board BBS
337-4950
Close Encounters
528-2582
Game Masters BBS
67-5713
Hawks Nest BBS
425-1000
New Horizons BBS
584-2453
Pleasure Island
544-4818
The Atrium BBS
785-6563
The Baywatch BBS
372-1779
The Beach Board
337-5480
The Pegasus Project-The Next Generation
481-5575
Underground
639-3887
Variety Connection
648-4732

814

The People's
684-7670.

815

Digital Dreams
227-9455
Electric Estates BBS
886-0109

File Cabinet
399-8978
Gateway Elite BBS
398-4678
Rockford College BBS
394-5153
The Boomtown BBS
868-2422

816

The Passport System
229-1841

817

BackAlley
831-2066
Chrysalis - Ft. Worth
540-5565
Snipe's Castle
757-0169
Stealth System
862-5500
Suzie's room BBS
446-4581

818

Computer One
763-9006
Electronic Access/Baseball
992-5627
KBTC BBS
967-0701
Merchants of Wonder
508-0214
Odyssey
358-6968
Panasia BBS
569-3740
Tele-Link BBS
966-4420
The Hard Drive Cafe
993-5516
The Nocturnal Sanctuary BBS
919-0777
The Sports Club BBS
792-4752
Wyrm
793-2426

901

After Hours
286-5517
Cue Ball BBS
642-0717
Lala Land of Memphis
753-8022
Second Wind BBS
88-8358
Smart Move BBS
632-1947
The Chessboard
854-2561

902

Color Nova BBS II
634-3095
The Final Frontier BBS
637-2515

903

Botany Bay
509-8518
The All Files transfer BBS!
675-4215
The Gate
872-0903

904

Beach BBS
426-8726
Esoteric Oracle
332-9547
Game Room
829-0315
Games And Grafix
389-7759
Games n More
282-3445
Jack's Review
563-0704
MCM BBS
581-3227
MSS BBS
248-1479
Mustang Valley BBS
726-3412
OLGA On Line Gamers Assc
478-1535

Other World
893-2404
SEA BBS
942-2403
StarportALFA!
249-5835
Steel Dog Cafe
654-9385
Terrapin Station BBS
939-8027
The Pack Rat BBS
799-4028
The Toy Shop-PC BBS
688-9124
The Virtual Gateway
376-6601
Titan Software Solutions
476-1270
Typnet BBS
224-0787

905

Alpha City BBS
579-6302
Mike's Gamesroom
828-6803
The Aardwark BBS
332-4127
The inner Sanctum
732-9826

906

Amiga Bitswap Central Dispatch
482-8050
InfoBase
632-4478
Sanctuary BBS
485-4246

907

Alaska Mineshaft
276-2416
Anchorage Select
333-7805
Forest Thru the Trees
344-5764
Rogue's Guild
688-2506
Steel Heart BBS

428-3130
The Bit Bucket
561-2185
The Drawing Board BBS
349-5412
The Northern Exchange BBS
479-3292
The Play Room
338-7049
The Story Teller
428-0804
The Unknown BBS
428-1001

908

After the Storm BBS
396-9571
Cheers Online!
972-2387
Cybersystems!
654-1290
Dateland
572-5762
Geno's Place BBS
525-0155
Hudson's Info BBS
525-8478
Intermania
624-2246
MicroFone InfoService
205-0189
NightWings BBS
286-6044
No Uploads BBS
925-0845
Phillipsburg's Phinest BBS
454-8340
The Attic BBS
396-0790
The Club House BBS
272-2073
The Mayhem BBS
929-1492
The POW / MIA BBS
787-8383
The TreeFort BBS
388-3496
Where Fantasy Beckons
905-3029
Xonk's World BBS
828-5008

Game Boards

909

Castle of the Dark Sun
468-0621
Empire BBS
980-2306
Game Master BBS
889-3219
Locksoft
654-5625
Nothin' But
338-6716
Seven Seas BBS
247-2972
The After Hours BBS
597-3004
The Enchanted Forest BBS
883-2552
The Library BBS
780-6365
Valley of the Falls Online
794-4426

910

Ansi-Mation Alley
346-6543
Deep Star BBS
721-9981
Earthlink
777-0022
Hawaiian Hang Time
326-5098
Ronnie's Private BBS
760-4087
The BillBoard BBS
292-1979
The Game BBS
744-9030
The Leap BBS
654-5593
The Undiscovered Country
841-5646

912

Baudville Station BBS
741-8722
Cornerstone BBS
538-7950
Microlink
786-5888

OS/2 Tower
439-4054
Software Corner BBS
432-6665

913

Colossus IV Systems
897-6667
The Crypt BBS
532-9028

914

Bill & Ted's Excellent BBS!
361-3887
Intercourse BBS
889-8361
Johnny Boy's PC-Mania
733-5697
Pokey's Palace BBS
858-2704
Prism
344-0350
The Apple-Wize BBS
779-0388
The GameRoom Deluxe BBS
344-0140
The Lost Carrier BBS
964-0419
The Road Less Taken
277-7305
The Space Station BBS
292-0670
The Voice BBS
664-1844
Tholian Web
227-4402
Ultra Tech BBS
227-7889

915

Game's Etc
520-4263
Games Online BBS
676-2920
Poseidon BBS
593-0639
The Clinic BBS
646-7509

916

Artisan Crafts BBS
331-7865
FAO Bulletin Board System
962-3973
Fatal Error
365-7456
The Compass Rose-Sacramento
447-0292
The Compass RoseDavis
758-3007
The Fortress
362-3350
The Gamer's Retreat
725-0403

918

Creepers Corner
749-2235
Tradewars Only BBS
683-2082

919

Bugman BBS
735-5914
Deep Space Nine
563-6199
DownTown! BBS
383-4905
Free Advice
934-1002
Night Forest BBS
563-9093
Sleepy Hollow
492-5353
The Flip Side BBS
946-4660
The Lizards Lair
537-8248
The Real World Entertainment Service
662-9918
The Vortex I
481-0368

Internet providers

National

CR Laboratories ☎ →*dial* 415-837-5300 (vox)/212-695-7988/713-236-9200/617-577-9300/415-389-8649 ✓ **INTERNET** ...→*telnet* crl.com→guest ...→*ftp* crl.com→anonymous→<your email address> ...→*email* info@crl.com ✍ *Email for automated info*

Delphi ☎ →*dial* 800-544-4005 (vox)/800-365-4636→JOINDELPHI→INTERNETSIG ✓ **INTERNET** ...→*telnet* delphi.com→joindelphi-free ...→*email* info@delphi.com ✍ *Email for automated info*

Millennium Online ☎ →*dial* 800-736-0122 (vox) ✓ **INTERNET**→*email* info@mill.com ✍ *Email for automated info*

Netcom Online Communication Services Dozens of area codes for many parts of the U.S. ☎ →*dial* 800-501-8649 (vox) ✓ **INTERNET** ...→*telnet* netcom.com→guest→guest ...→*ftp* ftp.netcom.com→anonymous→<your email address> →/pub/netcom ...→*email* info@netcom.com ✍ *Email for automated info*

PSILink ☎ →*dial* 703-709-0300 (vox) ✓ **INTERNET** ...→*ftp* ftp.psi.com→anonymous→<your email address>→/info ...→*email* all-info@psi.com ✍ *Email for automated info*

Your Personal Network (YPN) ☎ →*dial* 800-NET-1133 (vox) Run by the editors of this book. ✓ **INTERNET** ...→*telnet* ypn.com→guest ...→*ftp* ypn.com→anonymous→<your email address>→/pub ...→*www* http://www.ypn.com ...→*email* info@ypn.com ✍ *Email for automated info*

Alabama

Nuance Network Services ☎ →*dial* 205-533-4296 (vox) ✓ **INTERNET** ...→*ftp* ftp.nuance.com→anonymous→<your email address>→/pub/NNS-INFO ...→*email* jkl@nuance.com ✍ *Email for info*

Arizona

Data Basix ☎ →*dial* 602-721-1988 (vox)/602-721-5887→guest ✓ **INTERNET** ...→*telnet* Data.Basix.com→guest ...→*ftp* Data.Basix.COM→anonymous→<your email address>→/services/dial-up.txt ...→*email* info@Data.Basix.com ✍ *Email for automated info*

Evergreen Communications ☎ →*dial* 602-230-9330 (vox) ✓ **INTERNET**→*email* evergreen@libre.com ✍ *Email for info*

The Illuminati Online ☎ →*dial* 512-447-7866 (vox)/512-448-8950→new ✓ **INTERNET** ...→*email* info@io.com ✍ *Email for automated info* ...→*telnet* io.com→new ...→*ftp* io.com→anonymous→<your email address>

Internet Direct, Inc. ☎ →*dial* 602-274-0100 (vox)/602-274-9600/602-321-9600→guest ✓ **INTERNET** ...→*telnet* indirect.com→guest→guest ...→*email* info@direct.com ✍ *Email for automated info*

California

a2i communications ☎ →*dial* 408-293-8078 (vox)/415-364-5652/408-293-9010 ✓ **INTERNET** ...→*telnet* a2i.rahul.net→guest ...→*ftp* ftp.rahul.net→anonymous→<your email address>→/pub/BLURB ...→*email* info@rahul.net ✍ *Email for automated info*

Dial n' Cerf USA ☎ →*dial* 800-876-2373 (vox) ✓ **INTERNET** ...→*ftp* ftp.cerf.net→anonymous→<your email address>→/cerfnet_info/cerfnet-general info.txt ...→*email* info@cerf.net ✍ *Email for automated info*

E & S Systems Public Access ☎ →*dial* 619-278-8124/619-278-9127/619-278-8267/619-278-9837 ✓ **INTERNET**→*email* steve@cg57.esnet.com ✍ *Email for info*

Express Access 714-377-9784 908-937-9481 ☎ →*dial* 800-969-9090 (vox)/714-377-9784→new ✓ **INTERNET** ...→*telnet* access.digex.net→new→new ...→*ftp* ftp.digex.net→anonymous→<your email address>→/pub ...→*email* info@digex.net ✍ *Email for automated info*

HoloNet ☎ →*dial* 510-704-0160 (vox)/510-704-1058→guest ✓ **INTERNET** ...→*telnet* holonet.net→guest ...→*ftp* holonet.net→anonymous→<your email address>→/info ...→*email* info@holonet.net ✍ *Email for automated info*

Institute for Global Communications (IGC) ☎ →*dial* 415-442-0220 (vox)/415-322-0284 ✓ **INTERNET** ...→*ftp* igc.apc.org→anonymous→<your email address>→/pub ...→*email* info@igc.apc.org ✍ *Email for automated info*

KAIWAN Public Access Inter-

net Online Services ☎→*dial* 714-638-2139 (vox)/714-452-9166/818-579-6701/818-756-0180/310-527-4279/714-539-5726/714-741-2920 ✓**INTERNET** ...→*ftp* kaiwan.com→anonymous→ <your email address>→/pub/kai wan ...→*email* info@kaiwan.com ✍ *Email for automated info*

The Portal System ☎→*dial* 408-973-9111 (vox)/408-973-8091/408-725-0561→info ✓**INTERNET** ...→*telnet* portal.com→online→ info ...→*ftp* ftp.shell.portal.com→ anonymous→<your email address> →/portal.info ...→*email* info@por tal. com ✍ *Email for automated info*

The Well ☎→*dial* 415-332-4335 (vox)/415-332-6106→guest ✓**INTERNET** ...→*telnet* well.com→guest ...→*email* info@well.com ✍ *Email for automated info*

Colorado

Colorado SuperNet, Inc. ☎→*dial* 303-273-3471 (vox) ✓**INTERNET** ...→*ftp* csn.org→ anonymous→<your email address>→ /CSN/reports/DialinInfo.txt ...→ *email* info@csn.org ✍ *Email for automated info*

Community News Service ☎→*dial* 800-748-1200 (vox)/719-520-1700/303-758-2656→ new→newuser ✓**INTERNET** ...→*telnet* cscns.com→new→newuser ... →*ftp* cscns.com→anonymous→ <your email address> ...→*email* info@cscns.com ✍ *Email for automated info*

Old Colorado City Communications ☎→*dial* 719-632-4848 (vox)/719-632-4111→newuser ✓**INTERNET** ...→*telnet* oldcolo.com→ newuser ...→*email* thefox@oldcolo. com ✍ *Email for info*

Connecticut

The John von Newmann Computer Network ☎→*dial* 609-897-7300 (vox) ✓**INTERNET**→ *email* info@jvnc.net ✍ *Email for automated info*

DC & Maryland

CAPCON Library Network ☎→*dial* 202-331-5771 (vox) ✓**INTERNET**→*email* capcon@capcon.net ✍ *Email for info*

Express Access 714-377-9784 908-937-9481 ☎→*dial* 800-969-9090 (vox)/301-220-0462→new ✓**INTERNET** ...→*telnet* access.digex. net→new→new ...→*ftp* ftp.digex. net→anonymous→<your email address>→/pub→...→*email* info@ digex.net ✍ *Email for automated info*

Merit Network, Inc ☎→*dial* 313-764-9430 (vox) ✓**INTERNET** ...→*telnet* hermes.merit.edu→help ...→*ftp* nic.merit.edu→anonymous→ <your email address> ...→*email* info@merit.edu ✍ *Email for automated info*

Delaware

Systems Solutions ☎→*dial* 302-378-1386 (vox) ✓**INTERNET** ...→*ftp* ssnet.com→anonymous→ <your email address> ...→*email* info@ssnet.com ✍ *Email for automated info*

Florida

CyberGate, Inc. ☎→*dial* 305-428-4283 (vox) ✓**INTERNET**→*email* info@gate.net ✍ *Email for automated info*

The IDS World Network ☎→*dial* 401-884-7856 (vox)/305-534-0321→ids→guest ✓**INTERNET** ...→*telnet* ids.net→guest ...→*email*

info@ids.net ✍ *Email for automated info*

Illinois

InterAccess ☎→*dial* 800-967-1580 (vox)/708-671-0237→guest ✓**INTERNET** ...→*ftp* interaccess. com→anonymous→<your email address>→/pub/interaccess.info ...→*email* info@interaccess.com ✍ *Email for automated info*

MCSNet ☎→*dial* 312-248-8649 (vox)/708-637-0900/312-248-0900→bbs→new ✓**INTERNET** ...→ *ftp* ftp.mcs.com→anonymous→ <your email address>→/mcsnet. info ...→*email* info@mcs.net ✍ *Email for automated info*

Prairienet Freenet ☎→*dial* 217-244-1962 (vox)/217-255-9000→visitor ✓**INTERNET** ...→*telnet* prairienet. org→visitor ...→*email* info@prairienet.org ✍ *Email for automated info*

XNet Information Systems ☎→*dial* 708-983-6064 (vox)/ 708-983-6435→guest→new ✓**INTERNET** ...→*telnet* net.xnet.com→ guest ...→*email* info@xnet.com ✍ *Email for automated info*

Louisiana

NeoSoft's Sugar Land Unix ☎→*dial* 713-438-4964 (vox) ✓**INTERNET**→*email* info@neosoft.com ✍ *Email for automated info*

Massachusetts

Merit Network, Inc ☎→*dial* 313-764-9430 (vox) ✓**INTERNET** ...→*telnet* hermes.merit.edu→help ...→*ftp* nic.merit.edu→anonymous→ <your email address> ...→*email* info@merit.edu ✍ *Email for automated info*

NEARnet ☎→*dial* 617-873-8730

(vox) ✓**INTERNET** ...→*ftp* ftp.near.
net→anonymous→<your email address> ...→*email* nearnet-join@
near.net ✎ *Email for info*

North Shore Access ☎→*dial*
617-593-3110 (vox)/617-593-
4557→new ✓**INTERNET** ...→*telnet*
shore.net→new ...→*ftp* shore.net→
anonymous→<your email address>
→/pub/flyer ...→*email* info@shore.
net ✎ *Email for automated info*

NovaLink ☎→*dial* 800-274-2814
(vox)/508-754-4009/800-937-
7644→new ✓**INTERNET** ...→*ftp*
ftp.novalink.com→anonymous→
<your email address>→/info ...→
email info@novalink.com ✎ *Email
for automated info*

The World ☎→*dial* 617-739-
0202 (vox)/617-739-9753→new
✓**INTERNET** ...→*telnet* world.std.
com→new ...→*ftp* std.com→anony-
mous→<your email address>→
/world-info/description ...→*email*
world.std.com ✎ *Email for info*

Michigan

Merit Network, Inc ☎→*dial*
313-764-9430 (vox) ✓**INTERNET**
...→*telnet* hermes.merit.edu→help
...→*ftp* nic.merit.edu→anonymous→
<your email address> ...→*email*
info@merit.edu ✎ *Email for automated info*

MSen ☎→*dial* 313-998-4562
(vox) ✓**INTERNET** ...→*telnet* msen.
com→newuser ...→*ftp* ftp.msen.
com→anonymous→<your email ad-
dress>→/pub/vendor/msen
...→*email* info@Msen.com ✎
Email for automated info

Minnesota

MRNet ☎→*dial* 612-342-2570
(vox) ✓**INTERNET**→*email* info@mr.
net

New Hampshire

MV Communications, Inc.
☎→*dial* 603-429-2223 (vox)/603-
424-7428→info→info ✓**INTERNET**
...→*ftp* ftp.mv.com→anonymous→
<your email address>→/pub/mv
...→*email* info@mv.com ✎ *Email
for automated info*

NEARnet ☎→*dial* 617-873-8730
(vox) ✓**INTERNET** ...→*ftp* ftp.near.
net→anonymous→<your email ad-
dress> ...→*email* nearnet-join@
near.net ✎ *Email for info*

New Jersey

Express Access ☎→*dial* 800-
969-9090 (vox)/908-937-9481/
609-348-6203/714-377-9784/
908-937-9481→new ✓**INTERNET**
...→ *telnet* access.digex.net→
new→new ...→*ftp* ftp.digex.net→
anonymous→<your email address>
→/pub ...→*email* info@digex.net
✎ *Email for automated info*

**The John von Newmann
Computer Network** ☎→*dial*
609-897-7300 (vox) ✓**INTERNET**→
email info@jvnc.net ✎ *Email for
automated info*

New Mexico

New Mexico Technet ☎→*dial*
505-345-6555 (vox)

New York

Echo Communications ☎→*dial*
212-255-3839 (vox)/212-989-
8411→newuser ✓**INTERNET** ...→*telnet* echonyc.com→newuser ...→
email info@echonyc.com ✎ *Email
for info*

MindVox ☎→*dial* 212-989-2418
(vox)/212-989-1550→guest ✓**INTER-
NET** ...→*telnet* phantom.com→guest
...→*email* info@phantom.com ✎
Email for automated info

PANIX Public Access ☎→*dial*
212-787-3100 (vox)/212-787-
6160→newuser ✓**INTERNET** ...→*telnet* panix.com→help ...→*email*
info@panix.com ✎ *Email for automated info*

The Pipeline ☎→*dial* 212-267-
3636 (vox)/212-267-8606/212-
267-7341→guest ✓**INTERNET** ...→
telnet pipeline.com→guest ...→*ftp*
pipeline.com→anonymous→<your
email address> ...→*email* info@
pipeline.com ✎ *Email for automated info*

North Carolina

CONCERT-CONNECT ☎→*dial*
919-248-1999 (vox) ✓**INTERNET**
...→*ftp* ftp.concert.net→anonymous
→<your email address> ...→*email*
info@concert.net ✎ *Email for automated info*

Vnet Internet Access, Inc.
☎→*dial* 704-334-3282 (vox)/919-
406-1544/919-851-1526/704-347-
8839→new ✓**INTERNET** ...→*telnet*
vnet.net→new ...→*ftp* vnet.net→
anonymous→<your email address>
→/vnet-info ...→*email* info@vnet.
net ✎ *Email for info*

Ohio

APK Public Access ☎→*dial* 216-
481-9428 (vox) ✓**INTERNET** ...→*telnet* wariat.org→bbs ...→*ftp* ftp.
wariat.org→anonymous→<your
email address> ...→*email* info@
wariat.org ✎ *Email for automated
info*

Oregon

Rain Drop Laboratories
☎→*dial* 503-452-0960 (vox)/503-
293-1772/503-293-2059→apply
✓**INTERNET** ...→*telnet* agora.rdrop.
com→apply→<your name> ...→*ftp*
agora.rdrop.com→anonymous→
<your email address>→/pub ...→

email info@agora.rdrop.com ✍ *Email for automated info*

Teleport ☎→*dial* 503-223-4245 (vox)/503-220-1016→new ✓**INTERNET** ...→*telnet* teleport.com→new ...→*ftp* teleport.com→anonymous→<your email address> ...→*email* info@teleport.com

Pennsylvania

The John von Newmann Computer Network ☎→*dial* 609-897-7300 (vox) ✓ **INTERNET**→*email* info@jvnc.net ✍ *Email for automated info*

Telerama Public Access Internet ☎→*dial* 412-481-3505 (vox)/412-481-5302/412-481-4644→new ✓**INTERNET** ...→*telnet* telerama.lm.com→new ...→*ftp* telerama.lm.com→anonymous→<your email address>→/info ...→*email* info@lm.com ✍ *Email for automated info*

Rhode Island

The IDS World Network ☎→*dial* 401-884-7856 (vox)/401-884-9002→ids→guest ✓ **INTERNET** ...→*telnet* ids.net→guest ...→*email* info@ids.net ✍ *Email for automated info*

The John von Newmann Computer Network ☎→*dial* 609-897-7300 (vox) ✓**INTERNET**→*email* info@jvnc.net ✍ *Email for automated info*

Texas

The Black Box ☎→*dial* 713-480-2685 (vox)/713-480-2686→guest ✓**INTERNET**→*email* info@blkbox.com ✍ *Email for automated info*

DFW Net ☎→*dial* 817-332-6642/817-429-3520→info ✓**INTERNET** ...→*telnet* dfw.net→info ...→

email info@dfw.net ✍ *Email for automated info*

The Illuminati Online ☎→*dial* 512-447-7866 (vox)/512-448-8950→new ✓**INTERNET** ...→*email* info@io.com ✍ *Email for automated info* ...→*telnet* io.com→new ... →*ftp* io.com→anonymous→<your email address>

NeoSoft's Sugar Land Unix ☎→*dial* 713-438-4964 (vox) ✓**INTERNET**→*email* info@neosoft.com ✍ *Email for automated info*

RealTime Communications ☎→*dial* 512-451-0046 (vox)/512-459-4391→new ✓**INTERNET** ...→*telnet* vern.bga.com→new ...→*ftp* ftp.bga.com→anonymous→<your email address> ...→*email* hosts@bga.com ✍ *Email for info*

South Coast Computing Services, Inc. ☎→*dial* 713-917-5000 (vox)/713-917-5050→newuser ✓**INTERNET** ...→*ftp* sccsi.com→anonymous→<your email address>→/pub/communications ...→*email* support@nuchat.sccsi.com ✍ *Email for info*

Texas Metronet ☎→*dial* 214-705-2900 (vox)/817-261-1127/214-705-2901→info→info ✓**INTERNET** ...→*telnet* metronet.com→info→info ...→*ftp* ftp.metronet.com→anonymous→<your email address>→/pub/info ...→*email* info@metronet.com ✍ *Email for automated info*

Virginia

CAPCON Library Network ☎→*dial* 202-331-5771 (vox) ✓**INTERNET**→*email* capcon@capcon.net ✍ *Email for info*

Express Access ☎→*dial* 800-969-9090 (vox)/703-281-7997/714-377-9784/908-937-9481

→new ✓**INTERNET** ...→*telnet* access.digex.net→new→new ...→*ftp* ftp.digex.net→anonymous→<your email address>→/pub ...→*email* info@digex.net ✍ *Email for automated info*

Wyvern Technologies, Inc. ☎→*dial* 804-622-4289 (vox)/804-627-1828/804-873-0748→guest ✓ **INTERNET** ...→*ftp* infi.net→anonymous→<your email address> ...→*email* system@wyvern.com ✍ *Email for info*

Washington

Eskimo North ☎→*dial* 206-367-7457 (vox)/206-742-1150/206-367-3837/206-362-6731 ✓**INTERNET** ...→*telnet* eskimo.com→new→<your name> ...→*email* nanook@eskimo.com ✍ *Email for info*

Halcyon ☎→*dial* 206-455-3505 (vox)/206-382-6245→new ✓**INTERNET** ...→*ftp* ftp.halcyon.com→anonymous→<your email address>→/pub/info ...→*email* info@halcyon.com ✍ *Email for automated info*

Olympus ☎→*dial* 206-385-0464 (vox) ✓**INTERNET**→*email* info@pt.olympus.net ✍ *Email for automated info*

Canada

UUNET Canada, Inc. ☎→*dial* 416-368-6621 (vox) ✓**INTERNET** ...→*ftp* ftp.uunet.ca→anonymous→<your email address> ...→*email* info@uunet.ca ✍ *Email for automated info*

Communications Accessibles Montreal ☎→*dial* 514-931-0749 (vox)/514-596-2255/514-596-2250 ✓**INTERNET** ...→*ftp* ftp.CAM.ORG→anonymous→<your email address> ...→*email* info@CAM.ORG ✍ *Email for automated info*

Glossary

AberMUD   An adventure-based **MUD** program named after the University of Aberstywyth, where it was written.

AD&D   *Advanced Dungeons & Dragons.*

algebraic notation   The symbolic representation of a board game, especially *chess*, used in most nongraphical games played on the Net.

baud   The speed at which signals are sent by a modem, measured by the number of changes per second in the signals during transmission. A baud rate of 1,200, for example, would indicate 1,200 signal changes in one second. Baud rate is often confused with **bits per second (bps)**. See below.

binary transfer   A file transfer between two computers that preserves **binary** data.

bits per second (bps)   The data-transfer rate between two modems. The higher the bps, the higher the speed of the transfer.

bot   A computer program with humanlike behavior. In live-chat areas like IRC channels or **MUD**s, bots are often programmed to represent their creators, to moderate games, or to perform such tasks as delivering local **email** messages.

bye   A log-off command, like "quit" and "exit."

cd   "Change directory." A command used at an **FTP** site to move from a directory to a subdirectory.

cdup   "Change directory up." A command used at an **FTP** site to move from a subdirectory to its parent directory. Also **chdirup**.

challenge ladder   A ranking system whereby players of a specific game try to improve their standing by challenging the player above them on the ladder.

character   A term used in adventure or **role-playing** games to refer to the persona a player assumes in the game. Choosing a character name is usually one of the first things a player does.

cheat (noun)   Instructions for winning. See also **hint**, **walk-through**.

client   A computer that connects to a more powerful computer (see **server**) for complex tasks.

collaborative fiction   The literary version of **role-playing**, where players/authors write up their **characters'** adventures as part of a group effort to create an ongoing story.

compression   Shrinkage of computer files to conserve storage space and reduce transfer times. Special utility programs, available for most platforms (including

Glossary

	DOS, Mac, and Amiga), perform the compression and decompression.
demo, demoware	A crippled version of a commercial game that is given away as a free sample to whet the customer's appetite. Usually only the first level is included, or only one person can play at a time. With the advent of the Net, distribution of demoware has been vastly simplified and expanded.
DikuMUD	A combat-oriented **MUD** program with a sophisticated class and guild system. Named after Diku University, where it was developed.
dino	A long time **MUD**der.
dir	"Directory." A command used at an **FTP** site to display the contents of the current directory.
dungeon master	The organizer and referee of a multiplayer fantasy **role-playing** game such as *Dungeons & Dragons*, the offline game that originated the term.
Easter egg	A feature or message hidden within a game, usually unlocked by some code word or special joystick-keypad combination.
editor	A software utility that allows a game player to change certain aspects of the game: the number of ships, a weapon's strength, the scenario maps, etc. Editors are sometimes built into the game software, but more often they're distributed as **shareware**.
email	"Electronic mail."
Ethernet	A fast and widely used type of **LAN**.
FAQ	"Frequently asked questions." A file of questions and answers compiled for **Usenet** newsgroups, mailing lists, and games to reduce repeated posts about commonplace subjects.
finger	A program that provides information about a user who is logged into your local system or on a remote computer on the Internet. Generally started by typing "finger" and the person's user name.
flame	A violent and usually ad hominem attack against another person in a **newsgroup** or message area.
flame war	A back-and-forth series of flames.
freeware	Free software. Not to be confused with **shareware**.
frontend	A program used in conjunction with another program to alter the appearance—for visual appeal and ease of use—of the screen. The frontend is often run locally on a player's machine.
FTP	"File transfer protocol." The standard used to transfer files between computers.
furry	An anthropomorphic animal, popular with Net role-players embarking

on a sexual adventure.

game master The organizer and referee of a multiplayer play-by-email game such as *Diplomacy* or *VGA Planets*. The game master usually processes move lists from players and issues turn reports on the results of player moves.

gopher A menu-based guide to directories on the Internet, usually organized by subject.

handle The name a player wishes to be known by. A player's handle may differ significantly from his or her real name and user name.

hint Help with a particular puzzle within a game. See also **cheat**.

Home Page The main **World Wide Web** site for a particular game, group, or organization.

hypertext An easy method of retrieving information by choosing highlighted words in a text on the screen. The words link to documents with related subject matter.

IC "In character." A player who is IC is acting as his or her **character**'s persona.

IF "Interactive fiction." Text-based adventures of the *Zork* and *Classic Adventure* type. Also see **collaborative fiction**.

judge Generic term for an automated **game master**, and also the name for a play-by-email *Diplomacy* **server**.

LAN "Local area network."

LARP "Live-action role-playing." A mix of improvisational acting and gaming in which players act out scenes and adventures, often in costume.

LPMUD A combat-oriented **MUD** program. Named after the original creator, Lars Penji.

ls "List." A command that provides simplified directory information at **FTP** sites. It lists only file names for the directory, not file sizes or dates.

mget An **FTP** command that transfers multiple files from the **FTP** site to your local directory. The command is followed by a list of file names separated by spaces, sometimes in combination with an asterisk used as a wild card. Typing "mget b*" would transfer all files in the directory with the letter *b* in their names.

mob, mobile A monster in a game.

MOO An object-oriented **MUD**. Many MOOs have an education or research orientation. The LambdaMOO **server** is the most popular type of MOO.

MUCK A social **MUD** and a variation of **TinyMUD**. Also called a TinyMUCK.

Glossary

MUD "Multi-user dimension" or "multi-user dungeon." A computer program designed to create the illusion of rooms, worlds, and time periods through text descriptions. Players use commands to "walk" through the MUD, chat with other **characters**, solve quests, and fight monsters. Used generically to refer to any of the MUD variants like **MOO**, **MUSE**, **MUCK**, **MUSH**, etc. The first MUD was written in 1979.

MUD God The system administrator of a **MUD**.

MUSE A social **MUD** and a variation on a TinyMUSH that includes a class system and combat. Also called a TinyMUSE.

MUSH "Multi-user shared hallucination." A social **MUD** and a variation of a **TinyMUD** that allows building. Also called a TinyMUSH.

netiquette The rules of Cyberspace civility. Usually applied to the Internet, where manners are enforced exclusively by fellow users.

newbie A newcomer to the Net, to a game, or to a discussion.

newsgroups The **Usenet** message areas, organized by subject.

NPC "Non player **character**." Monsters and other programmed **characters** in a game.

null modem A serial connection used to connect a computer to another computer without a modem.

OOC "Out of character." Someone who is OOC is acting as himself rather than as his **character**.

patch A program designed to fix a software bug in a game. Many patches for commercial games are available from the game companies' BBSs.

PK, PKing "Player killer," "player killing."

port number A number that follows a **telnet** address. The number connects a user to a particular application on the **telnet** site. ToonMUSH II, for example, is at port 1941 of merlin.mit.edu (merlin.mit.edu 1941).

pwd A command used at an **FTP** site to display the name of the current directory on your screen.

real time The Net term for "live," as in "live broadcast." Real-time connections include IRC chat, where two or more people "talk" by typing messages back and forth; head-to-head flight simulators; and **MUDs**.

remote machine Any computer on the Internet reached with a program such as **FTP** or **telnet**. The machine making the connection is called the home, or local, machine.

RL "Real life."

role-playing	A type of gaming where players act and respond in the nature of the **character** they play. Role-play can be heavily moderated and tied to the rules and stories of a particular gaming system, like the *AD&D* or White Wolf gaming systems, or the play may be "free-form," with few rules.
RPG	"**Role-playing** game."
scenario	The setting for a game. Some computer games allow players to change aspects of the scenario, such as the map, the background story, or the opening positions.
server	A software program, or the computer running the program, that allows other computers, called **clients**, to share its resources.
shareware	Free software, distributed over the Net with a request from the programmer for voluntary payment.
SLIP and PPP	"Serial line Internet protocol" and "point-to-point" protocol." Connecting by SLIP or PPP actually puts a computer on the Internet, which offers a number of advantages over regular dial-up. A SLIP or PPP connection can support a graphical **Web browser** (such as Mosaic), and allows for multiple connections at the same time. Requires special software and a SLIP or PPP service provider.
soundcard	Computer hardware that enhances sound generation and playback on your personal computer. Most popular commercial games for DOS and Windows machines take advantage of special stereo and effects features of soundcards.
sysop	"System operator." The person who owns and/or manages a BBS or other Net site.
telnet	An Internet program that allows you to log into other Internet-connected computers.
terminal emulator	A program or utility that allows a computer to communicate in a foreign or non standard **terminal mode**.
terminal mode	The software standard a computer uses for text communication—for example, ANSI for PC's and VT-100 for UNIX.
TinyMUD	A social **MUD** where players explore and build. **TinyMUD** is the program used in the original **MUD**.
Tinysex	The use of **MUD** commands and "descriptive prowess" to imitate sex acts.
turn file	A "saved game" file that is sent to a judge or opponent. The opponent uses the turn file to respond with his or her next move.

Glossary

turn order, turn request	Also called a **move list**. A player's instructions to the **game master** in the form of commands for his or her **character** (e.g., "inquire about quests, rob shopkeeper"); maneuvers (for a country in *Diplomacy*, for instance); or military orders (in a war-gaming simulation). In most play-by-email **role-playing** games, the results of a move are returned in a turn report.
URL	"Uniform resource locator." The Web address of a resource on the Internet.
Usenet	A collection of networks and computer systems that exchange messages, organized by subject in **newsgroups**.
WAIS	"Wide area information server." A system that searches through database indexes around the Internet, using keywords.
walk-through	Step-by-step instructions for successfully navigating a game. See also **cheat**.
Web browser	A **client** program designed to interact with **World Wide Web servers** on the Internet for the purpose of viewing **Web pages**.
Web page	A **hypertext** document that is part of the **World Wide Web** and that can incorporate graphics, sounds, and links to other **Web pages**, **FTP** sites, **gophers**, and a variety of other Internet resources.
wiz (verb)	To win the game and be appointed **wizard**.
wizards	A player in a **MUD** who has won the game or been appointed to help run the **MUD** by **MUD Gods**.
World Wide Web	A **hypertext**-based navigation system that lets you browse through a variety of linked Net resources, including **Usenet newsgroups** and **FTP**, **telnet**, and **gopher** sites, without typing commands. Also known as WWW and the Web.

Index

Index

189
Atari Gaming Archive, 189
Atari Gaming Forum, 189, 199
Atari Jaguar, Lynx, 199
See also Atari
Atari SIG, 199
Atari-ST Games, 189
ATPUTIL, 47
Automatic MUD List, 214
Auto Racing, 149
Avalon Hill, 224
Aviation Log Book, 40
AvPlan Flight Planner v3.0, 40
Awakening, The, 71
Axis and Allies, 134

B

backgammon, 118–119
BadLandsII, 100
baseball, 149–151
Baseball Manager, 149
Baseball Stats, 149
basketball, 151–152
    NBA Jam, 203
BatMUD, 91–92
Battle Grid, 29
Battleship, 120
BattleTech and Mecha, 29–30
    support material, 30
    See also FASA
BattleTech Archive, The, 30
BattleTech Files & Discussion, 30
BattleTech VR, 30
BayMOO, 167–168
BBS Roulette, 131
BBSs, 4–5, 21–22, 232–246
Beginners (Netrek), 49
Beginner's Tactical Guide (Cyber-
    Strike), 26
Best game would have, The, 221
Bethesda Softworks, 224
Betting Doors—Football, 152
Beyond the Stars, 83
Big Hank's Guide to Air Warrior
    through the Internet, 42
Big League Basketball, 151
Bingo, 119
BlackDragon, 115

blackjack, 128–129
Black Lightning's Fast Tracker, 33
BladeRunner, 100
Blake Stone: Aliens of Gold, 24
Blankety Blanks, 169
Blitz List, 140
board games, 118–122
Board of Regents, 177
Bolo, 31–33
    hints, 33
    utilities, 33
#bolo, 32–33
Bolo Archives, 32
Bolo Discussion on AOL, 33
Bolo Finder, 33
Bolo Home Page, The, 32
BOLO Libraries, 32
BoloTrackers, 33
Boogers, 121
Bordello!, 206
Borderlines, 159
Boss, 110
Boxes, 121
Brain Programmers, 33
Brainstorm, 181
Bret Larwick's Page, 76
bridge, 129–130
Bridge Home Page, 129
British Legends, 92
Broderbund, 224
Brother Sean's MUD Guide, 212
BSD Empire, 140
BSD Empire Archives, 140
Btech 3056, 29–30
Budapest, 100–101
Bulls and Bears, 166

C

Cactus Jack Archives, 155
Camarilla-L, 72
card games, 128–132
    See also Magic: the Gathering
Cardiff MOO Page, 215
Cardiff's Crossfire Pages, 110
Cardiff's MUD Page, 214
Cardiff's Video Game Database
    Browser, 197
Cartel, 141

cartridge games, explanation of,
    14
    See also home gaming systems,
        video games, arcade games
casino games, 128–132
Categorically Trivial, 169
CaveMUCK, 208
CBNVEE, 213
Celebrity Trivia Games, 174
Center Stage Game Shows, 158
Cerebus Shadowrun Archive, 60
Champ-L, 64
Chaosium, 71
Chaosium Archives, 71
Chaosium Digest, 71
Charades, 159
chat, 8, 13–15
checkers, 119–120
Cheshire, Stuart, 32
chess, 123–127
    chess servers, 124–125
    Chinese, 127
    discussion, 126
    journals, 126
    play-by-email, 126
ChessBoard, 123
Chess Chow, 126
Chess Club, 123
Chess Forum, 123
Chess-L, 126
Chicago Player Registry, The, 33
children's games
    AJ Dakota, 162
    hangman, 179
    Match-it, 161
    MicroMUSE (Cyberion City),
        168
    NarniaMush, 108
    OceanaMUSE, 166–167
    Police Artist, 161
    Reverse, 165
    RocketQuiz, 161
    Silly Fill-ins, 160
    SmartKids Quiz, 173
    Square Off, 160–161
    State Your Capitals, 173
    Thinker, 165
    Trivia for Kids, 173–174
    Trivia for Teens, 174
    Twisted Tales, 160
    Where in the World is Carmen
        Sandiego?, 166
Chinese chess, 127

Index

Index

L

Labyrinth Door, The, 162
LambdaMOO, 210
Land of Devastation, 96
Larn, 111–112
LARP Archive, 88
Lasagna, 159
Last Outpost, The, 99
Laugh Lines, 180
Legend of the Red Dragon, 96
Lemmings FAQ, 28
Liam's Web Quiz, 170
Links Country Club Golf, 154
List of Arcade Game Manufacturers, 202
live-action role-playing, 88–89
    news, 88
    organization, 88–89
    regional, 89
Living History Forum, 88
Logic Puzzles and Brain Teasers, 164
Looking Glass Technologies, Inc., 225
Lord of the Rings RPG
    Evil Chat, 79
    Good Chat, 79
    See also Tolkien, J.R.R.
Lost Souls, 96
LPMud Archive, 215
LPMuds, general, 215
    See also MUDs
LucasArts, 225
LucasArts Historical Flight Sims, 43
LucasArts Sims, general, 40
LucasArts Space Flight Sims, 50
Lucky 7, 184
Lynx FTP Site, 199

M

MacDip, 139
MAC-GAMES, 190
Mach Numbers, 40

Macintosh, 190–191
    journals, 191
    utilities, 191
Macintosh Communications Forum, The, 191
Macintosh Compression Utilities, 191
Macintosh Games, 190–191
Macintosh Games Publications, 191
Macintosh ICONtact Games, 191
Macintosh Modem Players Server, 216–217
Mad Scramble, 182
Madvertising, 173
Mage-L, 71–72
Mage: The Ascension, 71–72
Magic: the Gathering, 76–77
Magic: the Gathering Archive, 76–77
Magic: the Gathering on GEnie, 77
mailing lists, explanation, 10
Major League Baseball, 150
Major Stryker, 25–26
Mallard Software, 46
Mapit, 139
Martial Champions, 37
Masquerade, The, 73
Masterbook, 65
MasterWord, 179–180
Match-It, 161
math and number games, 160–161
    AJ Dakota, 162
    Lasagna, 159
Maxis, 225
mazes, 162–163
    Adventurer's Maze, 90
McCaffrey, Ann, 80–81
Mecha, 29–30
Mech Warriors, 30
MEDIEVIA Cyberspace, 99
MegaWars I, 144
MegaWars III, 144–145
memory games, 161
Metaverse, 106
MicroMUSE (Cyberion City), 168
Microprose, 225
MicroProse Simulators, 40
Microsoft Flight Sim 4.0 Files, 46
Microsoft Flight Simulator, 46

Middle Earth, 78–79
    See also Angband
MiG-29 Challenge Ladder Rules, 45
mind games, 158–161
Mini-adventures, 116
miniatures, 134
Miniatures Archive, 134
Miniatures WWW Archive, 134
Mission from God, 139
Mixed Trivia Games, 174
Mixups, 184
Modem Games Forum, 217
modem-to-modem, 216–217
    explanation of, 13–14
Modem-to-Modem Challenge Board, 217
Modem-to-Modem Gaming, 217
Modem-to-Modem Gaming Lobby, 217
Monkey Island 2 Walkthru, 96
Monster Island, 96
Monster Island Mailing List, 96–97
Monster Macintosh Gaming Archives, 191
Monster MUD Archive, 212
Monster RPG Archives, 59
MOO Archive, 215
MOOcows, 215
MOOs, general, 215
    See also MUDs
MooseHead MUD, 97
Moria, 112
Mortal Kombat, 36
Mortal Kombat Guides, 36
Mortal Kombat Tips & Discussions, 36
Mortal Kombat II, 36
Motion Picture Trivia Games, 174–175
Movie Star Trivia Games, 175
MtG Files & Discussion, 77
MUCKs
    See MUDs
MUD Archives, 212
MUD Clients and GIF archive, 213
MUD Gopher, 214
MUD History Archive, 213
MUD RWHO Server, 214
MUDs, 212–215
    AberMUDs, 100–104

Index

Index

Index

Index

U

Ulrick, 105
Ultimate Universe, 146
Unix, 186
Unix Games, 186
Unofficial List of DikuMUDs, The, 215
Untanglers, 182
Upgrade Patch for FS5.0, 47
URL, 9
USA Today Baseball League, 151
USA Today Basketball League, 152
USA Today Football League, 153
Usenet newsgroups, 9–10

V

Valhalla, 99
Vampire-L, 74
Vampires, 72–74
    World of Darkness, A, 75
Vampire/White Wolf Discussion, 74
Variant Diplomacy Maps, 139
Vectrex, 201
VegaMUSE II, 83
VGA Planets, 52–53
    discussion, 53
    support, 53
VGA Planets Archive, 53
VGA Planets at the Gamer's Den, 52–53
VGA Planets—HINTS, 53
VGA Planets Players' Pub, 53
Video Game Cheat Sheet, 203
video games, 196–197
    Dune 2 FAQ & Strategy Guide, 84
    pinouts and cheats, 203, 197
    See also action games, arcade games, fighting games, home gaming systems
Video Games Forum, 196
Video Game SIG, 196–197

#vidgames, 197
Virtua Fighters, 37
Virtual Spaces, 214
Virtual Sun, 105
Vostag's Tavern, 64
V_RPG, 223

W

War Games, 133
War Game SIG, 133
war gaming and strategy, 133–135
Wargaming Club, 133
war simulations, 134–135
    Hundred Years War, 147
Werewolf-L, 75
Werewolf: The Apocalypse, 75
werewolves, 74–75
Wheel of Fortune, 184
Where in the World is Carmen Sandiego?, 166
Whicken's Page, 77
WhirlWind, 105
White Wolf, 75
White Wolf Archive, 75
Who Am I?, 160
Who Sings Me?, 160
Windows Games, 195
Windows Games WAVs, 37
Windows NT Games/Fun, 195
Wing Commander, 50
Wiretap Video Game Archives, 203
WisDOoM, 181
Wisseman, Tim, 53
Witty Write-ins, 207
Wizard Maze 3D, 163
Wizardry 6 FAQ, 69
Wizards of the Coast Archive, 59
Wolfenstein-3D/Spear of Destiny FAQ, 26
word association, 182–183
    Word Chains, 184
Word Builders, 184
Word Chains, 184
word games, 178–184
    Blankety Blanks, 169
    Borderlines, 159
.   Charades, 159

Danglers, 158
Ditto, 158–159
Fiction Therapy Group, 207
Parts Is Parts, 159
People, Places, and Things, 159–160
Poll Position, 160
Punchlines, 160
Quotables, 159
Silly Fill-Ins, 160
Storybook Writer, 207
Treasure Hunt, 160
Twenty Questions, 160
Twisted Tales, 160
Who Am I?, 160
Witty Write-ins, 207
    See also trivia games
Word Hunt, 184
Word Play, 184
Word Revenge, 184
World Empire Home Page, 141
World League Wrestling, 155
World of Darkness, A, 75
World of Darkness FAQ, 75
World of Video Games, 197
World Wide Web, explanation of, 8–9
wrestling, 155
Wumpus, 163
WWW Addict's Pop Culture Scavenger Hunt, 161
WWW Hangman, 180

X

XBoard, 127
Xpilot, 27–28
XPilot Home Page, 28
XPilot Maps, 28
XPilot Meta Server, 28
XSokoban Home Page, 163
XtraSlow, 40
X-Wing, 51
    See also Star Wars
X-Wing Archive, 51
X-Wing Mission Builder, 51
X-Wing Ship Editor, 51
X-Wing Silly Tour, 51
X-Wing Squadrons, 51

Y

Z

Michael Wolff & Company, Inc.

Michael Wolff & Company, Inc., digital publisher and packager, specializing in information presentation and graphic design, is one of the leading providers of information about the Net. The company's book *Net Guide*, published with Random House, has spent more than six months on best-seller lists. *Net Guide* debuts as a monthly magazine in November 1994. MW& Co. follows *Net Guide* and *Net Games* with *Net Chat*, *Net Money*, and *Net Tech*. MW&Co.'s Internet service, Your Personal Network (info@ypn.com), features a hypertext version of the largest Net directory available anywhere.

Among the company's other recent projects are *Where We Stand—Can America Make It in the Global Race for Wealth, Health, and Happiness?* (Bantam Books), one of the most graphically complex information books ever to be wholly created and produced by means of desktop-publishing technology, and *Made in America?*, a four-part PBS series on global competitiveness, hosted by Labor Secretary Robert B. Reich.

Kelly Maloni, who directed the *Net Games* project, is the managing editor of MW&Co. and, at 25, one of the most experienced travelers in Cyberspace. Senior editor Derek Baker spent six years at Prodigy, creating online content. Senior editor Nathaniel Wice, formerly an editor at *Spin* magazine, has written for *New York* magazine, *Esquire*, and *The New Republic*, among other publications, and in his spare time has played virtually every video game ever made.

EXPLORE the INTERNET
—— FREE! ——

DELPHI is the only major online service to offer you full access to the Internet. And now you can explore this incredible resource with no risk. You get 5 hours of evening and weekend access to try it out for free!

Use electronic mail to exchange messages with over 30 million people throughout the world. Download programs and files using "FTP" and connect in real-time to other networks using "Telnet." Meet people from around the world with "Internet Relay Chat" and check out "Usenet News," the world's largest bulletin board with over 5,000 topics.

If you're not familiar with these terms, don't worry; DELPHI has expert **online assistants** and a large collection of help files, books, and other resources to help you get started. After the free trial you can choose from two low-cost membership plans. With rates as low as $1 per hour, no other online service offers so much for so little.

5-Hour Free Trial!
Dial by modem, **1-800-365-4636**
Press return a few times
At *Password,* enter NETGM

Get Wired!

"Wired looks like Vanity Fair should, reads like Esquire used to and talks as if it's on intimate terms with the power behind the greatest technological advance since the Industrial Revolution."

David Morgan, Reuters

WIRED
Subscribe!

1 Year subscription (12 issues): $39.95
That's 33% off the newsstand price.
Call: 1-800-SO WIRED
Email: subscriptions@wired.com

NEIL SELKIRK

BUSINESS REPLY MAIL
FIRST CLASS MAIL PERMIT NO. 25363 SAN FRANCISCO, CA

Postage will be paid by addressee

PO Box 191826
San Francisco CA 94119-9866

GET WIRED!

GET WIRED!
AND STAY WIRED
BY READING NET SURF,
EXCLUSIVELY
IN WIRED.

If you want to keep up with the Digital Revolution, and the dozens of new sites that are appearing on the Net monthly, you need *Wired* and its Net Surf column – *Wired's* guide to the best of the Net.

From its online presence (gopher, WWW, Info-rama@wired.com, WELL, and AOL) to its focus on convergence and the communications revolution, *Wired* is one of the most Net-savvy publications in America today.

That's because *Wired* is the only place where the Digital Revolution is covered by and for the people who are making it happen – you.

Since its launch in January 1993, *Wired* has become required reading for the digerati from Silicon Valley to Madison Avenue, from Hollywood to Wall Street, from Pennsylvania Avenue to Main Street.

But *Wired* may be hard to find on newsstands (we're printing almost 250,000 copies and still can't satisfy demand).

So if you want to get *Wired* regularly and reliably, subscribe now – and save up to 40 percent. If for any reason you don't like *Wired*, you can cancel at any time, and get your full subscription price back – that's how sure we are that you will like *Wired*.

If you want to connect to the soul of the Digital Revolution, our advice to you is simple.

----- PLEASE FOLD ALONG THIS LINE AND TAPE CLOSED. (NO STAPLES) -----

I want to get Wired – reliably and regularly. Begin my subscription immediately, if not sooner, saving me up to 40% off the newsstand price. If for any reason, I don't like Wired, I can cancel at any time, and get my full subscription back. I would like (check one below):

		Can/Mex	Other
Individual subscription			
1 Year (12 issues)	☐ $39.95 (33% off single copy of $59.40)	☐ US $64	☐ $79
2 Years (24 issues)	☐ $71 (40% off single copy of $118.80)	☐ US $119	☐ $149
Corporate/Institutional subscription*		Can/Mex	Other
1 Year (12 issues)	☐ $80	☐ US $103	☐ $110
2 Years (24 issues)	☐ $143	☐ US $191	☐ $210

Foreign subscriptions payable by credit card, postal money order in US dollars or check drawn on US bank only.
* We have a separate rate for corporate/institutional subscribers because pass-along readership is higher. We felt it would be unfair for individual readers to, in effect, subsidize corporate/institutional purchasers.

Name _____

Job title _____

Company _____

Street _____

City State Zip Country _____

Phone _____ This is your ☐ home ☐ office ☐ both

E-mail address _____
Very important! This is by far the most efficient way to communicate with you about your subscription and periodic special offers, and to poll your opinion on *WIRED* subjects.

Payment method	☐ Check enclosed	☐ Bill me (for corporate/institutional rates only)	
	☐ American Express	☐ Mastercard	☐ Visa

Account number _____ Expiration date _____ Signature _____

Please Note: The "Bill Me" box above is only for corporations and institutions needing an invoice – which will be for the higher corporate/institutional rates. There is no "Bill Me" option for individuals.

WIRED rents its subscriber list only to mailers that we feel are relevant to our readers' interests. To remove your name from the rental list, please check this box ☐.

WIRED

AGL